A GENERATION OF CHANGE,
A LIFETIME OF DIFFERENCE?

British social policy since 1979

Martin Evans and Lewis Williams

D1438095

This edition published in Great Britain in 2009 by

The Policy Press
University of Bristol
Fourth Floor
Beacon House
Queen's Road
Bristol BS8 1QU
UK

Tel +44 (0)117 331 4054
Fax +44 (0)117 331 4093
e-mail tpp-info@bristol.ac.uk
www.policypress.org.uk

North American office:
The Policy Press
c/o International Specialized Books Services (ISBS)
920 NE 58th Avenue, Suite 300
Portland, OR 97213-3786, USA
Tel +1 503 287 3093
Fax +1 503 280 8832
e-mail info@isbs.com

© The Policy Press 2009

British Library Cataloguing in Publication Data
A catalogue record for this book is available from the British Library.

Library of Congress Cataloging-in-Publication Data
A catalog record for this book has been requested.

ISBN 978 1 84742 304 7 paperback
ISBN 978 1 84742 305 4 hardcover

The right of Martin Evans and Lewis Williams to be identified as authors of this work has been asserted by them in accordance with the 1988 Copyright, Designs and Patents Act.

The statements and opinions contained within this publication are solely those of the editors and contributors and not of The University of Bristol or The Policy Press. The University of Bristol and The Policy Press disclaim responsibility for any injury to persons or property resulting from any material published in this publication.

The Policy Press works to counter discrimination on grounds of gender, race, disability, age and sexuality.

Cover design by Robin Hawes
Front cover: image kindly supplied by Getty Images
Printed and bound in Great Britain by Hobbs the Printers, Southampton

Contents

List of figures, tables and boxes   iv
Acknowledgements   ix

one   Introduction   I

Part One: A generation of change   II
two   The changing British welfare state   13
three   Changing lives and a changing economy   35

Part Two: From the cradle to the grave   53
four   Childhood   55
five   Working age: taxation   79
six   Working age: safety nets and housing   99
seven   Working age risks: social insurance   123
eight   Working age risks: disability, caring and lone parenthood   143
nine   Old age and retirement   167

Part Three: A lifetime of difference?   195
ten   Taxes, benefits and national profiles of inequality and poverty 197
eleven   LOIS and model lifetimes   221
twelve   The Meades   241
thirteen   The Moores   267
fourteen   The Lowes   283
fifteen   Conclusion: a generation of change, a lifetime of difference? 305

References   317
Index   327

List of figures, tables and boxes

Figures

3.1a	Population distribution by age and gender, 1979	36
3.1b	Population distribution by age and gender, 2006	36
3.2	Dependency rates for pension age and children, 1971-2006	37
3.3	Fertility, 1971-2006 – total and age-specific fertility rates	38
3.4	Years of expected life at pension age, 1981-2056	40
3.5	Marriage, divorce and cohabitation	41
3.6	Household composition by pension age, presence of children and number of adults, 1975-2005/06	42
3.7	English households by tenure, 1971-2005	43
3.8	UK gross domestic product, 1971-2006 – real trend and annual growth	44
3.9	Employment growth, 1978-2007 – net employment change by industry and gender	45
3.10	Unemployment and economic inactivity rates, 1971-2007	46
3.11	Economic inactivity by reason, 1993-2007	47
3.12	Real earnings growth, 1971-2007 – median, 10th and 90th percentiles of male full-time earnings	49
3.13	Price and earnings inflation, 1971-2006	50
3.14	Household expenditure, 1971-2005	50
4.1	Maternity grants, 1971-2007	63
4.2	Maternity benefits, 1971-2007	63
4.3	Real value of Child Benefit, 1977-2007	64
4.4	Average awards in in-work transfers for families with children, 1972-2003	65
4.5	Real social assistance levels for children, 1979, 1997 and 2008	66
4.6	Coverage of children by means-tested transfers, 1972-2007	67
4.7a	The Meades' benefit income during childhood – benefit income as a percentage of original earnings	70
4.7b	The Meades' benefit income during childhood – net effects of taxes and benefits during childhood as a percentage of original earnings	70
4.8	The Moores – net effects of taxes and benefits during childhood	71
4.9a	The Lowes' tax and benefit income during childhood – benefit income as a percentage of original earnings	73
4.9b	The Lowes' tax and benefit income during childhood – net effect of taxes and benefits as a percentage of original earnings	73
4.10a	The Nunns' income profile during childhood, 2008 prices	75
4.10b	The Nunns' income profile during childhood relative to contemporary median earnings	75

5.1	Effective income tax rates under the 1979, 1997 and 2008 systems	84
5.2a	Parameters of the National Insurance system – main rate, 1975-2008	88
5.2b	Parameters of the National Insurance system – relative value of upper and lower earnings limits	88
5.3	Effective NIC rates under the 1979, 1997 and 2008 systems	89
5.4	Average rates and council tax, 1973-2008 (England)	90
5.5	Indirect taxes as a percentage of household disposable income, 1974-2004	96
6.1	Safety net benefit rates for a couple, 1979-2008	104
6.2	Average weekly local authority rent in real prices, 1971-2007 (England)	110
6.3	Housing benefits provision, 1979, 1997 and 2008 – percentage of rent met by benefits for a single earner couple without children	111
6.4	The Meades – effects of taxes and housing costs on contemporary median earnings, 1979, 1997 and 2008	116
6.5	The Moores – net effects of taxes and housing costs on twice median earnings, 1979, 1997 and 2008	117
6.6	The Lowes – net effects of taxes, benefits and housing costs on half median earners	118
7.1	Numbers in unemployment, 1971-2007 (UK)	125
7.2	Unemployed claimants by benefit entitlement, 1971-2007	126
7.3	Relative values of various earnings replacement benefits	127
7.4	Coverage of incapacity provision, 1971-2007	133
7.5	Income components and replacement rates for the Meades unemployment	135
7.6	Income components and replacement rates for the Lowes – unemployment	137
7.7	Income components and replacement rates for the Meades – incapacity	138
7.8	Income components and replacement rates for the Lowes – incapacity	140
8.1a	Disability benefits for extra costs, 1971-2008 – care allowances	147
8.1b	Disability benefits for extra costs, 1971-2008 – mobility allowances	147
8.2	Coverage of disability and caring provision, 1971-2007	152
8.3	Numbers of lone parent families in total and numbers receiving social assistance, 1971-2007	155
8.4	Social assistance income for lone parent families in real terms, 1971-2008	157
8.5	The Meades – lone parenthood	159
8.6	The Lowes – lone parenthood	161
8.7	The Lowes and the Meades – additional transfers as the result of having a severely disabled child	164
9.1	Real and relative value of basic state pension (single-person rate), 1971-2008	169
9.2	Real values of basic state pension and social assistance, 1971-2008	174
9.3	Social assistance coverage, 1971-2007	175

9.4	Income tax allowances for the over-65s, 1973/74-2008/09	177
9.5	Occupational pension scheme coverage (UK active membership)	180
9.6	Mr Lowe aged 70 – pension outcomes	186
9.7	Ms Lowe – pension outcomes	187
9.8	Mr Meade – pension outcomes	189
9.9	Ms Meade – retirement outcomes	191
10.1	Incidence of taxes and cash transfers, 2006	199
10.2a	Tax and benefit incidence by decile groups, 1979, 1997 and 2006 – transfers	201
10.2b	Tax and benefit incidence by decile groups, 1979, 1997 and 2006 – taxes	201
10.2c	Tax and benefit incidence by decile groups, 1979, 1997 and 2006 – net effect of transfers and all taxes	201
10.3	Household composition by income quintile, 1979 and 2006/07	203
10.4	Income inequality and tax and benefit incidence, 1978-2006/07	205
10.5	Real income growth at points in the income distribution, 1971-2006	209
10.6	Median male and female earnings relative to poverty line at 60% of median household income	211
10.7a	Relative poverty rates based on 60% of equivalised median income, 1971-2006/07 before housing costs	213
10.7b	Relative poverty rates based on 60% of equivalised median income, 1971-2006/07 after housing costs	213 213
10.8	Differences in child poverty from total poverty	217
11.1	Age weighting of earnings	226
12.1	The Meades' lifetime income profile, 2008 system	243
12.2	The Meades' net effects of taxes and benefits over the lifetime	253
12.3	Mr Meade's effective marginal deduction rates	255
12.4	The Meades' relative position in the income distribution	257
12.5a	The Meades' childhood poverty profile before housing costs	259
12.5b	The Meades' childhood poverty profile after housing costs	259
12.6	The Meades' pensioner poverty profile before housing costs	263
13.1	The Moores' lifetime income profile, 2008 system	268
13.2	The Evan-Moores' net effects of taxes and benefits	272
13.3	The Moores' net effects of taxes and benefits (with inflation modelled)	274
13.4a	Marginal deduction rates for Mr Moore	276
13.4b	Marginal deduction rates for Mr Evan-Moore	276
13.5	The Moores' relative position in the income distribution	277
13.6	The Moores' childhood income profile (AHC) and poverty clearance	278
13.7	The Moores' pensioner poverty profile	280
14.1	The Lowes' lifetime income profile, 2008 system	285
14.2	The Lowes' net effects of taxes and benefits over the working age lifetime (no inflation)	288
14.3	Mr Lowe's effective marginal deduction rates	294

14.4a	Replacement rates for the Lowes if Mr Lowe is not working – unemployment	296
14.4b	Replacement rates for the Lowes if Mr Lowe is not working – incapacity	296
14.5	The Lowes' relative position in the income distribution	297
14.6	Unemployment and incapacity events and poverty outcomes	299
14.7	The Lowes' childhood poverty profile (AHC)	300
14.8	The Lowes' pensioner poverty profile (BHC)	301

Tables

3.1	Children by family type, 1972-2006	41
4.1	The Meades' maternity income	69
4.2	The Lowes' maternity period income	72
5.1	The Meades' income tax position as a married or unmarried couple in 1979 and 1997	93
5.2	The Meades' tax position in 1979, 1997 and 2008	94
6.1	The Nunns' income as a childless couple in real and relative terms	105
8.1	The Lowes – disabled worker	162
8.2	The Meades – disabled worker	163
10.1	Periodic real income growth rates at different points in the income distribution	210
10.2	Periodic trends in AHC child poverty	216
12.1	The Meades' lifetime under the 1979, 1997 and 2008 systems	244
12.2	The Meades' lifetime under the 1979, 1997 and 2008 systems with behavioural change and policy maturation	250
12.3	The Meades' lifetime under the 1979, 1997 and 2008 systems with inflation modelled	252
13.1	The Moores' lifetime under the 1979, 1997 and 2008 systems	269
13.2	The Evan-Moores' lifetime under the 1979, 1997 and 2008 systems	271
13.3	The Moores' lifetime under the 1979, 1997 and 2008 systems with inflation modelled	273
13.4	Lifetime differences in outcomes of the Moores and Evan-Moores compared with the Meades'	282
14.1	The Lowes' lifetime under the 1979, 1997 and 2008 systems	286
14.2	The Lowes' lifetime under the 1979, 1997 and 2008 systems with behavioural change and policy maturation	291
14.3	The Lowes' lifetime under the 1979, 1997, 2008 systems with inflation modelled	293
14.4	Lifetime differences in outcomes of the Lowes compared with the Meades'	303

Boxes

5.1	Income tax calculation and terminology	80
5.2	An example showing the erstwhile 'kink' in the NIC system	86
6.1	Housing costs faced by the model families	115
7.1	Replacement rates	134
9.1	Pension scheme terminology	172
11.1	Inflation assumptions	231
11.2	Uprating assumptions[2] for whole lifetime profiles	233
11.3	Uprating assumptions for medium-term childhood and retirement profiles	233
11.4	Private pension parameters used in LOIS comparisons of 1979, 1997 and 2008	235

Acknowledgements

We owe many people appreciation for a lot of help with researching and writing this book. Of course, even with such help we are fallible and thus take all responsibility for any remaining errors or omissions. Jill Scarborough, LOIS' original creator, bequeathed a fantastic legacy for us to develop. The Joseph Rowntree Foundation (JRF) has been a constant source of support and encouragement and gave financial aid to us to develop LOIS further to be able to compare policy systems over time. Special thanks go to Chris Goulden and Ann Harrop at JRF. Our advisory group – John Hills, Holly Sutherland, David Piachaud, Stuart Adam, Iain Mulheirn, Janet Albeson and Trevor Huddleston – was outstanding in providing pointers, pithy criticism and patience as we developed the analysis. At Oxford, everyone in the Department of Social Policy and Social Work had a hand in supporting us and listening to and feeding back on research as it evolved, especially Pat Buckley and Bernie Parsons, who made sure everything worked around us and came together. But the research and book could not have happened without Michael Noble's explicit commitment and generosity and we owe him a special debt of gratitude. Martin Evans was Economic and Social Research Council (ESRC) Research Fellow during the writing of this book and additionally acknowledges support from the ESRC under grant number RES-000-27-0180.

ONE

Introduction

The year 2009 marks the historic 30-year anniversary of Margaret Thatcher's arrival as Prime Minister, universally acknowledged as a radical turning point in the British welfare state. The period of 30 years since 1979 has seen huge changes in both policy and in the British economy and society. This period is what we term 'the generation of change'.

But significant anniversaries have been coming thick and fast in recent years and remind us that 1979 was only the half-way point in the post-war welfare state. 2008 was the 60th birthday of the National Health Service (NHS), heralded by ministerial statements extolling the NHS as a proud achievement and black-and-white documentary footage of Nye Bevan, the Minister of Health responsible for its formation, on the main television news programmes. Forgotten was the simultaneous birthday of the 1948 National Assistance Act – a historic moment that marked the final abandonment of centuries of Poor Law and the introduction of a single, nationwide, national social assistance safety net. The pride shown through public remembrance of the NHS was a big contrast to attitudes to what has now been termed 'welfare' and subjected to continuous and relentless reform. The birthday passed unremarked; no cake or candles for the National Assistance Act. Instead, a Green Paper was published in 2008 that proposed to end Income Support, the modern-day equivalent of a general social assistance safety net, and replace it solely with provisions for unemployment and incapacity to work (DWP, 2008a).

2008 also marks a turning point, with an economic downturn and the move into recession after 16 years of uninterrupted economic growth. This is the fourth recession since the 1970s when the previous long uninterrupted period of post-war economic growth came to an end and new paradigms for both macroeconomic management and the welfare state began to emerge. While it is oversimplistic and premature to say that things have come full circle, the reputation of Keynes is undergoing a revival and those threatened with economic insecurity are looking at the British welfare state and wondering how it is going to cope with the consequences of recession, given the assumptions of continued economic growth, supply-side employment policy and the fact that benefit levels have fallen way behind the rising living standards of the general population over the past 30 years. Recent policy makers have assumed that there would be no more recessions and that growth and economic inclusion could reach down to bring everyone into the social and economic mainstream. These assumptions are likely to be tested to their limits. These are momentous times and everyone wants economic security accompanied by a health service, good education and other good public services, but the reputation and capacity of the tax and benefit system appear poorly matched to cope.

What happened to the idea of a welfare state based on comprehensive support protecting against the risks that occur over one's lifetime? The promise of a welfare state to protect and support people 'from the cradle to the grave' is one that still holds great resonance today; newspaper commentators often use the phrase and the majority of the population understand the concept. The language itself, 'from the cradle to the grave', is now hopelessly out of date. Cradles have long been abandoned along with the huge prams and the ration cards of the 1950s and cemeteries have increasingly been superseded by crematoria. But it is a reflection of the strength of the image in regard to the welfare state that people understand what is meant by provision 'from the cradle to the grave' – the theoretical commitment to a range of services and income maintenance in what most people understand as a comprehensive system – one that covers a lifetime of universally experienced events and most risky eventualities.

What stands in place of Beveridge's approach of 'the cradle to the grave' in Britain's social policy today? There has been a compartmentalisation of the lifetime in the design and implementation of programmes so that children, working age people and pensioners each have specific provision. Education and child welfare and other children's policies are in a single central department and Children's Commissioners are appointed locally to coordinate programmes and spending. Income maintenance for children has been given to the tax authorities with the combination of categorical child benefits and means-tested child tax credits to administer. Children's centres are being set up in each locality to provide a range of health, education and parental employment support services. For the older people, central government has given all responsibilities for pensions to a separate pension service for both contributory pensions and means-tested assistance. For low-income, non-employed adults of working age, the Jobcentre Plus service provides both benefits and employment services that are targeted more widely than the traditional and previous concerns for the unemployed.

Significant progress has been made in prioritising anti-poverty programmes for children and pensioners. The government committed itself to ending child and pensioner poverty in the medium to long term in unprecedented and historical promises made in 1999. The child poverty commitment is the least ambiguous, with clear targets and measures to halve 1998 levels by 2010 and to eliminate child poverty by 2020. Great progress has been made in the first years but unfortunately not sustained sufficiently to meet the interim target of quartering child poverty by 2005, and even before the economy slowed down the likelihood of meeting the target of halving child poverty in 2010 was seen as unlikely (Hirsch, 2006).

The three-way division of responsibility for the lifetime between children, working age adults and pensioners suggests that significant joining up of policy has been done *within* these segments of the lifetime, but a policy approach that adequately reconciles a lifetime approach with events and periods of the lifetime is still weak. Evans and Eyre writing in 2004 using an earlier lifetime analysis of the contemporary policy rules concluded there was no underlying theoretical problem with putting everyone into these three lifetime age compartments 'as long as there is the ability to reassemble such approaches into a set of sensible assumptions for the whole lifetime' (Evans and Eyre, 2004, p 83). Five years on, it is not clear that much progress has been made. An example is that adults of working age still have to trade off their children's needs against their own for pension provision – saving more today for one's own future takes money away from today's pressing needs and there is little recognition of how periodic risks and needs link over people's lifetimes. Having children, having high housing costs and having to put more away for a longer retirement are big demands to make on adults in their 30s and 40s. However, economic recession threatens to hollow out the earnings of many of those of working age, threatening their own and their children's livelihoods as well as their future pensions.

A policy approach that considers the lifetime enables a comprehensive look at the range of activities of the welfare state. An overview of this kind can thus demonstrate much about the overall policy design of the government of the day. When we stand back and ask of a policy system, 'what is covered from the cradle to the grave?', the answer says much about the assumptions of policy makers and how they have designed programmes to meet the widest range of circumstances and events.

This brings us neatly to the idea behind this book. How can the policy changes that have occurred since the 1970s be understood and interpreted in a lifetime perspective? Put more exactly, how differently did the welfare state treat the lifetime in the 1970s compared with now and what are the likely outcomes that arise from such differences? We use a model lifetime methodology to assess how far there has been significant difference in the outcomes of social policy, a 'lifetime of difference' since 1979.

The problem with simple and interesting questions of this type is that they hide a huge range of complexity in approach and difficulty in undertaking. The remainder of this introduction lays out how the book approaches the issues of bringing together change in policy with a lifetime perspective and analysis.

Policy change and lifetime

There is one big obstacle to showing a lifetime outcome of a set of policy rules: social policy is increasingly short to medium term in its nature. It responds and adapts to demographic, social and economic changes and is tied primarily to the electoral cycle. If a policy lasts the term of a government unchanged, it is unusual; to use the period of a lifetime to analyse policy is clearly running against the underlying time-frame for the majority of social policy. One area where policy has to be built to last a lifetime is pensions. A pensioner retiring in 2008 will be relying on entitlements built up in the 1960s onwards and the school-leaver of

2008 will rely on the maturation of today's policy promises sometime after 2060 for their retirement. Pensions thus require a lifetime approach but ensuring that pension policy has sustainability over the electoral cycles has not been one of the strong points of British social policy so far. However, change in pension policy has proceeded by protecting the cohorts of those who have built up entitlement thus far (to do otherwise would be electorally dangerous). Returning to our pensioner retiring today, this means that they will have a range of entitlements, to a basic state pension, to graduated pension from working in the 1960s and 1970s and to benefits from the State Earnings Related Pension Scheme and other state second pensions subsequently, but that these entitlements will be matched against today's rules for tax and means-tested benefits.

To calculate a set of consistent entitlement requires us to move to a theoretical world in which policy stands still and a single set of rules is applied consistently over the whole period. This is our approach and it builds on other work using *hypothetical model lifetimes* that is described more fully in Chapter Eleven.

However, the rapidity of policy change means that to capture such change in detail would mean looking at a large set of different rules. We could compare rules every five years but this would mean a huge amount of data and may still miss big changes that occur in in-between years. Our approach is to pick years that represent turning points since the 1970s.

Capturing Old Labour, Thatcherism and New Labour

We use electoral turning points in time to illustrate policy change. This means that the policy rules that existed in 1979 and 1997 compare the position in 1979 that James Callaghan handed over to Margaret Thatcher with the position in 1997 that John Major handed over to Tony Blair. We use 2008 rules to show how far things have changed since 1997 under Blair and Gordon Brown. How far does the choice of these years capture the essence of changing British social policy? It would be naïve to say that electoral turning points marked the crucial high points of either economic restructuring or ideological implementation. Indeed, by choosing dates based on electoral change, we are in danger of overemphasising regime change and understating the continuity in the evolution of social policy. Each government left unfinished business that was completed by their electoral nemesis. A more marked problem comes from regime change within government and our choice of 1997 marks the end of 18 years of Conservative government but misses the step-change in policy that occurred earlier around the resignation of Margaret Thatcher and her replacement by John Major. If we wanted to capture Thatcherism at a point of ideological purity, 1990 would probably be the year to choose. But if the 1990 version of Thatcherism was politically unsustainable, our choice of 1997 marks a more balanced reflection of what the Conservative Right represented after 18 years in power. Some watering down of the ideological high ground of the poll tax and a re-emphasis on elements of a rational economic approach to gender, family and fiscal policy that were anathema to Margaret Thatcher are thus part of a cumulative policy story. This approach also fits best with our long-term look at the lifetime and at sustained approaches to social policy rather than blips and u-turns that would seem more difficult to argue.

2008 is chosen to be as contemporaneous as possible at the time of publication. But we are writing at what increasingly looks like the end of an era and the government of Gordon Brown looks highly likely to change macroeconomic principles to deal with a historic downturn and recession in the British economy. The timing of budgets and uprating dates for benefits has changed over the past 30 years and this fact, combined with the aim of best capturing the approach of Old Labour in 1979, means that we use the rules that were in place in January 1979. The rules for 1997 are those in place in April of that year prior to John Major's defeat in the May 1997 election. The rules for 2008 are those in place in December 2008, allowing us to incorporate all of the changes that arose from the reversal of the abolition of the 10% income tax band and other minor changes that came into place over 2008. We do not attempt to model the changes that were announced in November 2008 in the pre-budget report on tax reductions and other fiscal stimuli for the flagging economy (HM Treasury, 2008a).

Social policy

This is a book about British social policy, but we are limited in what we can profile using our hypothetical lifetime approach to policies that directly influence income. This means that out of the five areas that are typically considered as comprising social policy, or at least comprising what might be termed 'the welfare state' – education, health, housing, the personal social services and social security – it is the last that forms the majority of our discussion and analysis. But we cover more than just pure social security by also looking in depth at taxation, a topic usually avoided by the mainstream of social policy. Additionally, throughout this book our approach necessarily broadens out to cover wider areas of social policy. Indeed, if we return to one of the founding texts of British welfare state analysis, Richard Titmuss pointed out in an influential lecture given over 50 years ago that consideration of welfare or social policy should not be restricted to obvious state-provided welfare, but should take into account the 'social division of welfare' through a consideration of what he termed 'fiscal welfare' and 'occupational welfare' in addition to 'statutory welfare' (Titmuss, 1958). Our discussions and analysis cover fiscal welfare and consider tax reliefs and exemptions that are provided through the tax system. We also capture elements of occupational welfare by including occupational pension provision together with sickness and maternity provision that has become mostly run and funded by employers.

But even our concentration on income-related social policy means that we have to address and incorporate other areas of social policy. Housing policy has changed the rents people pay and the way that they are subsidised. In education policy, the definition of school years has been expanded to encompass nursery education and, more recently, post–16 secondary education, and the changes to higher education finance are obviously pertinent to lifetime profiles because of loan repayment.

Finally, we acknowledge that purely looking in detail at the change in these specific areas of related policy gives us a very narrow ambit of policy context. Chapter Two will open up discussion on change in the British welfare state to a broader historical overview and put the past 30 years in context and place our concentration on income-related policies in both the longer-term and wider policy contexts.

Hypothetical profiles

The choice of a large range of policies that affect different parts of the lifetime and the need to look at the cumulative effects of policy over the lifetime mean that data are very inadequate. We have birth cohorts from a range of years since 1956 but not even the earliest have yet reached pension age, yet alone enjoyed a whole lifetime. Panel data begun in the 1990s give us much information about a wide sample of lives but nothing that allows us to look at whole lifetimes. Our use of hypothetical modelled individuals is thus chosen to allow us to provide extended profiles of the lifetime that can capture a range of different behaviours and income levels, but these will necessarily be illustrative rather than truly representative of any generation or cohort of the British population. We can and we will draw on empirical data to inform these profiles, but it is also worth stressing that our main aim is to use model lifetimes to analyse policy change and differences. This means keeping circumstances the same and changing policy in the first instance, so that the policy outcomes of different systems can be compared using the same underlying assumptions.

In our profiles we choose three hypothetical families. These families can be single people, couples or couples with children or lone parents – we match the underlying assumptions of benefit and tax credit rules for joining individuals and children together into family units. Our three hypothetical families are:

- the Meades, who have median full-time earnings at 1979, 1997 and 2008 levels;
- the Lowes, who are low earners with 50% of full-time median earnings in these years; and
- the Moores, who are high earners with twice full-time median earnings in these years.

These three hypothetical families are joined at times by a fourth, the Nunns, who are not employed and in Part Three of the book we additionally look at a very high-earning family, the Evan-Moores. The importance of these hypothetical families is that they are used to consistently measure policy outputs over time. They are not 'realistic' in that they are very simple and stereotypical by design. This approach is not intended to ignore the wide diversity in family types and formation and is not used to represent any fixed assumptions about wider issues of ethnicity or sexual orientation but to be consistent interpretable measurement tools to assess policy change, the inputs and outputs from taxes and benefits and the resulting outcomes.

The innovative and distinct approach of this book is to take this approach of hypothetical lifetime tax benefit modelling into a comparative perspective. In Part Three, we join up the treatment of children, working and pension provision in 1979, 1997 and 2008 to profile how policy has changed across the whole lifetime. This approach uses the Lifetime Opportunities and Incentives Simulation (LOIS), which is more fully described in Chapter Eleven.

Part Three takes this approach into new and conceptually difficult territory as the hypothetical approach has to be reconciled with real-time changes to outcomes for cohorts of the population, to inflation and to the huge growing complexity of the tax and benefit system and to changing risk profiles of the real world lives of British families since the 1970s. For the time being, let us put such detailed methodological considerations to one side and focus on the simple underlying question that hypothetical lifetime simulations explore: 'how different would the outcomes be for a whole lifetime lived under the rules of 1979, 1997 and 2008?'.

Questions and book structure

The main underlying themes of the book are to describe and analyse policy change in Britain since the 1970s and to do so by looking at lifetime design and outcomes. This approach means that we have to cover a lot of ground and to look at three large themes that cumulatively build to an understanding of how policy has changed, why, and the potential effect on lifetime outcomes.

Part One is called 'A generation of change' and in it we set the scene for a detailed look at British policy and society and how they have changed. Chapter Two looks widely at the past period of 30 years and at changing politics and social policy. This is a huge area and has been much covered by historians and others in recent years. Of course, *just* considering the period since 1979 would not allow us to fully understand the impact of Thatcherism without understanding the preceding events and policy structures, so we take a longer view and focus on the big political changes that influence social policy and signpost the elements of the story that will be crucial to cover for the main analysis of the book later. Chapter Three considers some of the main economic and demographic and other changes that have occurred in Britain over the latter period of 30 years and focuses on the changes that most directly affect lifetime outcomes of taxes and benefits – ageing, relationships, work and earnings and related matters. These two introductory and contextual chapters set the scene for the following and more detailed analysis of lifetime design of policy and the changes that have been made.

Part Two is called 'From the cradle to the grave' and in five chapters takes policy structures from the point of pregnancy and birth and childhood in Chapter Four through to retirement and death in Chapter Nine. Our approach is to try to map the description of change into the straightjacket of the current three-way split into childhood, working age and pensioners. But in reality there is much necessary signposting forward and referencing back – a lifetime perspective is in reality difficult to compartmentalise. Chapter Four outlines in detail changes to programmes for maternity and for the financial support of children. Alongside consideration of policy change, we look at changing coverage and value of benefits and then profile changing packages of programmes in 1979, 1997 and 2008 for our hypothetical families. Chapter Five is the first of four chapters that consider changing policy structures for the working age portion of the lifetime. Chapter Five considers taxation and looks across the various forms of taxation and then illustrates the impact on our model families in the three comparison years. Chapter Six looks at the schemes that form a national minimum safety net, mostly social assistance but also other forms of minimum income guarantee such as in-work benefits and the minimum wage. Because the means-tested safety net is so closely linked to paying the housing costs of the poorest people in Britain, Chapter Six also looks at housing support. Chapters Five and Six, with their coverage of population-wide issues of tax and minimum income provision and housing, pave the way for Chapters Seven and Eight, which look specifically at risks to adult livelihoods that occur during working age. Chapter Seven considers the risks that have traditionally been covered by contributory social insurance: unemployment and sickness and incapacity. Chapter Eight looks at risks that social insurance has mostly left out: disability, caring for disabled people and lone parenthood. Across all the chapters on adult working life – that is, Chapters Five to Eight – we describe policy change and changes to coverage and value of support and then illustrate the tax and benefit packages of 1979, 1997 and 2008 for our model families as appropriate. Finally, Chapter Nine reaches the latter part of the lifetime and looks at retirement, pensions and death. As in the early chapters, it describes how policy has changed and how coverage and the values of benefit have evolved before looking at model pension outcomes for our model families.

The first two parts of the book provide an evolving cumulative context for Part Three, called 'A lifetime of difference?', which moves into a more analytical overview of policy change using hypothetical lifetimes. Our questions at this point become more analytical. We profile the change in coverage of social and fiscal policies across the population and lifecycle using questions related to three themes:

- first, how does cumulative incidence of taxes and benefits alter and how different is this for periods of the lifetime between the systems of 1979, 1997 and 2008?;
- second, how do the outcomes of policy change over the lifetime, and for periods of the lifetime, when these three comparison years are considered?; and
- third, how does inequality change? Are our model families moving nearer or further apart?

Part Three outlines the methodology and assumptions used to create the individual hypothetical lifetimes and also join the hypothetical world of model lifetimes to the changing context of actual policy and incomes over the period. Chapter Ten looks at the changing overall incidence of taxes and benefits and their outcomes on income distribution and poverty. This allows the subsequent analysis of lifetime profiles to relate to the contemporary income distributions of 1979, 1997 and 2008 and support profiles of lifetime poverty and of tax and benefit incidence. Chapter Eleven looks in detail at the methodology of the hypothetical lifetimes that will be employed in profiling the changing policy systems of 1979, 1997 and 2008 and how differences in assumptions about the behaviour of individuals and families between 1979 and 2008 can be assessed. Additionally, the issue of inflation and uprating of tax and benefits is discussed and methodology described. With these two introductory chapters complete, the rest of Part three returns to our three model families and asks in turn how the policy outputs and outcomes would differ if they lived their whole lives under the rules in 1979, 1997 and 2008. Chapter Twelve looks at the Meades, median earners, and their lifetime profiles of inputs and outputs and the resulting position in the contemporary income distribution in those three profile years. Chapter Thirteen turns to the Moores, and a richer version of that family called the Evan-Moores. Chapter Fourteen assesses the Lowes and considers their lifetime of inputs and outputs and of poverty risk with profiles where employment is continuous, but also considers interrupted lifetime profiles where unemployment and incapacity occur. Chapter Fifteen draws the book to a close with discussion and conclusions about policy change and its effect on the lifetime. How has British policy changed in its support of people 'from the cradle to the grave'? Is there a lifetime of difference between the social policy of 1979, 1997 and 2008?

This overview gives an indication of the ambition of the book, but it is also important to put such conceptual ambition into some context. We straddle two very different approaches to policy analysis: one that sees things as systemic change driven by ideology and wider socioeconomic structures and another that is more empirical and aims to measure such change and understand its causation and association with other factors. Our approach is to try to capture policy and wider changes and to illustratively compare the effects of such change. We are empirical only in the sense that we consider historical events, rules and trends and then use these to provide illustrative models that can be consistently used to compare and contrast policy systems. Our models are empirically informed, but the only 'empirical facts' they contain are the policy rules and other contextual information. This means that we can contribute to an understanding of change and its potential effect on the lifetime, but that our evidence and interpretation does not match that undertaken by others to demonstrate actual long-term longitudinal experiences. Thus, the evidence that poverty in childhood has long-term consequences for the lifetime and wider repercussions and costs for society in general (Griggs and Walker, 2008), that youth unemployment has scarring effects on future employment and earnings (Arulampalam et al, 2001) and that early retirement is increasingly a risk for low-skilled men with problems of ill health (Lissenburgh and Smeaton, 2003), as well as other research, are all crucial findings that support a longer-term and lifetime approach to policy making, but that is empirically almost impossible to do as a lifetime is so long a period. Our approach steps around this problem and in no way solves it, but contributes considerably to building a better lifetime perspective.

On the other hand, political scientists, theorists and others will be looking for answers about the bigger conceptual world of changing social policy; a comparison of the 'isms' of Thatcherism and Blairism or of the differences between New and Old Labour. By choosing our comparison years as 1979, 1997 and 2008, we can help these commentators prime their arguments, but our approach is more about measuring differences using our particular methodology and we leave the wider interpretation to others. For instance, any question about how the change in systems represents 'regime change' in social policy is well beyond the scope of this book, but our results can help recent commentators such as Powell (2008) who are trying to put Blair's policy legacy into a historical overview, for instance.

We will return to these themes in the conclusion, but the whole period since the 1970s is a particularly difficult one for social policy in Britain. The academic project of social policy came of age at the same time as the expansion of policy in the mid- to late 1970s. It is thus understandable that the period since 1979 is seen as a souring of the ripest of fruit. Looking back over the generation of change to try to consistently capture the effects of change from the cradle to the grave is thus also looking back over the majority of the lifetime of British social policy.

Part One

A generation of change

TWO

The changing British welfare state

The spotlight may fall on 1979 as a turning point in social policy but it is notably only the half-way point in the post-war welfare state. This chapter puts the past 30 years of policy change into a longer historical context and broadens the focus to consider a wide range of policy and social policy, and governmental and political change. These wider and longer-term views allow us to concentrate more on programmes of taxes and benefits in later parts of the book. Looking back, how has social policy changed and developed in Britain and how do such changes fit into the policy history before and after 1979?

The first 25 years of post-war policy

The post-war welfare state was forged under the wartime coalition government and the 1945 Labour government. Inspired by a 'never again' attitude to the pre-war economic crash, and the experience of solidarity and planned economy during the Second World War along with a good dose of socialist idealism, a raft of social policy legislation effectively created the post-war welfare state between 1944 and 1948. This vision of a more egalitarian Britain, dubbed by some commentators as being one of a 'New Jerusalem' (Addison, 1975; Barnett, 1995), was based on a welfare state and full employment.

The 1944 Education Act enacted free secondary education up to the age of 15 as a right for all, removing the elementary 'all age' schools and fees from state secondary schools (Timmins, 2001). Nye Bevan's 1946 National Health Service Act introduced the National Health Service (NHS) based on universal healthcare free at the point of use, ending limited and uneven access to healthcare from a combination of fees and means tests. Bevan's legacy on housing was short-lived. His universal vision of council housing estates being communities of all classes and occupations was based on a high standard of housing and proved impossible to sustain due to cost and material and skills shortages. The severe housing shortage began to be solved by lower-quality mass building and this programme was basically adopted by the Tories in 1951. Private sector house building and private renting were restricted and highly regulated.

Local authorities as 'plannable instruments' became mainstream housing providers and holders of planning powers. The role of local authorities also expanded to include direct responsibility for the new education provisions and for personal social services, including domestic help, health visiting and residential care and child protection. On the other hand, local authorities lost responsibility for health and social assistance. The reviled Poor Law system of social assistance was finally ended by the 1948 National Assistance Act, which established a unified, cross-country, means-tested safety net for all and banished the hated old-style household means test (see Deacon and Bradshaw, 1983).

The 1946 National Insurance Act implemented most of Beveridge's publicly popular plan. The new unified and universal social insurance scheme paid flat-rate benefits in return for flat-rate contributions from workers and covered risks to livelihood from maternity, through unemployment and sickness to old age, widowhood and death. Alongside Family Allowance (introduced by the 1945 Family Allowances Act) and the NHS, this meant that Beveridge's vision of a comprehensive system to ensure freedom from 'want' that covered everyone from the cradle to the grave was essentially realised. National Assistance was seen as a minor element in the new post-war, full employment welfare state. Thus at the heart of the post-war welfare state was an approach that was both lifetime in conception and universal in coverage. This forms the background to all that follows in Parts Two and Three of this book.

The development of the welfare state from this point to the 1970s is subject to some controversy. Was there an evolving political consensus on economic and social policy, 'a commitment to the welfare state, support for full employment, Keynesian demand management, a corporatist approach to involving trade-unions in government considerations, a mixed economy and an Atlantic Alliance foreign policy' (Fraser, 2000, p 348)? Such views tend to emphasise 1979 as a fundamental turning point (Addison, 1975; Dutton, 1997; Kavanagh and Morris, 1989). This rosy picture of consensus has been criticised by Pimlot (1988), Jones and Kandiah (1996) and Glennerster (2000), all of whom describe it as a 'myth'. The truth lies somewhere in between. Conservative and Labour adhered to different belief systems during the so-called consensus period, placed different interpretations on the post-war settlement and differed in policy detail. Yet there was a demonstrable post-war settlement of sorts, a broad agreement on a commitment to the welfare state and Keynesian demand management until the mid-1970s. The notion of there being a 'golden age' of the welfare state might, though, truly be considered a myth, even if welfare spending as a percentage of gross domestic product (GDP) did grow year on year without check until the mid-1970s (Glennerster and Hills, 1998).

Radical talk, continuing consensus: Heath, 1970-74

A shift to the right was promised by the Conservative manifesto in 1970 that contained antecedents to Thatcherism: curbing inflation and trade union power, reducing income tax and shifting from direct to indirect taxation, controlling government spending, encouraging the sale of council houses and private pension provision and the highlighting of alleged 'shirkers and the scroungers' (Conservative Party, 1970). Edward Heath surprised most forecasters with his election victory and, in practice, his government remained grounded in the post-war Keynesian consensus as a series of policy u-turns led to the state playing a very interventionist role in the economy in the face of rising unemployment and a letting go of the right-wing model. Social policy emphasised a more targeted approach. These were the heady days of arguments over welfare principles; of universal versus means-tested approaches; and of Richard Titmuss arguing against the Institute of Economic Affairs that drew on Friedman, Hayek and the Chicago School of economists in the early days of British social policy. Overall, however, and in practice, elements of policy retrenchment (famously including the ending of free school milk) were generally outweighed by the huge rises in social expenditure that were also put in place.

Policy on secondary education between the two main political parties apparently stood in stark contrast. By 1970, Labour pledged to vigorously pursue comprehensivisation; whereas the Conservatives pledged to letting local authorities decide what sort of school was best for their area. However, comprehensivisation actually accelerated under Thatcher, despite her fundamental opposition to it in principle and her favouring of selection and grammar schools. To her later chagrin, and despite her rejection of many reorganisation proposals, Margaret Thatcher sanctioned the closure of more grammar schools than any other education minister. The percentage of children in comprehensives rose from 32% to 62% between 1970 and 1974 (Lowe, 1996).

Another architect of Thatcherism, Keith Joseph, was in charge of the 'super-ministry' of the Department of Health and Social Services previously created for Richard Crossman (overseeing health, the personal social services and social security). The NHS underwent extravagant reorganisation in 1974. The notion here was to create unity between hospital, general practitioner and local authority services and to introduce more efficient lines of management through a clearer hierarchy of regional, area and district levels of the NHS. Simultaneous local government reorganisation added to the ensuing short-term chaos, but even in the medium to longer term commentators agree that the 1974 reorganisation of the NHS was both expensive and had limited success (Lowe, 1996; Holmes, 1997; Glennerster, 2000; Timmins, 2001). The personal social services also saw large increases in spending under Joseph and faced two costly rounds of reorganisation, first as the unified social service departments were created in 1971 in the wake of the Seebohm Report (HMSO, 1968) and second as part of the NHS reorganisation in 1974.

In the area of social security, a number of new benefits were introduced under the Heath administration. Family Income Supplement (FIS, discussed in more detail in Chapter Four) was introduced in 1971 and was intended as a temporary measure while more radical plans to introduce a negative income tax or tax credits scheme were being considered. Attendance Allowance (discussed in more detail in Chapter Eight) was also born in 1971, albeit as an enactment of plans devised previously under Labour, and became the first categorical non-means-tested benefit to recognise the additional costs of disability. Invalidity Benefit (discussed in more detail in Chapter Seven) was also introduced, as a social insurance benefit that recognised the higher needs of the long-term incapacitated while short-term sickness remained covered by Sickness Benefit. In 1973, Supplementary Benefit was reformed to provide for higher 'long-term' rates for those claimants not required to sign on as unemployed – pensioners, lone parents and the long-term incapacitated. Other reforms with lasting impact initiated under the 1970-74 Conservative government included the introduction of category D pensions (payable purely on the basis of age to those over 80 regardless of contribution record), the 25 pence over-80 age addition to the basic pension[1], Christmas bonuses for pensioners and a commitment to annual rather than ad-hoc uprating of the basic pension. The Conservatives' version of secondary state pensions was enacted in 1973, but never implemented, as it was repealed by Labour.

Housing policy encouraged owner-occupancy but escalating house prices and interest rates meant that the rise in owner-occupation under the Heath government was only marginal. The 1972 Housing Finance Act, however, marked a fundamental shift in housing finance in the public sector towards income-related subsidies to tenants, while at the same time extending a parallel system of rent allowances to those renting in the private sector to allow for the deregulation of rent controls. Rent rebate schemes became nationwide and compulsory. Public sector house building continued under the Heath administration, but the number of new homes built fell as a result of policy preference for the improvement of existing housing. Despite this, the percentage of overall new-builds that were in the public sector was actually greater under Heath than it had been under the previous Labour government (Timmins, 2001).

The troubled economy and industrial unrest overshadowed social policy and led to the fall of the Heath government in February 1974. In the face of rising unemployment, which would exceed the then politically sensitive one million mark in January 1972, the government abandoned the approach of its manifesto in favour of the orthodox Keynesian response to unemployment of reinflating the economy through high public expenditure. To control inflation, which was at around 10% and rising in the latter part of 1973, the government's ultimate strategy was a statutory incomes policy legally restricting wage increases. This brought the government to a stand-off with the National Union of Mineworkers in the winter of 1973/74, a crisis that resulted in the 'three-day week', an early general election with Heath asking the country 'who governs Britain?' and Labour returning to power.

Universal vision under the economic cosh: Labour, 1974-79

Labour originally formed a minority government in a hung parliament and a second election in October 1974 resulted in an overall Labour majority of just three. Labour held power for a further four-and-a-half years, with Liberal Party support in the later stages. Inflation and unemployment rose to higher levels after external shocks to the economy, notably the global quadrupling of oil prices in 1973-74. So-called stagflation, with low growth and high unemployment combined with high inflation, was a combination of macroeconomic circumstances that challenged orthodox Keynesian approaches and the belief that a certain level of unemployment was associated with low inflation (the so-called Philips Curve). In 1976, the Labour government went to the International Monetary Fund (IMF) for a loan of £2.3 billion to save sterling. The loan was granted on condition that public expenditure would be substantially reduced and Prime Minister James Callaghan famously informed his Party conference in no uncertain terms that the orthodox Keynesian era was over:

We used to think that you could spend your way out of a recession and increase employment by cutting taxes and boosting government spending. I tell you in all candour that that option no longer exists, and that in so far as it ever did exist, it only worked on each occasion since the War by injecting a bigger dose of inflation into the economy, followed by a higher level of unemployment as the next step (Labour Party, 1976, p 188).

Labour had entered office on a left-leaning manifesto that promised 'a fundamental and irreversible shift in the balance of wealth and power in favour of working people and their families' (Labour Party, 1974) and began by increasing income tax and public expenditure to achieve this. By 1976, significant cuts were made to spending plans and the opportunities for further expansion of social policy were constrained. Even so, the five years of Wilson and Callaghan governments marked a final expansion and consolidation of social welfare.

Labour's manifesto promised to complete the comprehensivisation of secondary education and to withdraw all forms of funding and charitable status from private schools as well as expanding pre-school and higher education. After 1976, growth in education spending was held in check (Glennerster, 1998). Mandatory plans for going comprehensive were introduced and all authorities had to submit plans to do so. Only a small number of authorities managed to delay change until the Conservatives were returned to power, with the consequence that some selective grammar schools, around 150, remain to this day. Nevertheless, the battle for comprehensivisation had effectively been won when Labour left office and the percentage of children in comprehensives continued to rise after 1979. Against a background of growing concern over educational standards, Callaghan made clear his desire to see a core curriculum, closer involvement of parents and industry in schools and the monitoring of performance against national standards. Such views would later be reflected in Conservative and New Labour education policy.

In health policy, Labour came to power with an expansionist agenda and mildly socialist commitments. Rapid growth in government expenditure on the NHS and the personal social services were seen in the first two years, but these were followed by low and negative rates of growth (Evandrou and Falkingham, 1998; Le Grand and Vizard, 1998). Labour never made good its February 1974 manifesto pledge to abolish prescription charges. Reallocating NHS resources towards deprived regions on the basis of a better appraisal of health needs using the Resource Allocation Working Party was, however, 'quite successful' (Le Grand and Vizard, 1998; Le Grand et al, 1990). However, no real inroads were made on the promise to drive out private practice within the NHS. The proposed abolition of pay beds was eventually compromised to a reduction of around a quarter and had the perverse consequence of expansion of private sector medicine outside the NHS to replace capacity and to cater for those who perceived the NHS as in crisis and who wanted a private alternative.

Labour ended the Tory policy on council house rents and initially froze and then increased rents by less than inflation. The national rent rebate scheme remained in place. Left-wing opposition to owner-occupation was mostly ignored and policies continued the Conservatives' help for first-time buyers and the provision of mortgage interest tax relief. Even the sale of council houses was permitted to continue, albeit with the proviso of Circular 70/74 that it would be 'generally wrong' for local authorities to sell council houses in areas where there was unmet demand for rented accommodation (Young and Rao, 1997). Net capital expenditure on housing was increased in the early years of the Labour administration, only to be cut back after 1976. In particular, local authority new-builds fell substantially from around 135,000 in 1977 to 85,000 in 1979 (Hills, 1998). The 1977 Housing (Homeless Persons) Act placed a duty on local authorities to house homeless people in 'priority need', moving homelessness from a social services to a housing responsibility. However, this was a private member's bill; homelessness was never an official Labour policy initiative.

In social security, Labour followed a programme based on expanding new universal, categorical and contributory benefits in an attempt to permanently remove means testing as a major plank of provision. This clearly stood in contrast to the promotion of selectivity under the Heath government. The Conservatives' FIS and national rent rebates were retained, but their role was to be overtaken by improving incomes to families with children through the introduction of Child Benefit, a cash allowance for every child to replace the partial coverage of Family Allowance and the regressive child tax allowances. Additionally, a range of non-contributory provision to meet categorical needs was developed. The Non-Contributory Invalidity Pension (discussed in more detail in Chapter Seven) was introduced for those defined as incapable of work with no contributory record – often people with congenital or early onset disability. Invalid Care Allowance (discussed in more detail in Chapter Eight) was introduced for full-time unpaid carers. Mobility Allowance (discussed in more detail in Chapter Eight) was introduced to provide additional income to meet the travel and other mobility costs of those people with impaired mobility.

Pension reform introduced generous provision from improved contributory benefits and the contributory State Earnings Related Pension Scheme (SERPS) (discussed in more detail in Chapter Nine) was introduced with bipartisan support. The move away from flat-rate benefits also led to a reform of National Insurance contributions to be calculated as a percentage of earnings, entrenching the break with Beveridge of earlier reforms and making National Insurance contributions more progressive and more like income tax. In order to protect the relative value of new contributory and other commitments, long-term benefits were granted a statutory commitment to be uprated by the 'best of' price or earnings inflation.

The final plank of reform was to review Supplementary Benefit and the 1978 report supported moving further away from discretion towards a more rights-based approach. The review's recommendations (DHSS, 1978) were eventually implemented by the incoming Conservative government.

Old Labour's term in office ended in May 1979 with the collapse of the voluntary incomes policy, the 'social contract' and the resulting 'winter of discontent', a sustained period of widespread and far-reaching industrial action. At this point, we come to the supposed point at which the fortunes of the British welfare state changed. While it is debatable whether the door slammed shut on progressive welfare state development, there is no ambiguity about the rhetorical shift when the door of No 10 Downing Street was opened to receive Margaret Thatcher.

The radical right in power: Thatcher, 1979-90

Shifts and changes of direction rarely hinge on a single epoch-making event. The radical 1970 Conservative manifesto, the 1976 IMF crisis and the spending cuts were clear antecedents. Even so, the election of the Conservatives under Margaret Thatcher in 1979 and the embrace of monetarist economics, the shift away from universalism in the provision of welfare and the open embrace of short-term mass unemployment as a price for economic change all support a sudden and dramatic shift in approach. The consensus on full employment was gone; tax cuts and expenditure cuts were the priority. In terms of social policy, other than a desire to cut public spending and 'roll back' the welfare state, their goals were less well developed than economic ones. A restructuring of industry (including the privatisation of public utilities), the economy, taxation (including the shift from direct to indirect taxation) and the curbing of the power of the trade unions were priorities. It was the second and third terms of Thatcher that saw more change in social policy and a growing discontinuity with the social policy legacy of Old Labour.

New right ideology chimed with increasing criticism of the performance of social policy. Key areas of welfare provision had been tarnished by problems of performance or some media-heightened scandal or at least perceived outrage. The alleged excesses of progressive education had long been criticised in the series of *Black papers*[2]; the NHS had shown itself not to be immune from militant industrial action in the 1970s; the reputation of council housing was at rock bottom after tower blocks and poor management[3]; and the personal social services were tarnished by the tragedy of failed child protection such as the Maria Colwell case[4]. The image of the social security sponger or scrounger together with tales of fraud had become commonplace in the media. However, free NHS healthcare and education for all remained popular with the electorate and Child Benefit and the state pension were important, not just to those with low incomes but to the middle classes as well. The unpopularity of the welfare state should not thus be overstated. Radical ideas were thus developed in private in the early years of Thatcher's premiership, but rolling back the state not only meant cutting expenditure, but also direct or indirect privatisation and a fundamental challenge to the state – both civil servants and more so, local government, who stood in the way of the emerging agenda.

Writ large in the Conservatives' 1979 manifesto was a commitment to cut income tax 'at all levels' with a switch from 'taxes on earnings to taxes on spending' (Conservative Party, 1979). Geoffrey Howe's 1979 budget was a radical turning point, nearly doubling VAT from 8% to 15% and cutting income tax, particularly for higher earners. The highest rate of income tax raised under Labour to 83% was cut to 60%. Throughout the 1980s, headline income tax rates continued to be lowered, albeit at a more gradual pace, so that by the time Thatcher left office the basic rate of income tax had been reduced from 33% in 1979 to 25% in 1990 and the higher rates of income tax had been replaced by a single higher rate of 40%. These changes are discussed further in Chapter Five, which also demonstrates how far tax reductions were offset by increases in higher rates of National Insurance contributions as well as indirect taxation.

Rolling back the state also meant privatisation. This occurred in many forms and was a consistent theme for the whole of the 18 years of Conservative rule. Local authority and NHS workforces, particularly those in manual and low-skilled occupations, were forced to compete with privately out-tendered and contracted provision that over time replaced the vast majority of directly employed labour forces. Dustmen, cleaners, street sweepers, highways staff and all of the construction staff for repair and renovation of public housing stock all became private contractors. Gains to economic efficiency no doubt resulted but employment conditions and practices deteriorated and in the longer term the weakening of the public sector ethos had effects on hospital cleanliness and on the employment opportunities of many low-skilled men, especially those who were older or had health conditions. These privatisations were largely overshadowed by the selling off of publicly owned companies – airlines, power and utility companies and energy producers were often sold off with low-value initial share prices ensuring financial success in the stock market in the main.

Privatisation also seriously affected housing policy. The 1980 Housing Act granted council tenants the 'right to buy' their homes with generous discounts of up to 50% (and later 70%) of the market value of their home. The policy was spectacularly successful and popular. By 1990, nearly 1.5 million council homes had been sold to their former tenants. Subsidies to local authorities were cut and rents rose in real terms (see Chapter Six). Public house building was cut drastically and new-builds were cut by more than half between 1979 and 1983, and would grind to an effective halt by the mid-1990s. Housing associations were preferred to councils and in Thatcher's second term councils were encouraged to transfer housing stock en masse to housing associations. Legislation in the late 1980s also deregulated rents in the private sector and this kick-started a renaissance in private renting. But Thatcher's true passion was to promote owner-occupation above and beyond what pure market forces would dictate in order to build a political and electoral base. She fought hard to continue mortgage interest tax relief and opposed economic arguments for its abolition. The tax subsidy scheme became MIRAS (Mortgage Interest Relief at Source) operated at source by lenders and house prices surged along with deregulated access to credit and mortgage finance.

In education, the repeal of Labour's 1976 Education Act merely allowed a treasured few remaining grammar schools to survive. Selection was further encouraged through the introduction of the 'assisted places' scheme, means-tested funding of places in private independent schools, but this had limited impact. Capital expenditure and higher education were particular targets for cuts and public spending on education fell from 5.6% of GDP in 1980 to a low point of 4.7% in 1988 (Glennerster, 1998). A voucher scheme in education was considered, but it was not until the 1988 Education Reform Act that quasi-marketisation began through parental choice and formula funding of schools. Parents could specify their preferred choice of school, while schools would now manage their own finances (instead of it being under local authority control). Schools had to compete for custom, better information on school performance informed parental choice and funding reflected the number of pupils attracted to the school. Schools also were given the ability to fully opt out from local authority control to become 'grant-maintained' and directly funded from central government. The same Act also allowed private businesses to sponsor independent schools, called city technology colleges, that continued to have state funding. The National Curriculum was also introduced, requiring all state pupils to be taught a core common syllabus in key subjects with a series of attainment targets for pupils at different ages (Key Stages). Higher education funding was also reformed, although not to the extent originally envisaged, as initial proposals had led to students and middle-class parents taking to the streets in the mid-1980s. Student loans were introduced in an initial cautious form as 'top-up' loans to supplement the frozen maintenance grant, with fees continuing to be fully funded in the first instance.

Replicating these radical market-orientated approaches to the popular and fundamentally free NHS was more difficult and had significant electoral risk. Thatcher had declared the NHS 'safe in our hands' and the first two terms were cautious with 'apparent continuity', with the past being the most 'striking feature' of Thatcher's health policy (Le Grand and Vizard, 1998, p 79). Reorganisation rather than reform was the main approach, echoing the agenda of the 1970s, although there was a change of emphasis in favour of private sector management practices and of the private sector itself. Pay beds were encouraged, reversing previous Labour policy, limited tax concessions were granted to stimulate demand for private medical insurance, the growth of privately supplied healthcare was generally encouraged and some ancillary services such as catering and cleaning were contracted out. Core NHS services were sacred but not dentistry or optometry, which effectively became areas of private provision for the majority, with selective free provision for children, pensioners and the poorest remaining. Spending growth slowed. Thatcher's third term was more radical. The 1990 National Health Service and Community Care Act introduced quasi-markets to the NHS. An 'internal market' based on a split between purchasers and providers was introduced to improve efficiency through competition. Healthcare purchasers were both health authorities and general practitioners (GPs), now newly empowered as fundholders. GP practices could volunteer to operate a budget with which to purchase secondary healthcare for their patients from providers – essentially hospitals both public and private, but also other healthcare providers. Public hospitals could also on a voluntary basis elect to become self-governing and opt out of district health authority control to become independent NHS Trusts. But by the time the reforms were implemented in April 1991, Thatcher was no longer Prime Minister.

Community care became the big issue in personal social services. Care in the community, as opposed to long-stay institutional hospital care for frail elderly people, mentally ill people and those with learning disabilities, had been a common and consistent policy aim during the 1970s. However, the Conservatives switched emphasis towards non-state provision. In particular, capital and other financial constraints on local authorities, together with an ideological antipathy to state provision, meant that residential care in the private and voluntary sectors had to be encouraged to grow as an alternative. The social security budget was allowed to finance a large step-change resulting in the huge expansion of private and voluntary homes in the 1980s – individuals could opt to enter such care homes and have the bill picked up by Supplementary Benefit (or later Income Support). The 1986 Audit Commission report, *Making a reality of community care* (Audit Commission, 1986), was highly critical of the financing and organisation of that model of community care, with its inchoate mix of NHS, social services and social security responsibilities leading to gaps in coverage and perverse incentives. The 1990 National Health Service and Community Care Act granted local authority social services departments the key role in the provision and promotion of such social care services, but as 'enablers' of care rather than providers. Care services would be largely provided by the private or voluntary sectors, with social services departments buying services from whoever was the best-value provider. Additionally, the emphasis of enabling people to continue living in their own homes wherever possible was paramount, subject to an upper cost constraint equal to replacement institutional care.

So far we have highlighted macroeconomic concerns and policy changes, but in the field of social security policy was, alongside public expenditure control, also aimed at the micro level – at incentives and especially at incentives to work and this involved reform of social security. We discuss the changes in depth in Chapters Four to Nine, but some crucial headline changes should be highlighted here. In 1981, the statutory obligation to uprate long-term benefits by the higher of prices and earnings factors was repealed, leaving the basic state pension to be uprated solely by prices, a structural change with long-term consequences that still haunts pension policy today. Benefits to the unemployed were reformed to improve work incentives, earnings-related supplements were abolished and benefits made taxable for the first time. The definition of unemployment was revised many times to both reduce the headcount, a political millstone, and to promote supply-side efficiency. One outcome of this was to upgrade the relative benefits of being defined as 'sick' or being given any label other than 'unemployed', a long-lasting structural change that persists to this day over a period of declining relative demand for low-paid, low-skilled employment (Nickell, 2001)[5]. Union power was confronted head on and confrontation with a range of unions led to the miners' strike of 1984 and legislation altering financial support of unions and ending many areas of influence ensured that along with the decline in manufacturing industry, union membership and influence declined, allowing the market to dominate wage setting, in particular in low-paid occupations where real wages stagnated for many years. Privatisation was also an early element of social security reform. Statutory Sick Pay paid by employers in the wage packet replaced the National Insurance Sickness Benefit. Later, this benefit was extended and joined by Statutory Maternity Pay along the same lines.

The central piece of legislation on social security – called the Fowler reforms – overturned pension provision. Abolition of SERPS was proposed, both to lower and control future spending commitments and to reflect the belief that private provision of additional pensions from 'occupational and personal pensions are the right way to provide additional pensions above the basic national insurance pension' (DHSS, 1985a, vol 2, para 1.32). But the private pension industry did not want the bad risks of low-paid workers so the generosity of SERPS was cut back instead. Private pensions were encouraged (at the expense of SERPS membership) through the provision of incentive payments (as discussed in Chapter Nine). The result was an unseemly overselling of private pensions, even to those who would have been better off staying in SERPS, and the pension industry became discredited as a result.

The Fowler reforms also revolutionised means testing and reformed the system to operate on a mass scale. Social assistance, renamed Income Support (discussed further in Chapter Six), came into existence in 1988. Family Income Supplement was replaced by a more generous in-work benefit for low-paid parents; Family Credit and means tests across the whole system were harmonised. However, cuts in entitlement were also involved, especially in the treatment of one-off needs where grants were replaced with loans from the Social Fund, with, in most cases, available money coming under a fixed budget to remove demand-led increases in spending.

Part of the new means-tested social assistance was also restructured to fit in with the radical local taxation changes that Thatcher herself saw as crucial to restructuring the relationship between individuals and local provision. The individual liability for the community charge (known throughout as poll tax) operated even for the poorest, who would have to pay 20% of any charge from their basic social assistance, rebates being limited to 80%. The overall inequity of the poll tax played a part in its huge unpopularity and the tax became Thatcher's downfall. In November 1990, she resigned.

Major, 1990-97

Major was appointed replacement Prime Minister for the Conservatives at the end of November 1990 and went on to win the 1992 general election despite economic recession. The infighting within Conservatives over Europe, the catastrophic withdrawal from the Exchange Rate Mechanism (on so-called 'Black Wednesday') in 1992 and the atmosphere of sleaze that undermined the Major common man's 'back to basics' campaign all eroded the potency of government for the five years to 1997. The Major years took forward the majority of Thatcher's agenda, but with some marked softenings of approach and some new initiatives.

Major presided over the bedding in of the 1988 Education Act. In 1992, the first school league tables were published, ranking schools' performance on the basis of the percentage of their pupils who achieved five good GCSE grades. Other performance indicators would later be added. Such measures were supplemented by the creation of a new and rigorous schools inspectorate, the Office for Standards in Education (Ofsted). This approach – of improving information to, and the 'voice' of, consumers of services – matched Major's main idea of the Citizen's Charter, which was intended as a driver to improve public services through standards, measurability and accountability. Education spending also rose as a percentage of GDP recovering from a low of 4.7% in 1988 to 5.1% at the end of Major's premiership (Glennerster, 1998). The disappointing failure of grant-maintained schools to take off in any significant way led to legislation to encourage more schools to become grant-maintained in the 1990s but met with only limited success (Timmins, 2001). In higher education, there was a drive to increase student numbers; polytechnics were permitted to become new universities and universities old and new were subjected to market-like pressures in terms of competition for funds and students. Voucher schemes, for training for school-leavers and for nursery education were tentatively tried.

The story for health and personal social services under Major is similar; a bedding in of the previous radical legislation passed under Thatcher, new measurability and accountability initiatives, and increased spending. In health, the latter rose from a low point of 4.8% in the late-1980s to around 5.8% under Major (Le Grand and Vizard, 1998). The 1990 National Health Service and Community Care Act was implemented in 1991, although full implementation of the community care aspects was delayed until 1993. Research into the effectiveness of the quasi-market reforms in the NHS (Le Grand et al, 1998) concluded that they had relatively little measurable impact and a consensus among commentators is that the reforms were administratively expensive but neither as terrible nor as positive as their opponents and supporters suggested (Le Grand and Vizard, 1998; Glennerster, 2000; Timmins, 2001). The Patient's Charter was introduced as part of Major's Citizen's Charter initiative, setting out rights to care, new and existing, as well as targets for minimum standards of care, and it notably raised the profile of waiting list times, which were subsequently successfully targeted. NHS Comparative Performance Tables, were published giving detailed information on a whole series of performance indicators for hospitals and other services. There was also a move towards a more preventative approach in the 1992 White Paper, *The health of the nation* (DH, 1992), which set targets for the reduction of cardiovascular diseases, cancers, HIV, mental illness and accidents through a strategic approach including the improvement of information and understanding. These so-called 'top-down management tools' collectively but quietly took over from the internal market as a foundation for health service improvement.

Major introduced the Private Finance Initiative (PFI), which allowed private money to fund capital spending, with private consortia contracted to design, build or even manage new projects and lease them in the long term to a public authority. Initially introduced in respect of health and transport with limited outcomes, PFI would later be expanded and become New Labour's favoured method of funding new public sector projects.

Housing policy continued the Thatcher trends and approach. Right to buy sales continued, albeit with an inevitable slowing of pace; council rents rose in real terms; large-scale transfers of council housing stock to housing associations continued apace; and local authority new-builds ground to a virtual halt, leaving housing associations the only significant players in newly built social housing. 1996 legislation created the concept of 'registered social landlords' to take in a wider profile of providers and to encourage further stock transfers. By 1997, council housing had become increasingly marginalised and housing had slipped from the political agenda to the extent that 'housing policy' no longer existed in the sense in which it had done during the post-war 'consensus' years (Hills, 1998; Timmins, 2001). Owner-occupation was hit by the early 1990s recession, with repossessions and negative equity in the sector, but otherwise continued to thrive, and indeed expanded in the mid-1990s despite falling support from MIRAS. The private rented sector enjoyed a modest yet sustained revival in the aftermath of deregulated rents. Levels of homelessness had increased dramatically as access to social housing stock became more difficult. The 1996 Housing Act, however, effectively ended any commitment for local authorities to permanently house the homeless, restricting provision to two years of temporary accommodation.

In social security, there was a mix of carrying forward the Thatcherite agenda and a 'softening' of approach in certain areas. The overriding concerns, however, were cost constraint in the face of factors such as the rising numbers of lone parents on benefit (see Chapters Three and Eight) and the rising costs of paying housing benefit for higher rents. Hard measures were taken and cuts made in the areas of, for example, housing costs for owner-occupiers on social assistance (discussed in Chapter Six) and SERPS (discussed in Chapter Nine). Invalidity benefit for older 'hidden unemployment', especially among men, was reformed (see Chapter Seven) and unemployment benefits were made more conditional and renamed Jobseeker's Allowance (JSA) (also discussed in Chapter Seven). In contrast, Major reprieved Child Benefit (discussed in Chapter Four), initially uprating it above inflation and then pledging to uprate it in line with prices. Disability benefits introduced in the 1970s were developed into the more generous Disability Living Allowance (discussed in Chapter Eight), and social assistance claimants once again had full rebates of local government taxation as the hated poll tax was abolished. The generosity of the in-work benefit Family Credit was increased and the model of in-work benefits extended to disabled workers. The welfare-to-work approach that would dominate New Labour's thinking also began to appear. Lone parents were set to lose their additional benefit premiums and discussions were in place to invite US employment service providers for 'single moms' into the UK to help lone parents return to work. Compulsory employment programmes were introduced for long-term unemployed people. These first efforts at a more comprehensive welfare-to-work programme heralded more radical programmes to come.

New Labour: Blair and Brown, 1997 onwards

The landslide victory for Labour in the 1997 general election was for 'New Labour' and definitely not the Labour of 1979. The party had abandoned left-wing policies in favour of a new pragmatism – a 'what counts is what works' philosophy. A social justice agenda had firmly replaced any vision based on public sector provision or state ownership. The emphasis was placed on creating a 'modern' welfare state. In health and education policies this meant largely building on, rather than dismantling, Conservative reforms and carrying forward and intensifying the existing agendas of standards, performance measures and choice. In terms of social security and employment policy, the American term 'welfare reform' was embraced. Clinton's victory in the US elections in 1992 meant that after Labour's own defeat earlier that year, the Party turned to the US for policy models. The language of Etzioni and Mead was adopted on balancing rights and responsibilities and on the need to pre-emptively manage workless populations (Etzioni, 1993, 1996; Mead, 1993, 1997). Transatlantic lessons were absorbed on the importance of making in-work subsidies effective from Clinton's expansion of the earned income tax credit (EITC) scheme that 'made work pay'.

The Conservatives had left Labour a 'golden economic legacy' in their view – low inflation, relatively high economic growth and falling unemployment. The inheritance was also of a country where income inequalities had risen hugely since 1979 (Hills, 2004 and Chapter Nine); indeed, the growth in inequality was faster in the UK than in any other comparable industrial country (Hills, 1996). New Labour set out to meet five pledges rather than presenting a vision of a different social policy. One pledge focused on the economy and the setting of tough rules for government spending. Stung by the 1992 election defeat and the label of 'tax and spend', Blair's manifesto contained a commitment for a Labour government not to raise income tax rates in its first term and to stick to Conservative spending plans for the first two years of that term. Thus, despite the legacy of inequality, the popular mood for change and the opportunities a booming economy presented for revenue, this promise effectively ensured that progressive policy was largely hogtied until the new millennium.

Words thus spoke larger than action for the early years of New Labour. But what words! Tony Blair set the historic target of eradicating child poverty within a generation in the annual Beveridge lecture in 1999 and Gordon Brown subsequently announced the aim of ending pensioner poverty. Action followed and a series of measures were introduced, primarily through the tax and benefit system, aimed at increasing the incomes of families with children and of the poorest pensioners. The readoption of poverty as a government concern was clearly a huge step forward for progressive policy and overturned the previous approach of abandoning any commitment to poverty for any part of the population. Tackling social exclusion was also seen as central to the New Labour project, with Blair setting up the Social Exclusion Unit in 1997 to address areas such as homeless rough sleeping, children in care, teenage pregnancy and neighbourhood deprivation, where groups of people were seen as living apart from the overall social and economic growth of the country. The notion was to bring about 'joined-up' action across the traditional silos of departmental responsibility. Much progress has been made, but it has not prevented the UK becoming a still more unequal society. Income inequality is at the time of writing and according to the Institute of Fiscal Studies at its highest level since 1961 (Brewer et al, 2008).

Labour's promise not to raise income tax rates held. Early tax reform centred on a revenue-raising windfall tax on private utilities. By 1999, a confident Gordon Brown felt able to cut the starting rate of income tax from 20% to 10%. Such progressivity was accompanied by the abolition of National Insurance contributions for the lowest paid workers (to help make work pay) and a 1% cut in the basic rate of income tax. In 2003, reforms to National Insurance also brought in a gentle degree of progressivity by introducing the payment of contributions above the upper earnings limit for the first time. The high-profile cutting of the basic rate of income tax from 22% to 20% in 2007 was accompanied by the curiously regressive move of abolishing the 10% starting rate, which, while it may have created a simpler system of income tax, proved deeply unpopular, backfiring on the government in a blaze of controversy. However, it would be wrong to suppose that New Labour has to any significant extent put back into the tax system the progressivity that the Conservatives took out. Indeed, the higher rate of income tax is 40% today as it was in 1997. National Insurance contributions, some indirect taxation and local government taxation have all risen under Labour.

Devolution makes discussion of New Labour's social policy difficult, as health, education and housing are now devolved policy areas, with Scotland and Wales differing in some aspects from England. Our following description captures the English position as this best matches the main ambit of New Labour and the majority of the British population. However, we note large differences in approach where space allows.

The promotion of equality of opportunity was at the heart of Blair's vision, evidenced by the 'education, education and education' slogan for policy's priorities. New Labour has clearly invested significantly in education. The immediate overturning of Major's nursery voucher scheme and the assisted places scheme apparently showed a greater egalitarian approach, but grammar schools were allowed to continue and grant-maintained schools only abolished in name, becoming 'foundation schools'. The overriding trend was one of continuity for the existing policy agenda of diversity, testing, league tables, parental information and choice, inspection and intervention. The architecture of the Conservative reforms remained: the National Curriculum, Ofsted and local management were built on; 'Tory policy plus' is one commentator's verdict (Timmins, 2001). Spending increases followed, particularly during Labour's second term, with education spending enjoying a 7.7% per year rise in real terms during this period (Smithers, 2005). The 2007 Comprehensive Spending Review promises further, more modest, real-term increases in spending.

Class sizes in primary schools were reduced to meet the manifesto pledges and teacher numbers grew, together with the number of support staff and free nursery school provision. The expansion of choice and diversity was particularly apparent in secondary education where the amount of parental information available mushroomed and a plethora of school types came into existence, including community schools, foundation and trust schools, faith schools, grammar schools, academies and city technology colleges. The Specialist School Programme led to specialist schools now accounting for a majority of secondary schools. Private sector involvement increased in these and in academies (the successor to the Conservative's city technology colleges, state-funded independent schools sponsored by private business) and more significantly in New Labour's abounding adoption of the PFI as its favoured method of funding new public sector projects, including school new-builds and refurbishments.

Post–16 education has been encouraged under New Labour and the introduction of a new Education Maintenance Allowance provides a cash allowance for 16- to

18-year-olds from low-income backgrounds to stay on in secondary education. From 2013, the compulsory age for secondary education is planned to be raised to 18. These provisions reflect the continued presence of a consistent number of 16- to 17-year-olds – around 9% – who are not in education, employment or training – the so-called NEETs. The target of getting 50% of young people into higher education has been accompanied by radical changes to education finance. New Labour replaced the remaining maintenance grant entirely with loans and introduced partial tuition fees (that could be waived or reduced subject to a means test). This was followed, a major backbench rebellion notwithstanding, by legislation to permit universities to charge variable tuition fees (the controversial so-called 'top-up' fees). Scotland did not follow suit. There has been a reinvigoration of adult skills development through the Learning Skills Council in England.

Health, like education, enjoyed significant increases in spending after the original two-year spending moratorium. After 2000, the NHS witnessed unprecedented increases in spending, with real annual increases in spending averaging 8.2% during the government's second term in office (DH, 2008a). The 2007 Comprehensive Spending Review promises lower future real increases of 4% per year that are nevertheless historically high compared with any other year since 1979. These have narrowed the gap between health expenditure in the UK and in neighbouring countries such as France and Germany, but have not yet met the target of raising UK health expenditure to the European average. Labour abolished the internal market in the NHS, but at the same time retained the purchaser–provider divide while changing the language from one of 'competition' to one of 'cooperation'. Arguably, the practice of GP fundholding was not so much abolished as universalised. GPs were banded into Primary Care Groups, later to become Primary Care Trusts (PCTs), with directly allocated budgets and responsibilities for managing and planning local healthcare services. The degree of consumer choice and competition in the NHS (in England) was extended in a manner even more radical than that undertaken by Thatcher through the empowerment of patients to chose their provider for secondary care. Patients, advised by their GP, now have the right to choose at which hospital, including some private hospitals, they will have their operations, with money at a given NHS tariff following the patient (Glennerster, 2005).

Devolution of operational management down to PCT level left the role of health authorities to monitoring and overseeing the introduction of Hospital Foundation Trusts (semi-independent hospitals granted greater financial and operational autonomy), which are at the 'cutting edge of the government's commitment to de-centralising public services' (DH, 2008b). Target setting has been a significant theme and very publicly set targets (concerning waiting list times, increased staff and facilities and so on) have been largely successfully met. Spending reviews allocate funds that come attached to specific targets. The 'top-down management' approach is also reflected in New Labour's emphasis on uniform national standards of excellence. Under New Labour, the new independent National Institute for Clinical Excellence (NICE) is responsible for providing national guidance on healthcare; a new Health Commission (called the Commission for Health Improvement until 2004) provides inspection; and a new system of National Service Frameworks defines national standards of care for major health conditions and key patient groups. Public health promotion continued from the Major years, the most visible result of which is the ban on smoking in enclosed public spaces applying to the whole of the UK from 2007.

Other 'market-like' reforms in health are in place or are planned. Private sector involvement in the NHS has increased under New Labour through expansion of the PFI, which is behind a significant step-change investment in new hospitals, and from private treatment being provided for more NHS patients through public funds.

Housing policy has continued the process of demunicipalisation, with stock transfers of local authority housing to housing associations. Local authority stock fell by over 1.7 million between 1997 and 2006 (CLG, 2008a) and their new builds remained at a virtual standstill[6]. Social rents continued to increase in real terms, albeit at a slower rate than under the Conservatives (see Chapter Six). Elsewhere, the process of phasing out MIRAS begun under Major was completed and it was finally abolished in 2000. New Labour's housing policy has been distinguished by the pursuing of an agenda of neighbourhood renewal and social inclusion (with the problem of rough sleeping being targeted more proactively as part of the social inclusion project) and, post-2002, by intervention in the housing market to stimulate private sector new-builds in the face of a re-emerging housing shortage and escalating house prices. Private housing provision had been transformed by the long economic boom, with cheap access to credit and an unmet need for new housing translating into huge increases in house prices (see Chapter Three) and consequent problems of affordability and, more recently, a market crash and the threat of negative equity.

The model for personal social services in which local authorities are 'enablers' of private or voluntary sector provision continued apace under New Labour. The emphasis both on standards and inspection and on consumer choice grew. The Social Care Institute for Excellence, the equivalent to NICE in healthcare, was created in 2001 and tougher inspection regimes have led to the closure of many residential and nursing homes (Glennerster, 2005). Choice is very much in evidence in current government social services policy (see DH, 2005) and in the 'direct payments' scheme, whereby the provision of payments can replace the provision of services for certain groups of social care users.

Developments in social security are discussed in detail in Chapters Four to Nine, but the highlights are as follows. Blair enforced the commitment to carry out Conservative spending plans so that lone parents' social assistance and Child Benefit were cut to the same level as that of other claimants. A review, heralded as 'thinking the unthinkable' was announced, but in truth the Department of Social Security (DSS) was sidelined as the Treasury stepped forward to take control of and direct radical reform. First, the cuts to lone-parent benefits were effectively overturned by higher allowances for all children as both Child Benefit and social assistance for children were significantly raised. However, child poverty, now a high-profile policy target, would primarily be solved by more parents being employed. 'Making work pay' through a combination of in-work transfers and a minimum wage was the way forward. The introduction of the UK's first national minimum wage was a flagship New Labour policy that took effect from April 1999 and prevented employers taking advantage of increased in-work transfers to depress underlying wages. A new, more generous, Working Families Tax Credit (WFTC) replaced family credit but as a tax credit scheme run by the Inland Revenue[7]. The DSS also lost its role of collecting National Insurance contributions (which became the Inland Revenue's responsibility in 1999). Provision of social security moved significantly to the taxman.

Employment for lone parents increased overall as a result of WFTC (Blundell and Reed, 2000), but to effectively combat child poverty the level of child-orientated transfers had to be significantly increased. To do this solely through Child Benefit would be to insufficiently target the poor. A new Child Tax Credit (CTC) that operated across in-work and out-of-work populations and replaced social assistance (Income Support and JSA) elements for children was introduced in 2003 (see the discussion in Chapter Four). The approach, so-called 'selective universalism', extends help to most families with children but most to the poorest parents. Additional support for low-paid workers came from a parallel Working Tax Credit (WTC) (discussed in Chapter Six), which additionally was able to contribute to the costs of childcare. A national strategy for childcare sought significant expansion of provision to assist parental employment. Both CTC and WTC were operated by the Inland Revenue and Child Benefit too came over to the taxman.

Making work pay provided financial incentives to work, but other Labour policies focused on 'push' factors and a series of mandatory and other employment programmes have been introduced. The New Deal for Young People (NDYP) met an election pledge to improve the quality of employment programmes for young unemployed people (aged under 25) and to reduce youth unemployment, and was financed by essentially the only 'new' money raised from the windfall tax on privatised utilities. However, the NDYP became only the first of many New Deals that spread across the whole 'workless population' to encompass for the first time the idea that employment programmes should not solely focus on those defined as unemployed.

The DSS was renamed the Department for Work and Pensions and welfare reform adopted the mantra of 'work for those who can, security for those that cannot' to meet tough employment targets: 80% overall, 70% for lone parents and a narrowing of area- and ethnic-based differentials from the average. Originally, the only mandatory programmes were those for the unemployed. Over time, however, mandatory work-focused interviews were introduced for lone parents and the approach has been ratcheted up and expanded across the claimant population and now includes the mandatory requirement of lone parents with older children to seek work. Incapacity Benefit was replaced with Employment and Support Allowance (ESA), which expected employment orientation for the majority (see the discussion in Chapter Seven). The most recent Green Paper (DWP, 2008a) puts forward the abolition of Income Support and all working age claimants coming under JSA or ESA jurisdiction.

New Labour's policy on pensions and pensioners is a complex story, covered in detail in Chapter Nine. The key theme is that resources have been targeted at the poorest pensioners by greatly expanding the generosity of means-tested benefit provision for the over-60s, first through the Minimum Income Guarantee and then through Pension Credit. New Labour's policy has been to deliberately focus increases on means-tested assistance (therefore targeting those most in need) rather than on increasing the basic state pension (which would be to the benefit of all pensioners). However, it is now clear that this approach is medium term and that the adoption of the proposals of the Turner Commission (Pensions Commission, 2004, 2005) means that future pensions will be based on a combination of earnings-uprated basic pension with secondary state and private pensions (discussed in detail in Chapter Nine). The long-term prospect is thus for less means testing and improved incentives to save.

The latest policy changes in 2008 in social security bring to a close our brief historical overview of the policy changes that have occurred in the British welfare state since the 1970s and before. The country that saw Margaret Thatcher enter No. 10 Downing Street and wave from the window in May 1979 is very different from the one currently facing a threatened deep recession and election in 2009 or 2010.

Summary

This chapter has looked at the historical development of British social policy in order to give a background to more detailed analysis in Part Two of the book. We have looked at the longer-term history of social policy programmes that preceded the 1970s and our so-called 'generation of change', and we have looked at areas of social policy – education, health, social services and housing – that form some of the crucial context for our focus on taxation and benefits. The highlights of these themes are as follows:

- Radical right-wing reform of the welfare state was promised by the Heath government of 1970-74, but only certain elements were introduced, in housing and means-tested, in-work benefits.
- The Labour government of 1974-79 was faced with the first major economic recession since the Second World War, and introduced a raft of anti-discrimination laws and expanded universal benefits, non-means-tested

benefits and second-tier state pensions. Public spending after the IMF loan in 1976 was cut back, but mostly affected capital programmes.

- The Conservative governments of Margaret Thatcher from 1979 to 1990 sought to reduce state activity, increase the economic efficiency of the economy by marketisation and cut back public spending. This led to privatisation, a decline in union membership and power, and the restructuring of social policy to prioritise provision through private means in order to concentrate benefits on the poor and to ensure work incentives were optimised through lower-level benefits that only rose with prices. Tax reform moved to lower income tax rates and increase consumption tax, while local government tax reform led to the poll tax and Margaret Thatcher's resignation.
- John Major's governments from 1990-97 moved back to a property-based tax for local government finance and introduced individualised income taxation. Programmes for children, including Child Benefit, were reprioritised. Privatisation continued and this led to purchaser–provider models in health and social services operating on the basis of care in the community.
- From 1997 New Labour concentrated on welfare-to-work programmes and reshaping provision for children and for the over-60s to combat public commitments to end child and pensioner poverty. Large increases in public spending on health and education, together with increased target setting on performance, occurred, with schools and hospitals encouraged to adopt a more semi-autonomous status.

Notes

[1] Amazingly, at the time of writing, the 25p age addition is still payable to pensioners over 80 at exactly the same nominal value.

[2] The *Black papers* were a series of pamphlets critical of education policy published from 1969 onwards.

[3] This was despite high-rise blocks at their peak only accounting for 10% of council housing (Timmins, 2001).

[4] Seven-year-old Maria Colwell was killed by her stepfather in 1973, despite various reports of ill treatment having been made to various agencies.

[5] In a nutshell, '… the huge decline in the relative demand for unskilled workers has outstripped the fall in their relative supply. This had led directly to significant falls in their relative pay and very large increases in their unemployment, inactivity, and sickness and disability rates. These disadvantages then tend to interact with other local social and economic conditions to make their situation worse' (Nickell, 2001, p 623).

[6] Construction work began on 195 new council houses in England in 2006/07, 28 in Scotland and just 12 in Wales (CLG, 2008a).

[7] The Inland Revenue merged with HM Customs and Excise in 2005 to create Her Majesty's Revenue and Customs.

THREE

Changing lives and a changing economy

Changes in social policy described in the previous chapter have to be seen in the context of the changes in the demographic and economic structures of Britain. Indeed, social and economic policies change to reflect underlying structural changes and sometimes affect wider society and the economy, although mostly in non-measurable ways. This chapter takes a broad view and summarises the main themes of change over time in population, household formation and the economy since the 1970s. We focus on themes that are most relevant to our analysis of the incidence and performance of social policy over the lifetime in the latter parts of the book.

Population composition

There has been significant overall population growth that hides different trends in birth, longevity and migration since the 1970s. Overall, the British population has grown by 7.6% from 55 to 59 million between 1979 and 2006. Figure 3.1 summarises changes in population size and composition by age and gender using population pyramids for these two years. The increase in the number of older people in the population is evident from the lengthening of the bars in the upper parts of the graphs (those aged 60 and over), by 17% between 1979 and 2006. The over-60s grew from 20% to 21% of the whole population but the over-75 population grew much faster, by 50% overall and from 5% to 8% of the whole population. On the other hand, there are fewer children in 2006 compared with 1979, an overall fall in under-15-year-olds of 11%. However, more recent increases in births (discussed below) mean that the youngest age group of children (aged 0 to 4) has only fallen by 6% overall. Children aged under 15 years made up 21% of the population in 1979 and this fell overall to 18% by 2006. The remainder of the population, of working age, rose by 12% from 33 to 37 million.

In fiscal terms, both children and older people tend to be economically inactive and an underlying assumption about paying for welfare rests on the relationship between the working age population and children and older populations – the so-called 'dependency ratio' represented by the relationship of the populations of older people and children to the working age population. Figure 3.2 shows the trend in these crude dependency ratios over a longer period, 1971 to 2006. Child dependency ratios declined fastest from the mid-1970s to the end of the 1980s, falling from 44% to 32% before flattening and rising slightly in the early

Figure 3.1a: Population distribution by age and gender, 1979

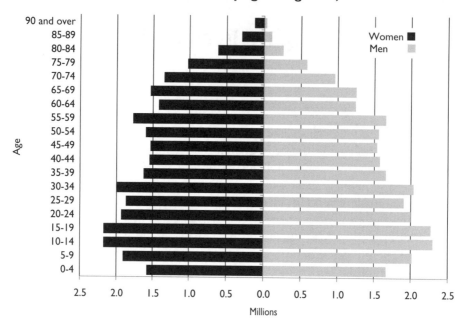

Figure 3.1b: Population distribution by age and gender, 2006

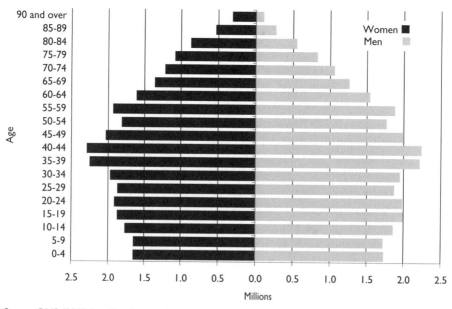

Source: ONS (2007a) and earlier versions.

Figure 3.2: Dependency rates for pension age and children, 1971-2006

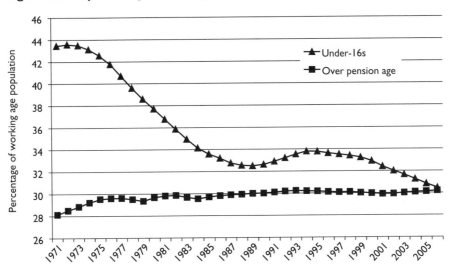

Source: Authors' calculations from ONS (2007a) and earlier versions.

1990s and falling again consistently from 1994. The pension age dependency rate has climbed slowly and consistently. In crude terms, some of the additional costs of supporting more elderly people have been counterbalanced by fewer children and a constant growth in working age population over the period. However, the expansion of higher education has meant that more children continue to be out of the main labour market until later in their early adult life and the actual dependency rate of children rises, leading in part to the changes in finance of higher education since the 1990s by shifting some of the burden of paying for higher education from contemporary workers (taxpayers) to the students themselves in the form of individual lifetime loans. The proposed extension of the compulsory education age to 18 will worsen crude dependency ratios, but it is crucial to note that education is partly funded by the increased productivity and wages that result from educated workers.

Births and fertility

The decline in the number of children stems primarily from changing fertility. Figure 3.3 shows the total fertility rate alongside age-specific rates for the period 1971 to 2006. The total fertility rate for all women of childbearing age (the solid black line and right-hand scale in Figure 3.3) rose in the late 1970s and then fell continuously until the mid- to late 1990s and has risen since. But the trends in fertility by age of mother (at first birth), shown by the various lines in Figure 3.3 that relate to the left-hand axis, clearly show an increase in delaying birth, as fertility has fallen steeply for women in their twenties who represent the main age group giving birth. Overall, the fertility rate among women aged 20-24 has fallen from 125 births to 70 per 1,000 and among women aged 25 to 29 from 130 to 100 per 1,000 since 1974. Teenage fertility has also fallen but less sharply. On the other hand, fertility rates in women over 30 have grown but they still represent a minority of births. The drivers of later childbirth are common across most developing countries and are due to increased postponement after women's participation in higher education and in career employment combined with later marriage and cohabitation (Rendall and Smallwood, 2003). Advances in fertility treatment have also enabled more success in childbearing among women in their late thirties and forties (albeit the probability of success is still low). Overall, the trend to later births is more strongly associated with higher earnings and thus with higher-income families. These changes over time in delayed age of first birth are important factors to incorporate into the development of our model lifetimes in Part Three of the book.

The other aspect of fertility that is crucial to understanding evolving differences in income and gender profiles is the occupational differences in timing of birth that come about from different education and earnings and that reflect social class. The mean age of the mother is higher in higher-skilled and higher-paid occupations at the time of birth of their first child when compared with the lowest occupational groupings[1] by 2.7 years in the 1970s. This difference rose over the 1980s to an average of 3.4 years and this came about mostly by the higher-income

Figure 3.3: Fertility, 1971-2006 – total and age-specific fertility rates

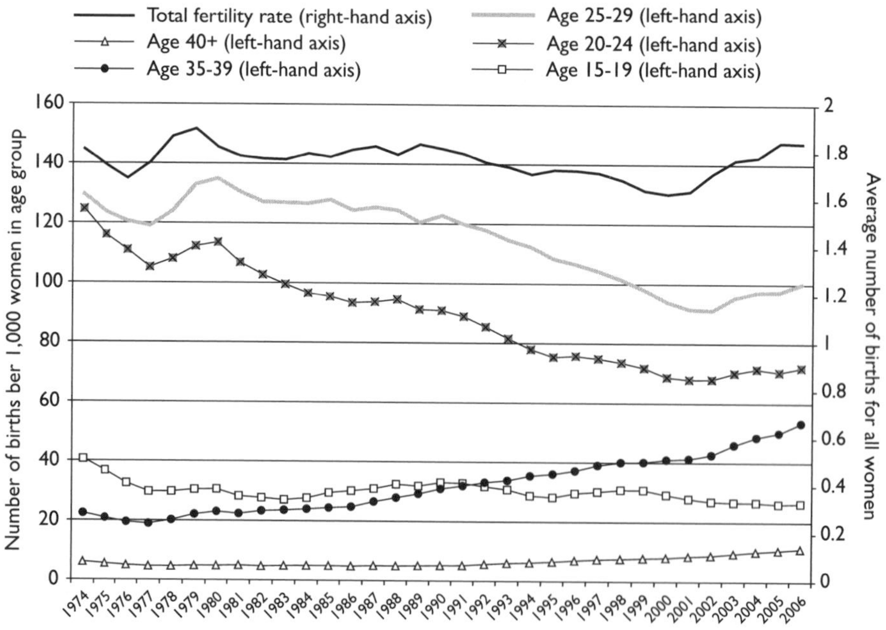

Source: Dunnell (2007, Figures 11 and 16)

mothers delaying birth by a further 1.4 years on average, with mean age at the birth of the first child rising to 29.7. Since the 1990s, the gap in birth timing has narrowed, with mothers in both low- and high-paid occupations further delaying first births (ONS, 2005). Since 2001 (using a changed definition of occupations introduced in that year and for figures that end in 2006), the first births to the highest qualified rose from the age of 31.3 to 31.9, while the same births for the lowest qualified rose from age of 27.7 to 28.4 – an average gap of 3.7 years but not comparable with the earlier figures (ONS, 2007b, Table 11). We use these findings in our later model building in Part Three.

Ageing and longevity

Let us look in more detail at the increasing longevity of the British population, as this has significant impacts on social provision and funding of pensions. Overall life expectancy increases through improved health across the lifecycle so that lower infant mortality and other factors will increase the average. However, in common with other industrialised countries with good public health and healthcare systems, the main factor in recent increases has been extended life for the older population; the fact that more people survive for longer and have longer retirements once past pension age of 60 or 65. Measuring life expectancy is not simple because over the lifetime the average number of years of expected life is not the same across the whole population. Those born today will have longer lives than those born 70 years ago and thus the cohort rather than the period of life expectancy best captures changes in age-specific mortality rates. These cohort life expectancy estimates enable a more accurate assessment of the number of years that someone of pension age will survive and how pensions and other social policy instruments have to adapt to meet the needs of increased years of retirement as each cohort of the population reaches pension age. Figure 3.4 shows the changes to expected years of life for 65-year-old men and 60-year-old women from 1981 through to 2056. The number of years of retirement for women aged 60 has risen by almost eight years since 1981, from 22.3 years to 28 years by 2008. Projections put further increases to 32.6 years by 2056. In 1981, men aged 65 had 14 expected years of life and this has risen to 20.8 by 2008 and is projected to rise to 25.5 years by 2056. However, such projections are averages for the cohorts and there are significant inequalities in life expectancy that arise from class. The most recent evidence showed the differences by occupational status for the period 1972 to 1999 (Donkin et al, 2002). The difference in life expectancy between the top professional and bottom unskilled classes rose over the period. Professional men aged 65 had 2.6 additional years of life expectancy compared with their unskilled peers in 1972 to 1976 and these extra years grew to 4.1 by 1997-99. The same class-based difference in women's life expectancy at 65 was 2.9 to 4.5, but with a less clear linear trend.

Figure 3.4: Years of expected life at pension age, 1981-2056

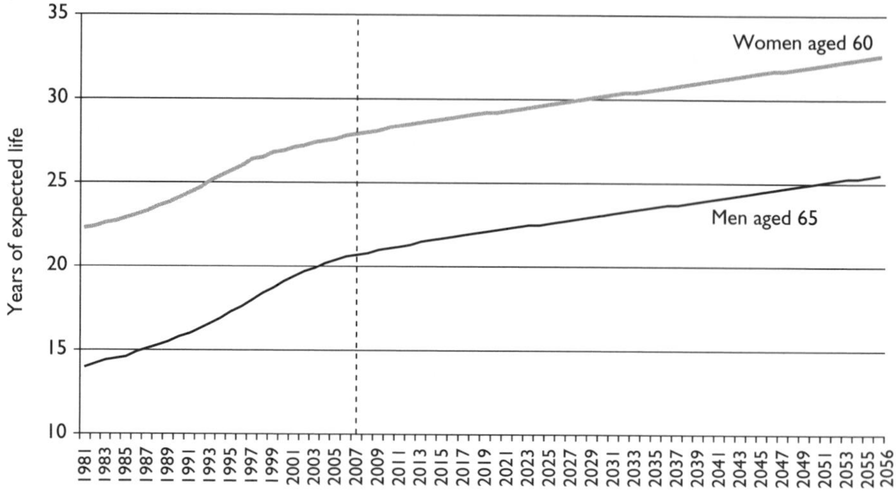

Source: GAD (2008a)

Family and household formation

Changes to the crude counts of population, however, are not always the driver of changes to policy. Often it is changes in the way that people live together in families and households that matter most. Marriage and divorce rates both reflect and drive other changes and falling marriage rates and increasing divorce and unmarried cohabitation are summarised in Figure 3.5 as indices of underlying rates. Divorce is now over twice as common as in the 1970s and marriage around half as common, while cohabitation has risen (figures only available from 1978) to be two-and-a-half times as prevalent.

Marriage, divorce and cohabitation

These trends in marriage and cohabitation meant that two trends were changing together: the move to having smaller families and the increase in the number of lone-parent families. Table 3.1 summarises these trends and shows that families with only one child accounted for 18% of children in 1972 and 26% by 2006. Over the same period, the proportion of children living with a lone parent grew from 8% to 24% of all children. The cumulative trends in ageing, family formation and break-up have resulted in more people living separately and consequently the number of households has risen faster than growth in families and in overall population – putting a strain on housing supply. The total number of households rose from 1971 by 31% from 19 to 25 million, but the number of single-person households more than doubled from 3 to 7 million, while the number of families only rose from 15 to 17 million (McConnell and Wilson, 2007, Figure 1.1).

Figure 3.5: Marriage, divorce and cohabitation

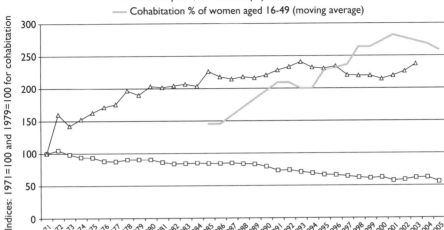

Source: Authors' calculations from ONS (2006), ONS (2008a)

The combination of family change and household formation has led over time to changes in the composition of households, as seen in Figure 3.6. Households containing pensioners have grown from a quarter (24%) in 1975 to nearly one third (30%), while households with working age adults but no children have grown from 35% to 49% of all households – nearly all accounted for by the rise in proportion of single-headed households. Couples with children have reduced

Table 3.1: Children by family type, 1972-2006

	% of all children				
	1972	1981	1997	2001	2006
Two-parent families					
With one child	16	18	17	17	18
With two children	35	41	37	37	36
With three or more children	41	29	25	24	22
Total two-parent families	*92*	*88*	*79*	*78*	*76*
Lone-parent families					
With one child	2	4	7	7	8
With two or more children	5	8	14	15	16
Total lone-parent families	*8*	*12*	*21*	*22*	*24*

Source: ONS (2007c)

Figure 3.6: Household composition by pension age, presence of children and number of adults, 1975-2005/06

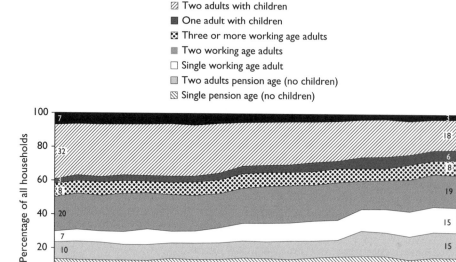

■ Other households with children
▨ Two adults with children
■ One adult with children
▩ Three or more working age adults
▨ Two working age adults
□ Single working age adult
▨ Two adults pension age (no children)
▨ Single pension age (no children)

Note: Great Britain from 1975 to 2004/05, then UK.

Source: DWP (2007a, Table 2.5); CSO (1990, Table 1); Department of Employment (1989, Table 1) and previous versions.

in proportion from 32% to 18%, while lone-parent households have doubled from 3% to 6%. All of these changes mean that the relationships between earnings, pensions and household formation have changed significantly, with potentially great impact on taxation and benefit programmes.

The final aspect of demographic change relates to the types of accommodation in which these changed families and households have lived. Figure 3.7 shows first that the number of households has grown as a consequence of the combination of population growth and the increasing trend for smaller households. The tenure basis underlying this growth shows clear evolution further towards predominant owner-occupation. The long-term decline of the private rented sector, observed from the Second World War, has been halted since the early 1990s as a result of changes in policy on rent and security of tenure for private lettings, discussed in Chapter Two. The largest change has been the huge decline in council housing run by local authorities since the early 1980s – driven by the programme of sales to sitting tenants in the first instance and then the transfer of stock to independent housing associations from the 1990s onwards.

Figure 3.7: English households by tenure, 1971-2005

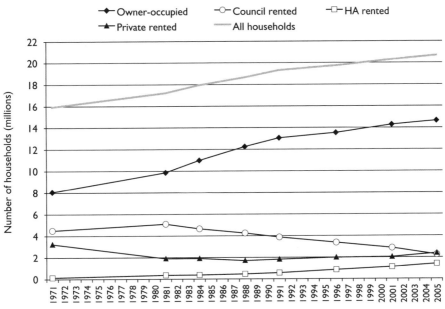

Source: CLG (2007)

The economy

The 1970s heralded the first economic recession since the Second World War and the subsequent period has seen two more with another imminent in late 2008. Despite periodic recession, however, the UK economy has still grown strongly overall over the past 30 to 40 years. Figure 3.8 shows overall trend growth in gross domestic product (GDP, using the left-hand axis), while the year-on-year annual growth figures (on the right-hand axis) give a clear indication of the cyclical fluctuations and the depressions of 1974, 1980 and 1991. The 16 years since 1991 are thus the longest period of sustained growth seen over the period, even if this has slowed recently in the face of a worldwide credit crisis.

Economic growth has come with restructuring and the service sector has become further dominant. The recession of the early 1980s was a major time of industrial restructuring that left manufacturing decimated, followed by the almost complete contraction of the mining industry. The 1990s' recession hit wider sectors of the economy, with financial and other services suffering more than in the 1980s. The structural changes in the macroeconomy affect households in a number of ways, but crucially in the creation and sustainment of jobs. Looking across the whole period from 1971, there has been significant job growth but huge shifts in the composition and nature of these jobs.

Figure 3.8: UK gross domestic product, 1971-2006 – real trend and annual growth

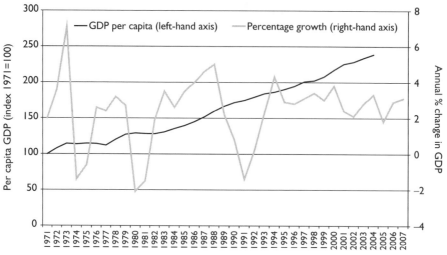

Source: ONS (2007c)

Figure 3.9 breaks down the overall change in employment (number of employed) since 1978 by industry and gender. Overall, there are over three quarters of a million more jobs for men and 5 million more for women over the whole period. However, it is clear that some industries have suffered net job decline across both male and female jobs – manufacturing, utilities, and agriculture and fishing. However, manufacturing clearly shows the largest volume of net job decline – over 2.8 million male and 1.5 million female jobs overall. The main job growth has been in the service sector, with finance and business, and distribution, hotels and restaurants being the largest net growth areas for men. These parts of the service sector are also important for women but the public sector is the biggest growth area for female jobs – an increase of more than 2 million.

These very significant changes in job growth and decline for men and women have been accompanied by a structural shift in the hours of work as more jobs have become part time. If we go back to 1984, the point at which data become consistently available on part-time employment, total employment has risen from 19 to almost 22 million people in the workforce. The proportion of these jobs that are part time has risen from just over a quarter in 1984 to over a third in 2007. Part-time jobs for women, always the majority, have slightly declined from 78% to 74% as increased labour market participation by women has also taken up full-time jobs – particularly in the public sector, as previously shown. It is thus clear that much of the underlying growth in employment has been in part-time jobs and while men have gained from this growth, they have done so far less than women. The overall story is that the growing economy has produced prolonged employment growth across cyclical fluctuations. However, the nature

Figure 3.9: Employment growth, 1978-2007 – net employment change by industry and gender

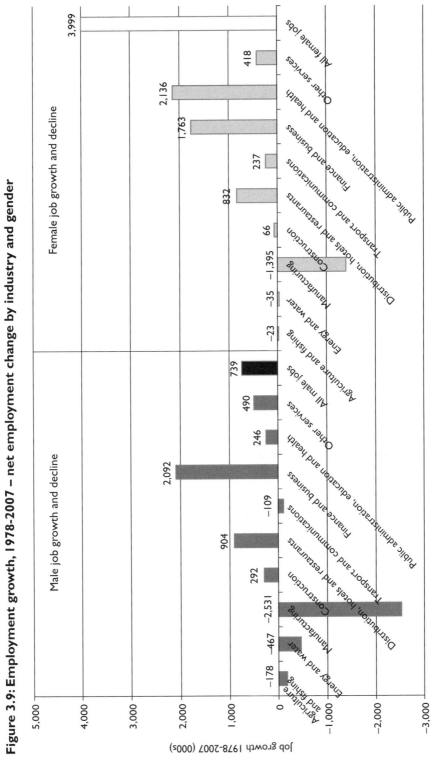

Source: Authors' decomposition of trends from ONS (2008b, Table 2.06).

of employment has become more female and more part time. These structural changes have had an effect on the numbers and characteristics of those who do not or cannot work.

Unemployment follows the economic cycle and Figure 3.10 shows with the tinted line and using the left-hand scale that unemployment (using the International Labour Organisation (ILO) definition rather than counting claimants of benefits who are defined as unemployed) was 4% in the early 1970s. This rose to over 5% in the late 1970s before the major depression and restructuring of the economy in the 1980s took unemployment rates to a peak of 12% in 1984. Unemployment then declined as the economy grew, but never fell to the levels of the 1970s before the next recession of the early 1990s took unemployment back up to a peak of 10.5% in 1993. The prolonged economic growth since then has allowed unemployment to fall to levels that are roughly those of the mid- to late 1970s again, around 5%. Figure 3.10 clearly shows the lag in reducing unemployment after each recession. However, the rates of economic inactivity are another potential sign of exclusion from the labour market as they reflect the number of people who are neither employed nor currently looking for work[2]. This group is diverse, made up of those who are looking after the home and/or family, traditionally women, of students, of retired people (essentially early retired as the figures are based on the working age population) and those who suffer from ill health or have a disability that excludes them from the labour market. Since the early 1970s, the rates of economic inactivity have varied between around 35% and 39% of the population, as shown by the black line and right-hand axis. Different scales in Figure 3.10 allow an easier comparison of trends between

Figure 3.10: Unemployment and economic inactivity rates, 1971-2007

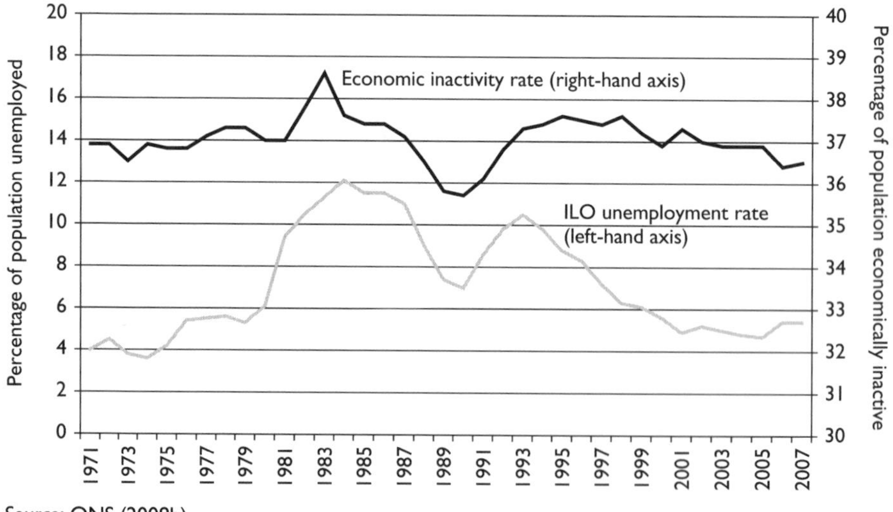

Source: ONS (2008b)

Note: Scales differ to show trends over time.

unemployment and inactivity. During the 1970s, inactivity rates were basically flat at around 37%, with some year-on-year variation. With the onset of the 1980s and the return of mass unemployment, inactivity rates also rose sharply, reaching a high point in 1983 of over 38.5%. Inactivity rates then fell and mirrored falling unemployment until the recession of the 1990s, when rates rose dramatically again mirroring unemployment. Since the early 1990s, recession rates of economic inactivity initially continued to grow slowly until 1998 and subsequently have slowly fallen to a point historically where they are at or below the level of the 1970s – around 36%.

Changing employment rates over time hide important underlying change in composition. We know from earlier figures on employment growth and on the growth of female and part-time work that one outcome of this is that female rates of inactivity due to family and home care have fallen. Figure 3.11 shows that this trend has been accompanied by a range of factors that outweigh falling inactivity from increased female employment: ill health has grown as a reason for inactivity and the numbers of students and early retirees have increased since 1993.

However, it is important to link both unemployment and inactivity to underlying skill levels, as over time the number of unskilled jobs has remained constant or fallen and the earnings returns from more highly skilled jobs and better education are greater. The risk of unemployment in 2007 is over four times higher for

Figure 3.11: Economic inactivity by reason, 1993-2007

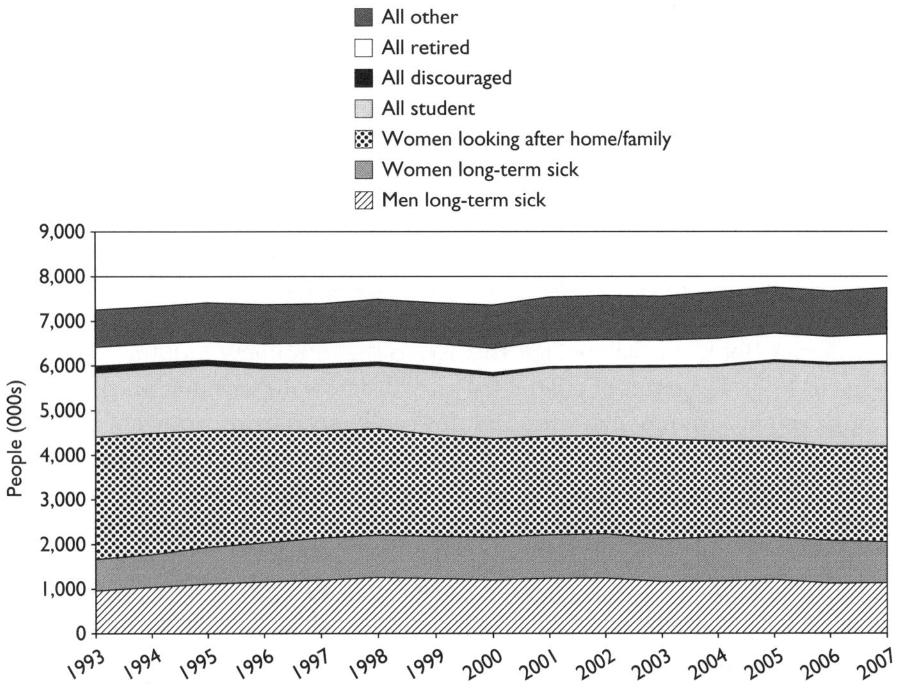

Source: ONS (2008b, Table 2.14)

'elementary occupations', at 8.7%, than managers and professionals, at 2% (ONS, 2008b, Table 6.11). The risk of inactivity from long-term ill health is also skewed to the low skilled, although this is best captured by using educational qualifications rather than occupation as an identifier of skill level, with 40% of people who are inactive due to long-term ill health having no qualifications and only 4% having higher education (authors' own calculations from ONS (2004)).

Another characteristic of the structural concentrations of unemployment and ill health among the low skilled is that household-level employment has become more polarised between 'workless' households and those 'work-rich' households where all or most adults work. One part of this trend in the growth of workless households is the growth in lone-parent households previously discussed, but the tendency for non-employment to concentrate in 'work-poor' households and for this concentration to grow over time is linked to low skills, disability or ill health (especially for men) and having a partner who does not work (Berthoud, 2007). It should also be remembered that selection is occurring as more highly qualified women return to work as mothers earlier and that the rising price of housing means that dual-income families are largely essential to maintain commitments to mortgages in the early years of the mortgage when costs are highest. In contrast, benefit and tax incentives for dual earning for the low paid during rising levels of part-time employment have not ensured equity of job entry opportunities for families over time – a point we return to in Part Two.

Earnings growth and dispersion

The growth in employment since the 1970s, despite cyclical fluctuation, has been accompanied by remarkable increases in inequality of earnings. Figure 3.12 shows real median full-time male earnings from 1971 to 2007 alongside the earnings levels at the 90th and 10th percentile points in the earnings distribution for the same period. Median earnings have grown in real terms by 65% over 35 years, but the higher paid have higher earnings growth. The 90th percentile has risen by 107% and the lowest-paid 10th percentile has only grown by 37%. Indeed, the very low paid, the bottom 5th percentile group, saw no real increases in earnings during the 1990s, one of the facts that led to the introduction of the minimum wage in 1999. The result of differential growth across the earnings distribution is a huge rise in earnings inequality and this can be seen by the growing distances between the lines in Figure 3.12, with the low paid falling further behind the median and the high earners pulling further and further away.

This evidence on increased inequality could, in theory, be the outcome of changes in volatility of earnings rather than permanent long-term changes in income mobility; however, Dickens and McKnight (2008) demonstrated that between the late 1970s and 2006 there was little evidence of long-range earnings mobility. Indeed, they showed that earnings mobility fell between 1979/80 and 1997/98 for low earners. These lowest-paid workers had a consistently high

Figure 3.12: Real earnings growth, 1971-2007 – median, 10th and 90th percentiles of male full-time earnings

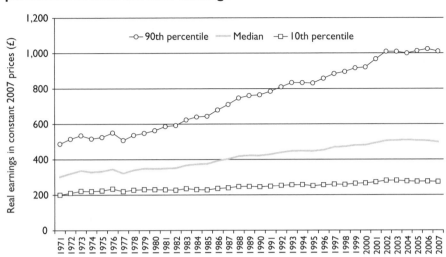

Source: ONS time series from New Earnings Survey/Annual Survey of Hours and Earnings provided to authors.

probability of being non-employed from one year to the next. Earnings mobility appears to have increased since the early 2000s (Dickens and McKnight, 2008). The rise in women's participation in the labour market has been accompanied by a narrowing of the pay gap, but such gaps remain substantial. Overall, comparing female and male *full-time* median earnings since 1971, it can be seen that women's earnings have risen from 60% to 80% of men's in crude terms, allowing no differences for occupation and skill profiles.

Prices and consumption

Real earnings growth has led to real changes in consumption patterns as the population's purchasing power has increased. Inflation, one of the main threats to living standards and purchasing power, particularly for those on low or fixed incomes, has been at historically low levels since the mid-1990s alongside sustained economic growth. The period of low inflation appears to have come to an abrupt end in 2008 with the rise in worldwide fuel and food prices and Figure 3.13 shows how inflation previously peaked in 1991 at 10% and 1981 at 22%, and in the late 1970s, at 18% in 1978 and 28% in 1976. Figure 3.13 also shows earnings inflation based on percentage rises in the average earnings index alongside price inflation and clearly shows that average earnings have kept ahead of inflation over the period as a whole.

Figure 3.13: Price and earnings inflation, 1971-2006

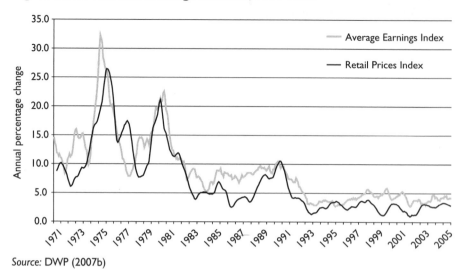

Source: DWP (2007b)

Real income growth for the majority has led to a change in consumption patterns; however, pensioners on fixed income and claimants of state benefits uprated solely with prices will not have shared in real income growth to the same extent. Figure 3.14 shows average household spending on a variety of items from 1971 to 2005 and shows how some elements of basics, such as food, clothing and footwear and fuel, have fallen. Spending on food shows the most dramatic fall, from over 25%

Figure 3.14: Household expenditure, 1971-2005

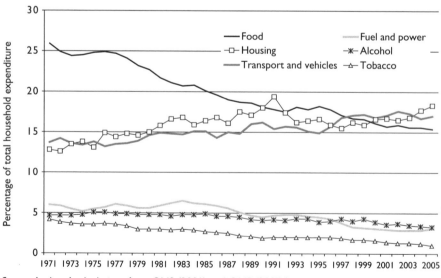

Source: Authors' calculations from ONS (2001) and ONS (2007d).

to around 15% of average household expenditure. These are trends that result from both higher incomes, as consumption of food and other necessities is known to fall as income rises, and from increased efficiencies in retail pricing through the expansion of supermarkets and from increased importing of cheaply produced products from developing countries in Asia. Housing costs, on the other hand, have risen on average from 13% to 18%, reflecting both the move to more market pricing of rents and the rise in house prices, making mortgages more expensive over time. It is also important to note the impact of changing preferences, as spending on tobacco has fallen greatly while spending on leisure goods and services (such as holidays, increasingly taken abroad) has risen.

Summary

This chapter has given a brief overview of changes in the economy and society since the 1970s, both to provide context to the general story of policy change and to help frame the model lifetimes that are adopted in Part Three of the book. Of course, there is much more to say on the changing culture and attitudes that accompany these changes in the population, household composition and the economy, but we leave this to other commentators. A more important theme that arises from the overview is one of increasing inequality. There is clear evidence that people occupying the top, middle and bottom tiers of British society have been moving apart, both drifting and perhaps driven, over the period. Evidence from the different generations gained from a series of birth cohort studies clearly shows that social mobility is at best static but probably falling (Blanden et al, 2005).

Britain has had a bumpy but overall upward growth in prosperity since the 1970s. Harold Macmillan's well-known aphorism that the most of us have 'never had it so good' applied to the late 1950s and is true again today. But 'never had it so skewed' is perhaps a parallel and more pertinent version for today. This chapter illustrates that the period since the 1970s, our so-called 'generation of change', has potentially very different impacts for the lifetimes of high, median and low earners that we look at in more detail in the remainder of the book. But unpicking the story of change and difference is complex. The impact of taxes and benefits will be a crucial determinant in both the drivers and outcomes of economic and social inequality and we now move on to look in more detail at the policies and programmes that have been in place to affect people's lifetimes. Then, in Part Three, Chapter Ten, we will look at how far such policies in the aggregate have affected income inequality.

• Demographic changes since the 1970s have led to a growing proportion of older people as life expectancy has increased, overall by eight more years for women and five more years for men after pension age since 1981. Fertility has fallen but has begun to rise again in more recent years. Significant differences in longevity exist between social classes and delayed childbearing is becoming more common.

- Rates of marriage have fallen by half and the incidence of divorce has more than doubled. Cohabitation has risen. One outcome is that the number of lone parents has risen and the percentage of children living in such families has risen from 8% to 24%.

- Household composition has changed, with single-person households rising from 21% to 30% and households with children falling from 42% to 27% of all households.

- The number of households has grown with both population growth and the underlying change in household composition. Owner-occupation has grown.

- The economy has grown by 230% in real per-capita terms since 1971, but four significant recessions have occurred, in the mid-1970s, early 1980s, the early 1990s and in 2009.

- Employment has grown over time and across the recessions but manufacturing employment has fallen; the service sector has grown and the number of part-time female jobs has increased significantly.

- Levels of unemployment peaked in the mid-1980s and then again in the early 1990s, since when a 16-year period of constant economic growth returned levels to those of the 1970s prior to the slowdown and recession in 2008/09. Economic inactivity has grown but has also changed composition and fluctuated over the economic cycle. Male inactivity from ill health has risen and female inactivity from household activity has fallen. Inactivity levels fell in the latter part of the 1990s and prior to 2008.

- Real earnings growth has been experienced on average but is accompanied by increasing earnings inequality. Wage growth for the lowest paid was poor throughout the 1980s and 1990s but has increased since 2000. Women's earnings have on average narrowed the gap with men's.

- Earnings growth has outstripped prices, resulting in real increases in living standards over the period for the majority of the population who rely on earnings. Consumption patterns have changed as real living standards have risen, with a falling proportion of household income spent on food, fuel and higher proportions spent on housing, goods and leisure services and travel.

Notes

[1] Occupational groups I and II (professional occupations and intermediate managerial and senior administrative occupations) compared with groups IV and V (partly skilled occupations and unskilled occupations).

[2] This includes those who want a job but have not been seeking work in the past four weeks, those who want a job and are seeking work but not available to start work, and those who do not want a job.

Part Two

From the cradle to the grave

FOUR

Childhood

This chapter looks at childhood, and how programmes to support children have changed since the 1970s. But when does childhood start and end? Policy provision for childhood precedes 'the cradle' because programmes for children and childhood begin to operate during pregnancy. Defining the end of childhood is more difficult. If children continue into further education, parents may find their economic obligations to support children continuing into the early twenties – beyond the teenage years that most usually signal the move from childhood into young adulthood. The earliest age at which a child can be considered either as an adult or be treated as independent of his or her parents' income is 16. This age has formed the basis for entitlement to benefits for a considerable period as it has coincided, since 1972, with the earliest age at which children can leave education. However, legally, the definition of children, as stipulated in the 1989 Children Act, is 18. Current transfers and benefits can continue in respect of those continuing in secondary education up to the age of 19, or, in some circumstances, 20. Our approach is to define childhood as including those up to and including the age of 18, assuming continued secondary education. This approach is consistent with recent proposals to extend the school-leaving age to 18 (DfES, 2007).

The chapter follows a three-part structure that is shared by all subsequent chapters in Part Two. First, we look at detailed policy history. Second, we consider aggregate outcomes for the value of benefits and their coverage of all children, and third, we consider the value of support for our three model families with low, median and high earnings.

Maternity programmes

Maternity provision dates from the first days of the British welfare state when the 1911 National Insurance Act provided for one-off, lump-sum maternity grants. The Beveridge-inspired post-war National Insurance system consolidated and extended provision by adding a 13-week Maternity Allowance alongside the lump-sum Maternity Grant. The reasons for improving provision for maternity stemmed from contemporary pronatalist concerns (Timmins, 2001)[1], which, given the post-war baby boom, were unfounded. Maternity Allowance was originally set at a relatively generous level compared with other national insurance benefits, Unemployment Benefit and Sickness Benefit[2].

How had such provision changed by 1979? Contributory maternity benefits introduced in 1948 were still in place. The Maternity Grant, £25 per baby born, had, however, not been uprated since November 1969. Maternity Allowance had been periodically uprated but was no longer more generous than unemployment or sickness benefits. Maternity Allowance had experienced the changes during the 1960s that introduced earnings-related supplements that could more than double the amount of benefit received if previous earnings were sufficiently high[3]. Maternity Allowance was payable for a total of 18 weeks. Means-tested maternity provision was available from Supplementary Benefit, the social assistance safety net in the 1970s. Supplementary Benefit, discussed at greater length in Chapter Seven, comprised set national rates of benefit accompanied by benefits in kind and large areas of discretionary additional help that could be tailored to individual circumstances. Pregnant women and mothers of babies receiving Supplementary Benefit were given free welfare milk and vitamins as a matter of right and could be considered for discretionary weekly exceptional circumstances additions and one-off extraordinary needs payments according to their individual needs. Low-paid expectant mothers not receiving Supplementary Benefit were also entitled to receive free welfare milk and vitamins subject to a means test. Finally, a truly universal provision was introduced in 1979 that continues to this day: the waiver of prescription and dental charges for all pregnant women.

Maternity provision was reformed radically by the Thatcher governments, but the story is not a simple one. In the first instance, entitlement to the Maternity Grant was extended by being made universal rather than contributory in 1982. This extension was subsequently reversed by the 1986 Social Security Act. This Act, the result of the Fowler reforms discussed earlier in Chapter Two, abolished the universal Maternity Grant and replaced it with a means-tested alternative, the Maternity Expenses Payment from the Social Fund. The Maternity Expenses Payment was only available to those new mothers who claimed a qualifying means-tested benefit, but was a grant rather than a repayable loan as the majority of Social Fund payments were. A savings limit of £500 that meant the grant would be reduced on a pound-for-pound basis by the amount of any savings in excess of that sum. This Maternity Expenses Payment was not regularly uprated and by the end of the Conservative years had not risen since 1990. Free milk and vitamins for expectant mothers remained, but were restricted to those in receipt of social assistance benefits.

Maternity Allowance meanwhile underwent two major changes in the 1980s. First, earnings-related supplements were abolished in the first term of the Thatcher administration as part of a wider abolition of such supplements across all social insurance that saw a return to the principle of flat-rate benefits in order to improve incentives to work (see Chapter Two). Second, in April 1987, Maternity Allowance was replaced by Statutory Maternity Pay (SMP) for all those who were in employment and effectively 'privatised'. This change followed the model of Statutory Sick Pay, introduced previously in 1983 (see Chapter Seven). SMP is administered by the employer rather than any government agency. Entitlement is non-contributory, resting directly on employment and earnings conditions and requiring continuous employment for at least six months and a recent earnings level above the threshold for paying National Insurance contributions. By 1997, SMP was paid for a maximum of 18 weeks, and was paid at two levels, 90% of average weekly earnings for the first six weeks and then at a flat rate for the remaining 12 weeks. Maternity Allowance continued as a flat-rate contributory benefit for the minority of working women who did not qualify for SMP because of their employment history but who had sufficient contributions.

New Labour has improved the generosity of maternity benefits but has done so primarily to benefit the poorest children. The Maternity Expenses Payment was replaced in 2000 by the Sure Start Maternity Grant, which was initially set at double the value of its predecessor (£200), and then quickly increased by 250% over the next two years to £500. However, there is no long-term commitment to maintaining this at real values over time and it has been subsequently frozen. Entitlement remained limited to those in receipt of a qualifying means-tested benefit, but the savings rule was abolished and thus it now goes to virtually all of the poorest children at birth.

Free milk for pregnant women was replaced in 2006 by the Healthy Start scheme, which provides vouchers (worth £2.80 per week) that can be exchanged for Healthy Start foods (essentially milk *and/or* fruit and vegetables). The scheme is targeted at low-income families and can be received by those claiming Income Support or income-based Jobseeker's Allowance and those with earnings below a threshold. Recent government legislation, the 2008 Health and Social Care Act, will introduce a universal one-off 'Health in Pregnancy Grant' from April 2009 to support additional nutritional needs in the last months of pregnancy. However, entitlement to this grant is dependent on taking up maternal health services from a health professional (GPs, midwives and so on) and is thus conditional on health-optimising behaviour.

New Labour has retained SMP and made it more generous. SMP is earnings-related at the earliest point at which work ceases and comprises payment of 90% of earnings for the first six weeks. It then moves on to a flat rate (in 2008/09 the lesser of £117.18 or 90% of average weekly earnings) for the remaining weeks. The length of entitlement has been progressively increased. Since April 2007, SMP has been payable for up to 39 weeks, with a further increase to 52 weeks promised by 2010 (CPAG, 2007). However, many employers provide both more generous maternity pay and leave conditions above and beyond the statutory minimum levels. These forms of occupational welfare particularly benefit those in the public sector as well as higher-paid and higher-qualified employees. Paternity pay and leave were introduced in 2003 and Statutory Paternity Pay, paid at the same rate as the standard rate of SMP and based on similar employment and earnings rules, is payable for up to two weeks to fathers of newborn babies[4].

Finally, the state-run Maternity Allowance continues to exist, but only as a fall-back provision for those who are ineligible for SMP, for example women who have just entered or left employment. In further erosion to the contributory insurance principle, this residual Maternity Allowance is no longer contributory, but like SMP now rests on direct employment and earnings conditions.

Policy for children

Social insurance saw maternity as an event that was an 'insurable risk', but the larger and longer lifetime risk of having children is beyond the approach of social insurance. The British welfare state took far longer to recognise the general needs of childhood, despite pregnancy and birth being part of the 1911 scheme. The potential to introduce transfers for children was hampered by the primacy of the wage system and the myth of the 'family wage' – that employers and unions would bargain for (male) wage levels that were sufficient to keep a family – that was prominent in the 1920s and 1930s. However, by the late 1930s, arguments that debunked this myth began to gather influential support (Brown, 1983). Analysis revealed the facts of family income: that a household's needs rise as children are born, but that there is no mechanism to cause wages to rise to match; added to this was the fact that children caused maternal employment to fall and thus caused family earned income to fall. Following the ceaseless campaigning of Eleanor Rathbone, MP and others, support for children slowly became a part of the social policy agenda (Glennerster, 2000; Timmins, 2001). Beveridge was convinced by Rathbone and his 1942 report (HMSO, 1942) rested on an underlying assumption that the state would introduce a family allowance. This was later enshrined in the post-war welfare state through the 1945 Family Allowances Act, which introduced a non-contributory, non-means-tested transfer for each child other than the eldest. These allowances were paid in addition to the allowances for children contained in personal income taxation that operated at the time and continued until the late 1970s.

The rediscovery of child poverty in the mid-1960s forced the issue on to the political agenda and challenged the post-war social policy settlement on children (Glennerster, 2000; Timmins, 2001). The campaign for improved benefits for children was helped by the fact that low-paid workers were demonstrably often not able to adequately support a one-child family on their earnings without state assistance and that the low rate of Family Allowance that had not been uprated since 1956 played a significant part in this problem. Harold Wilson's Labour government eventually uprated Family Allowance in the late 1960s, but it was left to the Conservative government of Edward Heath (1970-74) to introduce more fundamental benefit reform.

As part of its radical policy agenda, discussed in Chapter Two, the Heath government wanted to integrate taxes and benefits but introduced Family Income Supplement (FIS) in 1971 as a temporary first stage of a long-term and more radical process that eventually stalled in the face of considerable administrative and technical hurdles. The inherent problem was that tax allowances for children in income tax disproportionately helped richer taxpaying parents. Faced with the logistical impossibility of the 'perfect' reform of introducing a negative income tax – an option also toyed with by the US at the time – the Heath government introduced FIS as a means-tested, in-work benefit to aid poor families with children[5]. FIS, however, had notable problems of its own. It was dogged by a low take-up rate and presented its claimants with high marginal deduction rates, the so-called 'poverty trap' whereby £1 of extra earnings could translate into a very small increase in income as benefits were withdrawn and liabilities for tax increased. Indeed, rates of over 100% were possible, making income after taxes and benefits fall at the margin (see Chapter Fourteen).

The Labour government's commitment to avoiding means testing and adopting universal provision in the 1970s meant that Child Benefit was introduced as a universal categorical benefit that would replace *both* Family Allowance and income tax allowances for all the children in the family. Its introduction met with all-party support. The Conservatives' October 1974 manifesto had after all promised, as a prelude to the introduction of a full system of tax credits, a 'child credit' scheme along the same lines as Child Benefit[6]. The new universal benefit was phased in and tax allowances phased out so that Child Benefit became fully operational in 1979, just at the point where the political agenda changed dramatically.

Despite its positive role in supporting incentives to work and its public popularity, Thatcher governments were more hostile towards Child Benefit because it was expensive and not targeted (Bennett, 2006). Child Benefit was under serious threat of being cut and/or means-tested during the 1980s – a Cabinet review in 1982 proposed so. Instead, it was allowed to wither in value with intermittent uprating. Fortunes turned under John Major, who reprieved Child Benefit and introduced a series of upratings that almost returned the real value of benefit back to the 1979 level. The Major administration, however, introduced differential amounts of benefit paid in respect of the first child and following children.

The Thatcher governments saved their most radical changes in provision for children for means-tested benefits under the Fowler reforms in the mid-1980s. One driver of these reforms was the concern about the fall in fortunes of families with children, who, rather than pensioners, were seen to be the new priority for means-tested social security (DHSS, 1985a). The Fowler reforms emphasised both means-tested targeting and improved work incentives. Out-of-work benefits, in particular for unemployed people and for those in receipt of social assistance, were made less generous (Evans, 1996) and thus the overall incentives for parents to enter work were increased by a combination of this and improved wage supplements. The more generous Family Credit replaced FIS in 1988 to improve incentives for parents to take up low-paid work. Although more generous than its predecessor, the new benefit no longer carried entitlement to free school meals and welfare foods.

Income Support replaced Supplementary Benefit and together Family Credit, Housing Benefit and Income Support were aligned with common rules for income and savings to ensure greater consistency and simplicity and to end the worst instances of high marginal deduction rates. The original 1988 rules defined the difference between 'out of work' and 'in work' as being 24 working hours a week. Reform in 1992 lowered this to 16 hours a week and this meant that part-time maternal employment was more actively rewarded by the system, in particular for lone parents who were more likely only to work part time[7].

With their historical commitment to ending child poverty, the New Labour governments of Tony Blair and Gordon Brown prioritised provision for children. The initial reforms to lone parents' benefits inherited from Major threatened cash losses for this group but were offset by the significant uprating of Child Benefit and children's Income Support rates for all parents. The Department of Social Security joined with the Department for Education and Employment to become the Department for Work and Pensions (DWP) – and it took over two large lifecycle-based groups of responsibility: employment and the benefit system for the working age population, and pension policy for older people. Responsibility for children crossed into HM Treasury and to the tax system – even Child Benefit became the responsibility of the Inland Revenue (now Her Majesty's Revenue and Customs). However, the new DWP also took on the broader task of introducing a more employment-focused benefit system and reforming pensions; this coined the phrase 'welfare reform', a term that continues to be used today.

Raising levels of parental employment with the help of DWP's welfare reform process was the approach adopted to reduce levels of child poverty using the economic logic of labour supply that was consistent with all policy since the 1980s – raising in-work incomes to 'pull' people into work while 'push' factors from welfare-to-work programmes ensured that entitlement to benefits was increasingly based on job search. However, the increases to Income Support for children had raised *out of work* income for families with children and this meant that reform of in-work benefits had to be significant to make work pay. Family Credit was replaced by the Working Families Tax Credit (WFTC) in 1999, a more generous version of the previous system[8]. The small differences were, first, that responsibility for the administration of WFTC lay with the tax authorities and thus more resembled a refundable tax credit than a benefit, and second, that WFTC was paid as a wage supplement alongside earnings in the take-home pay of a parent worker. This meant that employers bore a large part of running costs and that intra-household targeting was worsened – WFTC often went to the 'male wage packet' rather than the 'mother's purse'. This arrangement proved to be unsustainable, as employers baulked at the costs and the poverty lobby pointed to poor intra-household consequences. Quietly things were reversed to resemble other cash benefits and WFTC was paid mostly to the mother.

But the long-term policy aim of integrating the tax and benefit systems resurfaced in an echo of Heath's unimplementable radical ideas from 1971. This involved a wider implementation of the principle of tax credits. A significant step towards tax benefit integration occurred in 2003 when WFTC was abolished and a wholly integrated tax benefit for children was introduced, Child Tax Credit

(CTC). CTC is payable at full rate to those with either no or low earnings and then tapered out for high earners. The system is a complex one, but simply put CTC is weighted to the low-paid and non-employed who receive full tax credits before they begin to taper out at roughly half of average earnings. Entitlement, however, is also carried much further up the income distribution through a second 'family element' of CTC that is subject to a second higher income threshold and means that CTC extends to a large number of parents on middle incomes who would not have qualified for WFTC, thus greatly extending the number of families eligible for tax credits. Significantly, the CTC system replaced dependent child additions to all other benefits. All financial support in respect of dependent children will be made through the tax credit system and additional elements of all other benefits phased out. The new system means, for example, that new claims for Income Support are 'adult only' and do not contain any additions for dependent children.

Alongside CTC, a new comprehensive low earnings supplement was introduced for all workers, Working Tax Credit (WTC, discussed in detail in Chapter Six). Parents can claim WTC alongside CTC in a single claim and at any age if they work more than 16 hours a week. Other claimants of WTC have to work 30 hours or more and be over 25. WTC also increased the generosity of payments towards formal childcare provision available to working parents. Once again, the new system (the combination of WTC and CTC) was more generous than its predecessor (WFTC) for low-paid families with children and especially so for those at the margins of Income Support where a move into work of 16 hours a week for a lone parent could raise his or her income above the poverty line. This new system was at the heart of the attempt to eradicate child poverty within a generation.

The result of the emphasis on policy for children since 1997 has been to target resources to the poorest as well as to make strategic interventions for all children, so-called 'selective universalism'. Childhood is seen as the crucial time for social investment and for building resources to ensure that the poor children of today do not become poor parents of the future. This longitudinal and developmental approach, boosted by evidence from the first British longitudinal panel study in the 1990s and the birth cohort studies of the 1950s and 1970s, has probably overplayed the idea of transmitted poverty in policy makers' minds – only 12% of today's poor children had parents who were themselves poor (Blandon and Gibbons, 2006). The principle of making an investment in all children was further supported by the Child Trust Fund introduced for every child born on or after 1 September 2002. This provides £250 (£500 in the case of low-income families) of start-up funding for a tax-free, long-term savings plan that matures when the child reaches 18.

Education subsidies

In the 1970s and earlier, local education authorities could provide a range of discretionary, education-related subsidies for clothing and travel, and additionally, in a small number of cases, for educational maintenance allowances for poorer children. Under increasing centralised control and spending constraints, these expenditures fell off and it was not until the Blair government that interest in providing financial incentives for poorer 16- and 17-year-olds to remain in secondary school or college was renewed. Since the 1980s, the proportion of this age group who appeared to take no part in education, employment or training (so-called NEETS – not in education, employment or training) had remained stubbornly high. From 2004, Education Maintenance Allowances (EMAs) were introduced as a national scheme to increase the numbers of young people from lower-income backgrounds participating in post-16 education. An EMA of up to £30 per week is paid directly to young people staying on in education after the age of 16 whose family income is below a given threshold.

The history of policy change on benefits for maternity and childhood provides a clear but complicated story that can be summarised as a move away from universal to more targeted approaches but with changing assumptions about generosity and of coverage. We now turn to consider these issues in aggregate profiles.

Generosity and coverage of maternity provision

Figure 4.1 shows the value of one-off maternity grants from 1971 to 2007 in real terms. Each programme has been allowed to erode over time between structural changes in 1987 and 2003, both of which increased generosity significantly at the point of change. The change from the Maternity Grant to the Maternity Expenses Payment in 1987 was in part paid for by far fewer mothers qualifying as provision moved from contributory/universal low-level grants to more selective generosity. Today's Sure Start Maternity Grant has double the purchasing power of the prevailing grant in 1971 and three times the purchasing power of that in 1987. However, the historical practice of what Sutherland and colleagues (2008) term 'benefit erosion' continues to operate today and the generosity of the Sure Start Maternity Grant has been allowed to erode in real terms since 2003.

Figure 4.2 shows the value of weekly maternity benefits (combining trends in Maternity Allowance and SMP) between 1971 and 2007. For consistency, it gives values based on the *basic rate* of maternity benefit. From the introduction of SMP in 1987, the real value of benefit has risen slowly, but dramatic above-inflation increases were made by New Labour in 2002 and 2003. Since then, levels have been flat in real terms. One of the roles of maternity transfers is to smooth incomes and weekly maternity benefits are a short-term replacement for maternal earnings. Figure 4.2 therefore also shows rates in relative terms as a percentage of average earnings (using the right-hand axis). With the exception of

Figure 4.1: Maternity grants, 1971-2007

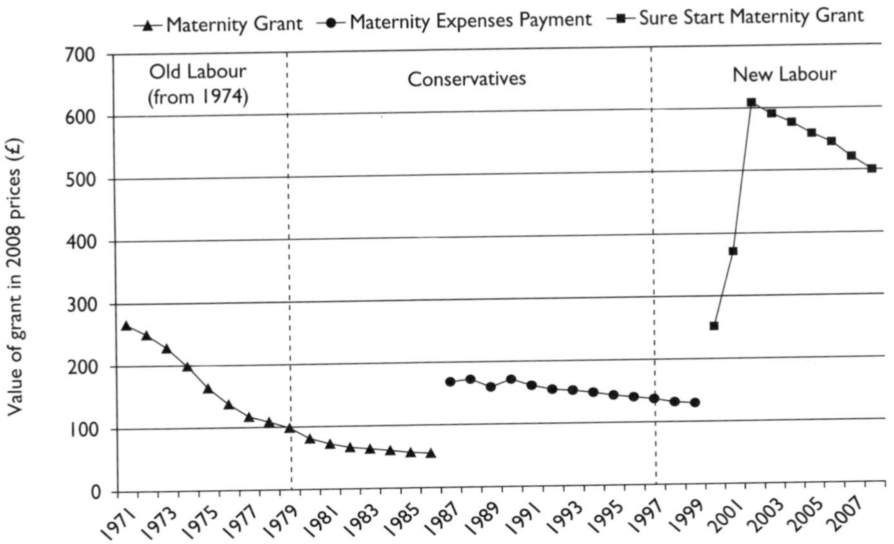

Note: Entitlement to the Maternity Grant was contributory from 1971-81 and universal from 1982-86; entitlement to succeeding grants rested/rests on receipt of a qualifying means-tested benefit. All plotted points are rates as at April each year.

Source: Authors' calculations from DWP (2007b) and IFS (2008a).

Figure 4.2: Maternity benefits, 1971-2007

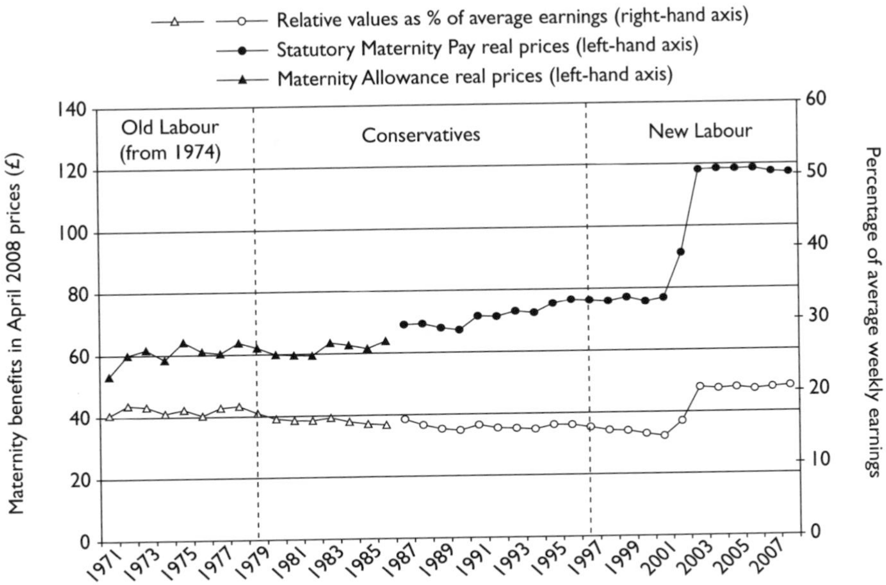

Note: Values of Maternity Allowance and SMP based on flat-rate values for each year. All plotted points are rates as at April each year.

Source: Authors' calculations from DWP (2007b) and IFS (2008a).

the 2002 and 2003 increases, the trend over time has been for levels to fall when compared with earnings.

One of the outcomes of changing from state to employer provision for SMP is that there are no statistics on caseload since 1987. Estimates of an annual caseload of 300,000 were given to parliament in 2004[9], but such an estimate provides no possibility to establish what proportions of births are covered by British maternity benefits, an incredible omission when it comes to the high-profile concerns of child poverty and its long-term consequences.

Generosity and coverage of benefits for children

How have benefits for children fared over time? Figure 4.3 shows Child Benefit rates in real prices from 1977 for three types of children: a single child of a lone parent; a single child of couple parents; and second and subsequent children in all families. The overall trend is most clearly seen in the trend of Child Benefit for the first child in couples (the tinted line). The period 1977-79 represents the phasing in of Child Benefit. Thereafter, Child Benefit suffered mixed fortunes under Thatcher followed by a revival under Major. Reform under Blair has taken Child Benefit to its highest-ever real value and a period of consistent price uprating has maintained this value. Child Benefit for lone parents is a parallel story until it was removed in 1999. Child Benefit for second and subsequent children can be

Figure 4.3: Real value of Child Benefit, 1977-2007

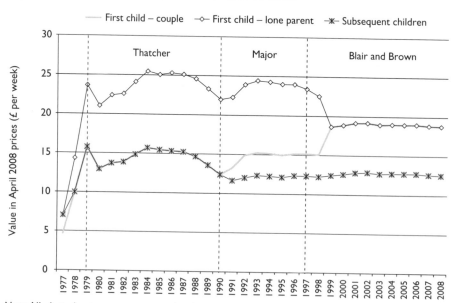

Note: All plotted points are rates as at April each year.

Source: Authors' calculations from DWP (2007b) and IFS (2008a).

seen to have maintained a constant value in real terms since the differential rate was introduced by Major in 1991.

While Child Benefit levels have been comparatively flat in nature over time, Figure 4.4 shows the contrasting fortune of in-work assistance to families with children, FIS, Family Credit and WFTC between 1971 and 2003. Figure 4.4 shows the average award of these benefits in real terms over the period and illustrates the increase in generosity of each reformulation of these benefits, although some of the growth will be due to changes in the composition of families claiming, for instance a greater number of single-earner lone parents.

Figure 4.4: Average awards in in-work transfers for families with children, 1972-2003

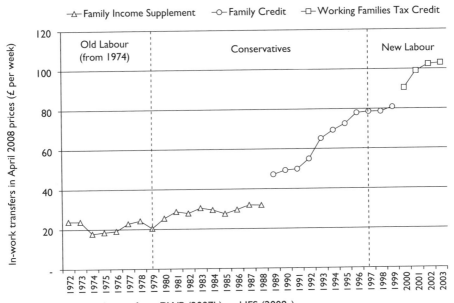

Source: Authors' calculations from DWP (2007b) and IFS (2008a).

However, the safety net of social assistance is crucially important for the poorest children and Figure 4.5 shows the value of safety net provision for children in out-of-work families[10]. These graphs clearly show that 2008 provision for the dependent children of safety net benefit claimants is more generous in real terms than that of the 1997 or 1979 systems. However, there are also two structural changes to consider: first, how has social assistance for children changed to take account of their age?; and second, how has social assistance met the needs for family size by the weights given respectively to first and subsequent children? Figure 4.5 shows that 2008 provision is completely flat for all children over the age of one up to and including age 16. In the first year, a greater amount of benefit is given through the 'baby element' of CTC, which is only paid where

Figure 4.5: Real social assistance levels for children, 1979, 1997 and 2008

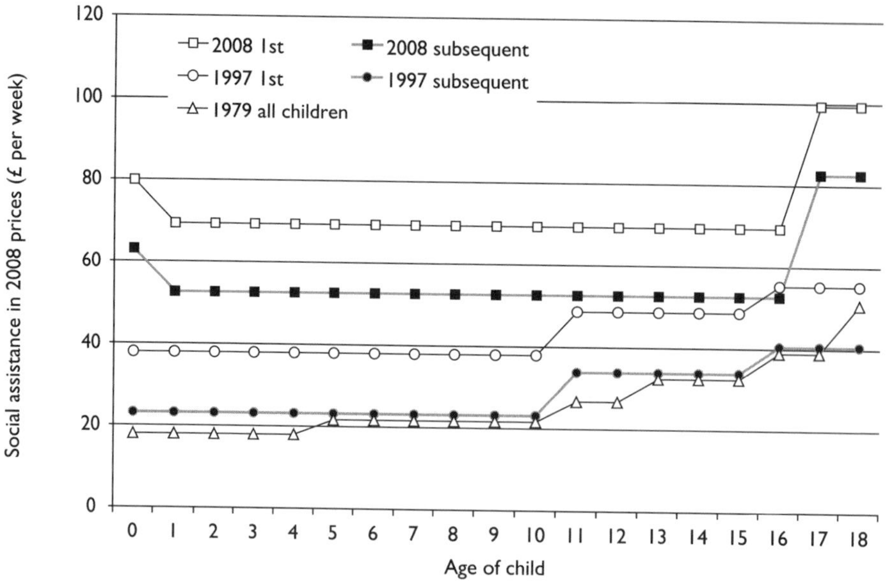

Source: Authors' calculations from CPAG (1978a, 1997b, 2008).

there is a child under the age of one in the family. At age 17 and 18, the child will receive an EMA if he or she remains in full-time education. Otherwise, the 2008 system does not distinguish needs on the grounds of child age. The 1997 system gave higher amounts in three age bands. The 1979 system, while being the least generous in respect of children[11], has the most age-related bands and does not distinguish between the first and subsequent children. In 1997 and 2008, rates for second and subsequent children are lower than for the first child. The combination of age-related and flat benefit structures for children, along with the differential rates for the first child, means that the systems differ most in the way that they treat large families or those with older teenage children.

One major policy story over the past 30 years has been the increased use of means testing and within that the increased generosity of in-work transfers for families with children. Combined with the increased levels of parental unemployment and inactivity for the low-skilled discussed in Chapter Three, the coverage of means-tested programmes for families with children has hugely grown, as shown in Figure 4.6. Greater generosity means that more families qualify and thus coverage grows. In 1972, as, in fact, throughout the 1970s, less than 10% of children were in families who received means-tested transfers. That figure is now over 70%, or over 50% if those receiving just the family element of CTC are excluded.

Figure 4.6: Coverage of children by means-tested transfers, 1972-2007

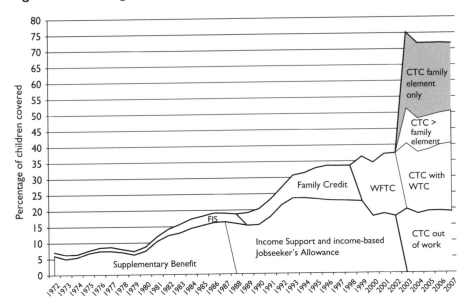

Note: All children aged 18 and under. Great Britain for 1972-2003 and UK thereafter.

Source: Authors' calculations using HMRC (2007) and DWP (2008b) and earlier versions.

Model families and childhoods

We now turn to profiling how the history of changing policy for children is reflected by our model families in the years 1979, 1997 and 2008. These hypothetical family models involve all elements of taxes and benefits and before we turn to the profiles it is important to remind readers of some of the assumptions involved and how the profiles will relate to the following chapters.

First, because our approach is to build the story of policy over the lifetime, we have only so far looked at children and by doing so have had to ignore significant drivers of family income that relate to their parents. Most notably, these include taxes and housing costs, which we will cover in detail in the next chapters.

Second, to reiterate points made in Chapter One, we will use simple hypothetical sets of circumstances to illustrate policy change. Our model families are not designed to be representative, but to capture the policy differences in response to families with different earnings levels. In this chapter, they are married couples and the different earnings levels are represented by the family names:

- the Moores, who are highly paid and earn twice the median;
- the Meades, who have median earnings;
- the Lowes, who are low paid and earn one half of median earnings.

Additionally, a non-working family, called the Nunns, are used to illustrate the position of out-of-work families.

Third, there are some key assumptions used to keep our three main profiles very simple. At this stage, each parent will have the same underlying earnings level, irrespective of gender or work history or whether he or she is working full or part time. This allows us to illustrate changing family work patterns using simple multipliers. For example, a two-earner household earns two times the family's earnings level; a one full-time earner and one-part-time earner household earns one-and-a-half times the family's earnings level; and so on. The assumption also allows us to have exactly the same history for each family for comparison. We begin our consideration before pregnancy when both parents are working full time. The mother ceases work the quarter before the birth of her child and does not return to work until her child reaches primary school age. At this point, she returns to work part time – which is equivalent to 50% of her partner's full-time earnings (thus representing 1.5 times their earnings level). When the child reaches secondary school age, the mother returns to full-time work and the family once again have twice their underlying earnings profile level.

Our final assumption is that each family has only one child and that this child continues in secondary education until the end of his or her 18th year. These simplistic circumstances are chosen to best set out how policy has changed over time. Of course, in reality the different families would have different histories and these would be determined in part by earnings level, in part by different behaviour over time across 1979, 1997 and 2008 and in part by influences of taxes, benefits and other important factors such as the costs of housing. At this point, we hold up our hands and ask readers eager for more realism and readers concerned about the obvious endogenous factors that interrelate according to income to bear with us. Final and more nuanced versions of these families will emerge as the book progresses and more realistic and different assumptions about how income level is related to earnings and child histories will be shown later in Part Three of the book.

The Meades

Table 4.1 shows how the Meades' maternity period income compares with previous income by asking two questions. First, we ask how much of total family income is covered during the final trimester of pregnancy when Ms Meade has ceased work. The results are shown in row A. The best 'replacement rate' is found under the 1979 system. Second, we ask how much of Ms Meade's earnings are replaced by the maternity benefits she receives. The results are shown for the first 18 weeks in row B1 and for the next 21 weeks in row B2. Once again, for the first 18 weeks the 1979 system provides the greatest level of replacement, 54% compared with 45% in 1997 and 52% in 2008. However, when we consider the extended period of maternity, the 19th to the 39th weeks, it is only in 2008 that Ms Meade receives any replacement of her earnings at all.

Table 4.1: The Meades' maternity income

	1979	1997	2008
A: family income during maternity leave prior to birth as a percentage of previous family income	77.3%	71.8%	72.4%
B1: Maternity benefits as a percentage of previous take-home pay for first 18 weeks	54.2%	44.6%	51.7%
B2: Maternity benefits as a percentage of take-home pay for the 19th to 39th week inclusive	0%	0%	32%

Note: Family income is measured after taxes and benefits but before housing costs.

Source: Authors' calculations using LOIS.

Apart from the longer duration of assistance provided under the 2008 system, why do median earners fare best in 1979? The answer lies in the cumulative effect of three factors. First, and most importantly, Ms Meade benefits strongly from the earnings-related supplement in 1979. Second, Ms Meade receives a maternity grant under the 1979 system only. Third, unseen changes to taxation make a difference. Maternity Allowance was not taxable under the 1979 system unlike SMP in the latter years, which is subject to both income tax and National Insurance contributions.

How do the Meades fare in benefit receipt over the 18 years of their child's life? The earliest period of pregnancy and postnatal weeks have already shown us that tax is important – so we will show before and after tax profiles separately to prepare readers for the full story of tax in Chapter Five.

Focusing our attention first on the effects of transfers, Figure 4.7a shows two main obvious trends. First, the 2008 system is overall more 'generous' than those of 1979 and 1997 respectively. Second, this increased 2008 generosity is most marked in the first year of childhood. Because their earnings do not take them above the second income threshold that protects it, the Meades will receive the family element of CTC in full for the duration of Meade Junior's childhood. It is this combined with Child Benefit that leads the 2008 system to be consistently more generous in gross terms over the whole of childhood, even at later points where Ms Meade returns to full-time work[12]. The particularly strong showing of the 2008 system during Meade Junior's first year is due to a combination of the increased duration of SMP under the 2008 system and the additional baby element of CTC, which is paid as part of the family element to families with at least one child under the age of one.

Figure 4.7b demonstrates that the *net effect* of taxes and transfers for median earners such as the Meades is negative across all three systems. They always pay more tax than they receive in transfers but the generosity of the 2008 system still means that it ranks highest of the three, albeit by a now small margin except during their child's first year where the difference remains dramatic. The underlying tax

Figure 4.7a: The Meades' benefit income during childhood – benefit income as a percentage of original earnings

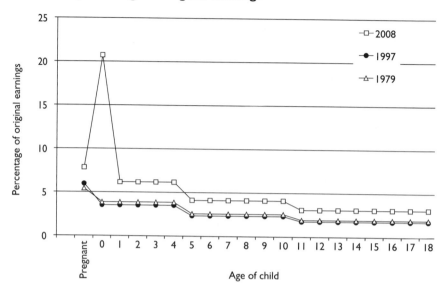

Figure 4.7b: The Meades' benefit income during childhood – net effects of taxes and benefits during childhood as a percentage of original earnings

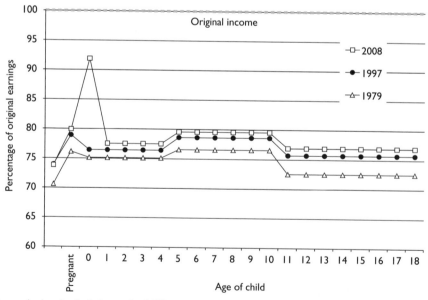

Source: Authors' calculations using LOIS.

position is indicated by the position of the Meades before pregnancy: two median-earning people face around the same tax burden under the 2008 and 1997 systems but higher tax under the 1979 system[13]. We can put this early and partial finding to one side until we discuss the position more fully in the next chapter.

The Moores

What of the Moore family, who have twice the earnings of the Meades? In terms of maternity benefits, the Moores receive the same benefits under all three systems as do the Meades. The only difference is that Ms Moore will receive a higher earnings-related supplement to her Maternity Allowance (1979 system) and higher SMP during the first six weeks (1997 and 2008 systems). In terms of childhood benefits, the Moores receive the non-means-tested Child Benefit under all three systems. While Mr Moore is the only earner, they also receive the family element of CTC, including the baby element for the first year. At all other times the Moores' combined earnings preclude them from receiving even the family element of CTC.

Transfer income plays a less significant role for the Moores than it does the Meades. Figure 4.8 shows the net effects of transfers and taxes for the Moores. It can be seen that only during the first year of their child's life do the Moores fare best under the 2008 system. This is due to the extended duration of SMP and to a lesser extent the baby element of CTC. Elsewhere, it is tax that most significantly affects outcomes for the Moores and they fare best under the system

Figure 4.8: The Moores – net effects of taxes and benefits during childhood

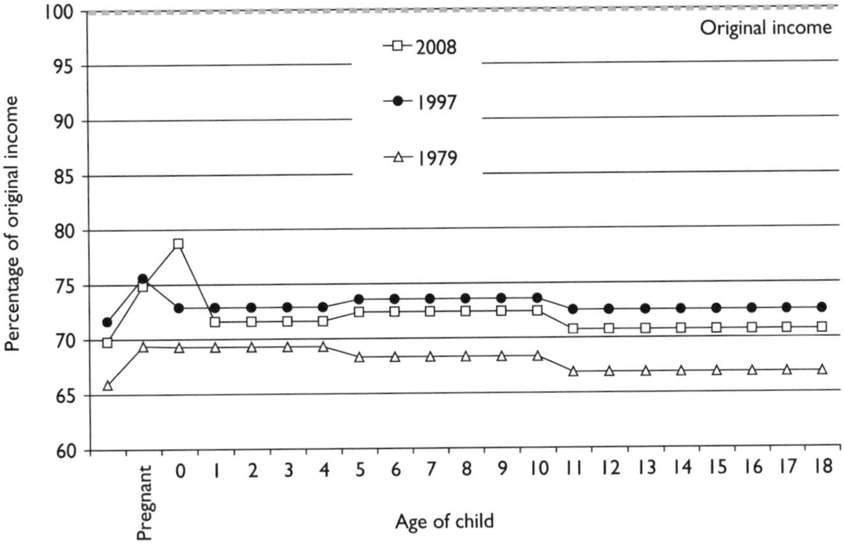

Source: Authors' calculations using LOIS.

that presents them with the lowest taxes, the 1997 system – a point we take up more fully in the following chapter.

The Lowes

Jumping to the other end of the earnings distribution, how do the Lowes compare on half of median earnings? Table 4.2 shows how maternity transfers replace Ms Lowe's earnings. On all measures, highest replacement rates result from the 2008 system, with the 1979 system second and then, in third place and displaying a large comparative reduction in generosity, the 1997 system.

Figure 4.9 shows the whole period of childhood and illustrates that the Lowes qualify for support from means-tested, in-work transfers under all three systems: in addition to receiving Child Benefit and in 2008 the family element of CTC exactly as the Meades do, the Lowes also receive FIS in 1979, Family Credit in 1997 and the combination of WTC and CTC in 2008. They also receive significant benefit assistance with their rent and rates under the 1979 system. However, this common qualification only consistently applies for the period when they rely solely on Mr Lowe's earnings – the first five years of childhood before Ms Lowe returns to work. Ms Lowe's return to part-time work (when her child is five) is clearly seen across all three systems in Figure 4.9a. Here the 2008 system provides the most generous package of transfers followed by the 1979 and 1997 systems in that order. Once again, the combination of longer SMP and higher CTC in the first year of their child's life makes a remarkable difference in 2008 when compared to 1997 and 1979. There is one additional factor under the 2008 system that will support the Lowes' child remaining in school past the age of 16: the EMA. However, The Lowes' income at this point (effectively equal to median earnings as it comprises the combined earnings of two full-time people at half median earnings) leads to the EMA being awarded at the middle as opposed to the standard higher rate (£20 rather than £30 in 2008).

Table 4.2: The Lowes' maternity period income

	1979	1997	2008
A: family income during maternity leave prior to birth as a percentage of previous family income	90.6%	79.8%	96.3%
B1: Maternity benefits as a percentage of previous take-home pay for first 18 weeks	75.9%	60.6%	83.6%
B2: Maternity benefits as a percentage of take-home pay for the 19th to 39th week inclusive	0%	0%	57.6%

Note: Family income is measured after taxes and benefits but before housing costs.

Source: Authors' calculations using LOIS.

Figure 4.9a: The Lowes' tax and benefit income during childhood – benefit income as a percentage of original earnings

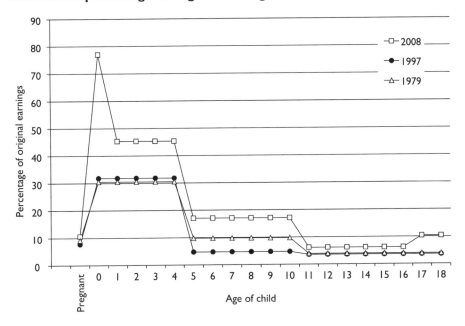

Figure 4.9b: The Lowes' tax and benefit income during childhood – net effect of taxes and benefits as a percentage of original earnings

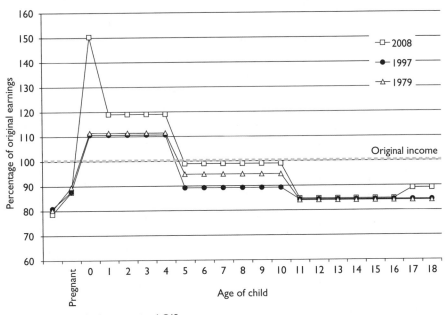

Source: Authors' calculations using LOIS.

The Lowes' net position after taxes and transfers is shown in Figure 4.9b. This clearly shows that for the first five years of childhood under all three systems they were net gainers – receiving more in transfers than they paid in taxes. Again, due to benefiting strongly from the tax credit system, the Lowes continue to fare best of all under the 2008 system as Ms Lowe returns to part-time work. The stronger result for the 1979 system for this period is the result of a quirk of the 1979 tax system in that it particularly favoured married couples where the wife had low earnings (see Chapter Five). However, once Ms Lowe returns to full-time work, excepting the effect of EMA, the apparent generosity of transfers under the 2008 system is nullified by the taxes with which the 2008 system presents the Lowes.

Non-employment and the Nunns

For simplicity, it is best to think about the position of an unemployed family who are equivalent to the Lowes but who never work. This, of course, is unrealistic as such a family would in reality have to have some serious constraint on employment from disability or similar to never work for 18 years or more of their children's lives. However, by having a continuous profile of a non-working unemployed family we are able to show how the benefit systems treated children of unemployed parents and how such treatment changed as children grew older. We call this model family the Nunns and profile them as being reliant on social assistance: Supplementary Benefit in 1979 and Income Support or income-based Jobseeker's Allowance in 1997 and 2008.

Figure 4.10 shows how the whole family income would change by age of child by benefit system in real and relative terms. To address these in turn, recalling that the Nunns are 'frozen in time' in 1979, 1997 and 2008 as their child ages, it is the 2008 system that would be the most generous – and especially so in the first year through the baby element of CTC and between 16 and 18 years of age with EMA. In purchasing power, the Nunns are best off in 2008, followed by 1997 and then 1979. There are some exceptions to this – 1979 is best for the Nunns before they have a child, as underlying adult rates of social assistance have fallen for the unemployed in real terms. Additionally, the age-weighting of social assistance for children in 1979 means that the Nunns received more in 1979 when their child was aged 18 than in 1997.

However, Figure 4.10b shows the results in relation to earnings – once more freezing the comparison for 1979, 1997 and 2008 to earnings levels in those single years rather than earnings rising as parents and children age. This comparison completely overturns the ranking of the benefit systems and 1979 is now more generous by a considerable degree followed by 2008 and then by 1997. The reason for this lies in the differential growth in earnings and prices over time. Families on social assistance are falling in relative terms to the majority of the population who rely on earnings, even though reform of benefits has increased their purchasing power. This is perhaps most clearly shown on the far left-hand side of the relative

Figure 4.10a: The Nunns' income profile during childhood, 2008 prices

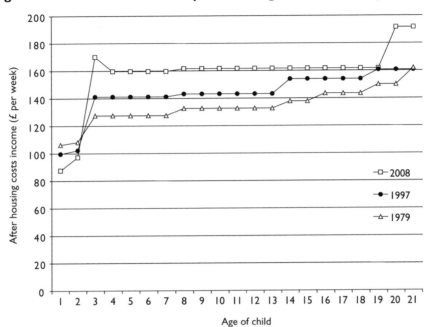

Figure 4.10b: The Nunns' income profile during childhood relative to contemporary median earnings

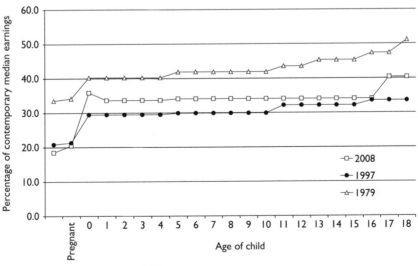

Source: Authors' calculations using LOIS.

earnings lines in Figure 4.10b where the Nunns begin by being 'worse off' in 2008 before having a child. The relative positions of 1997 and 2008 then change because of the additional generosity of the 2008 system to *children*.

Summary

- Programmes to assist maternity and childhood have moved towards increased use of means testing alongside the continued but varying political support for Child Benefit.
- Greater reliance on means testing has allowed the values of maternity grants to be increased with each structural change, but after each reform benefits have been allowed to erode.
- Maternity benefits now mainly comprise the employer-provided and funded SMP with no similar provision for those not in work.
- In-work support for families with children has increased in generosity over time with each structural change in policy. The most recent 2003 introduction of CTC alongside WTC reflects a 'selective universal' approach and the majority of parents receive financial support with most help for those on lowest earnings.
- Out-of-work support for children has increased in value, particularly since 1999 and now pays flat rates for children across all ages but targets most help on the first child.
- The models for families with earnings demonstrates that the outcomes of giving transfers to meet children's needs have to be assessed alongside their parents' tax liabilities.
- The poor working family, the Lowes, clearly receive a higher level of benefits under the 2008 system over childhood and even after taxation the net effects of the tax and benefit package are highest in 2008.
- The generosity of child transfers for the out-of-work family is also greatest in real terms in 2008. However, when put alongside the benefits of the parents, it still means that relative values have fallen greatly over time and are worse in 2008 when measured against contemporary median earnings and 1979 performs best.

These findings are important building blocks for the rest of the book and reflect underlying changes from inflation and uprating over time between 1979, 1997 and 2008 as well as the interaction of the system of taxes and benefits. We have also seen that in the end we cannot look at children without considering their parents of working age and cannot clearly see the impact of transfers for children without also looking at their parents' tax liabilities. These issues have important ramifications for the performance of the system in addressing child poverty and we will return to analyse poverty related incomes in Part Three. Before we do so, however, we must turn to the working lives of parents and others and to taxation.

Notes

[1] Beveridge himself also had eugenic concerns (Evans and Glennester, 1994).

[2] Historical benefit rates can be found at IFS (2008a).

[3] Authors' calculations from CPAG (1978a).

[4] It is also paid to partners of new mothers who are not the father.

[5] Similarly in the US, the Earned Income Tax Credit was introduced at a similar time and as a similar stop-gap measure. It is still in place today and has a recent history of generous reform under liberal administrations that has influenced New Labour (Holz and Scholz, 2003).

[6] The Conservative Party October 1974 manifesto states: 'Child credits will take the place of the family allowances and tax allowances ... [they] will be payable to mothers in cash in exactly the same way as existing family allowances, the only difference being that they will be worth more' (Conservative Party, 1974). Interestingly, the Labour Party's October 1974 manifesto also uses the term 'child credit' (rather than 'Child Benefit').

[7] By 1997, childcare costs were to an extent recognised by the benefit system. Since 1994, Family Credit has allowed for the possibility of including payment to meet up to 70% of childcare costs. Income disregards for childcare costs also in Housing Benefit, Council Tax Benefit and Disability Working Allowance.

[8] The Institute of Fiscal Studies described WFTC at the time of its introduction as merely a 're-badging of Family Credit' (House of Commons Library, 1998, p 28).

[9] Hansard House of Commons, 5 May 2004, col 1642W.

[10] The 1979 and 1997 values comprise additions to the prevailing safety net benefit in respect of dependent children. The 2008 values comprise Child Benefit, which no longer counts as income towards the now adult-only Income Support, maximum CTC, and, where the child is aged 17 and 18, the EMA.

[11] A word of caution must be added here because Supplementary Benefit rules in 1979 allowed for the discretionary award of additional weekly benefits, especially

for heating where there were young children. Such discretionary additions are not represented in Figure 4.5.

[12] It is worth repeating our zero assumption about both inflation and uprating at this point, as benefit erosion compared with earnings inflation will affect these results (see Part Three of this book and Sutherland et al, 2008)

[13] Taxes here refer to the sum of income tax, National Insurance contributions and local government taxation (rates under the 1979 system, council tax under the 1997 and 2008 systems).

FIVE

Working age: taxation

This is the first of several chapters that focus on the 'working age' portion of the lifetime and that show how policies have developed and changed to influence these years. This period forms the large majority of the lifetime and represents the economic powerhouse of lifetime events based on employment, forming relationships with other adults such as marriage, having children (although such events have been shuffled into the previous chapter to give a clearer lifetime perspective), buying houses or renting them and saving for retirement as well as establishing consumption patterns and lifestyle. It is also the time when we are asked most to contribute to the common pot and, while the end of childhood and the arrival of the first tax demand are not entirely synonymous events, the liability for income tax is a clear indication of adulthood. Indeed, National Insurance numbers and cards are issued to all individuals for their 16th birthday.

Taxation is also one of the most hotly political issues of policy since the 1970s and as we have seen in Chapter Two, much of the rhetoric of post-1970s governments has been based on 'low tax'. Such rhetoric is often misleading, as it mostly focuses on the issue of the headline rates of one tax, *income tax*. This chapter looks at the different forms of taxation and at the underlying components of income tax to put the issue into a more considered historical and analytical perspective.

The British tax system presents households with taxes that we approach under the following four headings:

- income tax;
- National Insurance contributions (NICs);
- local government taxation; and
- indirect taxation through consumption.

Income tax and NICs are direct taxes on personal income collected on a PAYE (pay as you earn) basis from wages. Local government taxation refers to council tax under the 1997 and 2008 systems and domestic rates under the 1979 system. The final heading, indirect taxation, comprises VAT and the range of excise duties on petrol/diesel, tobacco and alcohol, together with items such as car tax and TV licensing. There are other direct taxes, for instance inheritance tax, that we do not cover here.

Income tax

Before the Second World War, income tax had been collected on an annual or twice-yearly basis and was still confined to a minority of the working population – around 20% of workers. The war turned this minority into a majority. Additionally, collection of income tax moved to its current PAYE form of being deducted from contemporary earnings by employers in 1944. Income tax coverage continued to expand after the war so that by the end of the 1950s income tax essentially covered the whole of the working population (Kay and King, 1980).

Compared with today, the complex income tax system at the end of the 1970s was more progressive but was more discriminatory against women, particularly married women. Progressivity, the principle that higher earners pay higher rates of tax, was designed into the scheme through a large number of tax bands with progressively higher rates of tax – 11 in all in 1978/79. A basic guide to income tax calculation and terminology is provided in Box 5.1 to assist readers with the underlying concepts. In 1978/79, the *basic rate* of tax, the element with highest political profile, was 33%, with a lower starting rate of 25%. Above the basic rate were nine further tax bands with the top band having a tax rate of 83%. High earners were faced with very high marginal tax rates and thus high effective tax rates. The gender discrimination resulted from the joint taxation of married couples through the income tax system, which placed a lower tax burden on the married man than the married woman. We discuss this issue further below under the heading of marriage and partnership.

Box 5.1: Income tax calculation and terminology

Income tax allowances, rates and bands

Income tax is calculated through a system of allowances, bands and rates. Here we explain these terms with reference to the taxation of a single individual. A **tax allowance** is that sum of money a person can have as income before he or she has to pay any income tax, and on which sum regardless of income he or she will never have to pay income tax. Tax allowances are given to all taxpayers in the form of a basic allowance, and other allowances are available in addition to cover certain contingencies such as old age, marriage and the presence of children (withdrawn and replaced by Child Benefit by 1979).

Any income above the allowance is **taxable income**. Taxable income is subject to tax at different **tax rates** depending on the **tax band**, as taxable income level is split into bands to change tax at different levels of income.

All of this is best explained by the following example using 2008/09 tax allowances, rates and bands.

Mr A earns £45,000 a year. As a person under 65, his personal tax allowance is £6,035 a year. His taxable income is therefore £45,000 less £6,035, which is £38,965. The income tax rates and bands for 2008/09 are a basic rate 20% applying to the taxable income band £0-£34,800, and the higher rate 40% applying to the taxable income band £34,801 and above. Therefore, Mr A pays 20% tax on his taxable income up to £34,800; and 40% tax on his taxable income above £34,800. This means he pays £6,960 (20% of £34,800) plus £1,666 (40% of £38,965 less £34,800) in tax, presenting him with a total income tax of £8,626.

Marginal tax rates and effective tax rates

The **marginal tax rate** is that rate of tax an individual would pay on an extra £1 of income. In terms of income tax, Mr A faces a marginal tax rate of 40%. If he earned an extra £1, it would be subject to income tax at 40%.

We reserve the term 'marginal tax rate' for discussion of tax. In later chapters, when we discuss the phasing-out of means-tested benefits as income rises, the marginal rate of tax is part of a total combined rate of overlapping reductions to net income. We use the term **marginal deduction rate** for this combined effect of tax and means testing.

The **effective tax rate** is that amount of tax an individual pays on his or her income. It is calculated by dividing total tax by total income. In terms of income tax, Mr A faces an effective tax rate of 19.2% (£8,626 over £45,000 equals 19.2%).

Tax relief

In terms of income tax, tax relief refers to amounts that can be deducted from income before the income tax calculation is undertaken. For example, tax relief is granted on pension contributions. If Mr A makes £2,000 a year in pension contributions, his income tax will be calculated on the basis of income of £43,000, not £45,000.

Progressivity and regressivity

A progressive tax system can be defined as one where the proportion of a person's income paid in tax rises as his or her income increases. Simply put, with a progressive tax the rich pay relatively more than the poor. The opposite is a regressive tax system where the proportion of a person's income paid in tax falls as his or her income rises.

Tax reform over subsequent years was applied to all parts of the system, not just tax rates, and it is worth outlining such elements in the 1978/79 tax system[1], which offered particular tax allowances in respect of marriage (with a parallel higher tax allowance for lone parents to treat them the same as a married main earner) and an age allowance for people over 65. There were tax reliefs on mortgage interest payments (limited to certain price levels and discussed below under the heading of housing) and relief for private pension contributions that were fully tax-deductible and continue to be so today.

Reducing high rates of income tax was a core element of the Thatcher policy agenda. Chapter Two described the tax-cutting radical years of the early 1980s and income tax was at the forefront of such policy change. Big reductions in tax rates began in the 1979 budget, with the top rate cut from 83% to 60% and 3% cut off the basic rate. The basic rate took another seven years to fall a further percentage point to 29%, but in consecutive years was cut to 27% and then to 25% in 1988 alongside a reduction in the top rate of tax to 40%. Chancellor Nigel Lawson's promise was to eventually reduce the basic rate to 20%, a feat that was eventually implemented by New Labour in 2007. The basic rate remained unchanged during the late 1980s as the years of the 'Lawson boom' turned to recession. It was not until 1995 that basic rate fell by a further percentage point and then in Kenneth Clark's final budget it was reduced by a further 1% to bring it to 23%. But the consistent attitude towards lowering basic and top rates of income tax under the Tories did not extend to lower taxes for those on the lowest incomes. The lower starting rate of tax was abolished by Howe in 1980 but was reintroduced, at 20%, in 1992. The combination of reduced higher and basic rates and fluctuations on starting rates meant a clear decline in overall progressivity in the income tax system. The higher taxation of low-income households under the Conservatives was additionally implemented through taxation of previously tax-exempt benefits, in particular Sickness Benefit and Unemployment Benefit, during Margaret Thatcher's first term.

The regressive realignment of income taxation was also assisted through the continuation of tax relief on mortgage interest payments, which was maintained during Thatcher's premiership through her own stubborn defence of the tax subsidy for owner-occupation and against the advice of successive Chancellors who pointed to its distorting effects on house prices. Direct tax relief was abolished from 1983, replaced by the Mortgage Interest Relief at Source (MIRAS) scheme run through building societies and banks, which is discussed further in the Chapter Six. Tax relief for mortgages was readdressed on Major's arrival and phasing out began from 1990.

However, the other major structural change to the income tax system under the Conservatives was the abolition of joint taxation and its replacement by a system of independent taxation from 1990, where a simpler system of personal tax allowances replaced that of single-person tax allowances and married–man tax allowances. The abolition of joint taxation did not mean that the tax benefit to being married was abolished. Married men still received an additional tax allowance, the 'married couple's allowance'. The new system of independent taxation also introduced the 'additional personal allowance', which was available to lone parents with children under 18 in their care, but also to one member of unmarried couples with children under 18 in their care. From 1994 onwards, however, both the 'married couple's allowance' and the 'additional personal allowance' began to be phased out. These still remained in 1997/98, but were by then restricted to attract tax relief at the flat rate of 15%. Both were ultimately abolished in April 2000 with the exception that couples over the age of 65 at that time could continue to receive the married couple's allowance.

A new and higher tax allowance for those aged 75 or over was introduced in the 1990 budget and remains in place today, providing further relief against taxation for older pensioners, who already receive an age-additional allowance at age 65.

New Labour vowed no return to 1979's high rates of income tax on re-election in 1997. Effectively, after defeat in the 1992 general election on a 'tax and spend' agenda, New Labour became fiscal conservatives. Its manifesto pledged not to increase income tax basic rates and promised to cut the starting rate of income tax from 20% to 10%. This was implemented in 1999 once the self-imposed two-year moratorium on altering Conservative spending plans came to an end. Gordon Brown as Chancellor went further and continued to cut the basic rate of income tax, which was reduced by another 1% in 2000/01. No efforts have been made to raise rates for higher incomes and the top rate of tax remained at 40%, its current rate. Until 2007/08, the income tax system remained much as it did under the 1997/98 system and the phasing out of the additional tax allowances for marriage and mortgage interest was completed.

Structural reform in the 2007 budget, Gordon Brown's final one as Chancellor, saw the implementation of the promise by Geoffrey Howe and maintained by every Tory Chancellor subsequently to cut basic rates of income tax to 20%. However, this attempt from the right to outflank fiscal criticism came unstuck in the other part of this reform – the abolition of the starting rate of income tax[2]. The distributional effects of these changes and, in particular, the losses faced by some of the lowest earners, were a political time-bomb. Around 20% of taxpayers were losers, including those earning less than £18,500 per annum and those who did not qualify for tax credits to compensate for the loss (IFS, 2007). The disproportionate effect on low incomes caused by the abolition of the 10% rate led to high-profile criticism at a time when Gordon Brown, now Prime Minister, faced wider political difficulties. The resulting package of reforms to eradicate losers was not a u-turn. The 10% starting rate remained abolished but personal allowances were adjusted to remove the losses. With the starting rate abolished, the 2008 income tax system is simpler, comprising just two rates of tax in respect of earnings.

How have such changes to income tax affected the effective rate of taxation over time? Figure 5.1 shows the effective income tax rates on individual earnings under the 1979, 1997 and 2008 systems, in line with our choice of years for comparison. The first point of note is that liability for income tax starts at a consistent point,

Figure 5.1: Effective income tax rates under the 1979, 1997 and 2008 systems

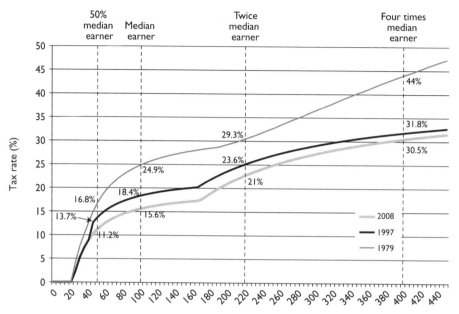

Earnings (percentage of full-time male median weekly earnings)

Note: Worker in question is assumed to be single. In respect of the 1979 and 1997 systems, the results would be different for a married male worker or a married female worker.

Source: Authors' calculations from IFS (2008a).

roughly 20% of median earnings for each of the years. This points to the fact that the underlying personal allowance for tax has risen with earnings over the 30 years. In other words, there has been no long-term fiscal drag[3]. This finding is an important one for our modelling of lifetime taxation in Part Three and we return to it in more detail in Chapter Eleven. The second point is that effective rates of income tax are highest under the 1979 system for all earners and lowest under the 2008 system.

The progressive nature of the 1979 income tax system in terms of its taxation of high earners is clear and a person earning seven times the male median wage would face paying nearly 60% of his or her earnings in income tax. The Conservatives changed all this and under the 1997 system our seven times median earner would pay 35.3% of his or her earnings in income tax, and in 2008, 34.6%. New Labour has in no way put back the progressivity that the Conservatives took out of the system.

But we can draw no definite conclusions about overall outcomes from taxation, its incidence, progressivity or other profiles, by *solely* looking at income tax. The story so far is clear, but the history of other forms of taxation have to be carefully considered *if* the 'tax-cutting' budgets of the 1980s and subsequently are to live up to their name.

National Insurance contributions

National Insurance contributions (NICs) are a form of tax that have better public relations than income tax. Many believe them both to be solely and completely used for National Insurance benefits – the myth of hypothecation – and many believe them to be actual contributions to a lifetime pot. There are some elements of truth in both of these suppositions, but NICs are effectively a tax[4]. Their underlying relationship with specific entitlements has weakened over time and they are used to fund wider aspects of the welfare state than just contributory benefits.

A system of social insurance had been in place in the UK since 1911, but only became a unified and national system on the implementation of the Beveridge Report (HMSO, 1942) after the war when the 1946 National Insurance Act introduced a system of compulsory contributions for unemployment, sickness, maternity and widow's benefits and retirement pensions from all employees and employers. Payments were deducted at source from employees' earnings as with the PAYE system for income tax. In return for NICs that were paid at a flat rate (all workers paid four shillings and 11 pence per week[5] and these could even be bought as 'stamps' to stick on to contribution cards), employees would receive entitlement to flat-rate benefits in the event of unemployment, sickness, maternity or old age. Employers would also make parallel contributions for each employee.

The first break with the principle of flat-rate benefits and contributions came in 1961 with the introduction of the graduated pension scheme. In April 1975, the notion of flat-rate, fixed-sum NICs was completely abandoned as NICs began to be calculated on the basis of a percentage of earnings. Since 1975, NICs have been calculated on the band of earnings between a lower earnings limit (LEL), effectively a parallel personal allowance to that for income tax, and an upper earnings limit (UEL). These are fixed sums set for each tax year as weekly earnings limits. In 1978/79, the first of our chosen years for modelling, any employee aged 16 or over, under pensionable age and earning more than the LEL was obliged to pay NICs equal to 6.5% of his or her earnings below the UEL. For a minority of workers, those who were contracted out of the then new State Earnings Related Pension Scheme (SERPS; see Chapter Nine), a reduced rate of 4% applied. Employers were then, as now, also obliged to pay NICs in respect of their employees.

NICs in 1978/79 had a so-called 'kink' in their rates as earnings rose, which is no longer present today. The reason was that no NICs were paid on wages below the LEL, but as soon as earnings reached or passed that level they became payable on all earnings (not just on the wages above the LEL, as in the relationship between income tax and personal allowances) up to the UEL. Thus, in the extreme case, a man earning £18 a week could be worse off than a man earning £17 a week, as shown in Box 5.2.

Box 5.2: An example showing the erstwhile 'kink' in the NIC system

In 1978/79:

A man earns £17 a week.

Because this is below the 1978/79 LEL of £17.50, he pays no NICs.

Therefore his weekly NIC is nil.

A man earns £18 a week.

Because his weekly wage is above the LEL (and below the UEL of £120), he pays NICs at the rate of 6.5% of his entire wages.

Therefore, his weekly NIC is 6.5% of £18, which equals £1.17 (thus making him worse off than the man who earns £17 a week).

How did National Insurance fare under the tax-cutting Thatcher governments? NIC rates rose as income tax rates fell. The main rate of NICs was incrementally increased from 6.5% in 1978/79 to 10% by 1997/98. The Thatcher governments also increased the ability to 'contract out' from NICs for additional pension coverage and the financial benefits of doing so (discussed in full in Chapter Nine) as a part of the Fowler reforms and in line with their aims to increase private market-based provision and roll back the state's provision.

New Labour has structurally reformed NICs to make them more consistently implemented alongside income tax in an overall aim to simplify taxation. The first structural change from April 1999 was to remove the 'kink' and the LEL began to operate as a non-taxable allowance with no liability on this first tranche of earnings. The second reform from April 2001 was to set a threshold (called the Primary Threshold) at a level slightly above the LEL but consistent with the employers' threshold for liability and the income tax basic personal allowance[6]. The third structural change was to introduce a liability for NICs on earning above the upper earnings limit (UEL) from April 2003, set at a rate of 1%. Fourth and finally, the budget of 2007 brought income tax and National Insurance closer together still from 2008/09. To match the simple two rates of income tax (see the discussion above), National Insurance would also operate with two rates: the main rate and the above-UEL rate, with the UEL gradually aligned over time to match the higher-rate threshold for income tax.

The process of simplification and reform to bring the income tax and National Insurance systems closer together built on the move to individual-level independent income taxation introduced in 1990. Administrative unification from 1999 took NICs from separate social security administration into Her Majesty's Revenue and Customs (formerly the Inland Revenue). Both NICs and income tax have been based on rates and earnings bands since 1975 and simplification and reform to harmonise the levels and number of income bands are now complete. The hypothecation of NICs has also weakened further, with increases introduced in part to pay for National Health Service expansion from 2003/04, for instance. Of course, as NICs increasingly resemble income tax, the ultimate act of fiscal consistency would be to merge the two into a single income tax. But this would be political madness, given the huge investment that has been made in the past 30 years in playing off decreasing income tax rates against more opaque increases in NICs. Despite the simplicity of a single basic rate of tax at 31% (20% income tax and 11% NICs), the public relations disaster of being seen to 'raise' headline income tax rates by 11% outweighs any gains from simultaneously abolishing NICs.

Taking a long-term overview, Figure 5.2 illustrates the parameters of the National Insurance system over the period from 1975 to 2008. Figure 5.2a shows the history of the main NIC rate. This reflects the history discussed and demonstrates that rates have doubled from 5.5% to 11% over the whole period. The sequential rises in NICs have occurred under Old Labour, the Conservatives and New Labour, but most dramatically under the Conservatives. Figure 5.2b shows the relative levels of the LEL and UEL measured against average earnings. The starting point for liability for NICs, marked by the LEL (or later primary threshold (PT)) measured as a percentage of average full-time earnings has remained roughly constant at around 20% over the whole period. However, the UEL rose relative to average earnings to the early 1980s and subsequently fell consistently until 2008 when it began to be realigned with the top rate of income tax. Given that earners paid no NICs above this level for the majority of the period and only 1% of earnings since 2003, this indicates that NICs became increasingly regressive over the period.

Figure 5.3 shows the effective rate of tax for NICs compared with contemporary median male earnings. The starting point for liability for NICs is fairly constant, at around 20% of median earnings for each of three systems. The different structure of the 1979 scheme to later systems is clear in Figure 5.3, with liability on all earnings beginning at the LEL and characterised as a sheer cliff at that point followed by a fixed rate until the income rises above the UEL (around 135% of median earnings in 1979) and leads to a fall in the effective rate. The 1997 and 2008 systems only take NICs as a percentage of earnings above LEL and this leads to a curved profile as effective rates rise once the fixed vale of the 'allowance' of untaxed income below the LEL falls relative to earnings. However, both the 1997 and 2008 systems still clearly show the regressive nature of NICs above the UEL

Figure 5.2a: Parameters of the National Insurance system – main rate, 1975-2008

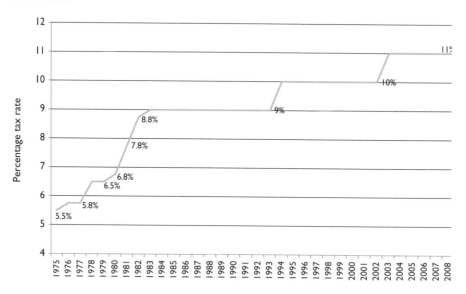

Figure 5.2b: Parameters of the National Insurance system – relative value of upper and lower earnings limits

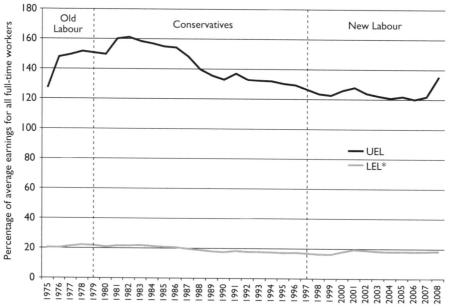

Source: Authors' calculations from IFS (2008a).

Notes: * LEL 1975-99; PT from 2000.

Figure 5.3: Effective NIC rates under the 1979, 1997 and 2008 systems

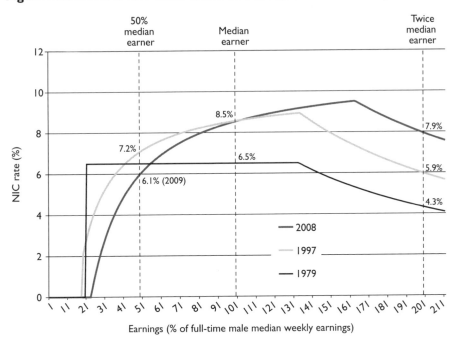

Earnings (% of full-time male median weekly earnings)

Source: Authors' calculations from IFS (2008a).

Note: Male median earnings used to ensure consistent time series from New Earnings Survey.

(at just over 130% of median earnings in 1997 and at 165% of median earnings in 2008) as effective rates fall off above these levels.

Local government taxation

Local government finance proved to be one of the most contentious areas of public policy in the 1980s and reform was to be the undoing of the Thatcher premiership (the 'poll tax' debacle discussed in Chapter Two). Local government taxation is one of the oldest forms of tax, predating income tax and stretching perhaps as far back as medieval times. Rates for householders to pay for local services were until the 20th century often a series of separate charges – for instance, for the fire brigade, water and sewerage, rubbish collection and to operate the Poor Law. In 1929, rates became a single unified charge. Both business and domestic charges were levied by local authorities until 1990 but since the introduction of the council tax in that year business rates have been centrally set. The earlier system of rates (we ignore the community charge as a short-term aberration in policy) was calculated on the basis of the 'rate poundage' (a tax rate expressed as the number of pence in the pound and set by the local authority) on the 'rateable value' (a value representing the annual amount for which the property might be let). Local government finance is determined by grants from central government and locally raised revenue. With falling central grants to local government in the 1980s, many local councils that wanted to maintain or expand levels of services, raised their rates to make up the shortfall and thus potentially frustrate central directions on rolling back public spending and state activity. Ideological conflict between 'hard left' local councils and No. 10 Downing Street overshadowed a wider problem of local government finance and response to increasing needs for local services. The Conservatives introduced a series of measures to increase central government control of local government, such as 'rate capping', but even so rates levels rose dramatically throughout the 1980s, as shown in Figure 5.4. From 1978/79 to 1989/90, the average domestic rates bill for England rose from £10.85 to £18.44 per week in 2008 prices.

Domestic rates were replaced from April 1990[7] with Thatcher's nemesis, the ill-fated community charge, which was replaced from April 1993 with council tax. Like domestic rates, council tax is levied on property rather than individuals as a head or poll tax. Unlike domestic rates, it is based on the capital value rather than notional rental value of a dwelling. No significant structural changes have been made to council tax since its introduction and the principles of the tax are as follows. Only those over 18 can be liable for council tax. With few exceptions, all dwellings are subject to council tax whether owned or rented. The amount of council tax a household is liable for will depend on which valuation band (from

Figure 5.4: Average rates and council tax, 1973-2008 (England)

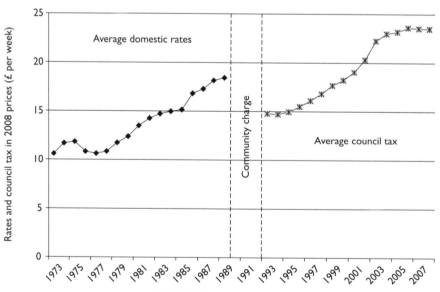

Source: Authors' calculations from DEWO (1976); CIPFA (1977, 1982, 1990); DoE (1989); ODPM (2005); CLG (2008b).

Note: All figures shown are before reductions due to discounts. Council tax figures are based on the average band C council tax.

A, the lowest, to H, the highest) its dwelling is classed as falling into. Band rates are set by the local authority each year, although council tax band rates have a fixed mathematical relationship with each other[8]. The council tax system allows for a 25% discount on the tax if only one adult lives in a property. Full-time students are not liable for council tax, being classed for its purposes as 'disregarded persons'.

But both rates and council tax have never been directly income-related as they rely primarily on the characteristics of the home rather than the income of those who reside there. Of course, it is likely that higher value and larger homes are owned by those on higher incomes, but this is not always the case and liability for a property tax for older people occupying the family home that previously housed a larger family is a common problem. Rebates based on a means test have thus existed to assist those on lowest incomes to pay rates and council tax and these are discussed further below.

While council tax rules have remained unchanged since its introduction, the size of the average bill has certainly grown in real terms. Figure 5.4 shows that on its introduction council tax was, in real terms, lower than rates had been. Since then, however, and especially since 1997, council tax has risen dramatically in real terms to more than overtake the highest real terms level of rates.

Indeed, if we compare rises in council tax and earnings and prices since 1994, we clearly see that council tax has consistently risen above price inflation *and* above wage inflation from 1994 to 2006. This is a very important factor when comparing the incidence of taxation over time and one that will be of importance when we come to look at our three model lifetimes later in Part Three of the book.

Rate rebates

Historically, rates were seen as an element of housing costs by social assistance and thus as part of a basic set of needs that had to be calculated as part of a minimum income safety net (see discussion in Chapter Six). We consistently treat rates and its descendent, council tax, as a tax but the policy history of rate rebates has in more recent years been part of the overall development of 'housing benefits' and this history is discussed more fully in the next chapter.

Rates were met in full by both National Assistance and Supplementary Benefit schemes. However, in the face of rising rates and revaluations, a separate national scheme of local authority-administered rate rebates was introduced in 1967. Separate forms of help for rates from social assistance and from the rate rebate schemes meant that many people, and in particular pensioners, claimed the wrong benefit and were worse off. Reform of help with both rent and rates to unify the system was put forward by the Supplementary Benefits Commission in 1978 but change in the form of the introduction of Housing Benefit occurred in 1983. The story of subsequent policy development is discussed in Chapter Six.

However, rate rebates have been made increasingly less generous over time. Under the original scheme, operating from 1967 through to 1983, while allowances were not aligned with social assistance scale rates, the taper for reducing rebates as income rose was 6%. This then rose to 7% from 1983 on unification of housing benefits. After the Fowler reforms, full rebates were granted at incomes equal to income support but the taper rose to 20% on all income above this. This system was carried forward into Council Tax Benefit and continues under New Labour in 2008.

These three forms of taxation – income tax, National Insurance and local government charges – form the main forms of direct taxation on households. Before moving on to discuss indirect forms of taxation, primarily on consumption, it is pertinent at this stage to consider how partnership and marriage are treated across the range of direct taxes.

Marriage, partnership and direct taxation

Partnership, cohabitation and marriage or civil partnership are events that occur in most adults' lifetimes. The policy treatment and recognition of being a couple and the status of the relationship are important factors when comparing tax and benefit systems. When it comes to tax, the incidence of direct taxation will change in some respects simply from the fact that household size changes if there is partnership or cohabitation, irrespective of the status of this relationship. The percentage of household income paid in income-related taxes will change unless the partners are earning exactly the same as each other and being taxed identically.

The status of marriage, however, has been given preferential treatment in income taxation. Until 1990, the British income tax system assumed that marriage required additional support because there were two people but only one primary earner: the assumption was that a wife was dependent on her husband who worked and paid taxes. A married man was granted a higher tax allowance through an additional tax allowance. Under these assumptions, joint assessment of taxes also was based on the principle that all income from both partners was treated as the husband's own for tax purposes. In the case of the wife's earned income, an exception to this principle was made in that the wife was granted her own personal tax allowance, termed the 'wife's earned income allowance'. This in effect taxed the wife's earnings in the same way as an unmarried worker's. All this meant that the married man received extra money for supporting his wife whether or not she was dependent on his income, and, assuming both partners were earning enough to pay tax, that a married man would receive more net pay per pound earned than his wife did.

The abolition of these principles and the introduction of independent taxation in 1990 did not, as we have noted above, mean the *immediate* abolition of the tax benefits of being married. Instead the 'married couple's allowance' was available to married men but could be transferred to the wife, either in whole or in part if not fully used. In the wake of the recession of the early-1990s, the married couple's tax allowance was initially frozen in value and then phased out from 1994 onwards. The phasing-out process was continued by New Labour. The married couple's allowance now survives only for the cohort of couples who were already 65 in April 2000. For all other couples, married or otherwise, their status makes no difference to the amount of income tax they pay.

A taste of the magnitude of the tax benefits of marriage under the 1979 and 1997 rules can be demonstrated using our median model family, the Meades. Table 5.1 contrasts the income tax position of the Meades as a married couple with all else being equal with their income tax position as an unmarried cohabiting couple under the 1979 and 1997 systems. We use three earnings profiles to show stereotypical changes to employment behaviour that arise with having children: beginning with two full-time earners, moving to one full-time earner when children are young, increasing to one-and-a-half earners and assuming the woman works part time when the child is older. This replicates the Meades' family history as it was given in the previous chapter.

Table 5.1 shows that the 1979 system outlined above[9] grants the Meades substantial tax benefits for being married under the joint taxation principles. In terms of the effective tax rate on the household, the benefits are greatest at the point where Ms Meade is not working. In the general case, the 1979 system would especially favour this situation or the situation where the wife was working for low pay and so receiving proportionately high benefit through the wife's earned income allowance. The higher relative benefits from these rules for low-paid couples is a matter that we will return to in Part Three of the book.

Table 5.1: The Meades' income tax position as a married or unmarried couple in 1979 and 1997

	Income tax as % of earnings		
	Two full-time earners (no child)	**Single full-time earner (very young child)**	**One-and-a-half times earnings (young child)**
1979			
Married	21.3%	19.0%	17.4%
Unmarried	23.5%	23.5%	20.3%
Tax benefit of marriage	2.2%	4.5%	2.9%
1997			
Married	15.8%	14.9%	13.3%
Unmarried	16.6%	14.9%	13.3%
Tax benefit of marriage	0.8%	Nil	Nil

Source: Authors' calculations from LOIS.

Note: Income tax shown as the effective tax rate (percentage of gross joint earnings).

With the 1997 system, the tax benefits of being married were substantially less. In fact, the only tax benefit to marriage we see is where the Meades are two full-time earners without a child. Once they have a child, they would as an unmarried couple qualify for the 'additional personal allowance' by virtue of having a child, this allowance having the same value as the 'married couple's allowance'. Thus their marital status makes no difference to the amount of tax they must pay once they have a child. Under the 2008 system, with its full implementation of independent taxation, the Meades enjoy no tax benefits to being married.

The National Insurance system has always been based on individual assessment. Neither marriage nor partnership makes a difference to the amount of NICs a person has to pay. An old rule existed from 1948 to 1977 that allowed married women to elect to pay a reduced rate of NICs and thereby forego their own entitlement to contributory benefits and pensions, instead relying on their husbands' contribution records. This option was withdrawn in April 1977, although women who had made such an election prior to this date could continue to pay NICs at the reduced rate.

Rates and council tax have never offered any tax benefits for marriage. However, the council tax system did try to include an element of per-capita taxation when it replaced the community charge that was purely individual. This exists in the form of a tax relief to sole occupants of property of 25% of the property-based tax. This means that the fact of co-residence matters rather than partnership or marriage.

Cumulative direct taxation and the Meades

Given that we have described a process of displacement across forms of direct taxation from income tax to other forms, we briefly consider here how our median model family, the Meades, fare in terms of overall direct taxation under the 1979, 1997 and 2008 systems. This approach will be fully integrated with a full life history later in Part Three, but a snapshot gives an indication of that overall change in composition of direct taxation. Table 5.2 shows the position

Table 5.2: The Meades' tax position in 1979, 1997 and 2008

	Income tax	National Insurance	Rates/council tax*	Total tax
1979	21.3%	6.5%	1.6%	29.4%
1997	15.8%	8.4%	1.9%	26.0%
2008	15.1%	8.6%	2.5%	26.2%

Source: Authors' calculations from LOIS.

Note: All taxes shown as effective rates (percentage of gross earnings for two full-time earners).

* Based on average rates and council tax.

when both Meades are in full-time work, say when their child is of secondary school age, for each of our comparison years.

These results clearly show the outcome of the political fixation on reducing rates of income tax: highest in 1979, drastically less under the 1997 system and slightly less still in 2008. National Insurance rises over time to counter some of these gains and, based on average liability for rates and council tax, so does local government direct taxation. The cumulative net effective rate of tax is thus still highest in 1979 but falls in 1997 are only by three percentage points, nowhere near the headline fall in income tax of 9% for the Conservative years. Between 1997 and 2008, these crude estimates leave overall direct tax rates as constant, despite the 4% fall in basic rates of income tax.

However, these illustrative calculations do not include the additional move from direct to indirect taxation that has also occurred over the period and it is to these other taxes that we now turn our attention.

Indirect taxation

There are a considerable number of indirect taxes, including duty on fuel, tobacco and alcohol, specific taxes on air passenger travel and insurance policies, and the general tax of valued added tax (VAT) on goods. Indirect taxes on consumption are preferred by right-wing policy makers because they reflect choice in consumption rather than obligatory calls on income. We focus most on VAT as this has had the most significant and relevant history since the 1970s and is the most significant form of indirect taxation, as shown in Figure 5.5. Introduced in the UK in 1973 as a condition of its becoming a member of the European Community, VAT replaced the existing purchase tax and selective employment tax. On its introduction, the standard rate of VAT was 10%. Food and certain commodities such as children's clothing and books were not subject to VAT. The Labour government in 1974 cut the standard rate to 8% but introduced a higher rate of 25% to apply to 'luxury' goods. This luxury rate was subsequently cut so that in 1979 the standard rate of VAT was 8% and the luxury rate 12.5%.

VAT was a high-profile element in the Thatcherite transformation of tax. In their 1979 manifesto (Conservative Party, 1979), the Conservatives promised both to 'switch to some extent from taxes on earnings to taxes on spending' (p 14), reflecting their clear aversion to income taxation, and to 'simplify VAT'. As discussed in Chapter Two, the month after entering power, the radical Howe budget of 1979 replaced the 8% and 12.5% rates with a single higher rate of 15%, thus almost doubling the standard rate. This 15% rate was raised to 17.5% in 1991 to fund a reduction in the community charge. Since then, the standard rate (apart from its temporary reduction in December 2008) has not been changed. In 1994, a rate of 8% was applied to domestic fuel, an item that had not previously been subject to VAT. New Labour cut this fuel rate to 5% in 1997. Other items seen as social benefits, such as children's car seats, nicotine patches and energy efficiency goods, have also been moved to the lower rate of VAT.

Other forms of indirect taxation comprise the excise duties applying to alcohol, tobacco, petrol and diesel, vehicle excise duty (commonly known as the tax disc), and sundry other taxes that might be grouped under the category 'other'. In real terms, duty on spirits and wine has fallen greatly since 1979, but has remained comparatively constant in respect of beer. Duty on cigarettes has seen an increase in real terms of over 150% since 1979. Duty on petrol has seen an increase in real terms of 58% since 1979, mainly accounted for by increases made in the 1990s under both the Conservatives and New Labour. Vehicle excise duty has since 1998 been a graduated tax based on engine size or carbon emissions, thus precluding a simple comparison between rates today and in 1979. However, it can be said that for all vehicles except for those with the highest emissions vehicle excise duty has either fallen or remained roughly constant in real terms. Indirect taxes falling under the category 'other' comprise such items as television licences, stamp duty on house purchase, customs duties, betting taxes and, since 1994, the newly introduced insurance premium tax, the national lottery fund and air passenger duty.

Figure 5.5 shows indirect taxes as a percentage of disposable income for all (non-retired) households. The amount of a household's disposable income that goes on indirect tax will depend on two factors, first, the rate of the indirect tax, and second, the household's spending decisions – for example, the proportion

Figure 5.5: Indirect taxes as a percentage of household disposable income, 1974-2004

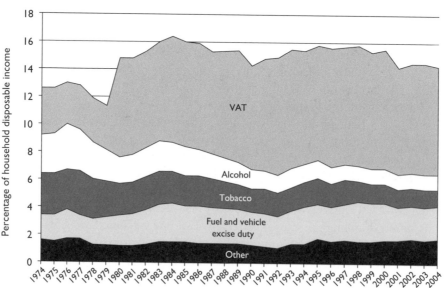

Source: Authors' calculations from ONS (2001, 2007d).

Note: All households from 1974-82; all non-retired households from 1983 onwards.

of income spent on goods and services subject to VAT. The importance of the second factor is seen by considering the percentage of household income that goes on duty on tobacco. This has fallen dramatically since 1974, but this is not because the rate of duty has fallen (on the contrary it has risen dramatically), but because fewer people smoke and therefore less tobacco is purchased.

More importantly for the overall history of tax incidence, Figure 5.5 shows that the amount of household income that goes in indirect taxation has risen from around 11% in 1979 to anywhere between 14.5 to 16% thereafter. If we refer again to Table 5.2 and remind ourselves that the combined effective rates of direct taxes have fallen by around 3% for the median earners, this counteracting rise in indirect taxation clearly has significant repercussions for overall taxation rates. Headline deductions of rates of income tax appear to have been overcompensated for by the combined effect of both rises in other forms of direct taxation and rises in indirect taxation. We will return to this important theme in Part Three of the book.

Before we move on to other policy provision for the 'working age' adult period of the lifetime, we highlight a few aspects of tax that will be covered in later discussions: the treatment of housing is discussed in Chapter Six and the treatment of old age by the tax system is covered in Chapter Nine with the other programmes for older people. We have not looked at taxation for our low- and high-paid families in this chapter; we leave this to Part Three of the book when we bring together all the policy elements for all the stages of the lifetime into a discussion of model lifetimes in our three comparison years.

Summary

In this chapter, we have looked at taxation: direct taxes, income tax, national insurance, local government taxation and indirect taxes. We have seen that:

- income tax has moved from being a very progressive system in the late 1970s to a much less progressive one today;
- income tax rates have been cut by the Conservatives and to a lesser extent by New Labour;
- such income tax cuts have been to a large extent offset by increases in National Insurance, local government taxation and indirect taxes;
- the cumulative effect of reforms, especially recent reforms, to National Insurance has been to bring NICs much closer to income tax;
- in the area of marriage and partnership, we have seen that the 1979 income tax system, and to a much lesser extent the 1997 income tax system, provided tax benefits to married couples that are not provided under the 2008 system.

Notes

[1] Our comparison year '1979' refers to the tax and benefit system as it stood in January 1979 and thus refers to the tax year 1978/79; see discussion in Chapters One and Eleven.

[2] That is on non-savings income – the 10% rate remains on income from savings, producing considerable complexity.

[3] Fiscal drag occurs when tax instruments keep pace with income growth. The short-term position may well be that tax allowances do not keep pace with earnings growth and rise with prices or other assumptions. If this is the case, it allows the tax take to grow. See Sutherland et al (2008).

[4] For example, see Kay and King (1980), IFS (2006).

[5] 24½ new pence or approximately £6.90 in 2008 prices. Married women who worked could opt for a lower rate and rely on their husbands' contribution record.

[6] Employees paid NICs on earnings above this threshold and were credited with contributions on any liability arising from difference between the threshold and LEL.

[7] Earlier in Scotland and kept in place in Northern Ireland.

[8] All other bands can be calculated from band D. For example, band A is always equal to 6/9ths of band D.

[9] A complication peculiar to the tax years 1978/79 and 1979/80 was that in addition to the wife's earned income allowance the wife was granted her own lower income tax band.

SIX

Working age: safety nets and housing

Adulthood brings financial independence and access to a range of social rights. This chapter considers two of these in tandem: first, the right to a basic income, and second, the need and rights to somewhere to live. Once again, the exact age at which childhood ends and independent living as an adult begins is hazy. The age at which young people gain a right to independent treatment of income and are seen as being in need of a minimum income was 16 for social assistance purposes until 1988, when the Fowler reforms upped the age to 18 on the basis of there being training and education schemes available for all 16- and 17-year-olds and to encourage young people to remain in the parental home. The minimum age at which a legal tenancy may be granted is 18 years old, a reflection of underlying assumptions on both responsibility and having the legal capacity to enter into contracts.

This chapter takes major issues of the treatment of working age individuals and families first by looking at means-tested safety nets and then moving on to outline the ways in which the tax and benefit system supports housing costs.

The benefit safety net and minimum income guarantees

The evolution of the social assistance safety net

Beveridge's plan from the 1940s was to build universal and comprehensive coverage for all life's main needs on the social insurance principle and thus to relegate social assistance to a small residual safety net for the few who fell through or outside such coverage. Beveridge foresaw this residual group as 'cripples and deformed, deaf and dumb, mentally deficient, and vagrants and moral weaklings'[1]. The contemporary inappropriate language should not get in the way of the clearer analytical point that Beveridge missed some important factors, such as divorce and lone parenthood, that would make potential coverage wider; he also made assumptions about rent and flat-rate needs and benefits that were irreconcilable (Evans and Glennerster, 1994). The story of social assistance in the post-war years is thus the playing out of these irreconcilabilities and gaps in coverage together with the overall change since the late 1970s to sponsor rather than avoid means testing. The result is that today social assistance is a major form of support designed to meet the majority of working age needs when out of work.

The National Assistance Act came into force in 1948. This centralised national social safety net replaced the provisions of the locally run Poor Law and moved to see needs at the level of family units rather than whole households, so that

co-resident adults such as adult relations and lodgers were no longer required
to be means tested alongside the core family. Supplementary Benefit replaced
National Assistance in 1966, but both these variants of social assistance had the
same underlying logic – a set of fixed weekly rates based on the assumption of
normal needs combined with liability for actual rent, rates and water rates. On top
of these basic weekly sums was the ability to add exceptional regular or one-off
assistance to meet particular needs. From 1973, Supplementary Benefit changed
its basic rate into two rates: a higher long-term rate for pensioners and long-
term claimants such as the long-term sick or lone-parents (after two years) and
basic short-term rates for everyone else (the unemployed and short-term sick in
the main). Discretionary additional weekly exceptional circumstances additions
(ECAs) and one-off grants, extraordinary needs payments (ENPs), could be paid
in addition. Sixty per cent of Supplementary Benefit claimants in 1979 were
receiving weekly ECAs for heating, dietary or laundry requirements and a total
of 1.13 million ENPs were made for a claimant caseload of 2.86 million people
(DHSS, 1980). Discretion thus represented a significant part of the system. The
logic of the Supplementary Benefit system meant that one-off payments were
supposed only to supplement normal needs, and as the majority of ENPs were
made for clothing and footwear, the underlying assumptions on a minimum
normal stock of clothing were made apparent. It is a sign of those paternalistic
but ungenerous times that a stock of just two pairs of (under)pants was seen as
adequate for everyone's normal needs[2].

   The rise in social assistance claimant numbers in the 1970s and the administrative
costs of a system based on both discretion and individual assessment of additional
needs meant that reform was needed. A DHSS review published in 1978 (DHSS,
1978) proposed adapting the scheme to its now mass role by removing large
amounts of discretion from the system. The Thatcher government implemented
many of the recommendations of this 1978 review, replacing discretion by a more
rights-based approach, albeit still with individual tailoring. However, a rights-
based approach combined with a demand-led budget meant that this expansion
was short-lived. More radical reform of the social assistance system had to wait
until the Thatcher government's second term in office. As discussed in Chapter
Two, the 1984 review of the whole social security system and the consequent
1986 Social Security Act, the Fowler reforms[3], replaced Supplementary Benefit
with Income Support.

   The main effects of the change from Supplementary Benefit to Income Support
were to:

- introduce the claimant's age as an important factor in the amount of benefit paid
  – in particular, single householders under 25 were entitled to less benefit;
- reduce the benefit rights of 16- and 17-year-olds – during the late 1980s
  most 16- and 17-year-olds were excluded from the Income Support system

altogether, instead being eligible for training allowances if they accepted places on youth training schemes;

- replace the system of weekly extra payments with a simpler system of automatic additions for specified groups of claimants – Income Support 'premiums' were paid at differential rates to claimants with dependent children, single-parent claimants, disabled claimants, pensioner claimants, disabled pensioner claimants and claimants with a disabled child;
- end the practice of there being long-term and short-term benefit rates – the long-term and short-term Supplementary Benefit rates were replaced by a single set of Income Support rates together with the above-mentioned premium system;
- end the practice of water rates being specifically covered by additional benefit – instead claimants would need to meet this cost from their weekly benefit;
- slightly reduce the couple rate in terms of its relationship to the single rate of benefit – under Supplementary Benefit, the standard couple rate was consistently around 1.6 times the single rate; under Income Support, the couple rate has been consistently around 1.57 times the single rate of benefit;
- require claimants to pay 20% of their local government tax bill (rates, or later community charge) from their weekly benefit;
- replace the system of one-off extra payments with the Social Fund, a smaller system that provided the majority of one-off help through a system of interest-free loans that had to be repaid from weekly benefit.

These last two measures were the most controversial, and the former was abandoned along with the community charge. The Social Fund, however, continues to operate under the same basic principles to this day. The net effect of the above reforms was, allowing for social and demographic factors, a marked reduction in benefit coverage and spending. The change from Supplementary Benefit to Income Support created some winners as well as losers across different family types. In real terms, households with children tended to receive more income under the Income Support system, but pensioners under 75 and households without children received less income under Income Support than the Supplementary Benefit system (Evans, 1996)[4].

The introduction of Income Support additionally signalled something of a change in emphasis away from the notion of an individually tailored safety net benefit for all towards a categorical system with some significant holes. In order to claim Income Support, a person has to fit into one of a series of prescribed groups. On the introduction of the benefit the key groups were: those over 60[5], the unemployed, lone parents, full-time carers and people who are long-term sick and disabled. The next reform was to remove the unemployed from Income Support into a separate Jobseeker's Allowance (JSA) that operated for both the insured unemployed (who could claim JSA as if it were unemployment benefit for six months) and those who had no contributory record or who needed social assistance to top up their contributory benefits. From 1996, these newly combined unemployed claimant groups faced more stringent tests of availability for work and active work search under a compulsory 'jobseeker's agreement' with the Department for Education and Employment (later joined to the Department of Social Security to form the Department for Work and Pensions and Jobcentre Plus service).

Since 1997, New Labour has increasingly reduced the remit of Income Support by making it only a 'working age' benefit first, by removing older people into a separate system (Pension Credit – effectively a more generous version of Income Support for those over 60; we will discuss this in more detail in Chapter Nine) and second, by removing children's needs from coverage and into the Child Tax Credit system from April 2003, as explained in Chapter Four.

An additional way in which Income Support has been changed is through a series of realignments with the employment focus of working age benefits and welfare-to-work programmes. This means, in the first instance, large structural changes in the treatment of those with limited capability to work (discussed in greater length in Chapter Eight) by way of a new unified benefit called Employment and Support Allowance (ESA), which was introduced in 2008 by the 2007 Welfare Reform Act. In terms of new claims, people with long-term sickness or disabilities that affect their ability to work are no longer one of the groups of people who can claim Income Support, but must claim income-based ESA alongside those with contributory entitlement to ESA that replaces Incapacity Benefit[6]. In the second realignment to employment, lone parents, who had been a major claimant group for Income Support for many years, must switch to JSA or ESA when their youngest child reaches a younger age than 16 (school-leaving age), which formed the previous, long-standing requirement for eligibility. Current proposals under the same 2007 Welfare Reform Act will make this age 12 in late 2008, 10 in October 2009 and, eventually, seven in 2010. The final manifestation of this move to change Income Support to fully reflect employment assumptions for all its claimants was announced in July 2007, with a Green Paper that proposes its abolition – to be replaced only by JSA or ESA for all (DWP, 2008a).

Marriage and partnership in social assistance

The social assistance system has never made a distinction between married and non-married couples but has consistently based its approach on co-residence and cohabitation and thus on a couple's status as 'living together *as* husband and wife'. Social assistance rates have always assumed that there are economies of scale from co-habitation and thus rates for couples, married or unmarried, are set below those of two single people. This meant that determining how far a man and woman were cohabiting has been an important part of policing the Supplementary Benefit system over the period of rising divorce and cohabitation in Britain since the 1960s. The absence of a clear definition for social assistance meant that legal consideration of single or couple status rested on a number of factors such as whether there was a stable relationship that actually shared a household; public acknowledgement as a couple; a sexual relationship; joint finances; and so on. However, such guidelines did not stop it being commonplace in the 1970s for 'a woman to have her benefit withdrawn if she slept with a man on, say, three consecutive nights' (CPAG, 1980, p 106). Lone parents on social assistance were commonly targeted for cohabitation checks and this approach may well have led to incentives to delay re-partnering and cohabitation. Since 2005, the same assumptions apply to same sex relationships and civil partnerships.

However, the designation of which member of a couple is the 'claimant' has had to change over time to move away from the assumption that it was always the man. Of the rules discriminating between men and women, the vast majority were removed following the coming into force in December 1984 of the European Union's directive on equal treatment for men and women in matters of social security (Council Directive 79/7/EEC).

Living standards on social assistance

What income standard has been maintained by social assistance since 1979? Uprating of social assistance has consistently been with prices, apart from the period from 1979 to 1981 when Old Labour's approach of uprating pensions and other long-term benefits with earnings was applied *solely* to long-term Supplementary Benefit rates (DWP, 2007b; IFS, 2008a). This means that a constant approach to uprating short-term social assistance – for the unemployed, in particular – exists across all governments and only operates to keep pace with prices. This has important repercussions for comparing the relative living standards of non-employed periods of the lifetime in Part Three. However, the changes in the 1980s to remove rent from social assistance (discussed later in this chapter) changed the price basis for indexation to an index that excluded rent (the ROSSI index). Figure 6.1 shows the relative value of the social assistance safety net in consistent terms by showing the basic couple rate of the prevailing safety net benefit from 1979 to 2008 as a percentage of average earnings. To illustrate the different assumptions for the long-term rates of Supplementary Benefit (the period 1979 to 1987), these are shown separately. It is clear that a primarily price-based uprating will see values fall significantly over time and the gap in relative position ever widen, with severe implications for poverty if this is also measured in relative terms. Basic (and short-term) rates have fallen from 28% of average weekly earnings in 1979 to 17% in 2008. Long-term rates kept their relative value fairly constant until 1983 and subsequently fell dramatically after real earnings rose and uprating changed from 1982 to be based on prices only.

In real terms, the purchasing power of social assistance for a couple has remained roughly flat over time, fluctuating at around £100 per week for a couple in 2008 prices. However, it should be remembered that average retail prices may understate inflation for poorer families with low purchasing power who are less likely to

Figure 6.1: Safety net benefit rates for a couple, 1979-2008

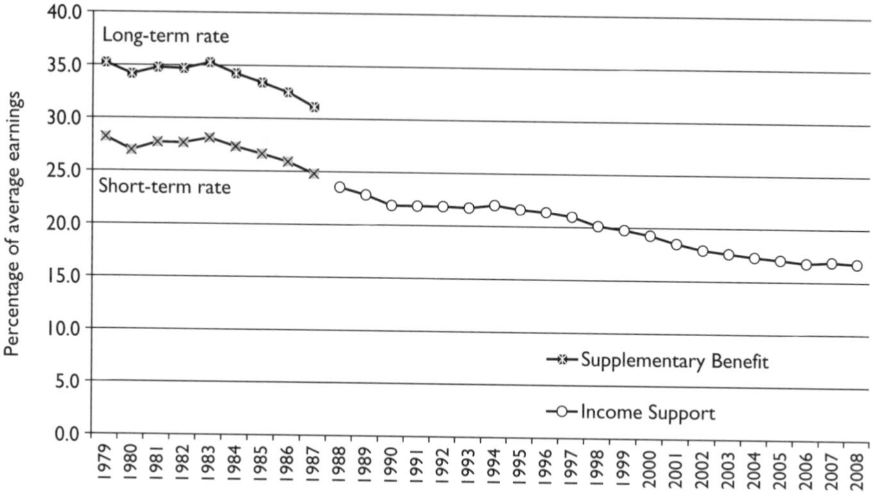

Source: Authors' calculations from DWP (2007b) and IFS (2008a).
Note: Only basic rate of benefits shown for 18-59 age group.

be able to benefit from discounts in bulk or pre-payment and have less access to competitive pricing. Additionally, we saw in the previous chapter that consumption taxes have increased dramatically over the period so that an increasing proportion of spending is taxed back.

However, it should be stressed that a long time series of this type hides many changes and has particular difficulty in consistent valuation of benefits between Supplementary Benefit and Income Support. For instance, the long-term rate of Supplementary Benefit was not simply replaced by the lower single rate of Income Support, as the majority of people who qualified for the long-term Supplementary Benefit rate would have had premiums under Income Support rules. However, the reform of social assistance to take out entitlement to one-off support payments and the introduction of loans from the Social Fund does produce more significant problems of comparison over time – losses at the time were estimated in the region of £2.50 a week in 1988 prices (Evans, 1994). A better and more accurate illustration of the changing value of social assistance is related to a more tightly specified family situation and we therefore conclude our discussion of the safety net benefit system by revisiting our non-working model family, the Nunns, to see how they have fared over time.

The Nunns

Let us say the Nunns are an unemployed couple without a child who are reliant on social assistance. How do they fare under our comparison year systems of 1979,

1997 and 2008? Under the 1979 system, they receive Supplementary Benefit and we include a sum in the Nunns' income calculated from 1979 statistics to represent the average benefit of ECAs and ENPs to unemployed claimants. Under the 1997 and 2008 systems, the Nunns would receive the couple rate of income-based JSA but no premiums in addition. We adjust for water rates to be consistent with the 1979 system that covered these separately in full. We consistently assign no value to 'passport' benefits for healthcare.

Table 6.1 shows the values of benefits in both real and relative terms. In 2008 prices, taking account of the underlying changes outlined above, we see a fall in consistent real value from £106 to £89, a 19% fall ignoring differential inflation and increased taxation in consumption. When we compare these rates of benefits to median earnings, to equate more to the position of the Meade family and to take out some of the effect of the increased inequality of earnings that draws the mean upwards over time, we see that relative values have fallen from 34% to 19%, an incredible 15 percentage point fall. The Nunns will be falling further behind the working Meades over time, even without the different lifetime events and profiles that we will come to consider in Part 3.

Minimum earned income guarantees and minimum wage

Social assistance prior to the 1970s was always seen as provision for those that

Table 6.1: The Nunns' income as a childless couple in real and relative terms

	1979 system	1997 system	2008 system
Weekly income in 2008 prices	£106.23	£99.63	£88.95
Weekly income as a percentage of median earnings	34%	21%	19%

Source: Authors' calculations using LOIS.

Note: Income calculated in after housing cost terms to ignore effect of rent.

did not work and the boundaries between employment and means-tested social assistance were based on an assumption of full-time working. Supplementary Benefit operated under the 'rule of thumb' that full-time work meant working 30-36 hours per week (CPAG, 1978b). Part-time workers could, for instance, not claim Supplementary Benefit if their hours were to the 'full extent normal', even if they qualified on income grounds. The introduction of in-work benefits to support low pay (initially for families with children) led to a clearer separation of in-work and out-of-work support. In the 1980s Fowler reforms, the boundary between in-work and out-of-work benefits was moved from 30 hours a week to 24 and then, in 1992, reduced further to 16.

From 1971, the only specific in-work support for low pay was Family Income Supplement for low-paid parents; the remaining low-paid workers would rely on wage bargaining, a system of minimum wages set by wages councils, discussed below, and the system of rent and rate rebates that operated to help with affordability for those with low incomes and were relatively more generous than today's Housing Benefit and Council Tax Benefit. The full-blown Conservative tax-credit system as proposed by a Green Paper in 1972 would in effect have provided transfers to any low-paid worker with or without children (DHSS, 1972), but it never happened. Labour under Wilson and Callaghan in the 1970s opposed further means testing and boosted coverage of categorical benefits for children and disability and kept rents low as part of a programme of expanding the social wage and keeping unionised labour happy. Such an approach was the antithesis of Thatcherism, which additionally indefinitely shelved the commitment to pursue tax benefit integration that had been a low-profile statement of policy. The market was allowed to set wages and unions were confronted and their power diluted. However, over time the problem of real wage stagnation at the bottom of the earnings distribution became a recognised problem for work incentives for the low paid. In the latter part of Major's term, a pilot scheme of wage supplements for low-paid workers not covered by Family Credit was introduced and evaluated (Marsh, 2001) and this pilot programme ran over the period of the change of government in 1997 and thus reported to New Labour. New Labour's approach was to improve low-paid incentives through two routes: first, a minimum wage and second, by expanding the generosity, and later the coverage, of in-work benefits. We discuss these in turn.

Britain had never before had a minimum wage because it was left to unions and employers to set wages, notwithstanding several infamously unsuccessful attempts at an incomes and prices policy in the 1960s and 1970s. However, trade boards and later wages councils had set minimum wage rates for the certain low-paying industries where trade union representation was low or ineffective. This meant that any moves to introduce a standard minimum wage across all industries were stymied by a consensus of effect arising from the different ideological perspectives of the left and the right. By the mid-1990s, the trade union movement was considerably weakened in both industrial relations and wider civil society and its hold on the Labour Party weakened after the 1992 election defeat and the emergence of New Labour. There was also increasing economic evidence from the US that minimum wages had little effect on employment levels and a new economic orthodoxy that accepted there was a market failure in wage setting caused by employers not competing properly for low-paid work (so-called 'monopsony') in the absence of a minimum wage standard. A national minimum wage became a flagship policy for the first Blair government and, introduced from April 1999, the National Minimum Wage Act requires that all workers be paid a minimum hourly wage at three age-related levels.

The introduction of a minimum wage also helped avoid the worst effects on employer incentives to reduce pay rates in the face of higher government subsidies to workers with low wages. New Labour first revamped the Conservative programmes of in-work benefits to parents by introducing Working Families Tax Credit in 1999 (discussed in Chapter Four). In 2003, after the evaluation of the earnings top-up pilots and early evidence of the effect of the minimum wage were considered, a new tax credit was introduced to 'tackle poor work incentives and persistent poverty' among working people (HM Treasury, 2002, p 3) for those with and without children. Working Tax Credit (WTC) extended support to all workers aged 25 or over, working 30 hours or more a week, in effect providing them with a minimum income guarantee. For example, WTC will currently (in 2008/09) guarantee a minimum income of £232 per week to a single-earner couple without children or a disability, aged 25 or over and working full time on the national minimum wage. Low-paid parents were further helped by the Child Tax Credit system that operates in parallel to WTC, as discussed earlier in Chapter Four.

Housing

The issue of choosing a home and paying for it is a central facet of adult life. But so far we have assumed that the treatment of children, tax and social assistance are independent of tenure and housing costs. Of course, this cannot be true in the real world. The development of housing policy, and in particular the issue of rent affordability, sat awkwardly across social assistance and between central and local responsibilities.

Renting

Early 20th-century social research into poverty, by Rowntree, the Webbs and others, saw it as axiomatic that rent was part of any national minimum income standard (Evans and Glennerster, 1994). Paying the rent was a fundamental part of a basic set of needs, and thus had to be covered by any programme that addressed monetary poverty, and remains so today (see, for instance, Bradshaw et al, 2008). Beveridge agreed with the principle, but couldn't handle the consequences in the design of a flat-rate system of National Insurance benefits. Rent liability was irreconcilable with a flat-rate system, as it varied according to household size, location and other factors. A proposal for a flat-rate weekly allowance for rent to be included in National Insurance benefits was not taken forward because when Beveridge's proposals came to be implemented it was more pragmatic to leave any difference in needs that arose from rent levels and the level of flat-rate benefits to be taken up by social assistance – a scheme based on the logic if not the costing of a national minimum income standard when it was introduced as National Assistance in 1948.

This logic for social assistance, that basic rates for weekly needs did not cover any element of rent, which was paid in full in addition to such basic rates, continued through to the Supplementary Benefit system. However, as part of a radical overhaul of housing finance by the Heath government, social rents would move to a more market level. This produced a problem of affordability for those on low incomes and the 1972 Housing Finance Act introduced means-tested rent rebates payable to tenants to replace some of the subsidies that went to buildings. The result was two overlapping but separate schemes to ensure that rent was affordable for the poorest tenants, one run by central government through the Supplementary Benefits Commission and the other run by every local authority on a national set of rules. Some people were potentially eligible under both schemes and could be better or worse off depending on which they claimed. According to the Child Poverty Action Group, this difference could amount to over 25% of basic weekly Supplementary Benefit needs (CPAG, 1978b). Contemporary estimates suggested that around 360,000 households had made the wrong choice and were claiming the benefit that made them worse off (Timmins, 2001, p 376). Clearly, the situation of having two benefit systems fulfilling the same need was far from ideal. A call for a unified system of rent payment came from the Supplementary Benefits Commission and some exploratory work was done to flesh out details. However, the intervention of the 1979 election meant that implementation of reform was left to the first Thatcher administration.

The decline of the private rented sector meant that while the 1972 rent rebates scheme also included rent allowances for private rents, the majority of funds for means-tested rent went to local authority housing revenue accounts. This, alongside the system of rate rebates that local authorities operated, meant that in theory they were best placed to take on the payments or rent (and rates) benefits for the poorest population. Having control of larger proportions of rent revenue through administering the scheme for social assistance claimants was attractive to finance and housing managers in local authorities. The reform of policy to unify housing benefits was also subject to cost controls by the Thatcher government to reduce civil service staff numbers and to keep any change a cost-neutral reform. The result was that unified payments, called Housing Benefit, were administered solely by local authorities but that entitlement from non-supplementary benefit cases was cut back to pay for reform. The change in 1983 caused administrative chaos for a considerable period of time. Claimants were faced with higher transaction costs and hassle as two agencies with quite different organisational cultures now dealt with their claim. The new system, much resembling the old with separate entitlements calculated for Supplementary Benefit cases and other cases, had hardly settled down when the Fowler reforms of social security began in 1984.

Of course, the new Housing Benefit system was dealing with growing demand due to higher unemployment, depressed incomes and higher rents, as housing finance policy once again raised rents and Conservative policy was set to transform the landscape of tenure in the UK forever by council house sales. The Fowler reforms were partly concerned with the need for increased cost containment in the main area of demand-led spending. Entitlement to Housing Benefit had to be further cut back, despite, or indeed partly because of, higher rents. The 1986 Social Security Act radically reformed Housing Benefit and came into effect in 1988. Claimants of the new Income Support, which replaced Supplementary Benefit, would receive 100% of their rent (subject to much higher assumed contributions from co-resident family members and others). For those with incomes above Income Support levels, Housing Benefit was now withdrawn at the steep taper of 65%. The effect of this was to target Housing Benefit on the very poorest and the overall numbers receiving Housing Benefit fell drastically from 5.5 million in 1987 to 4.1 million in 1988 (IFS, 2008a). Many people on low incomes were simply excluded from the reformed system and those that were in the system and not receiving Income Support paid more for rent. These reforms coincided with the introduction of the poll tax and the requirement for even the poorest to pay 20% of their income in un-rebated poll tax and the introduction of the Social Fund with loans rather than grants for large one-off needs (see earlier discussion in this chapter).

Since 1988, reforms of Housing Benefit have taken the form of minor adjustments to ensure that underlying structures reflect reform elsewhere in the system, such as the introduction of carer's premiums and of an allowance in respect of childcare costs in the 1990s, both under the Conservatives. Similarly, since 1997 under New Labour, Housing Benefit has remained largely unreformed, with changes made to reflect the new tax credit system to ensure its compatibility. However, radical reform has been implemented in 2008 for private tenants. Following trials in 18 local councils, a local housing allowance scheme was rolled out nationally. For private tenants, this means that Housing Benefit will be calculated not on the basis of actual rent but on the basis of a set local housing allowance based on a mid-range market rent in that locality. In this way, policy has finally resolved the 'irresolvable' problem of Beveridge – that of rent and flat-rate benefits. However, it has done so by abandoning a commitment to meeting full rent as a fundamental part of basic needs and thus potentially overturns the best part of a century of standard poverty assumptions.

Rents and affordability

Has gross rent before rebates become less affordable? Figure 6.2 depicts average weekly local authority rent in real prices. The graph clearly shows how local authority rents were increased first by the Heath government's housing finance reforms, then pegged back by Old Labour before rising dramatically under the Conservatives and that this trend, albeit to a less marked extent, has continued under New Labour. If we analyse Figure 6.2 in terms of the four different political periods indicated, we see that Thatcher and Major governments raised rents most

Figure 6.2: Average weekly local authority rent in real prices, 1971-2007 (England)

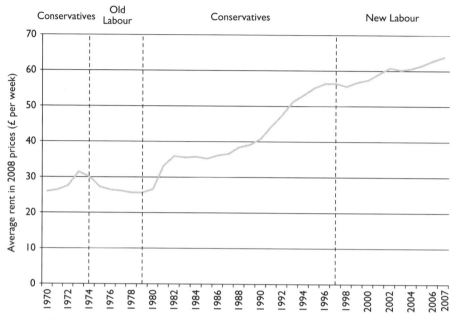

Source: Authors' calculations using DoE (1984) and earlier versions, and CLG (2008a).

– 6.7% per year on average – and that the Heath government also raised rents far ahead of inflation – 4% per annum. New Labour has also raised rents in real terms but at a lesser rate – 1.3% per annum on average.

But, of course, real growth in rents would not provide any problems of affordability if the incomes of tenants were rising at the same rate. However, if we were to bring forward the findings on earnings growth for the low paid at the bottom of the income distribution from Chapter Three, we would clearly see that real rises in social rents have in general outstripped rises in the earnings of the tenants of social housing.

The changes to reduce the generosity of housing benefits ensured that these higher rents were not met in full by higher benefit payments. Figure 6.3 shows the relationship between rent rebates for an average local authority rent and median full-time male earnings in 1979, 1997 and 2008. The calculations are all based on an assumption that the tenant is not claiming social assistance and thus receives a rebate on income from earnings or an equivalent. In 1979, the system continued to pay full rent rebate on earnings of 35% of contemporary median earnings; help then tapered out so that some assistance (equal to around 6% of the rent) continued at 75% of median earnings and tapered down to zero at 80% of median earnings. By 1997, help with 100% of contemporary rent ·ended at around 25% of median earnings and the far steeper taper meant that all

Figure 6.3: Housing benefits provision, 1979, 1997 and 2008 – percentage of rent met by benefits for a single earner couple without children

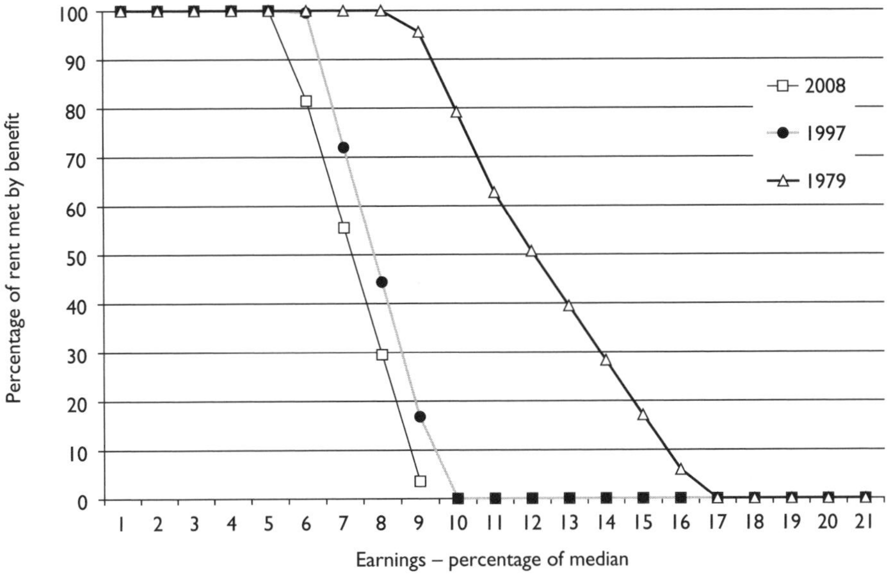

Source: Authors' calculations using CPAG (1978b, 1997b, 2008); ONS (2003, 2007e).

entitlement ended at 45%. By 2008, further falls in generosity relative to earnings have occurred so that entitlement ends at a level equivalent to 20% of median earnings and the same tapers as 1997 take entitlement to zero at around 40% of median earnings. Housing benefits have thus both structurally changed to be less generous between 1979 and 1997 (primarily as a result of the Fowler reforms), but have also been eroded in relative value, as help with 100% of rent is fixed at income levels equivalent to Income Support levels that have only risen with prices and thus fallen further behind median earnings over time.

Owner-occupation

Historically, both the tax system and the benefit system have supported home ownership by providing assistance with housing costs but based on very different assumptions. The income tax system saw mortgage interest as applicable for income tax relief, while the benefit system saw mortgage payments as a necessary cost of basic needs to maintain a roof over one's head. The trend over the past 30 to 40 years has been to withdraw both forms of support, although announcements in October 2008 heralded a sense of reversal for benefits, with increased potential for assistance for mortgagees who become unemployed in the 2009 recession.

Occupying and purchasing a house results in several direct costs: paying back the loan (mortgage interest and capital payments), insuring the structure of the home and keeping it maintained. Mortgage costs change over time as the loan is taken out for a fixed purchase price at a single point in time (ignoring remortgaging or other ways of releasing equity) and this means that over the lifetime of the mortgage the costs fall in relation to rising income – most people first purchase in their relatively early adult years and both earnings growth and their lifetime earnings profile mean that their housing payments decline over time relative to income. The composition of mortgage repayments also changes over time; interest payments are at the highest proportion at the point of purchase, while capital repayments rise as the mortgage progresses. Two crucial factors alter this simplistic linear view of mortgages: first, interest rates tend to fluctuate and thus the amount of interest changes and payments change periodically; and second, most people do not buy one home in a lifetime but move and change homes through a succession of purchases. However, when it comes to our model lifetimes later in Part Three, we will use a simple set of constant rates and a single lifetime house purchase to more clearly illustrate and analyse policy change and other change.

Owner-occupation and benefits

Support for owner-occupier housing costs was part of social assistance's commitment to cover a minimum set of basic needs that included housing costs. However, the state would never provide subsidies for purchase of the equity of a home and thus only the interest paid could be covered, as a direct equivalent to rent, to owner-occupiers who claimed National Assistance, Supplementary Benefit and Income Support. Prior to the introduction of Income Support, water rates and a fixed weekly allowance to cover house repairs and insurance were also covered in full. The only serious proviso was that housing costs, both for mortgages and rent, could be limited if the property concerned was seen as 'unreasonably luxurious' or too large.

The fundamental principle that all housing costs would be met consistently by social assistance was abandoned during the period of the Fowler reforms. Since 1987, a waiting period has applied on all new claims from owner-occupiers before mortgage interest payments would be met in full. Initially, this was set at 16 weeks, during which time only 50% of mortgage interest payments would be met. When Income Support was introduced a year later in 1988, the payment of specific sums to cover water rates and the allowance for house repairs and insurance were abolished outright. The waiting period for mortgage interest payments for Income Support was then extended in 1995 after discussions with banks and buildings societies about arrears and repossession procedures and the up-take of income protection insurance. The period of waiting for full mortgage interest payments rose to 26 weeks for those with mortgages taken out before October 1995 and 39 weeks for the remainder who no longer received *any* assistance with mortgage interest payments during the waiting period in normal circumstances[7]. Mortgage support costs were also constrained by moving to a fixed interest rate on a maximum of a £100,000 loan rather than actual interest paid. Until 2008, no significant change to these rules had been made since 1995; while house prices at the same time surged, the £100,000 limit was not uprated.

With the fast-gathering economic downturn in the latter part of 2008 and the attendant increased risk of unemployment and increased potential for defaulting on mortgages, the policy of less and devalued assistance with mortgage costs has changed. In September 2008, proposals were made to reduce the waiting period from 39 to 13 weeks and increase the ceiling of costs to £175,000, but to limit the total time that help with mortgage interest payments could be given to two years.

Income tax and owner-occupation

The income tax rules for the 1970s provided mortgage interest tax relief. This was the last remnant of a historical set of tax assumptions that had eroded to that point. Tax relief had once been granted on *all* interest payments for any loan on the basis that income from interest was taxed and therefore setting off interest payments would avoid a form of double taxation. Over time, the majority of interest payments were systematically brought under income tax but setting off mortgage interest payments remained because the notional income from rent that householders gained from living in the home they owned or were purchasing was taxable under then current rules. These so-called 'Schedule A' tax rules were abandoned in 1963 but relief for mortgage interest was not[8]. Such tax expenditure did not 'count' as public spending and could be presented in part as a counterbalancing subsidy that produced some fairness across tenures compared with the subsidies that went to tenants.

Prior to 1974, mortgage interest tax relief was granted in full, meaning that owner-occupiers would pay no income tax on any of their income that went towards paying mortgage interest. From 1974, tax relief was confined to interest on loans of £25,000 (when the average house price was then around just £10,000) and this limit only affected an affluent minority. Labour in the 1970s saw the political costs of withdrawing mortgage interest relief as too great. The Conservatives were more open to the idea and wanted to reap the political gains from advancing owner-occupation as a preferred tenure for a 'property-owning democracy'. However, free-market new right Conservatives had an alternative view: these subsidies distorted the market and made house prices higher than they had to be by subsidising demand. As outlined in Chapter Two, it was Thatcher herself who put market ideology to one side and opposed all economic arguments to protect her natural electorate in the suburbs of the Home Counties and elsewhere.

In April 1983, the method of administering mortgage interest relief changed from the pay as you go income tax system to a more sensible one of mortgagees paying their lenders interest less the tax relief, through the Mortgage Interest Relief at Source (MIRAS) scheme. With the introduction of MIRAS, the limit for attracting tax relief was increased to £30,000 (albeit an increase far below house price inflation). However, this was to be the last time any move was made to increase mortgage interest tax relief. Post-Thatcher, the Major government began phasing out MIRAS and cut it to a flat rate of 20% and, in subsequent reforms, to 15% and then 10%. With the dramatic rise of house prices in the late 1990s leading to further erosion in the significance of MIRAS, it was a relatively small matter for New Labour to abolish it completely in April 2000.

Of course, one of the major tax subsidies to owner-occupation is through disregarding the significant gains in capital value that occur when homes are sold. The 'private residence relief' in capital gains tax for the primary home has had an obvious effect on house prices but is politically untouchable. Capital gains tax applies in general to the sale or disposal of all other assets.

Modelling taxes, benefits and housing costs

In our discussion of the lifetime we have now reached the point where, having looked at taxation and means-tested benefits, it is time to consider together all the different forms fiscal policy in the context of our model families, the Meades, the Moores and the Lowes.

The Meades

In Chapter Four, we asked how the benefit and tax credit systems for children affected our model families in 1979, 1997 and 2008. We stick with this approach and the underlying assumptions about the ages for partnership (28), marriage (30) and house purchase (32), but keep things simple by taking out the child and any child-related transfers to focus more on matters concerning housing, means testing and tax taken together. In all these profiles, no inflation is taken into account other than the change in prices and earnings level between the comparison years. Earnings are kept constant over time in a very basic 'Groundhog Day' approach, with no reflection of changes that arise from age and experience or earnings growth. These assumptions on earnings allow us to concentrate on underlying structural differences in housing costs and fiscal incidence and should be interpreted as based on a constant contemporary measure of median earnings for each year as the household 'ages'.

> **Box 6.1: Housing costs faced by the model families**
>
> The analysis in this section requires values to be put on house prices, weekly rent, weekly water rates and weekly house repair/insurance costs in order to calculate housing costs. In the interests of consistency and simplicity, common average values are used. House prices and rent are treated as follows:
>
> The families that buy houses buy them at the average house price a first-time buyer would have paid in 1979, 1997 and 2008. We keep interest rates constant over the duration of the mortgage repayment and assume no remortgaging. We assume a real mortgage interest rate of 3% under all three systems. Only mortgage interest is taken as a 'housing cost' in line with income definitions currently used by government for the households below average income series (DWP, 2007a).
>
> All families pay weekly rent at the average weekly cost for a local authority dwelling for 1979, 1997 and 2008. No change in rent occurs as the household moves from comprising one member to comprising two.
>
> *Respective sources for values:* Nationwide (2008); CLG, (2008a)

Figure 6.4 shows the net effects of taxation and housing costs on the Meades' earnings under the 1979, 1997 and 2008 systems by plotting the net income after taxes, benefits and housing costs as a proportion of gross earnings, shown on the vertical scale, against age. The arrows aid interpretation by showing the points in the life history where underlying events occur and assumptions change. We consider the five stages that result from these changes in turn. From age 24-27, Mr Meade is single and rents and thus faces the best outcome for this period of his life under the 1979 system, where, although he faces the highest taxation, housing costs are that much lower, leaving him overall with a higher percentage of his income after tax and housing costs.

At age 28, Mr Meade begins cohabiting with his partner and the sharing of housing costs under all three systems lowers the percentage of their joint earnings after tax and housing costs. However, the improvement is less profound under the 1979 system because housing costs are less significant. The improvements under the 1997 and 2008 systems are offset slightly by Mr Meade losing his single person's discount from his council tax. Marriage at age 30 produces no change in their tax outcomes in 2008; under the 1997 system, their outcome improves slightly and under the 1979 system more so due to income tax benefits.

The Meades become owner-occupiers aged 32 and comparison between policy years is most affected by the changes in house prices and comparative costs of renting versus mortgage payments. Under the 1979 system, the comparatively low rent and comparatively low house prices mean that in the first instance the Meades are no significantly worse or better off by becoming owner-occupiers, as rent and mortgage interest payments are roughly equal. Under the 2008 system,

Figure 6.4: The Meades – effects of taxes and housing costs on contemporary median earnings, 1979, 1997 and 2008

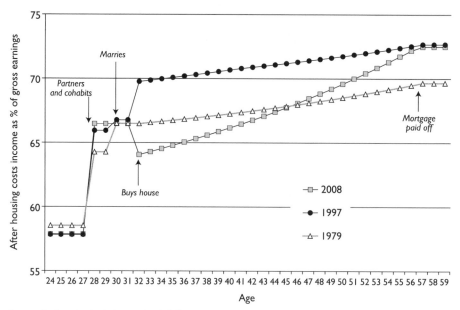

Source: Authors' calculations using LOIS.

Note: No price or earnings inflation.

high post-boom house prices mean that despite rent being the highest in terms relative to their income under the 2008 system, the Meades face initial mortgage interest payments that are much higher than the rent they had been paying. Under the 1997 system, comparatively low pre-boom house prices coupled with rent that in terms relative to their income is much higher than under the 1979 system, mean that the Meades face initial mortgage payments that are much lower than the rent they had been paying. Obviously, these results are driven by the assumptions of prices at the particular point of time. Over the period of the mortgage across all comparison years, the falling relative value of mortgage interest payments is apparent. Although it is not easily discernable from the graph, under the 1997 system, the Meades receive some tax benefits from making mortgage interest payments (through MIRAS), greater tax benefits under the 1979 system (through mortgage interest tax relief) and no such tax benefits under the 2008 system. At age 57, the 25-year mortgage ends and thus the Meades' housing costs fall considerably and cease to be a very significant factor in their net income. From this point they simply fare best under the systems that present them with the lowest taxes – the 1997 and 2008 systems.

The Moores

The Moores have double the income of the Meades (twice the median earnings), but otherwise have identical lives.

Figure 6.5 shows the Moores faring consistently better under the 1997 system, with its comparatively low housing costs and comparatively low taxation when measured by the amount of their earnings they get to keep after taxation and housing costs. The 2008 system, with low taxation, is worse primarily because of its comparatively high housing costs. The 1979 system of taxation takes most from gross income leaving the Moores much worse off under the 1979 system, even with its comparatively low housing costs. The Moores face a much higher effective income tax rate under the 1979 system and face a marginal tax rate of 60% compared with both lower effective and marginal rates in the 1997 and 2008 systems. They are also better off opting for separate rather than joint taxation under the 1979 system and we model this optimising behaviour, leaving the 1979 system result unaffected by the Moores' marriage. Elsewhere, the story of the Moores is similar to that of the Meades, except, of course, their housing costs are comparatively lower because here we assume that the Moores face the same housing costs as the Meades but have more income. Later, in order to make more realistic comparisons in Part Three, we will increase the housing costs for the Moores in a more realistic direction to recognise the fact that they could buy a

Figure 6.5: The Moores – net effects of taxes and housing costs on twice median earnings, 1979, 1997 and 2008

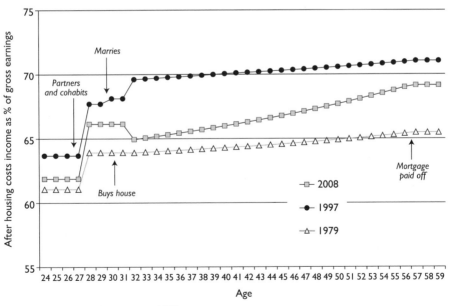

Source: Authors' calculations using LOIS.

Note: No price or earnings inflation.

bigger, better located home, but for the moment we keep house prices constant, allowing us to compare tax incidence alongside housing costs for these earnings levels more clearly.

The Lowes

Figure 6.6 shows the combined effect of lower levels of earnings (at half of contemporary median) and continuous renting. Under the assumptions of no earnings or price inflation, the Lowes' housing costs stay constant. We make no attempt here to put a value on other housing subsidies (that keep their rent low) and that would give them a notional income in kind. The profile for the Lowes' working age is thus much simpler, with the same partnership and marriage assumptions as the Meades and the Moores. When Mr Lowe is single he has a low enough income to entitle him to receive rent and rates rebates to the value of around 28% of his total rent and rates bills under the 1979 system but nothing similar from Housing Benefit in 1997 and 2008, illustrating again the decline in relative generosity over time that was discussed earlier. In 2008, once he is over 25 and remains single, he will also receive a small amount of WTC under the 2008 system, although it is a characteristic of WTC for this sort of claimant that it is rarely taken up. As Mr Lowe partners, the household's two-earner income precludes it from receiving benefit income any more, but on marriage, the 1979 and 1997 systems present the couple with lower taxation, most dramatically so

Figure 6.6: The Lowes – net effects of taxes, benefits and housing costs on half median earners

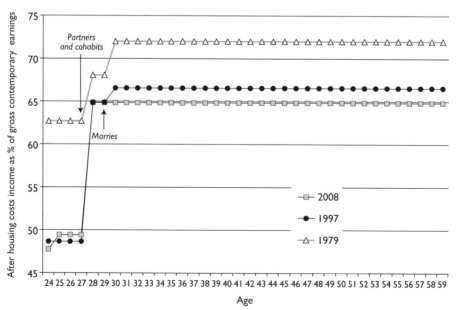

Source: Authors' calculations using LOIS.

under the 1979 system whose tax allowances for marriage actually favour them as low earners. This, combined with low rents, means that the Lowes fare much better under the 1979 system.

Summary

This chapter has considered two policy areas that potentially affect all adults' lives. First, we discussed the development of the range of benefits that support minimum standards of income, out-of-work social assistance, in-work benefits and the minimum wage, as well as their changing coverage. Second, we considered programmes that support housing costs through means-tested measures to ensure affordability and through tax relief.

In the area of social assistance and minimum income guarantees, we have seen that:

- social assistance, originally intended as a necessary but small safety net in the benefit system, has become the major form of support;
- elements of discretion in the social assistance system have been replaced by categorical elements of right;
- reforms in the 1980s reduced real safety net provision in various areas;
- the recent trend has been towards replacing the notion of a safety net benefit for all with a series of categorical social assistance benefits respectively reserved for different groups of claimants;
- the value of the safety net has fallen drastically in relative terms over the past 30 years as wages have risen faster than the prices used to uprate benefit; and
- minimum income guarantees for those in work without dependent children were not introduced until New Labour's national minimum wage and Working Tax Credit.

In the area of housing costs, we have seen that:

- the 'biggest stories' in terms of change have been those outside the tax and benefit system, notably the post-1997 housing price boom, and the change in the UK's tenure profile brought about by the sale of local authority housing in the 1980s;
- in the 1980s, there was a policy move from subsidising housing to subsidising people, resulting in higher social housing rent but greater claims on the housing benefit system;
- the coverage of Housing Benefit was markedly cut in the late 1980s so that the benefit only covered the lowest income groups;
- the 1979 benefit system provided housing costs support to owner-occupier claimants that was effectively removed from the late 1980s onwards;

- the 1979 tax system, and to a much lesser extent the 1997 tax system, provided tax benefits to owner-occupiers with mortgages that are not provided under the 2008 system.

Our model family analysis considered the portion of the lifetime that can be considered the main 'home-building' element of adulthood, from partnership and marriage through to buying or renting the home that forms the basis of adult life. The main differences we saw over the three comparison years reflect historical differences in underlying housing costs, in the costs of buying a home as house prices have risen and the costs of rent. Alongside historical differences in the tax and benefit systems, our analysis indicates that:

- median and above-median earners without children generally fare best in terms of the proportion of income they get to keep after taxation and housing costs under the 1997 system; and
- low earners fare best under the 1979 system, with its combination of low rents and more generous housing benefits, and generally fare worst under the 2008 system.

However, these profiles do not take into account the increased levels of support for children in low-income families in 2008 outlined earlier in Chapter Four.

Notes

[1] Beveridge's remit for the subcommittee to discuss assistance, as quoted in Evans and Glennerster (1994).

[2] The B/040 Clothing Needs Checklist is given in full in CPAG, 1978b, pp 27-8.

[3] Referring to the then Secretary of State for Social Services, Norman Fowler.

[4] For comparison analysis of model family types under Supplementary Benefit and Income Support, see Evans (1996, pp 243-5).

[5] Or even aged 50 for those aged between 50 and 60 who had been out of the labour market for 10 or more years. This was mostly targeted at women who had not worked previously while being primarily at home looking after the family who used to be permitted to claim income support without being required to register as unemployed and seek work.

[6] For details of ESA, see Chapter Seven and DWP (2007c); OPSI (2007a, 2007b).

[7] Special case rules and exceptions to the waiting period rules exist, including exemption for those aged 60 and over, although cynics may point out that the level of interest for older people with more mature mortgages will be lower than for younger people with more recent mortgages.

[8] If an individual owns a house and rents it to another, rental income is taxable. If an individual owns a house and is an owner-occupier, effectively renting it to himself/herself, no such tax liability occurs. This waiver of 'notional economic' income can still be interpreted as a subsidy for owner-occupation.

SEVEN

Working age risks: social insurance

We now turn to consider a series of risks that can interrupt or erode earnings during working age. Obviously, there are a significant number of such risks so for the purposes of this chapter we split them into two main groups: risks that have historically been approached through social insurance, namely unemployment, sickness and incapacity for work, and other risks, which we leave to Chapter Eight.

Unemployment

Unemployment dominated social policy in the 1930s and the post-war commitment to full employment was one of the bedrock assumptions of Beveridge and others when redesigning the welfare state. Unemployment benefits had existed in an insurance-based form since 1911, but coverage, in terms of both workforce and duration, was insufficient to cope with global recession and high levels of unemployment. The 1948 National Insurance Act had a comprehensive unemployment benefit for all unemployed workers who had paid sufficient National Insurance contributions, as long as they weren't blameworthy for losing their job and fulfilled the conditions of looking for and being available for work.

The 1948 Act did not carry forward Beveridge's own recommendations for indefinite benefits. Instead, Unemployment Benefit was payable for a maximum of one year to cover short-term unemployment. The flat-rate unemployment insurance benefits fell foul of Beveridge's core irreconcilable rent problem, discussed in Chapter Six. Anyone who paid rent and became unemployed would need both insurance and social assistance to cover their basic needs and this meant means testing was still important if not dominant in the treatment of unemployed people. After 1948, the basic rate of Unemployment Benefit declined relative to National Assistance. Originally, it was 8% higher but by 1996 (when the benefit changed to become Jobseeker's Allowance) the basic rate of Unemployment Benefit had been at or below the basic single person rate of social assistance for a total of 19 years of the benefit's 48-year existence. In 1979, it was just 1% higher.

In the 1970s, Unemployment Benefit still existed with its original 1948 assumptions, was still contributory in its nature and payable for up to one year with additional benefit for a dependent spouse and dependent children. Earnings-related additions had been available with the first six months of benefit receipt since 1966.

The election of the Conservatives in 1979 was a bigger change for unemployment and the unemployed than for any other group. In the 1980s, monetarist economic policies deliberately drove unemployment rapidly to levels that would have been deemed politically unacceptable in the 1970s. The two-pronged policy approach of improving work incentives and cutting back on government spending applied especially to unemployment provision[1]. Unemployment Benefit was targeted for early reform. Earnings-related supplements were abolished in 1980 legislation, described as 'the great welfare state chainsaw massacre' by one contemporary commentator (Mesher, 1981). Unemployment Benefit was made taxable (along with Supplementary Benefit when paid to the unemployed) for the first time ever in 1982. Other incremental reforms to Unemployment Benefit followed over much of the 1980s, including the abolition of dependent child additions and the tightening of contribution conditions. This cumulative incremental approach to reform with changes 'limited in their individual impact' amounted overall to a significant reduction in generosity of unemployment benefit and a weakening of the role of the contributory principle (Atkinson and Micklewright, 1989.

In 1996, the Conservatives under John Major replaced Unemployment Benefit completely with contributory Jobseeker's Allowance (JSA) and also replaced Income Support for unemployed claimants with a means-tested JSA. In contrast to Unemployment Benefit, contributory JSA is payable for a maximum of six rather than 12 months, includes no dependent additions and is payable at exactly the same rate as the means-tested JSA. All three of these changes clearly marked a further weakening of the role of insurance-based unemployment support and marked a further stage in the expanding role of means testing. Both the changes in duration and coverage of needs led to an increased role for means testing. The alignment of rates between contributory and means-tested benefit removed any last vestiges of recognition of or reward for having a contribution record.

Under New Labour, JSA has not undergone any major reform. However, New Labour's approach to unemployment support and labour market policy has been characterised by three distinct aspects of change (Clasen, 2007). First, receipt of JSA has been made more conditional, requiring compulsory participation in New Deal programmes for claimants under 25 after receiving the benefit for six months, and for over-25s after receiving the benefit for 18 months. Second, employment and benefit services have been brought under the same administration, with Jobcentre Plus now fulfilling the combined role of employment agency and social security office. Finally, the target of employment policy has been widened in scope to 'worklessness' as opposed to just unemployment, thus including those in receipt of incapacity benefits as well as those in receipt of unemployment benefits.

Levels of unemployment and coverage by benefits

Figure 7.1 shows the history of unemployment in terms of numbers unemployed and complements the earlier discussion of levels of unemployment in Chapter Three. It shows the 'claimant count' – the number of people who present themselves to Jobcentre Plus offices (and their predecessors) and sign on looking for work – alongside the International Labour Organisation's (ILO) definition of unemployment based on the numbers estimated from national surveys. The two measures reflect broadly the same story – large rises in the numbers of unemployed up to around the three million mark during the economic downturns of the early 1980s and early 1990s. The two measures are further apart during periods of low unemployment but converge more when unemployment rises. However, since the 1990s recession and during the long sustained period of 16 years of economic growth, the 'Brown boom', there has been a growing divergence between ILO and claimant count measures. This reflects the fact that more non-working people are looking for employment but not being counted by the Jobcentre as being unemployed. Part of this trend comes from economically inactive people becoming more interested in employment but not registering as unemployed. These groups may well include lone parents and those with long-term health problems who are becoming more employment-orientated as a result of the New Deals and other employment programmes that do not require them to define themselves as 'unemployed' to receive cash benefits.

Figure 7.1: Numbers in unemployment, 1971-2007 (UK)

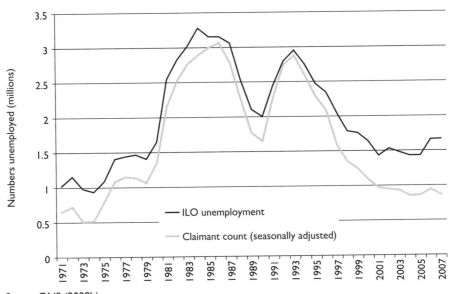

Source: ONS (2008b)

Note: Plotted values are figures as at May each year.

Figure 7.2 shows the claimant count measure of unemployment broken down by the underlying type of benefit received. The claimant count includes those registering as looking for work to maintain National Insurance contributions rather than receive cash benefits, but their number has fallen from 20% to 10% over the whole period, in part a reflection of the changes in the growing employment of partnered women, who used to be a large proportion of such cases. Figure 7.2 clearly demonstrates the declining role of contributory benefit and the rise in means testing. In 1971, a majority (54%) of unemployed claimants were receiving contributory benefit either on its own or with a means-tested top-up. By 2007, a mere 16% of unemployed claimants received contributory benefit with or without a means-tested top-up; 75% received means-tested assistance alone. The point at which means testing becomes the majority is, unsurprisingly, 1983 – the peak of the 1980s' recession – but despite subsequent booms and recession the proportion of those receiving means-tested benefits rises relentlessly.

Figure 7.2: Unemployed claimants by benefit entitlement, 1971-2007

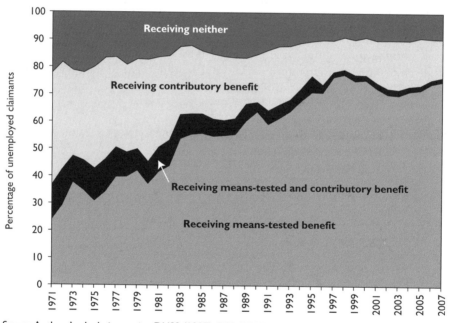

Source: Authors' calculations using DHSS (1987), DSS (2000) and DWP (2008b).
Note: Figures used are as at May of each year.

There are two important qualifying factors to remember at this point. First, the changes to social assistance discussed in Chapter Six have, over time, reduced generosity for the unemployed for a number of reasons, including the loss of one-off payments and weekly discretionary payments in the 1980s. Second, the disproportionate risk of unemployment on the low skilled and low paid means that repeated unemployment is not unusual for those groups. Repeated unemployment for low-skilled workers means that they have little to gain from contributory rewards in traditional perception of risk, and policy has increasingly moved to focus purely on short-term job-entry objectives and the incentives that arise at the margins of being in and out of work.

Figure 7.3 takes forward this issue of benefit value over time and shows trends in the relative values of all income replacement benefits compared with average earnings. This allows us to show Unemployment Benefit alongside other National Insurance benefits and its relative value to such benefits over time as well as to average earnings. We discuss these other benefits later in the chapter and refer back to these results then. Figure 7.3 also shows individual social assistance rates, so that they can be compared with the levels of unemployment benefits. The levels of contributory unemployment benefits have never differed widely from the safety net over the period, confirming our earlier findings in the discussion of the longer period since 1948. However, it is also worth remembering at this point that cuts in value are not shown in this comparison, including the abolition of earnings-related supplements, the introduction of lower rates for the under-25s and the cut in maximum duration of entitlement.

Relative to other risks in adult working life, the benefits for unemployment have consistently been lower than those for long-term incapacity (discussed

Figure 7.3: Relative values of various earnings replacement benefits

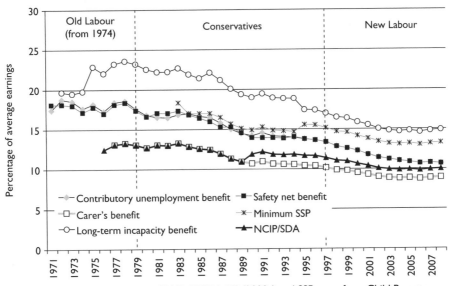

Source: Authors' calculations using DWP (2007b), IFS (2008a) and SSP rates from Child Poverty Action Group benefit guides (CPAG, 1978b, 1980, 1997a, 1997b, 2007, 2008).

Notes: April values in each year. The contributory unemployment benefit line shows the basic adult rate for Unemployment Benefit and the single adult over-25 rate for contributory JSA. The safety net benefit line shows the basic single person rate for Supplementary Benefit and the single adult over-25 rate for Income Support (and JSA) from 1988. Average earnings are of all adults.

later) and higher than those for carers. They have also consistently been higher than non-contributory income replacement benefits for disabled people, also discussed later. The rates for short-term Sickness Benefit were exactly the same as Unemployment Benefit until the introduction of Statutory Sick Pay in 1983, when provision subsequently become more generous. Relative to earnings, there has been overall a dramatic fall in the value of contributory benefits over the period, with for example, contributory Unemployment Benefit for a single person over 25 being equivalent to 18.8% of average weekly earnings in 1972 but just 10.7% of average earnings in 2008. This reflects the consistent approach to the uprating of unemployment benefits that has not changed from Old Labour in the 1970s to the present day.

Sickness and long-term incapacity

In 1948, social insurance to cover interruptions in earnings resulting from illness operated alongside free healthcare from the National Health Service to tackle the two fundamental problems arising from ill health: loss of income and the cost of healthcare. Unfortunately, the separate health and income insurance provisions of the British system have meant that there have never been incentives to join up healthcare and income transfer issues, unlike continental health insurance systems and occupational rehabilitation. This has been an enduring weakness in the system. Sickness Benefit in 1948 was exactly like Unemployment Benefit and provided flat-rate income replacement benefits during periods of incapacity for work that arose from ill health. Sickness Benefit had identical rates and the same dependent adult and child additions and contributory qualifications as Unemployment Benefit. Sickness Benefit, however, was not time-limited and a period of long-term incapacity to work was covered by the same provisions as short-term illness until the introduction of Invalidity Benefit in 1971.

Invalidity Benefit, introduced by the Heath government, was paid at higher rates than Sickness Benefit, but entitlement was only for those who had been receiving the contributory Sickness Benefit for six months beforehand. There were two components, the Invalidity Pension, a flat-rate benefit, and the Invalidity Allowance, paid according to three age-related levels – the younger one the age at which one's incapacity began, the higher the Invalidity Allowance. Invalidity Benefit included dependent adult additions and substantially more generous child additions than those offered on Sickness Benefit. The recognition that longer-term or permanent conditions needed greater levels of income assistance than short-term interruptions in work was extended into the social assistance system in 1973 and Supplementary Benefit had a long-term rate that could be claimed by, among others, the long-term sick who had been in receipt of the benefit for two years.

Old Labour further extended the generosity of Invalidity Benefit and in the 1970s brought in other benefits to cover people with ill health and disabilities.

Invalidity Benefit became one of the benefits to be uprated by the higher of earnings or prices as it was a 'long-term benefit'. Additionally, the introduction of the State Earnings Related Pension Scheme (SERPS), discussed more fully in Chapter Nine, meant that recipients of Invalidity Benefit could receive SERPS alongside their Invalidity Benefit prior to reaching state pension age[2]. Take-up of such SERPS additions was slow and nobody was set to benefit quickly from this provision, but SERPS increases to Invalidity Benefit levels would in time become potentially dramatic, as we demonstrate at the end of this chapter.

A new non-means-tested incapacity benefit was introduced in 1975 for those incapacitated for a period of over six months. Non-Contributory Invalidity Pension (NCIP) was aimed at those with congenital or long-standing conditions that meant that they could not be covered by social insurance. The benefit, while not aimed at non-working women, the most significant group at that time likely to be lacking a contribution record, excluded economically inactive housewives by including a rule that to be eligible a woman must be incapable of 'performing normal household duties' as well as be medically certified as incapable of work if they were living with or were married to a man. Such blatantly discriminatory rules were part of Housewives' Non-Contributory Invalidity Pension (HNCIP) as opposed to standard NCIP.

This expansion of entitlement and generosity did not last long under the Conservatives in the 1980s. The 1980 Social Security (No 2) Act abolished earnings-related additions to benefits and thus altered Sickness Benefit. The abolition of earnings-related uprating also affected Invalidity Benefit and meant that this benefit would be uprated with prices alongside Sickness Benefit. Radical reform came with the effective privatisation of Sickness Benefit and the introduction of Statutory Sick Pay (SSP) from 1983. SSP is administered by employers rather than any government agency. On its introduction, SSP covered only the first eight weeks of sickness and costs were for the most part ultimately borne by the National Insurance fund rather than employers themselves. It was paid at three wage-related levels, with the higher and middle rates being significantly more generous than Sickness Benefit. In 1986, SSP coverage was extended to six months and by 1994 funding from the National Insurance fund had been completely withdrawn, leaving employers to meet all the costs. Sickness Benefit itself remained for those who could not qualify for SSP but who had social insurance contributions (a fairly small group) until later reforms and the introduction of Incapacity Benefit in 1995. At this point, SSP changed to a single rate.

European directives on equal treatment meant that the sexist assumptions of HNCIP were no longer tenable and in 1984 the whole ambit of non-contributory benefits for invalidity changed with the introduction of a single benefit, Severe Disablement Allowance (SDA). Although SDA was more gender neutral, it restricted eligibility to those either whose incapacity began before age 20 or who were classed as being '80% disabled'. Effectively, the benefit became more of a disability benefit as opposed to an incapacity benefit; we return to discuss subsequent developments in the next chapter.

Invalidity Benefit continued throughout the 1980s and faced no major changes until 1995. Indeed, under the Conservatives, rates of Invalidity Benefit were increased, as shown in Figure 7.3, and the numbers of claimants increased hugely: 612,000 people were claiming at the end of 1978/79 but this rose by 190% to almost 1.8 million at the end of 1994/95 (DSS, 1997). This increase was in part an increase in 'hidden unemployment' and included significant numbers of people who moved from being classed as unemployed to being classed as long-term sick as they had chronic underlying health conditions. Three drivers of this movement can be identified. First, there were organisational incentives. In the 1980s, unemployment offices were encouraged to keep unemployment figures down and not have people with constraints of ill health signing on as unemployed (Campbell, 1996). Second, long-term unemployment itself can have a detrimental effect on health. Third, there is what might be termed the 'discouraged worker syndrome'. If a long-term unemployed person cannot see any prospect of employment, it may well suit him or her to be redefined as long-term sick. Additionally, GPs were found to be willing to sign people off as incapable of work to an extent that may not have accurately reflected their true ability to work (Ritchie and Snape, 1993).

Reform was inevitable in the face of such huge increases in caseload and an underlying acceptance of the role of incapacity status in hidden unemployment. In 1995, Incapacity Benefit replaced both Invalidity Benefit and Sickness Benefit. The introduction of Incapacity Benefit marked a number of significant changes. First, it introduced a new tougher 'all-work' test for incapacity for work, which, unlike the previous equivalent test, was deliberately designed to be 'objective' and excluded consideration of the claimant's age, education and training. Second, it changed the system's definition of long-term incapacity from six months to one year. Under the old system, a claimant could receive Invalidity Benefit in full after six months of receiving SSP. Under Incapacity Benefit, a claimant in the same position would only receive the 'short-term higher' rate of Incapacity Benefit and would have to wait a further six months to receive Incapacity Benefit at its higher long-term rate. Third, the age-related components of the old Invalidity Benefit were replaced by a different and overall less generous set of age additions to the long-term rate of Incapacity Benefit. While these still paid higher amounts to those whose incapacity began at a younger age, it reduced generosity for those whose incapacity began after 35 and removed all additional benefits to those whose incapacity began after 45.

New Labour's welfare reform programme began with minor changes[3]. Incapacity Benefit rules were tightened to reduce the inflow from long-term unemployment and incentives to retire early were reduced by offsetting benefit against pension income. These reforms aside, New Labour's early strategy to reverse the rise in Incapacity Benefit claims was concentrated on helping claimants back into the labour market. As part of the wider set of employment programmes to address 'worklessness' rather than purely unemployment, there was a New Deal for Disabled People (NDDP) and a Pathways to Work programme aimed at Incapacity Benefit claimants rather than disabled people per se. The scheme provides advice and assistance in finding employment through the use of personal advisers. The scheme is voluntary and in May 2007 had 186,000 participants (DWP, 2008b). The Pathways to Work programme, rolled out nationally during 2008, is aimed specifically at people in receipt of Incapacity Benefit (or Income Support on health grounds). Like the NDDP, it is voluntary and makes use of personal advisers, but also allows for a return-to-work credit to be paid to participants securing employment.

The 2007 Welfare Reform Act, however, took the employment focus further and introduced a change to both means-tested and contributory benefits for those with long-term ill health. From 2008, Employment and Support Allowance (ESA) replaced both Income Support on the grounds of incapacity and Incapacity Benefit, in a similar way to the single Jobseeker's Allowance for the unemployed in 1996 (discussed earlier). Contributory ESA replaces Incapacity Benefit for new claimants with a contribution record. The introduction of ESA will result in a further significant lessening in the contributory principle in the area of incapacity benefits (Williams, 2009); there is no differential in benefit rates between contributory and means-tested support and a contribution record will only assist claimants who additionally have substantial savings or whose partner works.

ESA differs radically from the benefits it replaces by being a two-tier system, with claimants being distinguished between those who cannot engage in any work or work-related activity because of the severity of their condition and those whose capability for work is 'limited'. The former category of claimants will receive the 'support' component on top of their basic allowance. The latter category will receive the 'employment' component on top of their basic allowance and may be required to attend work-focused interviews and undertake work-related activity, with a penalty of reduction in benefit if these requirements are not met without good cause. The clear expectation is that the vast majority of claimants will fall into the 'employment' rather than 'support' category (DWP, 2007c). Alongside ESA, a new 'work capability assessment', intended to be a positive assessment of capability, replaces the previous assessment procedure for incapacity.

Coverage and generosity of sickness and incapacity benefits

How have benefits for sickness and incapacity changed in value since the 1970s? Returning to Figure 7.3 allows us to consider relative values. Contributory Sickness Benefit was paid at exactly the same rate as Unemployment Benefit until 1983 and the same plotted line for 'contributory unemployment benefit' therefore also reflects the rates of Sickness Benefit between 1971 and 1982. From 1983, SSP has always had a slightly higher value than the social assistance safety net and the minimum rate of SSP fluctuated slightly during the 1980s and early 1990s but mostly kept up with prices prior to the consolidation of rates in 1995 when the rise in value marks the point at which SSP became payable at one rate only. It has been consistently price uprated since that point and has thus fallen in relative value.

Long-term incapacity benefits have had higher relative values compared with sickness and unemployment benefits. Figure 7.3 shows the basic adult rate for Invalidity Benefit up until 1995 and the basic adult long-term rate for Incapacity Benefit thereafter. In both cases, the rates shown are those for an adult whose incapacity began at age 50, both for consistent comparison over time and to approximate the median age of new claimants. It is clear that the real value of Invalidity Benefit since its introduction in 1971 increased under both Old Labour and to a lesser extent the Conservatives and its relative value only shows consistent decline from the latter part of the 1980s onwards. The step-change fall in value in 1995 reflects the introduction of Incapacity Benefit on a consistent assumption of claimant profile. Since 1995, Incapacity Benefit has been consistently uprated in line with prices and has thus fallen in relative terms alongside the other contributory benefits shown.

Chapter Three showed that rates of economic inactivity due to ill health had risen over the whole period since the 1970s and it is thus predictable that coverage of incapacity benefits will also have grown. Figure 7.4 depicts coverage of incapacity benefits in terms of the percentage of the working age population receiving benefit. The plotted line labelled 'Invalidity Benefit' straightforwardly shows coverage of Invalidity Benefit. The plotted line labelled 'Incapacity Benefit (long-term and short-term higher rates)' excludes the short-term lower rate of Incapacity Benefit that replaced Sickness Benefit and thus facilitates direct comparison with Invalidity Benefit coverage. The plotted line labelled 'including credits only' includes all such Invalidity and Incapacity Benefit claimants as well as claimants in receipt of Income Support (or earlier Supplementary Benefit) on the grounds of incapacity. (Directly comparable data are unfortunately not available to allow this line to be plotted for points earlier than 1983.) It can be seen that during the 1970s less than 2% of people of working age were on Invalidity Benefit. Dramatic increases in the numbers claiming incapacity benefits in the 1980s and early 1990s led to over 5% of the working age population receiving Invalidity Benefit by 1995 and around a further 2% receiving means-tested incapacity benefits. The replacement of Invalidity Benefit with Incapacity Benefit clearly led to a fall in the numbers receiving contributory incapacity benefits, but this fall has been accompanied by a rise in the numbers receiving means-tested incapacity benefits (Income Support on grounds of incapacity). In May 2007, 3.86% of the working population (1.425 million people) were receiving Incapacity Benefit, but a further 2.69% (993,000 people) were receiving means-tested incapacity benefits. The rate of the working age population receiving either contributory or means-tested incapacity benefits has remained between 6.5% and 7% since 1995.

Figure 7.4: Coverage of incapacity provision, 1971-2007

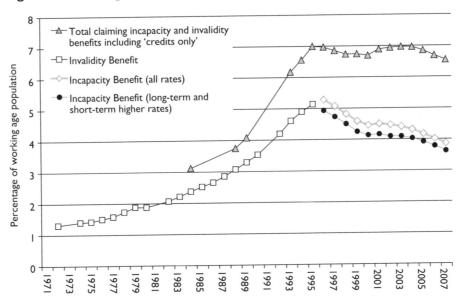

Source: Authors' calculations using DHSS (1987), DSS (2000), DWP(2008b) and ONS (2008b).

Note: Working age population comprises men aged 16-64 and women aged 16-59.

Model families and the risks of unemployment, sickness and incapacity

How would our model families, earning median, high and low wages, be protected against the risks of unemployment, sickness and long-term incapacity, and how has such protection changed? We concentrate exclusively on the Meades and the Lowes and thus on the position of median and low earners respectively in 1979, 1997 and 2008, as the high-earning Moores have little probability of such risk events.

We continue to cumulatively build the profile of working age lives and to incorporate the information we have gained so far from Chapter Four onwards. This approach enables us to make the Meades more realistic in profile and comparison – we suppose that they have a child and are buying their home. The Lowes, meanwhile, have a child identical in age to the Meades', but they live in social rented accommodation. We can thus show all benefit income, taxation and housing costs when considering and comparing their outcome profiles over time.

Box 7.1: Replacement rates

Economists and others concerned with the efficient working of the labour market worry about how far income out of work compares with income in work. When out-of-work benefits are at a level where the gains to being in work are seen as small, there is a potential work incentive problem. As we have seen in this and earlier chapters, policy since the 1980s has been consistently concerned with work incentives and the potential problem of benefit levels. A comparison of income in and out of work provides what is known as an earnings replacement rate: the value of income out of work compared, as a percentage or ratio, with the income in work. These calculations are called 'replacement rates'. This is a term that will be used fairly often in the remainder of the book and it is worth consideration at some length here.

Crude replacement rates can be seen in Figure 7.3 when benefit levels are compared with average earnings. But there are two problems with such an approach:

- First, incomes out of work do not just rely on the specific benefits for unemployment or sickness or incapacity, as families will claim other benefits – for children, to help them pay the rent, or for other reasons.

- Second, average earnings is a poor overall measure of replacement rate because, as we have seen previously, the risk of interruptions of work differ by levels of earnings – the low paid are far more likely to be unemployed or inactive due to incapacity.

These two crucial facts mean that comparing incomes in and out of work is best done using income packages that include a full range of tax and benefit assumptions rather than just the benefit rates of individual types of benefits. Additionally, the comparison is best made with earnings that match the risk. Calculating the income package and net replacement rates thus means first calculating net *household* income when in work and when unemployed. A clearer picture of replacement rates is also gained if *after housing cost income* is calculated, as the benefit system is set up to meet housing costs for those on low incomes and will operate when out of work if there are no other sources of income.

Where replacement rates are near to or above 100%, income out of work is close to that gained from working and the term 'unemployment trap' is employed.

Unemployment – the Meades and the Lowes

How do the 1979, 1997 and 2008 systems treat unemployment and which replacement rates arise for the Meades and the Lowes? Unemployment as a risk to family income will obviously be worse if all earners are unemployed and worse if the timing of unemployment coincides with the period of highest constraints on dual earnings – when children are young and have most effect on their mothers' employment. In the following profiles, we compare the Meades and the Lowes at the point when both families have a pre-school child and Mr Meade and Mr Lowe are the sole earners in the household. We suppose there is an 18-month spell of unemployment and look at the changes to income over that period. It is wise at this point to say that the replacement rates we calculate are on the net income from *previous* earnings; obviously, if re-entering work included a pay cut, the rate based on future earnings would differ and be higher.

For the Meades, as illustrated in Figure 7.5, the 1979 system is characterised by comparatively high replacement rates, of 63% of after housing costs (AHC) income for the first six months and then 60% after six and 12 months. There is a comparatively significant role for contributory Unemployment Benefit, as it makes up the majority of income for the first six months, comprising basic benefits, adult and child dependent rates and earnings-related supplements. But faced with the Meades' mortgage interest, it still requires a top-up from Supplementary Benefit. This figure only falls slightly to 60% once payment of earnings-related supplement ends after six months. Unemployment Benefit ends after 12 months and the Supplementary Benefit system, which includes payment in full of the Meades'

Figure 7.5: Income components and replacement rates for the Meades – unemployment

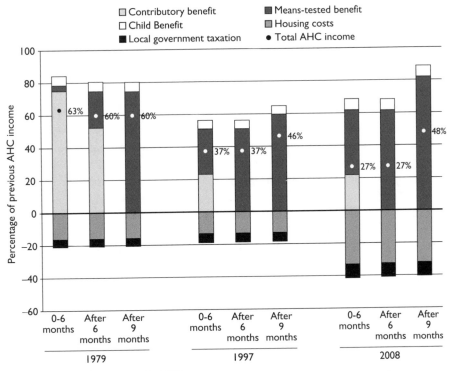

Source: Authors' calculations using LOIS.

housing costs, tops up income to a constant level as underlying contributory entitlement changes over time.

By 1997, the replacement rates for the Meades are much lower. This is partly due to 18 years of earnings inflation and the relative decline of unemployment benefits (now JSA) that have only been uprated by prices in the meantime, leading to an overall fall in earnings replacement value against median earnings. However, the abolition of earnings-related supplements and dependent additions also brings the crude replacement value of contributory unemployment benefit to a much lower level than seen in 1979. Means-tested JSA tops up income, together with other means-tested assistance, and altogether the replacement value is 37% for the first six months of unemployment. When contributory JSA ends, this replacement rate does not change, as means-tested JSA makes up the difference. After nine months, the Meades, if they have managed to avoid repossession, will receive benefit payments towards mortgage interest that raise the amount of benefits overall and increase replacement rates to around 46%. Thus, under the 1997 system, outcomes improve for the Meades after nine months, whereas under the 1979 system they decline slightly after six months. Also under the 1997 system, contributory benefit clearly plays a much less significant role than under the 1979 system.

In 2008, the same benefit structures that were seen in 1997 still operate, but since then the value of benefits has fallen further behind median earnings and thus replacement rates have fallen further. Exactly the same unfolding timetable of benefit entitlement changes affect the Meades as in 1997, but starting from a replacement rate of 27%. After nine months and the beginning of payment of mortgage interest (on a lower proportion of a higher loan due to increases in house prices since 1997), replacement rates rise to 48%.

How do the Lowes fare if they are unemployed in analogous circumstances? Figure 7.6 shows the same set of calculations for them. Help with the Lowes' rent is 100% under all three systems. Unlike the Meades, they are not faced with a period when they have to pay housing costs with no direct help towards these costs. This means that the outcomes for the Lowes are much more straightforward and it is only under the 1979 system that the Lowes' AHC income will vary at all throughout Mr Lowe's unemployment. Under the 1979 system, Mr Lowe receives an earnings-related supplement with his Unemployment Benefit for the first six months of his claim, which leads to a replacement rate of 93% for the first six months followed by 82% thereafter. By 1997, the underlying value of both contributory and means-tested benefits for the unemployed have fallen relative to earnings and the Lowes face a much lower replacement rate of 48%. This rate remains constant during unemployment as means-tested JSA tops up income to the same level on the expiry of entitlement to contributory benefit.

In 2008, the underlying income package for the Lowes is higher *despite* continued falling value of unemployment-related benefits against earnings. This is because of greater generosity in respect of their dependent child from a combination of Child Tax Credit and the disregard of Child Benefit by means-tested JSA. This

Figure 7.6: Income components and replacement rates for the Lowes – unemployment

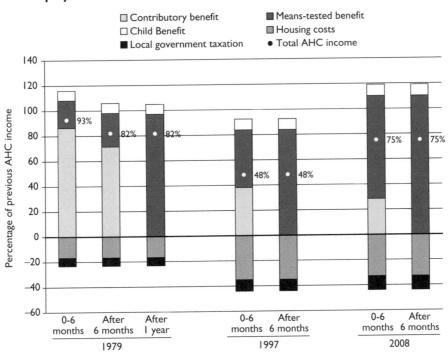

Source: Authors' calculations using LOIS.

results in a higher replacement rate of 75% throughout unemployment. One point to note from the underlying assumptions about housing costs, discussed earlier in Chapter Six, is that rent levels remain relatively constant between 1997 and 2008 for the Lowes, in contrast to the Meades' higher cost of mortgage.

Incapacity – the Meades and the Lowes

We now turn to sickness and incapacity and Mr Meade and Mr Lowe in exactly the same circumstances, with the same housings costs, earnings and family profiles, facing an interruption from work that begins with sickness and develops into long-term incapacity.

Figure 7.7 shows the position of the Meades. There are two new elements of benefit that we have to consider and that will also apply to the Lowes later. First, in 1979, there is the 'SERPS addition', an entitlement under the State Earnings Related Pension Scheme that would have been paid along with Invalidity Benefit under the 1979 system. This is shown separately for the reason that any entitlement rests on a supposition that the person in question has built such entitlement by working up until the point of his incapacity under 1979 rules. A real claimant in real-time 1979 could not receive such an entitlement to SERPS. For this reason,

Figure 7.7: Income components and replacement rates for the Meades – incapacity

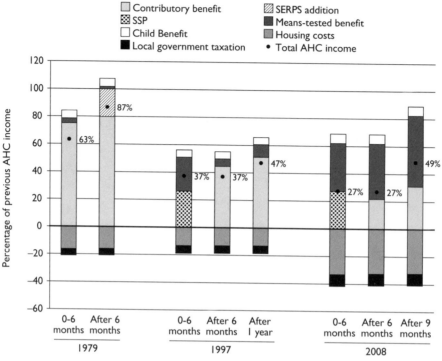

Source: Authors' calculations using LOIS.

we demonstrate the difference made by the SERPS addition and in the text give replacement rates with and without its inclusion. Second, for both 1997 and 2008, we identify SSP, which means that Mr Meade is actually still being 'paid' by his employer for the first six months of sickness and incapacity.

Figure 7.7 illustrates the plight of the Meades. We see that, under the 1979 system, for the first six months the Meades receive exactly the same level of benefits as for unemployment because Sickness Benefit under the 1979 system was at the same rate as Unemployment Benefit. After six months of incapacity, Mr Meade moves to Invalidity Benefit and for the remainder of incapacity this means the Meades face a replacement rate of 87% if the SERPS addition is included or 67% if it is not.

By 1997, the relative value of benefits to median earnings has fallen, with corresponding lower replacement rates. Mr Meade receives SSP for the first six months followed by Incapacity Benefit for the next year. Both benefits are topped up with means-tested assistance in the shape of Income Support and/or Council Tax Benefit with replacement rates of 37%. Only after a year does Mr Meade receive Incapacity Benefit at the long-term rate, and this additionally leads to a disability premium in Income Support and means the household's replacement rate rises to 47%.

In the 2008 system, the Meades can claim means-tested assistance to top up household income while in receipt of SSP for the first six months. However, despite the increased generosity of the 2008 system for the child, once again, as with unemployment, the high housing costs erode any such generosity and the Meades face a replacement rate of 27% during this time. Once SSP ends, the Meades' fortunes will not improve immediately. Mr Meade will now receive Employment Support Allowance (ESA), which will include a contributory element, but his total ESA will initially remain at the basic Income Support level. After nine months, benefit income will increase for two reasons. First, after a total of nine months in receipt of social assistance, support towards housing costs will be provided. Second, after he has undergone the assessment phase for ESA[4], it is supposed that Mr Meade will become entitled to ESA's 'work-related activity component'. These factors combine to grant the Meades replacement rates of 49%.

A similar profile for the Lowes is shown in Figure 7.8. In 1979, the first six months on sickness benefits duplicate the outcomes when unemployed and shown in Figure 7.6, with a high replacement rate of 93%. However, after six months and when entitlement to Invalidity Benefit begins, the rate rises further, to 115% if the SERPS addition is included and 105% otherwise. These replacement rates of over 100% do reflect a theoretical position where income out of work is higher than that from previous earnings, but the assumption of policy makers of the time was that there was little potential to return to work at all – benefit was, in effect, an early pension. Replacement rates under the 1997 system, despite higher nominal rates of SSP, remain the same as those for unemployment, 48%, but rise to 56% after 12 months of incapacity once the higher long-term rate of Incapacity Benefit is paid. Under the 2008 system, replacement rates are higher than 1997 for the first nine months, at 76%, again due to the higher amounts of transfers paid for children rather than real changes in underlying support for incapacity. After nine months and the start of the 'work-related activity component', rates rise to 88%.

These profiles show clearly the decline in contributory coverage and the rise of means testing for both the Meades and the Lowes, but one of the outcomes of this change has been to differentiate the risk of adequate income provision between the Lowes as tenants and the Meades as owner-occupiers. The other clear conclusion is about the role of child-related transfers, which in 2008 have made up for some of the decline in underlying support for sickness, incapacity and unemployment and have raised comparative replacement rates. In addition, the overall chronology of the response to sickness and incapacity has changed – higher levels of support for incapacity now begin later and have become more conditional.

Figure 7.8: Income components and replacement rates for the Lowes – incapacity

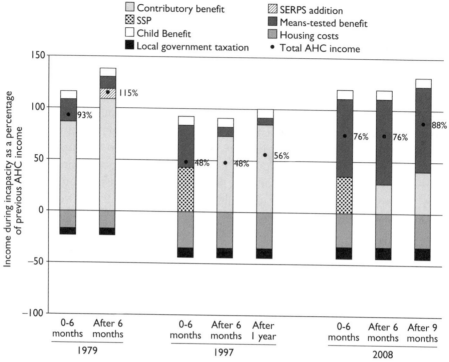

Source: Authors' calculations using LOIS.

Summary

In this chapter, we have considered the risks to adult working lives and livelihoods caused by unemployment and incapacity to work due to ill health.

Our main findings are as follows:

- Unemployment benefits have become more means-tested and economic changes have led to peaks in claimant numbers over the past 30 years.
- An increased focus on job searching was attached to unemployment benefits during the 1980s and 1990s and since 1997 this has been extended to other forms of out-of-work benefits.
- Sickness benefits changed to employer-paid SSP in 1983.
- Invalidity Benefit, with more generous provision than Sickness Benefit for long-term conditions, was introduced in 1971 but claimant numbers rose and in 1995 eligibility criteria to long-term incapacity benefits were tightened. In 2008, the new ESA replaced all short-term and long-term benefits for ill health and is geared towards re-employment.

- Prior to the 2008 downturn, falling unemployment and a rise in employment levels generally had reduced the number of unemployment benefits claims to their lowest levels since the 1970s and incapacity benefits claims to the levels found in the late 1980s.
- Replacement rates for unemployment have fallen since the 1970s, encouraging re-entry into low-paid employment.
- Replacement rates for incapacity benefits in 1997 and 2008 are also much lower than the 1970s.

Notes

[1] For example, Margaret Thatcher said in 1980: 'People ... say, "Look, why should we work when some of us are as well-off not working as we are working?" And you have to tackle that' (TV interview, 'Weekend World', 6 January 1980).

[2] Moreover, Invalidity Benefit claimants who had contracted out of SERPS would still receive SERPS payments as if they had been contracted in.

[3] Plans to simplify the SSP system, including the removal of the three waiting days currently required, reached the Green Paper stage in 2006, but a 2007 review concluded against significant reform (DWP, 2006a; DWP, 2007d).

[4] The assessment phase is expected to last '13 weeks in most circumstances' (DWP, 2007c).

EIGHT

Working age risks: disability, caring and lone parenthood

Social insurance systems find it difficult to respond to risks that are not directly related to interruptions to work that can be covered by a history of contributions. Disability is covered by social insurance if it arises from serving in the armed forces, or from an industrial accident or occupationally related disease, but health and safety procedures enforced by regulation in all workplaces means that cases falling in the latter two categories are a very small proportion of overall incidences of disability. Other types of transfer have been developed to cover cases that relate to congenital conditions, genetic predisposition or from other illness in early life, and there are others still that respond to the needs of carers who find themselves in a situation of informal, unpaid employment. Family-related risks of divorce were considered briefly by Beveridge but not included in his 1942 report (HMSO, 1942) or subsequent legislation. Again, the problem of how to link the risk to a work and contribution record has not been solved and provision has mostly been left outside of social insurance.

Once again, it is difficult to shoehorn the notion of disability and caring solely into the working age portion of the lifetime, as children and older people also have disabilities or are carers, but we do so for the purposes of this chapter, returning to issues that continue to be pertinent for older people in Chapter Nine. These three areas of risk – disability, caring and lone parenthood – form the main focus of this chapter and we cover them in turn. How does the tax and benefit system respond to such risks and how have such responses changed over the past 30 to 40 years?

Disability

Disability is not the same as incapacity, despite both media and government commentators being apt to employ the terms as though they were synonymous[1]. Indeed, the benefit system can be much better understood once the terms are clearly distinguished. Incapacity refers to being incapable of work on health grounds. Disability refers to an impairment that may or may not prevent a person from working. This means both that a person can be incapacitated and not consider him or herself disabled, and that a person can be disabled but not incapacitated. Indeed, the employment rate among disabled people, albeit much lower than that among non-disabled people, is currently said to be around 50%

(Parckar, 2008), meaning that *at least* half the disabled working age population are not incapacitated in fact and that more wish to work.

Until the 1970s, the only specific provisions for people with disabilities were those relating to war disablement, industrial accidents and occupational disease. Pensions from these schemes calculated compensation on the basis of 'loss of faculty', for instance, loss of a limb or sensory organ, and saw disability primarily as physical functional impairment. Benefits were based on earnings replacement but were based on fixed tables of percentage loss that could build to total impairment of 100% or pay pensions pro rata for lower assessments. Under such an approach, there was no provision for many forms of disability, such as learning or other cognitive disabilities, and the system was not sufficiently developed to recognise mental ill health. No provision arose from disability caused by anything other than working. The only recourse for support for people with non-work-related disability was social assistance and it is worth repeating Beveridge's stated assumption about the remit of social assistance here: it was for '*cripples and deformed, deaf and dumb, mentally deficient*' (our emphasis) as well as 'vagrants and moral weaklings' (see Chapter Six) (Evans and Glennerster, 1994). Prior to the 1970s, disability support was primarily left to National Assistance or Supplementary Benefit schemes and to local authority social service departments, which often used residential care rather than supporting people with disabilities in their homes.

Since the 1970s, four changes have occurred in social policy's response to disability. The first was the gradual adoption of a 'care in the community' approach that moved away from residential care and towards supporting disabled people and their carers in their homes or in day centres or other community centres. In the benefit system, three strands in the provision of income transfers were developed:

- benefits that sought to compensate disabled people for the 'extra costs' that arose from their disability;
- benefits that replaced earnings as a source of income for those who were not in work; and
- in-work benefits that supplemented earnings that were constrained by disability.

We leave the changes in social service provision and community care to one side and discuss its contextual importance as it arises, but first we address each of these three strands in benefit provision.

Extra-cost benefits

In the 1970s, a growing concern about poverty among disabled people and powerful pressure group activity helped to expand social security coverage. 1971 saw a new benefit that recognised additional costs generated by disability

–Attendance Allowance. This benefit was determined solely on a test of the *need* for care and attention that a non-disabled person would not experience. This was a categorical approach and there was no means test and no need for a contributory record. Eligibility for Attendance Allowance depended on demonstrating a need for frequent or constant attention from another person either during the day or night. Shortly after its introduction, the benefit was paid at two rates, with the higher rate applying to those judged to require constant attendance.

This new form of benefit was then followed five years later by the introduction of Mobility Allowance under Labour in 1976. Again, this benefit was a categorical one, based on a population that had limited physical mobility, and was neither means tested nor contributory. Mobility Allowance was introduced to replace the invalid tricycle scheme, whereby the government had leased purpose-built, small, blue single-seat 'Invacars' to those disabled people who could drive themselves. Mobility Allowance was instead a weekly payment made to those who were unable to walk or virtually unable to walk as the result of a physical handicap.

Both Attendance Allowance and Mobility Allowance, however, were not based purely on needs, but also sought to act as compensatory provision to cover those needs that would arise during a normal lifetime, so that infants and young children (aged under two unless specific additional reasons applied) were excluded from Attendance Allowance and those aged under five and over pension age were excluded from Mobility Allowance (those that claimed prior to retirement age could continue to receive benefits). This approach stopped the early needs of attendance and inability to walk and the deterioration of mobility in old age from qualifying in their own right.

Both benefits were ignored in the calculation of other benefits, so that an award of Attendance Allowance or Mobility Allowance would always mean an increase in income for the recipient. Indeed, qualification for these benefits became a signpost to entitlement to additional assistance from means-tested social assistance, for both weekly and one-off needs. After the Fowler reforms in the 1980s and the introduction of clear categorical groups of social assistance, both Mobility and Attendance Allowances signalled additional premiums.

These original benefits were designed to assist quite severely disabled people, leaving a range of people with lower levels of disability that received inconsistent and patchy help. In 1992, both Mobility and Attendance Allowances were reformed in part to meet such an expanded profile of need. Attendance Allowance continued in name but was purely for those aged 65 and over. For the working age and younger populations, a new Disability Living Allowance replaced both benefits. There was a clear improvement in administration as a result of considering both care and mobility needs in a single claim, but the change also represented a significant increase in the scope of disability benefits for extra costs. Disability Living Allowance (DLA) consists of a care component (DLA care) and a mobility component (DLA mobility), the former replacing Attendance Allowance for the under 65s, the latter replacing Mobility Allowance. DLA care is payable at three as opposed to two rates, with the new lower rate effectively extending entitlement to a group of people whose care needs would not have been severe enough to qualify them for Attendance Allowance. Similarly, DLA mobility is payable at two rates, with the new lower rate effectively extending entitlement to a group of people whose impaired mobility would not have been severe enough to qualify them for Mobility Allowance. As with Mobility Allowance, DLA mobility is not available to those whose impaired mobility began after age 65. This reformed structure of extra needs benefits continues in 2009.

The receipt of DLA has increasingly been seen by local authority social service departments as a signifier that user charges for domiciliary services (home helps, meals on wheels, care assistants and so on) can be made and, even though DLA is ignored when calculating social assistance, it can be taken into account when levying charges (DH, 2003).

There are other non-social security schemes that provide benefits for disabled people and we can only mention these briefly here. The Motability scheme has been providing vehicles for disabled people since 1978. The current arrangements allow for anyone receiving the higher level of DLA mobility to buy or contract-hire a car, powered wheelchair or scooter on subsidised terms. Accompanying the shift to provide more care in the community as opposed to institutional care, the Independent Living Funds scheme, established in 1988, provides financial support to disabled people to enable them to live in the community rather than in residential care. It is funded by central government, but administered through local authority social workers.

Disabled people may be entitled to tax relief on local government taxation. However, such tax relief has never been granted purely on the grounds of disability. Rather, it operates on the principle that extra space or rooms required because of a disability ought not to be taxed. Under the general rates system, from April 1979 rate relief was granted on 'required facilities' within a disabled person's residence. Under the council tax system, a band reduction scheme operates, whereby if a substantially disabled person is living in a property and if the property has additional space or rooms required by that disabled person, the council tax charged will be that in respect of the valuation band below the actual valuation band for the property.

Changing value of extra-costs benefits

How has the value of extra-costs benefits changed over time? Figure 8.1 shows the value in real terms of the disability benefits for extra costs from 1971 to 2008 for working age people. Figure 8.1a covers the different elements and rates for care allowances, while Figure 8.1b covers those for mobility allowances.

Figure 8.1a shows that the real value of Attendance Allowance rose fairly continuously from the point of introduction and it has only been from the introduction of DLA since 1992 that rates have remained flat in real terms. Up

Figure 8.1a: Disability benefits for extra costs, 1971-2008 – care allowances

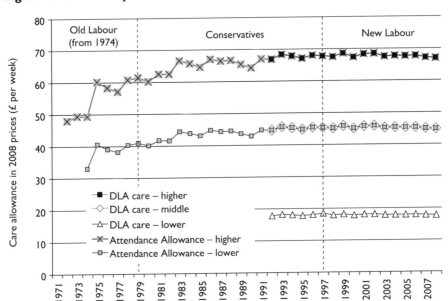

Figure 8.1b: Disability benefits for extra costs, 1971-2008 – mobility allowances

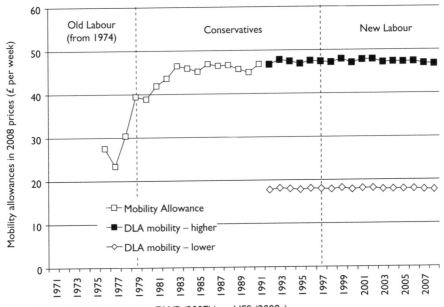

Source: Authors' calculations using DWP (2007b) and IFS (2008a).

Note: All plotted points are rates as at April of each year.

to 1979, Attendance Allowance at both high and low rates rose by almost 5% per annum in real terms on average. Under the Conservatives through the 1980s to reform in 1992, the rates rose more slowly, by 0.8% to 0.9% per annum in real terms on average. It is clear that while the Conservatives did uprate just ahead of prices, they did not uprate to either match the earlier period or keep up with earnings. If one thinks of what attendance needs consist of, they depend on paying someone to care, and thus an underlying assumption to maintain their purchasing power would logically be to follow earnings to allow a consistent payment for services. However, since 1992, both the Major government and New Labour have uprated DLA purely by prices.

Figure 8.1b shows the real value of mobility benefits over time from their introduction in 1976 to 2008. Early increases in the first three years raised the original rate of Mobility Allowance by over 40% and in the early years the value of benefit continued to grow in real terms under the Conservatives. Overall, however, from 1983 until 1992 the real trend value remained flat. Since 1992 and the introduction of the DLA mobility elements, real prices have remained consistently flat.

However, when assessing the impact of extra-costs benefits on the real and relative living standards for disabled people, it is not just the purchasing power or level of income they provide that is important. Extra-costs benefits recognise extra underlying needs that disabled people have in particular. In comparing disabled and non-disabled people and in ranking their income consistently, such additional needs should be taken into account to ensure that they are equivalent. However, as we will discuss further in Chapter Ten, no such adjustments to ensure equivalent comparison are made in official British poverty figures or analysis of the overall income distribution. Indeed, the extra-costs benefits are counted as pure income despite the fact that they are designed to be spent on particular needs and thus to leave living standards neutral. The apparent high rates of benefits and their generosity when compared with underlying social assistance or other flat-rate benefits must therefore be carefully contextualised and the position of disabled people in official poverty measures treated with great caution.

Out-of-work benefits for disabled people

Clearly, the out-of-work benefits that replace income during periods of incapacity for work discussed in the previous chapter – that is, Invalidity Benefit, Incapacity Benefit, and, most recently, Employment and Support Allowance – are all potentially paid to disabled people who have a contributory record. However, as emphasised earlier, these benefits are not designed to address disability specifically and the development of alternative non-contributory and social assistance benefits has been an important area for income maintenance for people with disabilities. We now look at these in turn.

In Chapter Seven, we outlined how severe disablement allowance replaced non-contributory invalidity pension in 1984 and we pick up that story here for disabled people. Figure 7.3[2] in Chapter Seven showed how low rates were for Non-Contributory Invalidity Pension (NCIP) and Severe Disablement Allowance (SDA). These benefits have always had a lower value than social assistance safety net benefit rates and thus a majority of SDA claimants have always received Supplementary Benefit or Income Support in addition. The introduction of SDA in 1984 saw a shift towards a specific benefit for disability because, alongside being available for those who developed an incapacity to work during childhood (before the age of 20), it provided for others who could qualify as being '80% disabled'. This test was a cumulative assessment of loss of faculty and function drawing on the assessment of industrial injuries, although more attuned to cognitive and learning disabilities. However, the fact that 70% of recipients' benefits were topped up by Income Support meant that in 2001 New Labour announced that SDA would be abolished for new claimants. Incapacity Benefit rules were changed to allow young people access without a contributory record, but the quiet abolition of SDA affected a significant group of people – primarily women living with partners with 'no relevant National Insurance record, no chance of getting Income Support because of a working partner and now no state benefit to meet basic living expenses' (Vaux, 2001, p 3). However, with an overall emphasis on means-tested targeting, the removal of SDA and its effective replacement with Income Support for the poorest fitted overall aims for social security. SDA was abolished for new claimants from 2001. Although over a quarter of a million people were still receiving the benefit in May 2007, this cohort of claimants will eventually age out, and SDA coverage has predictably declined since 2001, as shown later in Figure 8.2.

One reason why social assistance was seen as an appropriate alternative to SDA was the fact that over time it had developed specific provisions and higher rates for disabled people. Under the old Supplementary Benefit system, prior to 1982 these additional weekly additions operated on a discretionary basis, as discussed in Chapter Six. The Supplementary Benefits Commission, in charge of policy over that period, defined certain illnesses and disabilities as acceptable grounds for receiving certain additional payments, for example those in respect of special dietary or laundry needs, but these directions were not binding. Statistics from 1979 indicate that only around 40% of sick and disabled claimants were receiving exceptional circumstances additions (ECAs), but that this group received higher amounts than other claimant groups (DHSS, 1980). In the codification of Supplementary Benefit in 1982, these ECAs were replaced by a system of 'additional requirements' set down in regulations. Additional requirements for disabled people included a range of extra benefits, including heating and other specific costs, help in the home and attendance needs. Income Support in 1988 replaced individual assessment of such needs with a system of categorical premiums. These included a 'disabled child premium' payable in respect of each disabled child in the family, a 'disability premium' payable in respect of disabled *or* long-term incapacitated adults, and a 'severe disability premium' payable in respect of severely disabled adults with severe disability being defined with reference to receipt of extra cost disability benefits. These premiums continue to apply in the 2008 system[3]. The disability and severe disability premiums have been joined by a third adult disability premium, the 'enhanced disability premium', payable in respect of adults receiving the highest rate of DLA care. Disabled child provision, which for new claimants is now handled through the tax credit system in Child Tax Credit, includes an additional payment in the case of a severely disabled child. Disability premiums also apply in the calculation of Housing Benefit and Council Tax Benefit.

In-work benefits for disabled people

Promoting the employment of disabled people did not form part of the mid-1970s' legislation on equality; the equal pay and sex discrimination and race relation provisions of that period had no disability equivalent. The post-war legacy for disabled people and employment was based very much on an approach taken to place war-disabled in employment in the 1944 Disabled Persons (Employment) Act. This approach persisted and those with congenital disabilities and cognitive and learning disabilities were largely left outside of employment rehabilitation, and such rehabilitation as there was tended to be geared towards low-paid, unskilled assembly, clerical and other jobs (Lonsdale, 1986). Training and sheltered forms of employment existed for disabled people with adult training centres run by the voluntary sector, which were often where young people with learning difficulties were referred to on leaving school. Remploy and other specific, designated employment programmes had a long record of low pay and very poor job progression opportunities. Subsidised places in mainstream employment were introduced in the Sheltered Placement Scheme but pay and advancement profiles did not significantly improve (Barnes, 1992). By the 1990s, greater emphasis came to be placed on self-provision and equality of opportunity. In employment law, the 1995 Disability Discrimination Act made it unlawful to discriminate against disabled people in connection with employment.

The additional financial help given to people with disabilities when they were out of work, together with the constraints on their earning ability in work, meant that the incentives to work for disabled people were weak, even where discrimination was absent. In 1992, Disability Working Allowance (DWA) was introduced as a tax-free benefit available to low-paid workers with a disability that put them at a 'disadvantage' in getting a job. The benefit was closely modelled on Family Credit and the history of in-work disability transfers has followed a similar pattern to that of in-work transfers for low-paid families. With New Labour's reform of in-work credits in 1999, DWA was transformed into the more generous Disabled Person's Tax Credit scheme alongside Working Families Tax

Credit. Since 2003, in-work transfers for disabled people have been made through additionally more generous provisions of Working Tax Credit (WTC). Among other objectives, WTC is designed to significantly increase the earnings capacity of those with impairment. Its test of qualifying disability is wide to the extent that it covers periods of rehabilitation. WTC includes a disability element and a severe disability element. The former is available to low-paid workers working at least 16 hours per week who are disabled or have a disabled partner. The latter is additionally available if the disabled claimant or partner is receiving the highest rate of DLA care or Attendance Allowance. In addition, the Child Tax Credit system provides assistance in respect of disabled children to low- to moderate-income families as well as those out of work.

Caring

The benefit system began to explicitly recognise the role of unpaid carers alongside the introduction of specific disability benefits in the 1970s. Invalid Care Allowance (ICA) was introduced in 1976 as a categorical non-means-tested benefit for people of working age who stayed at home to care for a disabled relative on a full-time basis. However, like NCIP, ICA did not escape the overt sexism of the times. Married or cohabiting women were not eligible to receive ICA, presumably on the grounds that they were expected to fulfil an unpaid caring role anyway. This rule was eventually removed in the 1980s as the result of a European Court ruling. Subsequent reforms have included the renaming of the benefit to Carer's Allowance in 2003 and the extension of eligibility to include persons over working age.

Figure 7.3 in Chapter Seven demonstrates that carer's benefit (ICA or Carer's Allowance) has, like NCIP and SDA, always been something of a 'second-class' benefit in that its rate has always been below that of the prevailing safety net benefit. Predictably, this means that receipt of Carer's Allowance is often accompanied by the receipt of means-tested benefit. However, a significant number of claimants (275,000 in May 2007) receive the benefit in isolation, either not claiming means-tested assistance or being precluded from receiving it by household savings, partner's income or possibly their own pension income. However, for a majority of carers receiving benefit (means-tested and/or Carer's Allowance), receipt of Carer's Allowance itself makes no difference at all to the amount of income they receive. Rather, it is the 'carer's premium' to Income Support (or the equivalent 'carer's addition' in Pension Credit) that actually makes a difference. The carer's premium was introduced from October 1990. Assuming full entitlement to Income Support in 2008/09, it provides carers with an additional £27.75 per week. Figure 8.2 depicts coverage of carer's benefits in terms of people receiving ICA/Carer's Allowance *and/or* carer's premium. It can be seen that coverage has steadily increased – from less than 0.01% of the population aged over 16 in 1977 (a mere 5,370 claimants) to 1.74% of the population aged over 16 in 2007 (over 834,000 claimants).

Coverage of disability and caring benefits

Figure 8.2 illustrates the coverage of extra-costs benefits along with that of carer's benefit and NCIP/SDA. The line labelled 'benefits for care needs' refers to numbers receiving DLA care or Attendance Allowance as a percentage of the population. The line labelled 'benefits for mobility' refers to numbers receiving Mobility Allowance (MA) (from 1976-91) and DLA mobility from 1992 onwards. The figure shows that take-up of the benefits was comparatively low at the time of their introduction, despite their comparative generosity. Coverage grew dramatically during the 1980s and even more so following the introduction of Disability Living Allowance in 1992. There are many reasons for this, the first being that because extra-costs benefits are typically received on a long-term basis, in many cases for life, outflow from these will be limited, thus leading to an inherent trend of increasing coverage. Second, there are factors that specifically help to account for the dramatic rises in coverage after 1992. These include the fact that the new lower rates introduced along with Disability Living Allowance extended

Figure 8.2: Coverage of disability and caring provision, 1971-2007

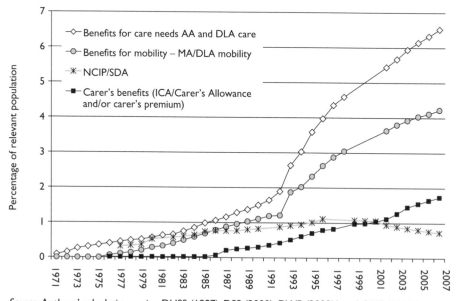

Source: Authors' calculations using DHSS (1987), DSS (2000), DWP (2008b) and ONS (2008c).

Notes: Coverage rates given refer to rates out of different populations depending on the eligibility conditions/target population of the benefit concerned. Coverage of carer's benefit is a percentage of the population aged 16 or over. Coverage of disability care benefit and disability mobility benefit are measures as a percentage of the whole population. Coverage of NCIP/SDA is a percentage of the working age population. NCIP figures include HNCIP from 1980.

eligibility to groups of people who would not have been eligible for extra-costs benefits under the old schemes; the proactive publicity that accompanied the introduction of Disability Living Allowance; and the fact that in the early 1990s self-assessment was the dominant method of determining awards (Walker and Howard, 2000). Third, there have been more general attitudinal changes both in society's conception of disability and individual willingness on the part of disabled people to claim benefits. Fourth, there are demographic changes; for example, as we saw in Chapter Two, there are more people living into their eighties and nineties now than in the 1970s, which has undoubtedly increased levels of disability among the retired population. In addition, disability rates will have been influenced by labour market changes, in particular high and long-term unemployment, affecting the working age population.

Lone parenthood

The only lone parents formally recognised by the 1948 enactment of Beveridge's social security system were widows. Widow's Benefit was paid to bereaved wives on the basis of their late husbands' contribution records. Other forms of lone parenthood hardly fitted into the contributory model and were not seen as a big enough social problem to warrant any special treatment. Divorced, separated and single mothers without any other means of support could turn to social assistance.

By the end of the 1960s, lone parents were no longer a small number of exceptional cases among those receiving social assistance. As our discussion in Chapter Three has shown, divorce and/or separation had risen very significantly across the population and this easily overtook loss of a spouse as the most common reason for lone parenthood. Non-widowed lone mothers formed a significant group of social assistance claimants. The emergence of lone parenthood, in part due to rising rates of divorce, coincided with the 'rediscovery' of poverty in the mid-1960s and in particular child poverty. In 1969, the Labour government commissioned the Finer Committee to report on the problems faced by one-parent families.

The committee reported in 1974 with a wide ranging study that was critical of the way in which family law was currently administered by three separate overlapping and poorly coordinated systems (the magistrates' courts, the higher courts and the benefit system) (House of Commons, 1974). It proposed that the benefit system itself rather than the courts should assume the primary responsibility for determining and collecting maintenance liabilities from liable relatives (primarily absent fathers), thus for the most part meaning that no- or low-income lone parents would have no need to use the court system. Moreover, the report proposed that a new non-contributory benefit payable at a higher rate than Supplementary Benefit and termed the Guaranteed Maintenance Allowance be introduced for lone parents, payable whether or not the benefits agency was successful in obtaining maintenance income.

The publication of the Finer Report coincided with a time of economic crisis and the newly incumbent minority Labour government[4], and its main proposals were never implemented. Instead, a number of lesser measures to help lone parents were introduced in piecemeal fashion. For example, higher-income disregards in the benefit system were introduced for lone parents during the 1970s, lone fathers were recognised as having the same status as lone mothers, and, on its introduction in 1977, Child Benefit was made payable at a higher rate for lone parents. This Child Benefit increase was later named 'One Parent Benefit', but it clearly fell far short of the Finer Committee's notion of a new benefit for lone parents. For one thing, One Parent Benefit would not increase the net income of lone parents in receipt of social assistance because it, like Child Benefit itself, counted in full as income for the purposes of benefit assessment.

Taking a snapshot of provision for lone parents under the 1979 tax and benefit system, we can identify both explicitly targeted provisions for lone parents and other provisions that benefited them disproportionately and such provisions operated both in and out of full-time work. Lone parents not in full-time employment with at least one dependent child under 16 could claim Supplementary Benefit without having to register for work. After two years, Supplementary Benefit would be paid at the higher long-term rate. In part-time work, lone parents had a higher disregard on their earnings. Lone parents in work could, in addition to the Child Benefit increase, benefit from a higher income tax allowance and, if low paid, receive Family Income Supplement. In December 1979, more Family Income Supplement awards were going to single-parent families than to two-parent families and also at a higher average amount (DHSS, 1980). Court decisions on maintenance for lone parents continued to be arbitrary and unpredictable by all accounts, even after the Finer Report, and lone mothers claiming Supplementary Benefit were pointedly given the choice between taking court proceedings themselves against fathers not paying maintenance or letting the Supplementary Benefits Commission do so (SBC, 1976). If maintenance payments were eventually made by the absent father, the mother's Supplementary Benefit would be decreased pound for pound and not raise her income while she remained on benefits.

Between 1971 and 1998, the number of lone-parent families tripled and the number claiming social assistance quadrupled. Figure 8.3 shows the rise to over 1.7 million lone parents by 1999 and the subsequent stabilisation of numbers at around this level. From 1971, the growth of those claiming social assistance would reach a peak of just over a million in 1996, a rise that Beveridge and his contemporaries could not have imagined. In 1971, less than 40% of lone-parent families were claiming social assistance and in 1993 that figure peaked at 69%.

Despite these trends, the Conservatives in government under Margaret Thatcher did not specifically target parsimony in benefit reform towards lone parents. Unemployment was clearly viewed as more significant at the time. The policy

Figure 8.3: Numbers of lone parent families in total and numbers receiving social assistance, 1971-2007

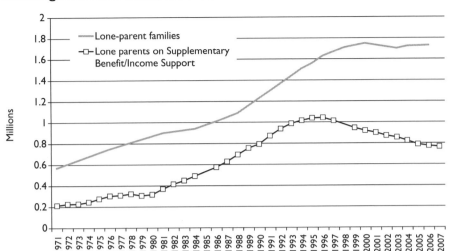

Source: One-parent families: Haskey (2002) and authors' calculations. One-parent families in receipt of Supplementary Benefit/Income Support: DHSS (1987), DSS (2000) and DWP (2008b).

approach of providing extra-costs assistance to one-parent families through tax and benefits continued into the 1990s. The Fowler reforms consolidated provision for lone parents, with the possibility of extra weekly payments and a specific lone-parent premium replacing both the long-term rate previously paid to lone parents. Lone parents under the age of 25 were also granted the same basic level of benefit as other claimants over 25. But the fundamental Conservative support for the traditional family meant that things changed; the 1979 Conservative manifesto had expressed concern for the 'hardship' faced by lone parents, but at the 1992 Conservative Party conference, the then Secretary of State for Social Security, Peter Lilley, was happy to characterise single mothers as feckless manipulators of state provision in his infamous 'little list' speech based on Gilbert and Sullivan.

The 1991 Child Support Act was morally driven by a view that 'implicitly discouraged illegitimacy, separation, divorce and the creation of subsequent children' (Timmins, 2001, p 451). In some ways, the Child Support Act was also a belated following of the recommendations of the Finer Report to introduce a child maintenance regime outside the court system. In the case of lone parents claiming benefits (social assistance or in-work benefits), the Child Support Agency, created by the Act, would be automatically involved in initiating and recovering maintenance. Income obtained originally resulted in no increase of income for lone parents receiving social assistance up until 2002 when a limited disregard of child support payments was introduced in Income Support rules. Lone parents claiming Family Credit or subsequent in-work benefits could keep all maintenance in a 100% disregard and this produced significant additional incentives to work in such cases. However, the Child Support Agency had a troubled history from its introduction in 1993 and has almost universally been deemed a failure. The formula used to calculate maintenance from absent fathers was changed to try to improve performance, but no reform, relaunch or change of management appeared to help. Current government intention is to replace it with a smaller and more focused body that will not have automatic involvement in the case of benefit claimants (DWP, 2006b).

Returning to the issue of the core treatment of lone parents by the benefit system, the approach to reviewing and removing more generous treatment for lone parents began under Major, but was eventually implemented by long-term, high-profile feminist Harriet Harman when she was Secretary of State for Social Security in the first Blair government. Forced to abide by the previous administration's spending assumptions by their own explicit promise to do so, she abolished the lone-parent premium in Income Support and the higher rate of Child Benefit payable to lone parents in 1998. The additional tax allowance for lone parents was completely phased out by 2000. However, as discussed in Chapter Four, any reductions in income that arose from these changes were annulled by compensatory increases in Income Support allowances for children and by the subsequent reforms that introduced tax credits aimed at improving work incentives and reducing child poverty. Lone parents in receipt of Income Support have thus seen significant real increases in income under New Labour. Figure 8.4 illustrates this by showing real values of income after housing costs from social assistance from 1971 to 2008 for two model lone-parent families, one with one child under five and another with two children under five. The dramatic real-term increase can be clearly seen (as can a more moderate increase over the Conservative period). Post-1998, this is a reflection of the higher levels of benefit provided to all workless families with children rather than an endorsement of lone parenthood through extra-costs benefits.

New Labour's approach that 'work is the best form of welfare' has increased employment among lone parents. We have already outlined the changes to benefits and tax credits that have increasingly 'made work pay' in Chapter Four. The key measures of tax credits to supplement earnings give additional incentives to lone parents as they received the same credits as a couple. In-work benefits can cover up to 97% of childcare costs (80% from WTC and a further 17% from Housing Benefit and Council Tax Benefit) for those on the lowest earnings. The tax credit system ignores all child maintenance payments providing additional gains from working compared with not working. And from 2008, a new In-Work Credit payment of £40 per week payable for up to one year has been made available to lone parents returning to work. The In-Work Credit might well be regarded as the latest 'carrot' or at least a 'pull factor' to encourage lone parents back into the labour market, but other reforms have introduced more 'sticks' or 'push factors'. A gradual but consistent move to reorientate lone parents to consider themselves as jobseekers has taken place since 1997, accompanied by improved provision of

Figure 8.4: Social assistance income for one-parent families in real terms, 1971-2008

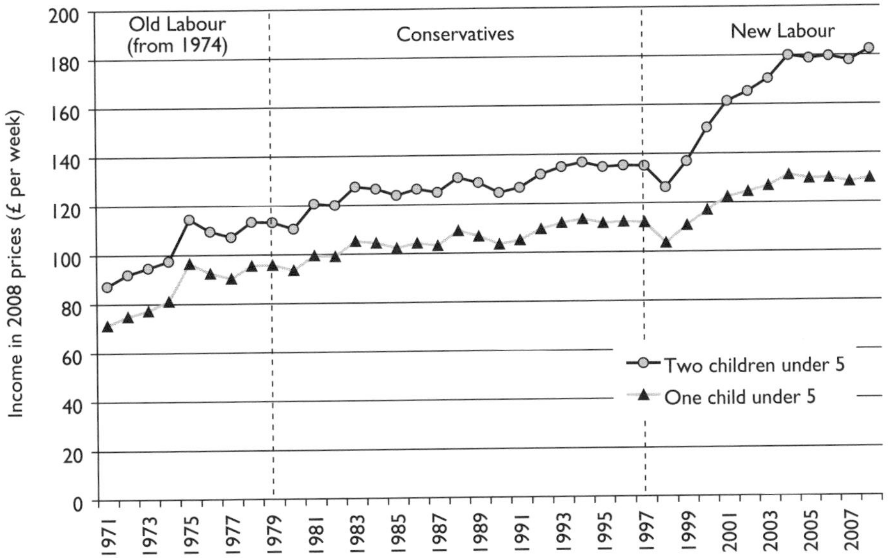

Source: Authors' calculations from DWP (2007b), IFS (2008a) and Child Poverty Action Group guides (CPAG, 1978b, 1980, 1997a, 1997b, 2007, 2008).

childcare. From 1998, the New Deal for Lone Parents provided more employment services to lone parents who wished to work. This was very successful for those lone parents who came forward to participate (Evans et al, 2003). Over time, gradual obligatory work orientation became a feature of eligibility for Income Support. First, work-focused interviews became a necessary part of claiming and reviewing entitlement to benefits and more recently the definition of lone parents has changed so that they become Jobseeker's Allowance (JSA) or Employment and Support Allowance (ESA) cases when their youngest child reaches the age of 12 (rather than 16). From 2010, lone parents with a youngest child aged seven will be covered by the same rule. In addition, under consideration in late 2008 were the proposals in the Green Paper to remove Income Support in its entirety; if this were implemented, all lone parents would have to be treated as either JSA or ESA cases.

Model families

We now turn to repeat the approach of earlier chapters and bring together the different elements of taxes and benefits into an analysis of how total income packages change when disability, caring or lone parenthood is introduced. This means returning to our model families, and in particular the median-earning Meades and the low-paid Lowes. How do the systems of 1979, 1997 and 2008 treat these hypothetical families as they experience the risks outlined in this chapter? We begin with lone parenthood.

Lone parenthood – the Meades and the Lowes

How does lone parenthood affect the Meades if the Meades separate when their child is of pre-school age? We profile four possibilities for the newly separated Ms Meade:

A. Ms Meade now has no income other than benefit income.
B. Ms Meade receives maintenance income from an absent Mr Meade. (We give such maintenance income a fixed relationship with earnings across the three historical systems.)
C. Ms Meade works part time for half full-time median earnings but receives no maintenance income. We keep this profile 'simple' by ignoring the issue of formal childcare.
D. Ms Meade works as in C and also receives maintenance income.

Figure 8.5 shows the results for profiles of income packages after separation on these four scenarios. Maintenance income where assumed is a constant percentage of Mr Meade's income. Figure 8.5 shows the level of income as a percentage of income after tax and housing costs prior to separation based on Mr Meade's contemporary median earnings.

Let us consider the first scenario, A, where Ms Meade continues to live in the marital home but receives no maintenance. This shows a situation of something akin to abandonment. Under 1979 rules, Ms Meade would receive Supplementary Benefit, which would include payment of rates and housing costs in full. After two years (not shown), she would receive higher levels of benefit as she moved to the long-term rate. The initial income after housing costs would be 42% of the original level the household enjoyed while Mr Meade was present and working full time. Under 1997 rules, the comparable contemporary replacement rate is much lower at 26%. This lower figure results from the fall in relative benefit levels over time and to a lesser extent the different social assistance rates under the 1997 system that include the partial and delayed eligibility for mortgage interest support discussed in Chapter Six. Under the 2008 system, the comparable figure is lower still – only 17% of previous income. The increased generosity for children, highlighted in Chapter Four, is eroded by the higher housing costs that have arisen from rising housing prices combined with both structural changes to Income Support, such as the withdrawal of the lone-parent premium, and the erosion of value of underlying Income Support against earnings. Ms Meade's situation is clearly not sustainable and an arrangement to cover mortgage arrears until benefits become available to cover the interest will be critical unless there is some other arrangement in place such as enforcing Mr Meade's maintenance.

Figure 8.5: The Meades – lone parenthood

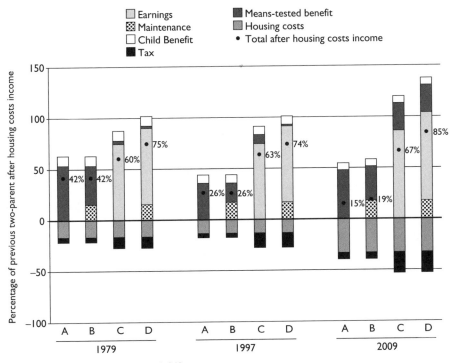

Source: Authors' calculations using LOIS.

Note: 'Tax' comprises income tax, National Insurance contributions and local government taxation.

When we move to consider the impact of receiving maintenance on Ms Meade's claim for social assistance, scenario B, we get a clear illustration of the difference between the systems of 1979 and 1997 on one hand and 2008 on the other in the way they treat maintenance income. Under the 2008 rules, £10 per week of any child maintenance income is disregarded for the purposes of income assessment for Income Support[5] and this raises income from 15% to 19% of previous family income; however, there is no difference between the 1979 and 1997 systems.

The impact of employment in scenarios C and D can be seen by making two comparisons, first with original pre-separation income and second with income after separation on social assistance. The percentage figures in Figure 8.5 enable us to do this, but there is a caveat. The profiles of social assistance in Figure 8.5 show the position in the early period of separation and 1997 and 2008 systems will increase social assistance after a period to reflect mortgage interest costs and thus change underlying rates. These are not shown and therefore the 1997 and 2008 profiles overestimate the relative gains from employment compared with incomes on social assistance.

How have the 1979, 1997 and 2008 systems treated lone parents who work part time? Three factors – housing costs, taxes and in-work transfers – affect outcomes alongside Ms Meade's part-time earnings equivalent to 50% of median earnings. Over time, due to house price inflation, Ms Meade faces the highest contemporary housing costs under the 2008 system, followed by the 1979 system and finally the 1997 system. Comparatively, Ms Meade faces the highest taxes under the 2008 system, but the lowest under the 1979 system where the lone parent's additional tax allowance then in place works to her significant advantage. In terms of in-work benefits, Ms Meade clearly receives the greatest support under the 2008 system, where she receives both CTC and WTC. The effect of maintenance can be seen by comparing scenarios C and D. Under the 1979 system, her income is too high for Family Income Supplement but she receives a rate rebate that is reduced if she receives maintenance income. Under the 1997 system, she receives Family Credit, but this only has a small maintenance income disregard and entitlement is mostly reduced by this. By contrast, the 2008 system has the most generous level of in-work transfers and any such income she receives is not at all affected by maintenance income. These factors are sufficient to ensure the highest replacement of pre-separation income for Ms Meade under the 2008 system despite its higher taxes and housing costs.

Figure 8.6 shows a similar set of profiles for Ms Lowe, who has exactly the same circumstances as Ms Meade apart from being a tenant and previously relying on a lower level of income (Mr Lowe's earnings at 50% of median contemporary earnings). With this lower comparison level of earnings and set benefit rates, we see that the rates for replacement of pre-separation income are higher overall than for the Meades.

Compared with Ms Meade's dire position as a mortgage payer, the Lowes' tenancy acts as a protective factor when faced with the income shock of lone parenthood because social assistance consistently meets 100% of housing costs across all three systems, repeating the findings from the profiles in Chapter Seven on unemployment and incapacity and differential treatment for the Meades and Lowes. In scenarios A and B, in Ms Lowe's case under all three systems we see income replacement profiles that follow the assumptions of 100% of housing costs being met. This leads to basic rates of 57% for 1979, 62% for 1997 and 59% for 2008 in scenario A when income on social assistance is compared with pre-separation income. The treatment of maintenance in scenario B across all three systems replicates the situation for Ms Meade discussed earlier: only in 2008 is any element of maintenance disregarded while she is out of work and claiming social assistance.

In-work benefits for Ms Lowe raise income after housing costs from 57% of pre-separation income on social assistance to 72% or 76% with maintenance in 1979. Under 1997 rules, the differential between out-of-work and in-work income grows. Out-of-work income was 62% of pre-separation levels and in-work 89% or 101% with maintenance, and thus incentives to enter work have proportionately increased. In 2008, surprisingly, despite the increased real-term generosity of tax credits, the underlying incentives to work have fallen compared with 1997 when

Figure 8.6: The Lowes – lone parenthood

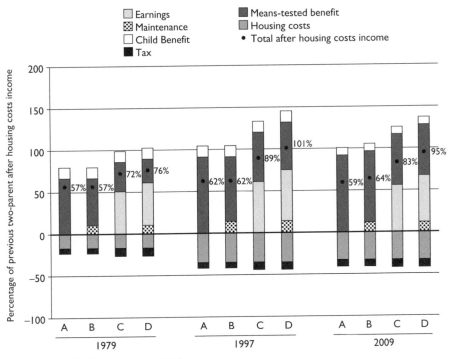

Source: Authors' calculations using LOIS.

Note: 'Tax' comprises income tax, National Insurance contributions and local government taxation.

measured as percentages of pre-separation income. Out-of-work incomes are between 59% and 64% of pre-separation income and in-work incomes are 83% and 95% in 2008. In terms of *percentage point difference* between in-work income and remaining on income support, the 1997 system gives a boost of 27 points for non-maintenance and 39 points for maintenance scenarios, while the comparable figures for 2008 are 24 and 31 points respectively.

There are some crucial points of context when interpreting these results. First, comparing the 1997 and 2008 systems of in-work transfers before and after separation and lone parenthood implicitly means comparing the treatment of the tax benefit position of couples (before) and lone parents (after). The high replacement rates seen under the 1997 system are straightforward not because the 1997 system is the most generous to low-paid lone-parent families but because it is comparatively generous towards lone parent families while at the same time being the *least generous* towards low-paid two-parent families. Second, one of the reasons that the 2008 system does not have as big an effect as expected is that our measurement is a relative one – a percentage of earnings – and since 2003 the relative generosity of tax credits has fallen overall in relative terms because many elements of the system are not uprated with earnings to match uprating of the headline rate of Child Tax Credit (Sutherland et al, 2008). Finally, there are other aspects of the 2008 system that we have not shown here because we are not focused totally on the immediate period of return to work but on overall comparative packages. The 2008 system will give additional rewards during the first year only of any return to work of an additional £40 per week 'In-Work Credit' payment (£60 for London residents) if the period out of work has lasted more than one year. This would raise the differential in 2008 to similar levels as seen in 1997 but only for the first year in work.

Disability – the Meades and the Lowes

We have already considered the position where disability leads to incapacity for work in Chapter Seven and we turn in this section to consider how being employed and having a disability affects Mr Meade and Mr Lowe. We compare first the effect of the introduction of means-tested, in-work benefits for more severely disabled people on low incomes (exemplified by Mr Lowe) and second the extension of extra-cost disability benefits to less serious conditions of disablement for median earners (Mr Meade). Finally, we look at the impact of assistance for children with disabilities over time.

Let us begin by looking at the combined effect of extra-costs benefits and in-work benefits for the Lowes. We suppose that Mr Lowe has mobility needs only and that he is able to work full time. As previously, we consider outcomes for the Lowes at the point at which Mr Lowe is the sole earner and their single child is of pre-school age. Table 8.1 shows the outcomes for the Lowes in two ways. The first (A) is to ask how much transfer income the Lowes will receive that they would not do otherwise if Mr Lowe were not disabled. The second (B) is to address the 'why work?' question and to ask how much better off the Lowes are in terms of income after housing costs if Mr Lowe works full time than if he does not.

Clearly, as a disabled worker Mr Lowe faces the best outcome in terms of taxes and benefits under the 2008 system, where the Lowes benefit strongly from the disability element of WTC. Given the replacement rates we have previously seen for the Lowes in respect of incapacity, it is perhaps not surprising to learn that the Lowes would actually be better off in terms of income after housing costs if Mr

Table 8.1: The Lowes – disabled worker

	1979	1997	2008
A: additional income solely due to disability (in 2008 prices)	£42	£50	£95
B: percentage by which the Lowes are better off with Mr Lowe working than they would be without Mr Lowe working	–7%	19%	32%

Source: Authors' calculations using LOIS.

Note: Measure A, transfer income, includes benefits, tax credits and tax relief. Measure B is calculated by comparing AHC income when Mr Lowe is working full-time with AHC income after one year of Mr Lowe claiming incapacity benefits. SERPS addition is not included in the 1979 calculation.

Lowe did not work. The same is not true of the 1997 or 2008 systems, with the 2008 system showing the better result in terms of work 'paying' for the Lowes. This is in part due to out-of-work benefits being lower relative to earnings in 2008 than in previous periods, but also due to Mr Lowe receiving significant WTC while in work.

Moving on to look at the impact of minor disability for median earners, we suppose that Mr Meade has a relatively minor disability[6] such that he finds it difficult to work more than 30 hours per week (which we assume is equivalent to three quarters of full-time hours). Table 8.2 shows the same measures of disability-related transfers and difference between working and not working.

Table 8.2: The Meades – disabled worker

	1979	1997	2008
A: transfer income solely because of disability and reduced hours (in 2008 prices)	£2	£48	£96
B: percentage by which the Meades are better off with Mr Meade working than they would be without Mr Meade working	15%	38%	87%

Source: Authors' calculations using LOIS.

Note: Measure A, transfer income, includes benefits and tax credits. Measure B is calculated by comparing AHC income when Mr Meade is working 30 hours with AHC income after one year of Mr Meade claiming incapacity benefits. SERPS addition is not included in the 1979 calculation.

There are two triggers to transfer assistance: the reduced hours and thus lower earnings, and the disability. Under the 1979 system, Mr Meade receives no assistance for his disability directly but the lower earnings mean that the family qualifies for a small sum in rate rebate. The 1997 and 2008 systems provide lower rates of DLA care and relevant in-work transfers. Clearly, the overall picture is that in real income terms Mr Meade fares best under the 2008 system and by a large margin. Work also pays best under the 2008 system; however, one driver is that out-of-work benefits are falling over the period up to 2008 alongside the generosity of in-work transfers.

Caring – the Meades and the Lowes

Finally, we consider the possibility of the Meades and the Lowes having a disabled child. In both cases, we suppose that the child is severely disabled and needs a full-time adult carer. To make this consistent with our previous assumptions about earning and caring responsibilities, we make Mr Meade and Mr Lowe the sole full-time earners, at median and 50% of median full-time earnings respectively, and their partners the full-time carers. Figure 8.7 illustrates additional transfer income that the families will receive under the three systems in 1979, 1997 and 2008.

Figure 8.7: The Lowes and the Meades – additional transfers as the result of having a severely disabled child

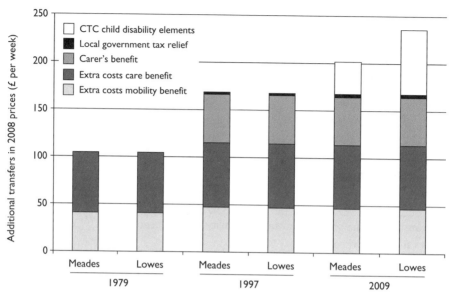

Source: Authors' calculations using LOIS.

Under the 1979 system, assistance for both families would be limited to the extra-costs benefits of Attendance Allowance and Mobility Allowance in respect of their child. Both Ms Meade and Ms Lowe are precluded from receiving any carer's benefit because they are married women and thereby not eligible for Invalid Care Allowance. By 1997, both women qualify for the carer's benefit as gender discrimination has been outlawed in the meantime. Both families continue to receive extra-costs benefits and receive a council tax band reduction[7]. In 2008, both families remain entitled to the 1997 package but also qualify for the CTC child disability elements. Because these elements are means-tested (by being tapered away according to income), the Lowes will receive more money through them than the Meades. Otherwise, the Meades and the Lowes receive exactly the same levels of additional transfers.

Summary

This chapter has looked at a wide range of needs and transfers that cover disability, caring and lone parenthood. Our findings are as follows:

- Benefits for disability were not part of the Beveridge's 1948 vision of social security but have increased since the 1970s to provide wider availability to people with lower levels of disability and to assist employment.

- The level of disability benefits has remained constant in real terms since the early 1990s but underlying costs of care have risen ahead of general prices.
- In-work disability provision has improved incentives to work in 1997 and 2008 compared with 1979.
- The rate of carer's benefits are lower than those of social assistance and have fallen increasingly behind earnings growth since their introduction.
- Lone parenthood rose as a percentage of underlying social assistance claimants during the 1970s, 1980s and 1990s. However, the proportion of lone parents out of work and on benefits has consistently fallen since the mid-1990s.
- The level of benefits for lone parents has increased since the late 1990s and in-work incentives have greatly improved.

Notes

[1] See, as an example, the government's New Deal for Disabled People, mentioned in Chapter Seven, or BBC broadcast news (19 November 2007), which referred to incapacity benefits as disability benefits.

[2] For consistency with long-term Incapacity Benefit, this figure shows rates of benefit for a person whose incapacity began at age 50. The step increase in rate that can be seen reflects the introduction of age-related additions to SDA in 1990.

[3] At least for claimants whose claims pre-date October 2008. The disability premium is not payable with Employment and Support Allowance; instead, it is replaced by the support or employment components.

[4] There were two general elections in 1974, in February and October. The first resulted in Labour forming a government without a parliamentary majority. The second granted Labour an overall majority of just three.

[5] From 2009, a £20 disregard.

[6] This disability may be one that affects manual dexterity such that Mr Meade is unable to prepare a cooked main meal for himself – one test of the lower-rate DLA care element.

[7] We assume that both the Meades and the Lowes will live in homes in some way modified to meet the needs of their child.

NINE

Old age and retirement

This chapter considers the final portion of the lifetime – old age – and considers the range of tax and benefit support for old age and retirement and death. The core of this chapter focuses on pension funding and outcomes, and this is a true reflection of how much the tax and benefit system is geared to retirement and old age. We follow the structure of the earlier chapters in this section and first look at the policy history before moving on to consider pension and retirement profiles for our model families on low, median and higher earnings.

State benefits for pensioners

State pensions

The Department for Work and Pensions treats the state pension as being the oldest extant benefit, recording it as being introduced 1 January 1909. However, as with unemployment and sickness benefits, the post-war settlement superseded existing arrangements. The Beveridge scheme envisaged a state retirement pension being payable to any person having paid National Insurance contributions over his or her working lifetime. However, on its introduction, pensioners who had not built up entitlements to the new retirement pension were still able to claim it at the full amount. Such a full implementation of flat-rate pensions rather than their gradual build-up over time undermined many of the funding assumptions in the original Beveridge Report (HMSO, 1942). These pensions were never unequivocally accepted in the 1950s, especially by the Treasury, and all attempts to raise the pension level significantly during this period were fought tooth and nail. The pension thus found itself continually at the margins of National Assistance rates.

Other aspects of the post-war settlement on pensions have had a similarly long-lasting impact. Pensionable age then was 65 for a man and 60 for a woman, and remains so at the time of writing. The five-year age differential was introduced in 1940 and accepted by Beveridge without discussion. The motivations for its introduction, that women generally had shorter working lives than men and that wives were generally younger than their husbands, clearly do not withstand scrutiny today and higher pensionable ages for women will be phased in from 2010, with pensionable ages for men and women being equalised at 65 by 2020. Pension age will then be increased by three years for the next generation. Since 1948, a flat-rate basic pension has been paid to any person reaching pensionable age who has retired and who meets the National Insurance contribution conditions that are based on a 40-year working life. Those, typically women, with shorter working lives can face a lower proportional entitlement to the basic pension. Also surviving for a long time was the notion that a significant proportion of married or widowed women would rely on their husband's contribution record for state pension entitlement.

The history of state pension reform since 1948 has been less one of reforming the basic state pension than one of providing for earnings related additions to it – that is, the dominant issue historically has been one of providing *secondary pensions* alongside Beveridge's flat-rate basic pension. After the Second World War, occupational pensions grew to cover many people, but there remained a substantial proportion of people who had limited or no access to private pensions (occupational or otherwise). A constant and legitimate theme of policy since the late 1950s has been the provision of incentives for workers without occupational pensions not to rely solely on the basic state pension and to build up additional funds to avoid slipping into social assistance in old age.

The mid-1950s saw the Labour Party put forward a National Superannuation scheme that would ensure earnings-related pensions in retirement and included part-investment funding of contributions collected through the PAYE system. The Conservatives were forced to respond and the 1961 graduated pension scheme was introduced. To a great extent, the graduated pension contributions were actually enabling greater funds to pay the contemporary flat-rate pensions and support the beleaguered National Insurance fund. The scheme deliberately provided limited benefits to avoid competition with occupational schemes (Hannah, 1986; Timmins, 2001) and was never properly inflation proofed.

Pension reform in the 1970s focused on replacing graduated pension with a better scheme to ensure reasonable second pensions. Remarkably, the introduction of the State Earnings Related Pension Scheme (SERPS) was a bipartisan measure. The scheme that came into effect from April 1978 was in its original guise a comparatively generous one. It was intended to provide an additional pension of 25% of band earnings (band earnings being those between the lower earnings limit and upper earnings limit for National Insurance) with the calculation of band earnings being made with reference to the individual's 20 best years of earnings revalued in line with earnings inflation. This 'best 20 years' rule would act as protection for those with fluctuating earnings or who spent years outside employment, fulfilling caring roles or in self-employment, for example. Membership was automatic for all, although arrangements were made for employers to contract out employees from SERPS if they could demonstrate that the employees had been granted an occupational pension scheme at least as good as SERPS. In 1978, nine million people were contracted out in this way[1] (CPAG, 1978a).

The introduction of SERPS helped women's entitlement to pensions in their own right through the 'best 20 years' rule but still left the issue of how years out of the labour market could be recognised for the basic state pension. The supposed solution 'home responsibilities protection' was introduced from 1978 and provided for a discounting of years caring for a child or a disabled person from the assumptions of a working life (subject to a minimum working life of 20 years) and thus would maintain basic pension entitlement. However, home responsibilities protection was not retrospectively applied to years before 1978/79 and thus, as with any contributory entitlement, it would take years before any claimant could derive benefit from it.

The other crucially important reform undertaken by Labour in the 1970s was the commitment to uprate the basic state pension in line with the higher of prices and earnings. This, as mentioned in earlier chapters, was overturned early in the Thatcher years. The effect of this decision on the value of basic pension is illustrated by Figure 9.1. where the value of a single person's basic pension can be seen to fall by around 25% from 22% of average weekly earnings in 1979 to just 16% of average weekly earnings 20 years later.

The effect of such a long-term decline in the relative value of basic pension has a huge impact on second pensions. If the aim of policy is to ensure incentives to save and have other forms of pension, when pensions fall in value these savings and private pensions have to do more to provide reasonable living standards in old age and to avoid means testing. Providing such better benefits for those with low to median earnings or with interrupted work histories is difficult for the market to do. Private providers are wary of taking on such customers with high

Figure 9.1: Real and relative value of basic state pension (single-person rate), 1971-2008

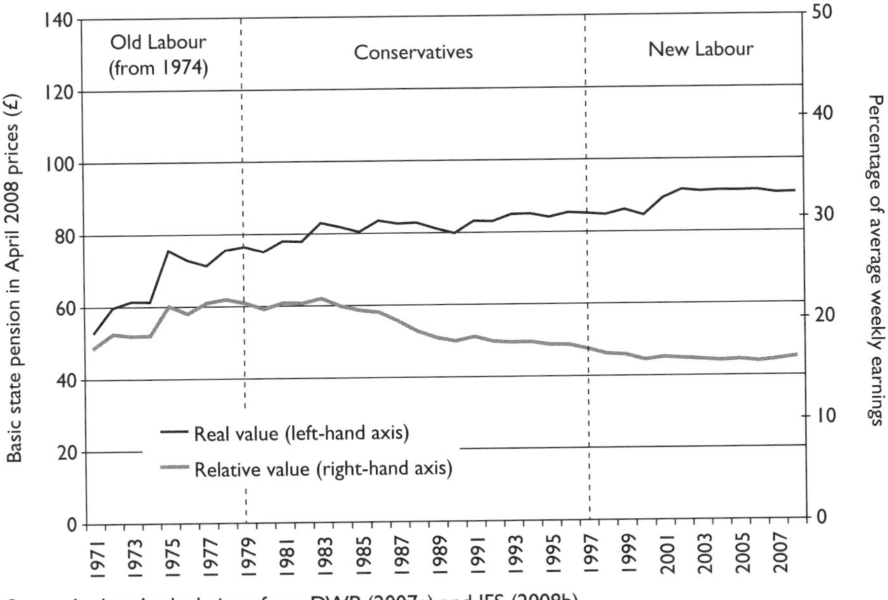

Source: Authors' calculations from DWP (2007a) and IFS (2008b).

Note: All plotted points are rates as at April each year.

administrative costs and low returns. These factors meant that when the Fowler reforms first mooted the complete abolition of SERPS[2] and its replacement with private pensions, the pension industry was not entirely happy with being given the whole portfolio of pension risk. SERPS ended up reformed in 1986 and not abolished as planned.

The macroeconomic costs of SERPS were increasingly being seen as unsustainable and the projections of the first Government Actuary's report suggested that National Insurance contribution rates would have to rise significantly to fund the scheme in the medium to long term. This was anathema to the Thatcher government, which prided itself on reducing tax and spending and on fiscal constraint. It strongly believed that private provision could fill the gap, if it was not crowded out by state provision of anything but the minimum basic pension. Original SERPS provisions foresaw a gradual reduction of the tax subsidies of contracting out to assist in the finance of SERPS and to make the scheme more universal. Such reductions were never implemented and the assumptions never featured in any cost projections in the 1980s.

The 1986 Social Security Act cut back on some of its most generous and progressive features and reduced the future cost of the SERPS. Significantly, the 'best 20 years' rule was abolished and the accrual target of 25% of band earnings was reduced to 20%. There were further comparatively minor reforms to SERPS in the 1995 Pensions Act that both changed the calculation method to reduce the generosity of the scheme and allowed Family Credit and other in-work benefits to be treated as though they were earnings to the benefit of the entitlement of low-paid workers with children or a disability.

Pension reform under New Labour can be split into two phases: first, 1999 legislation that led to the introduction of the State Second Pension (S2P) in 2002 and second, the 2007 Pensions Act.

From April 2002, SERPS was replaced by S2P. Although broadly similar to SERPS, it differs significantly in that it is explicitly redistributive. A more generous accrual rate (40%) applies to band earnings below a lower earnings threshold (£13,000 in 2007/08) than earnings above that threshold. Moreover, people with caring responsibilities for a child under six or a sick or disabled person, as well as the long-term incapacitated, are granted S2P accruals as though they had earnings equal to the lower earnings threshold. Thus S2P targets provision towards the low paid and those for defined reasons not in employment, while at the same time, through its somewhat complicated structure of different band earnings and accrual rates, it offers roughly the same benefits to other categories of employees as SERPS.

However, poor take-up of 'stakeholder pensions' (to be discussed later in this chapter) and continued large gaps in private pension uptake meant that the whole area of pensions had to be reviewed again and the Pensions Commission was set up to do so in 2002. Two of its reports, the first empirical and thorough, the second, analytical and prescriptive, represent perhaps the best example of 'evidence-based policy' to emerge since 1997 (Pensions Commission, 2004, 2005). A consensus on what markets can and cannot do in pension policy, together with changing demographic demand and financing options, led to a set of proposals that were difficult for any government to ignore. The 2007 Pensions Act resulted from the Pensions Commission's second report and has two broad aims. The first is to introduce a new quasi-private pension scheme, termed 'personal accounts', to which all eligible employees will be automatically but not compulsorily enrolled from 2012. We discuss the details of these proposals below under the heading of 'personal pensions'. The second broad aim is to reform state pension provision, including S2P, in order to 'provide a solid foundation on which people can save' (DWP, 2006c, p 17). This solid foundation meant first, a commitment to uprate basic pension in line with earnings in the near future (2012 or thereabouts) and second, a series of reforms to better enable those with caring responsibilities to build up entitlement to basic state pension. Notably, the qualifying contribution conditions (in terms of number of years of contributions required and number of actual as opposed to credited contributions required) will be made easier to meet for all, and home responsibilities protection will be replaced by weekly credited contributions for which those with caring responsibilities (for a young child or sick or disabled person) will qualify. In terms of S2P, it means converting the benefit to a simple, flat-rate weekly top-up to the basic pension by 2030. In simple terms, fully reformed S2P will (in 2008 prices) grant £1.40 per week in additional state pension for each year a person works for earnings above the lower earnings limit for National Insurance or has caring responsibilities or a long-term qualifying incapacity.

The reforms of the 2007 Pension Act will take many years to have their full effect, but it is worth noting that the fully realised vision of the Act represents an abandonment of the state directly providing earnings-related pensions. In a way this can be seen as a return to one of the principles of Beveridge, who saw benefits as a basic flat-rate measure on top of which individuals could arrange private provision. However, the new approach grants flat-rate benefits in return for earnings-related contributions, turning Beveridge's approach on its head. The contributory principle has also been taken in a more welcome 'un-Beveridgian' direction with the extension of contributory entitlements to those fulfilling defined caring roles, and the 2007 Pensions Act will eventually mean that anyone who has worked *and/or* fulfilled caring roles throughout his or her lifetime will qualify for a combination of full basic state pension and additional state pension.

Box 9.1: Pension scheme terminology

Defined benefit/defined contribution

Pensions can be distinguished between those that are 'salary-related/defined benefit' and those that are 'money purchase/defined contribution' schemes.

The terms 'salary-related' and 'defined benefit' are synonymous, as are the terms 'money purchase' and 'defined contribution'.

A salary-related scheme provides a pension that is based on final earnings (or some measure of average earnings over the last few years of employment). Scheme members will typically pay in a percentage of their earnings (say 6%) and on retirement will receive a pension calculated on the basis of an accrual rate (say 1/80th) multiplied by the number of years of membership multiplied by final earnings. For example, 40 years of membership and an accrual rate of 1/80th will grant a pension of one half of final earnings.

With a money purchase scheme, the provider will invest contributions made into a fund. On retirement, that fund is used to purchase an annuity (that is, an annual pension income). The amount of pension is not defined and will depend on a number of factors, including: the amount of money that is paid into the scheme; the performance of the fund into which it is paid; the administration charges made by the provider; the commission charged on annuity purchase; the rate used to calculate the annuity; and whether a flat or escalating (inflation-proofed) annuity is chosen.

Occupational/personal

Pension schemes can be distinguished between those that are 'occupational' (employer provided) and those that are 'personal' (where the contract is between the individual member and the pension provider).

Occupational pension schemes can be either defined benefit or defined contribution schemes, although traditionally they have been defined benefit.

Personal pension schemes are always defined contribution schemes.

Social assistance

Our discussion of social assistance in Chapter Six has already shown how the flat-rate assumptions of Beveridge's pensions and other benefits were not properly reconciled against social assistance and essential items such as rent. Under the Supplementary Benefit system of the 1970s, people of pensionable age were awarded the long-term benefit rate immediately and Department of Health and

Social Security statistics from 1979 show 79% of pensioner claimants getting higher than average weekly exceptional circumstance additions. When Income Support replaced Supplementary Benefit from 1988, the differences in generosity of treatment were enshrined in a new system of categorical premiums where all claimants over 60 (thus including men aged 60-64 who could not strictly speaking be termed 'pensioners') received a 'pensioner premium' at three rates that rose with age, with an enhanced rate for those aged 75-79 and a higher rate for those aged over 80 (or who met certain disability conditions).

Income Support for those over 60 was renamed the Minimum Income Guarantee (MIG) in 1999, administered by the newly separated Pensions Agency. Minimum Income Guarantee was more generous than the old Income Support and did away with different age-related benefits for pensioners and paid a single higher rate, but otherwise kept other elements of Income Support. In 2003, MIG became Pension Credit, or more exactly it became the 'guarantee' element of Pension Credit (Pension Credit guarantee or PCG). In effect, PCG introduced a single set of rates that form the standard minimum guarantee of income for single and couple pensioners. These can be increased in the event of qualification for set additional allowances for severe disability, carer or housing costs.

However, the problem of introducing higher social assistance rates is that incentives to save are reduced. This was recognised and policy changed to improve the treatment of income for pensioners around social assistance levels of income. The Pension Credit's 'savings' element (PCS) was conceived as a 'reward' for those who have some additional provision for their retirement over and above the basic state pension. It is payable alongside the guarantee element in cases where the claimant has an income that falls between the basic pension and Pension Credit guarantee levels, and is payable at its maximum amount at the point at which income (excluding Pension Credit) is equal to the PCG level. This savings credit is tapered away so that those with moderate to high levels of additional pension or income will receive no PCS. The savings credit of the Pension Credit system is, however, only available to those aged 65 and over, whereas Pension Credit guarantee can be claimed by those aged 60 and over. This creates a (temporary) anomaly that, in line with other changes to pension age, will be phased out from 2010.

Means-tested benefits for those of pension age have consistently had poor take-up and Pension Credit is no exception. For those eligible for PCG only, or for a combination of PCG and PCS, take-up for 2005/06 was estimated at between 68% and 82%. For those who are only eligible for savings credit (that is, those with incomes above PCG levels but low enough to be eligible for some PCS), take-up was estimated to be in the very low range of 42% to 48% (DWP, 2007e).

Figure 9.2 shows the levels of social assistance available to a single person over 60 who would qualify for the pensioner premium at the standard rate. For comparison, the level of basic state pension for a single person is also plotted. It can be seen that during the 1970s and early 1980s, social assistance rates were very close to basic

Figure 9.2: Real values of basic state pension and social assistance, 1971-2008

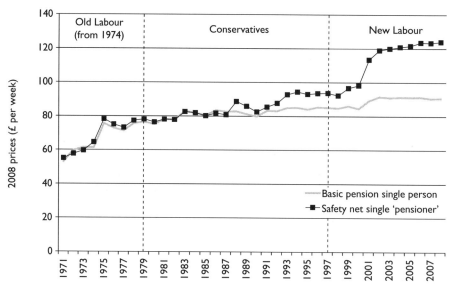

Source: Authors' calculations from DWP (2007a) and IFS (2008b).
Note: All plotted points are rates as at April each year.

pension rates. Since the 1990s, social assistance rates have pulled further ahead of basic pension. This trend can be seen to have begun under the Conservatives but has been intensified under New Labour. One reason stems from the commitment to end pensioner poverty. Combating pensioner poverty meant addressing the problems of a substantial minority of pensioners at a time when average pensioner incomes were rising due to the expansion of occupational and other pensions in the 1950s onwards that were now being drawn by the latest generation of pensioners. The most economically efficient and cost-effective way of targeting poor pensioners was thus to means test specific help and not to raise the basic pension. The series of significant and historically large increases in means-tested benefits for those of pensionable age under New Labour demonstrate this.

Figure 9.3 illustrates coverage of social assistance for pensioners between 1971 and 2007 as a proportion of the pension age population. The problem is that since 1988 social assistance has effectively overwritten pension age as a sensible denominator because Income Support and subsequent social assistance for pensioners operated from a lower harmonised age of 60. Figure 9.3 joins these two trends. The proportion of those of pension age claiming social assistance fell dramatically in the early 1970s, probably due to a growing number of pensioners with occupational pension income (SBC, 1976) and then levelled off in the 1980s. Since 1998, there was a rise in the proportion of over-60-year-olds claiming social assistance in the early to mid-1990s, which was probably an effect of the recession and increased early retirement. Claims fell in the latter part of the 1990s

Figure 9.3: Social assistance coverage, 1971-2007

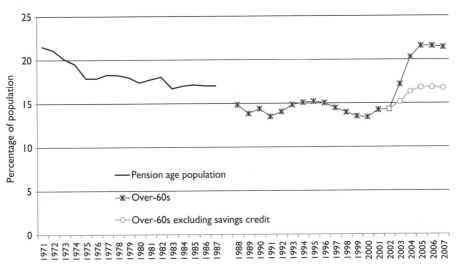

Source: Authors' calculations from DHSS (1987), DSS (2000), DWP (2008b) and ONS (2008c).

until the introduction of the more generous Pension Credit clearly resulted in a substantial increase again. If claimants of savings credit are additionally included, then social assistance covers around 22% of over-60s in 2007.

In addition to core social assistance benefits, means-tested help with housing costs and local government taxation has always been an important part of income maintenance for pensioners[3]. However, Housing Benefit and Council Tax Benefit are plagued by low take-up among claimants in old age. Estimates of caseload take-up of Council Tax Benefit in 2004 are 53%-58% among the over-60 population (DWP, 2006d).

Pensioners have also been historically entitled to receive other benefits on age grounds. Such provision has been expanded under New Labour. Free NHS prescriptions and sight tests have long been available (under current rules to those over 60)[4]. Those over 75 will qualify for a free TV licence. Winter fuel payments since 1997/98 have provided a one-off payment to assist with winter fuel costs[5] and these have been increased dramatically, partly to offset political criticism of the failure to uprate the basic pension sufficiently, and the current level of payment is at two age-related rates (£200 and £300 in 2008/09), with an additional age-related per household addition (£50 or £100 in 2008/09). Concessionary bus travel has recently been expanded to include free national off-peak bus travel to all those over 60.

One final and rather incongruous feature of pensions is that there is an additional 25 pence payable each week at the age of 80. Introduced in 1971 to reflect the additional cost of a bag of coal, it has never been uprated and is now insufficient to buy a second-class stamp.

Death and funeral expenses

We have finally got to the 'grave' in our lifetime profile of policy; time to discuss provision for death and funeral expenses. The ignominy of a Poor Law burial and the inefficiency and selectivity of private life assurance policies before the Second World War meant that Beveridge put a contributory Death Grant in his scheme that was introduced in 1948. However, much like the Maternity Grant, it was allowed to wither in real value. One-off payments of discretionary social assistance were available for funeral expenses as an addition or alternative. Both these forms of support were amalgamated in the Fowler reforms of 1988 and became part of the Social Fund. Since then, funeral expenses payments have been available as a grant from the fund to meet 'necessary' funeral expenses, but with restrictions, and only to those receiving qualifying means-tested benefits.

Survivorship benefits have traditionally been covered by social insurance and contributory widows' benefits formed part of the 1948 social security system, comprising Widow's Allowance (a short-term weekly benefit for working age widows to cover the 'readjustment' period), Widowed Mother's Allowance (a weekly benefit available long-term for widowed mothers with dependent children) and Widow's Pension (a weekly benefit available long-term for widows 'nearing' retirement). Receipt of all three benefits depended on the assumption that men worked and their wives did not and thus on the widow's late husband's contribution record. In 1988, these three benefits were joined by a fourth – the Widow's Payment – a one-off lump-sum payment for working age widows that effectively replaced the Death Grant (but calculated on the dead spouse's contribution record). In 2001, the system of widow's benefits was replaced by the current unisex system of bereavement benefits. Effectively, Widow's Pension was abolished. Widow's Allowance has been replaced by Bereavement Allowance, which is available to both sexes and is payable for a maximum period of one year. Widowed Mother's Allowance has been replaced by Widowed Parent's Allowance, again available to both sexes. And finally the Widow's Payment, which had been £1,000, was replaced by the Bereavement Payment, available to working age widows and widowers in the sum of £2,000, although at the time of writing this sum had not been uprated since its introduction.

Taxation

Taxation continues to the grave. One exception to this rule is that people over pension age no longer have to pay National Insurance contributions, even if they continue to work. There is, however, no upper age limit on payment of income tax and all forms of pension, state or private, have always been taxable. The income tax burden on pensioners usually falls because retirement income is typically much lower than employment income. Social assistance income is not taxable. Pensioners also benefit from higher age-related income tax allowances once they are 65 (although at higher levels of income, these taper away). Figure 9.4 illustrates tax allowances from 1973/74 to 2008/09 in real weekly terms for a single person. Throughout the period, any person over 65 would need to have significant taxable income above the level of the basic pension to have to pay any income tax. From 1987, a second higher tax allowance has applied for older pensioners and from the mid-1990s onwards the over-65 tax allowances have enjoyed above-inflation increases. This is most markedly so in 2008, with further above-inflation increases promised thereafter. A current government commitment is that by April 2011 no pensioner over 75 will pay any income tax unless his or her income exceeds £10,000.

Figure 9.4: Income tax allowances for the over-65s, 1973/74-2008/09

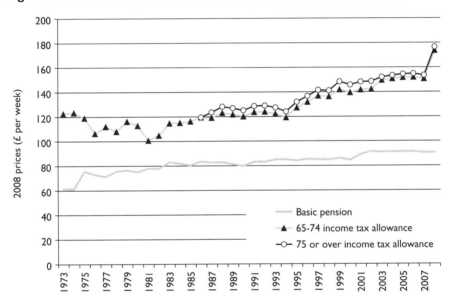

Source: Authors' calculations from DWP(2007b) and IFS (2008a).

Note: During the tax years 1987/88 and 1988/89, the higher tax allowance applied to those over 80 rather than 75.

Private provision

Saving and contributing

Government support of the provision of pensions is not limited to the direct expenditure of the state pension and other benefits. In addition, support for private pension provision is granted through the indirect expenditure of tax relief on occupational and personal pensions. This is a significant and often neglected policy area that is discussed in this section along with the ways in which policy encourages or discourages saving more generally.

Government initiatives to support saving in general terms can be traced back at least as far as the 19th century and the founding of the Post Office Savings Bank to encourage saving among ordinary workers. In more recent times, the tax system has been explicitly used to provide incentives for savings and investment. Notably, under Margaret Thatcher's premiership, Personal Equity Plans (PEPs) were introduced, allowing those taking them out to receive the profits from stock market-related investment without facing income tax or capital gains tax on them. The introduction of PEPs in 1987 was followed in 1991 by the introduction of Tax Exempt Special Savings Accounts (TESSAs), which were targeted at a broader range of savers and offered savings interest free from income tax. Faced with the situation of half of the population having less than £200 in savings (HM Treasury, 1998), New Labour had explicit policy intentions to encourage everyone to save. To this end, PEPs and TESSAs were replaced by a system of Individual Savings Accounts (ISAs). This was built on the principles of its predecessors and offered all adults the possibility of investing within limits in savings accounts or stocks and shares without incurring income tax on their profits, but with greater flexibility, including the promise that ISAs would be 'available over the counter in supermarkets' (HM Treasury, 1998). A further New Labour initiative is the Savings Gateway scheme, to be rolled out nationally from 2010, which offers cash savings accounts for those on low incomes with direct financial incentives to save via 'matched' payments for each pound saved.

However, incentives for the poorest to save are deterred by social assistance capital rules that are not regularly or consistently uprated. For example, between 1988 and 2006, the lower capital limit for social assistance and Housing Benefit remained frozen at £3,000. The application of different rules across tax credits and social assistance and between pensioners and working age claimants make for a complicated and inconsistent set of incentives. Additionally, in the case of social assistance and Housing Benefit, a deemed 'tariff' income assumption is applied irrespective of contemporary interest rates.

The tax system has long been used to support private pension provision and saving for retirement. Tax relief on contributions made can be traced back as far as the mid-19th century and the 1921 Finance Act confirmed the principle that private pensions meeting certain conditions would only be subject to tax when in payment (Hannah, 1986). Subsequent legislation has in different ways extended and limited this principle but never overturned it. Reform in 2002 introduced single lifetime and annual limits to the amount of tax-free pension saving a person could make. However, such limits are not intended to prevent the vast majority from receiving tax relief on whatever pension contributions they can afford to make.

Tax relief in respect of private pensions has been criticised for being regressive, expensive and ineffective. Certainly, the better off derive the most benefit from tax relief on pension contributions and indeed the regressivity has been extreme. Figures from the tax year 1996/97 show half the benefit of tax relief on pension contributions going to the top 10% of taxpayers (Agulnik and Le Grand, 1998). Tax expenditure of this kind is expensive when considered purely in cross-sectional terms and in its own right. The Pensions Policy Institute estimated the overall net annual cost to be in excess of £19 billion in 2004 (PPI, 2004). While there is some argument that such tax subsidies may have historically encouraged the growth of occupational pension provision in the post-war years up until the 1980s (Hannah, 1986), there is an increasing scepticism about the current effectiveness of such tax reliefs as incentives (PPI, 2004; Sinfield, 2007) and therefore in particular a concern that New Labour's reforms have failed to address or correct an unwarranted regressivity in this area (Sinfield, 2007). The problem is that tax expenditure on pensions should not be considered as simply a gross spending figure that could be reduced in its own right without compensatory additional spending on public pensions. The fundamental question for this complex area is thus the balance of private and public provision and the funding mechanisms for such provision to achieve the desired policy outcomes (Fry et al, 1985).

Occupational pensions

At the turn of the 20th century, only a small minority of employees, perhaps 5% in the public and private sectors combined (Hannah, 1986), belonged to any type of formal pension scheme. Principally through expansion in the post-war years, occupational pensions came to dominate private pension provision in the succeeding years and until the late 1960s the growth in occupational pension coverage was inexorable. By 1967, Government Actuary estimates suggested that the proportion of workers in occupational schemes had reached 53%.

Increasing life expectancy effectively created the market for pension provision in the first place and employers saw the provision of pension schemes as a way of improving the length and quality of service of their employees. The state helped occupational pensions to grow and tax relief on pension contributions produced a tax-efficient way to save. Sustained income growth and full employment in the post-war period encouraged the growth of occupational pension coverage, leading to it becoming the norm, at least among the full-time male employees of medium-sized to large employers. Occupational pensions became a part of a wage package that employers needed to offer in order to compete for staff in a period of full employment and part of the terms and conditions of employment at the heart of union negotiations.

The growth in coverage of occupational pensions was accompanied by an improvement in their quality. Historically, public sector pension schemes, notably those granted to civil servants, offered generous defined benefits to their members. A combination of the post-war Labour government's nationalisation programme and subsequent Conservative government policy had, by the 1950s, led to comprehensive and attractive occupational pension coverage in the now greatly expanded public sector. Final salary schemes, which became the defined benefit

norm, effectively offered benefits in real income rather than money terms. In the
1970s, the desire to meet the conditions required for contracting out of SERPS
led to improvements in many existing occupational pension schemes.

Figure 9.5 illustrates occupational pension coverage in 1979, 1995 and 2007,
the closest years to our comparison years that are covered by the Government
Actuary's Department surveys.

By 1979, occupational pension coverage had fallen slightly from its late 1960s
level and was 46% of all employees. Occupational pension coverage subsequently
declined, as illustrated in Figure 9.5, driven by economic restructuring, increased
competition on employers' operating costs and profitability and the growth of
other forms of pension that were cheaper and less risky for employers. Membership
of occupational pension schemes fell by 1.3 million between 1979 and 1995, but
with greater numbers of women and fewer numbers of men becoming active
members of occupational pension schemes, particularly in the public sector. The
overall decline in numbers is accounted for by falling numbers of active members
in the public sector, with private sector active membership totals actually being
slightly higher. Privatisation under the Conservatives had a significant role in
these changes. Two million fewer people were employed in the public sector
in 1995 compared with 1979 (ONS, 2008b). Changes between 1995 and 2007
show falls against the backdrop of rising employment – there were over 3 million

**Figure 9.5: Occupational pension scheme coverage (UK active
membership)**

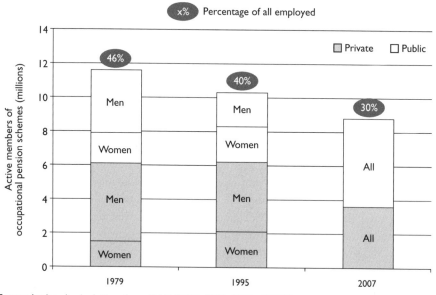

Source: Authors' calculations from GAD (1986, 1999, 2008a, 2008b).

Note: 'All employed' is the Labour Force Survey result for all people in employment aged 16+ in the
spring quarter of the applicable year.

more people in employment in 2007 than there were in 1995. Consequently, in terms of the percentage coverage of those in employment as opposed to absolute numbers, the decline has been more dramatic. By 2007, less than one third of people in employment enjoyed active occupational pension scheme membership. Private employers increasingly chose alternatives to expensive defined benefit occupational pension schemes, increasingly favouring defined contribution schemes and group personal pensions. The latter is in effect not to provide an occupational pension at all. A group personal pension remains essentially a personal pension, even though the employer may facilitate employee membership and payment of contributions, because the legal contract is between the individual scheme member and the pension provider. Following accepted terminology (for example, that of the Government Actuary's Department), group personal pensions are 'employer-sponsored pensions', but not 'occupational pensions'.

A marked reduction in both the number of private occupational pension schemes and the proportion of open private occupational schemes has occurred in recent years. In 2000, there were 105,000 private occupational pension schemes; by 2007, that number had fallen to 54,114, with a significant proportion accepting no new members (GAD, 2008a). In 1995, 4.9 million belonged to defined benefit schemes, while 1 million belonged to defined contribution schemes – a clear ratio of 4.9:1 in favour of defined benefit schemes. By 2007, the corresponding figures were 1.3 million belonging to defined benefit schemes and 0.8 million belonging to defined contribution schemes, reducing the ratio to just 1.6:1 in favour of defined benefit schemes.

Personal pensions

Prior to 1988, direct saving with pension companies through Retirement Annuity Contracts was possible, but was effectively the reserve of the richer strata of self-employed and other workers with no occupational pension. The Fowler reforms encouraged flexible, fully portable personal pensions and employers were prohibited from compelling employees to join their occupational pension scheme; the possibilities for contracting out of SERPS were greatly increased and its value undercut. It became possible to be contracted out of SERPS to defined contribution occupational pension schemes, but more significantly individuals were permitted to use personal pensions to contract themselves out from SERPS. In this case, instead of building up a SERPS entitlement, individuals would receive rebates into a personal pension. Thus contracting out was extended from being something that employers could do on behalf of employees, if they provided an appropriate occupational pension, to also being something that individuals could decide to do *for themselves* if they had or chose to start a so-called 'appropriate personal pension' (APP). A personal pension could even be taken purely on the strength of such rebates. There was no obligation for employees who had contracted out to personal pension schemes to pay any money themselves into the scheme. Moreover, generous incentives were provided through the payment of additional rebates into personal pension schemes if individuals contracted out of SERPS.

The effect of these reforms was to create a mass personal pension system almost from nowhere. The generous incentives designed to 'kick-start' the personal pensions sector apparently succeeded 'beyond the government's wildest dreams' (Timmins, 2001, p 400). Contemporary Department of Social Security estimates had it that, by 1992, 5.5 million people had contracted out of SERPS into a personal pension (DSS, 2000), representing one of the most significant, if least recognised, privatisations of the Thatcher era. From then on, growth in contracted-out membership of APPs was partially checked. Incentives to contract out were reduced from 1993/94. A mis-selling scandal also broke, as significant numbers of people were thought to have been the victims of high-pressure sales practices and wrongly advised to start personal pensions. Indeed, the Securities and Investments Board, the regulator, estimated that the number of pensions mis-sold could be as high as one and a half million, and ordered that all personal pensions sold between 1988 and 1994 be reviewed and in cases of mis-selling individuals be appropriately compensated. After eight years, the review process had resulted in approximately 1 million offers of redress. Compensation cases were restricted to mis-selling with reference to occupational pension schemes. It did not cover the significant numbers of those with low earnings or older workers who did not in general stand to benefit from contracting out of SERPS into APPs but were advised to do so. Research suggests that as many as 63% of personal pension contributors were apparently unsuitable for a personal pension in the mid-1990s (Ginn and Arber, 2000).

The first phase of New Labour pension reform, the 1999 Welfare Reform and Pensions Act, addressed personal pension reform. Stakeholder pensions were introduced from 2001. Stakeholder pensions are a type of personal pension and are thus defined contribution schemes, but are importantly characterised by compulsory minimum standards, a distinct governance structure and guaranteed workplace access. Stakeholder pensions have stipulated maximum administration charges (initially set at 1% of fund value), carry no entry and exit charges, and are flexible to the extent that the minimum contribution level is low (£20 per month) and contributors can start and stop contributing as they wish. Moreover, since their introduction, employers with five or more employees who do not offer occupational pensions have been required to give employees access to a stakeholder scheme through the workplace and, on behalf of those employees choosing to join the scheme, make deductions from pay and pass them on to the scheme provider. The aim of stakeholder pensions was to encourage saving for retirement amongst those on low to middle incomes without occupational pensions. However, according to analysis by Chung et al (2005) and Disney et al (2007), the introduction of stakeholder pensions had no effect on take-up of private pensions among such middle earners. Those who did take up stakeholder pensions

– over one million people by 2002 – appeared to be individuals switching from other pension schemes rather than people with no private pension coverage to start with (House of Commons Treasury Committee, 2006). In fact, overall, taking stakeholder pensions into account, private pension coverage has been in decline in the 21st century. By 2006, the Select Committee on Treasury had concluded that 'stakeholder pensions have not been successful in halting the decline of non-state pension provision among middle earners' (House of Commons Treasury Committee, 2006, para. 21).

The Pensions Commission discussed earlier in the chapter has reviewed pension provision and has offered a generally pessimistic view of the future of pensioner income in the UK if present trends continue. Its report found non-state pension saving to be in 'significant decline' and around nine million people were estimated to be under-saving for their retirement; without policy change, it predicted, the medium- to long-term future would produce poorer pensioners and greater inequality (Pensions Commission, 2004). A second report published the following year recommended 'the creation of a low cost, national funded pension savings scheme into which individuals will be automatically enrolled, but with the right to opt out, with a matching level of compulsory matching employer contributions and delivering the opportunity to save for a pension at a low annual management charge' (Pensions Commission, 2005, p 18).

It is believed that the approach of 'auto-enrolment' can succeed by overcoming the behavioural barriers to saving among under-savers without introducing compulsion that would fail to allow for the diversity of individual's preferences and circumstances. The Committee's report was met with a broad consensus in favour of the approach of 'auto-enrolment' and this is the approach embodied in the 2006 White Paper, *Security in retirement: Towards a new pensions system* (DWP, 2006c), and the subsequent 2007 Pensions Act. From 2012, a new scheme of 'personal accounts' will be introduced in accordance with the principle recommendations of the Pensions Commission.

Longer lives and longer working lives

Chapter Three outlined increasing life expectancy and the growth in older people as a percentage of the population, indicating that fertility and immigration trends may well be inadequate to keep dependency ratios constant. Pension systems must adapt to an ageing population in order to be sustainable, as funding the additional years of life after retirement requires more contributions and a larger pension pot. This is true of both the state system, based on 'pay as you go' transfers from the working population to older people, and of funded private pensions.

It is important to distinguish between pension age and retirement. Pension age is a set condition of entitlement to pension, so that pensions start on reaching that age. Retirement is the period in the latter part of the lifetime when a person no longer works. There are thus two overlapping aims to ensuring sustainability in pension provision: first, delaying entitlement to pensions and second, promoting later retirement.

Raising the pension age has been approached in three ways. First, the pension ages of men and women have been set to equalise at 65 by 1995, legislation that raises the pension age for women incrementally over a 10-year period beginning in 2010. Second, the general pension age for both men and women will be raised to 68 from 2044 as a response to general financing of pension provision. Finally, the de facto 'pension age' that exists in means-tested provision for both men and women based on the age they qualify for Pension Credit and no longer have to be treated as looking for work will additionally be incrementally increased to match the raising of the formal equalisation of contributory pension ages in 2020.

It is this latter lower age of entitlement to means-tested provision as an older person, or 'pensioner', that manifests the bigger problem since the 1980s of increasing levels of early retirement. Recent estimates show that just 53% of women are employed at age 59 and only 42% of men at age 64 (Pensions Commission, 2004, p 34). In the 1950s and 1960s, the economic activity of those aged 65 and over fell, but after the economic restructuring of the late 1970s and 1980s falling employment rates among men aged 50-64 became prominent (Pensions Commission, 2004, p 34). Labour market demand, and the skill profiles and relative productivity of older men are important driving factors, but policy also helped to increase early retirement. Occupational pensions were often paid early on the grounds of ill health as part of redundancy packages. The benefit system adapted in the 1980s reduced the claimant count of unemployment by allowing 60-year-old men to claim without being considered unemployed, as discussed in Chapter Seven. Invalidity Benefit and, albeit less so, Incapacity Benefit, catered for older non-employed people with ill health, as discussed in Chapter Eight.

The recent 15-year period of economic growth that began in 1993 and ended in 2008 has seen a slow but steady improvement in the employment rate for people over 50 (Hotopp, 2005), with a consequent rise in the average retirement age (Pensions Commission, 2004). Again, labour demand has combined with a deliberate policy shift in favour of encouraging employment among people aged 50 and over. In contrast to the 1980s and 1990s, there are a number of areas in which the benefit system now reflects a desire to encourage employment among the over-50s. Most obviously, there is the 50-plus element of Working Tax Credit, which is payable to those over 50 returning to employment after an absence of at least six months. This is a part of the wider New Deal 50 Plus scheme, which also allows for training grants and personal advice and support in finding employment. Incapacity Benefit conditions were changed to reduce benefit if occupational pensions are in payment. Since 2006, employment legislation has made it illegal for employers to discriminate against employees or jobseekers on grounds of age.

Model families and retirement

How would our model families, the Lowes and the Meades, fare with pensions under the 1979, 1997 and 2008 rules? We obviously have to 'freeze' the rules for the whole lifetime as they existed in these years and additionally we base our profiles at the individual level. These assumptions together allow us to simply profile the change in policy-related outcomes most clearly.

Mr Lowe

First, we consider pension outcomes for Mr Lowe, a single man with a lifetime history of low-paid work (working for 50% of the median male wage); and for Ms Lowe, his female counterpart, who has a lifetime history of low-paid work (working for 50% of the median female wage) but one interrupted by some years of caring responsibility. Let us look at them in turn.

Figure 9.6 illustrates outcomes for Mr Lowe at the age of 70 following a lifetime lived out under each policy system but held in contemporary income and price levels, thus not modelling uprating policy. We continue to presume that the Lowes are tenants and, given the continued problem of affording rent at the margins of basic pension and social assistance across all the comparison years, it is the most illuminating to think of income in after housing cost (AHC) terms and in constant 2008 prices. To illustrate the outcomes of the 2007 Pension Act, we show the results for a further version of the 2008 system based on the assumption that the proposals are fully implemented and this result is shown as '2008M', or the mature 2008 system.

In general, the use of net income after housing cost assumptions gives a more rounded idea of overall policy outcomes. Studying Figure 9.6 and looking across all years, we see Mr Lowe paying no income tax in retirement under any system and the contemporary real level of basic pension he receives stays at approximately the same level[6]. Turning to the pension income package in more detail, under the 1979 system Mr Lowe receives a full original SERPS pension alongside his basic state pension. However, this does not clear him of the need for means-tested assistance towards his rent and rates. Under the 1997 system, he receives basic retirement pension and reduced SERPS. Higher housing costs under the 1997 assumptions leave him with a lower AHC income in real terms. Under the current 2008 system, the basic retirement pension is supplemented by S2P that for Mr Lowe is more generous than SERPS in 1979 and 1997. This S2P means that the savings credit form of Pension Credit is payable in addition to means-tested assistance towards his rent and council tax. Turning to the 'future' and a mature version of 2008, outcomes appear even better, subject to our assumptions about constant rent and council tax. In addition to his basic pension, the now flat-rate S2P accrual system combined with the extra three years he now works (we presume the pension age and thus retirement has moved to 68) provides a higher level of

Figure 9.6: Mr Lowe aged 70 – pension outcomes

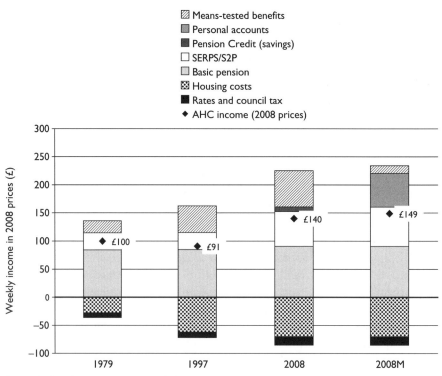

Source: Authors' calculations using LOIS.

Notes: No inflation over each hypothetical lifetime.

state second pension than earlier years and versions. When we also assume that Mr Lowe has been making contributions to the personal accounts scheme since the age of 22 we estimate on currently available information that this will lead to a pension of around £60 a week from paying 2.3% of his lifetime earnings in personal accounts contributions. The combination gives him the highest income in retirement of the four profiles.

It is worth stressing a series of caveats at this point as these apply to both Mr Lowe and subsequent profiles in the remainder of this chapter. First, this profile is illustrative only and not designed to be representative. Second, the hypothetical individuals live out their entire lives under the systems of our comparison years, so that, for example, the 1979 results for Mr Lowe are representative of a hypothetical individual building up entitlement to SERPS under its original rules for a whole working lifetime. Our results illustrate the outcomes that arise from extrapolating the intentions of policy makers in our comparison years and assume full take-up.

Ms Lowe

Ms Lowe's lifetime is based on 50% of female median earnings and we assume that she takes a total of 15 years out of paid work to engage in full-time childcare. We keep these assumptions constant to make consistent comparisons and Figure 9.7 shows the resulting profiles. Ms Lowe receives a full basic state pension despite her absence from paid work in each year due to home responsibilities protection or credited contributions. Breaks in earnings history and her lower earnings level, however, make her entitlement to SERPS under the 1979 and 1997 systems much lower than Mr Lowe's. Under S2P rules in the 2008 system, Ms Lowe fares much better from both the underlying greater generosity to the low paid and continuing to build up entitlement when she is at home caring for a child aged under six. Under the mature 2008 system (2008M), this coverage is extended to cover periods when she is caring for a child under the age of 12. We also assume under the mature 2008 system that Ms Lowe works until age 68. Ms Lowe will pay 2.1% of her lifetime earnings in personal accounts contributions to achieve a £25 a week personal account pension in the mature 2008 result. As

Figure 9.7: Ms Lowe – pension outcomes

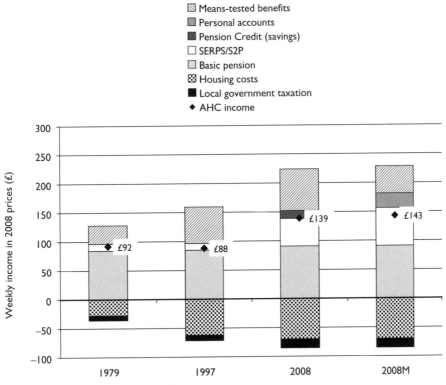

Source: Authors' calculations using LOIS.

Notes: No inflation over each hypothetical lifetime.

an individual, Ms Lowe gets help from means-tested benefits under each of the four systems but receives a higher income under the 2008 rules and the lowest under the 1997 system.

Of course, in reality the Lowes would be treated as a couple for means testing, but seeing the Lowes as individuals provides us with a measure of outputs from pensions and other elements of the different tax and benefit systems and allows us to compare these with contemporary social assistance.

Mr Meade

For median earners, we change our assumptions about the balance of state and private pension provision. Both Mr Meade and Ms Meade are profiled as individuals using the same assumptions about inflation and constant 1979, 1997 and 2008 policies as the earlier profiles of the Lowes, but we consider the outcomes of joining either an occupational pension or joining a private pension and contrast this to relying solely on state provision. We also assume that the Meades are owner-occupiers and at the age of 70 have no outstanding mortgage. We show their incomes before housing costs (BHC) to reflect these assumptions. We keep the sets of assumptions on occupational and private pensions constant across the comparison years to remove effects of interest and annuity rate differences. Unlike the Lowes, the Meades income in retirement is often high enough to be subject to income tax.

Figure 9.8 depicts the outcomes of three scenarios for Mr Meade's retirement. In the first and most unlikely scenario, Mr Meade relies solely on state pension. If so, in 1979 Mr Meade would receive not only considerable SERPS in addition to his basic pension but also a small rate rebate, and he would also pay income tax[7]. In 1997, a smaller SERPS entitlement would actually not leave him that much worse off than in 1979, as he would receive no help with council tax but would pay less income tax. In 2008, his state second pension would be higher, but he would additionally qualify for Council Tax Benefit, making his income here the highest of the three comparison years.

The more realistic scenario is that Mr Meade joins a private pension scheme to better safeguard living standards in retirement. The profile of Mr Meade's pension under the occupational pension scenario is based on a defined benefit occupational pension scheme into which he contributes for 44 years to grant him a pension of 55% (which is 44 times 1/80th) of his (final) earnings[8]. We hold these assumptions constant across each year, but use contemporary median male earnings in each estimate. This means that increasing real earnings between 1979, 1997 and 2008 affect the outcomes even when we assume no earnings or price inflation over the frozen lifetimes lived in each policy year. Basic state retirement pension is roughly the same real level for the three comparison years and, given that the different levels of occupational pension reflect the different levels of contemporary earnings, the only significant changes in pension outcomes

Figure 9.8: Mr Meade – pension outcomes

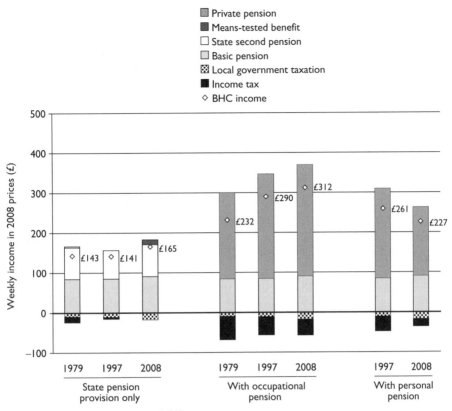

Source: Authors' calculations using LOIS.

Notes: No inflation over each hypothetical lifetime.

from policy reflect changing tax. Mr Meade faces highest rates of income tax in 1979[9], partly reflecting the steeper tapering off of age allowances in that year compared with the others.

Turning to look at personal pensions, the situation in 1979 does not lead to a sensible profile. Mr Meade would not be able to opt out of SERPS, as rules to do so did not cover such pensions, so any profile would show the combined effect of both SERPS and a private pension – and very high pension levels that would be difficult to interpret as an illustrative case. For these reasons, results are shown for the 1997 and 2008 systems only. Our estimates of personal pension outcomes are on the assumptions of Mr Meade continually contracting out of SERPS/S2P and paying 6% of his earnings into a personal pension on top of the contracted-out rebate that also goes towards building up his pension fund. The personal pension scheme's parameters are constant across the two profiles and have been chosen to represent a typical personal pension scheme[10]. As can be seen, Mr Meade's personal pension income is in real terms smaller under the 2008 system than the 1997 system. Given that underlying earnings growth should be reflected in pension outcomes, why does this occur? The first reason is that while inputs into the pension remain constant on higher earnings, the annuity will be calculated differently in 2008 to 1997 to reflect long life expectancy. The bigger pot from real earnings growth has to stretch further. The main difference, though, stems from changing levels of contracted-out National Insurance rebates. For employees, these were higher in 1997 (1.32% of earnings) than in 2008 (1.27%). However, it is the change in employer rebates that makes the biggest difference, falling from 3.01% of Mr Meade's earnings to 1.11% in 2008.

Ms Meade

Figure 9.9 shows pensions for a single median female earner, Ms Meade, who takes 15 years out of paid employment to undertake childcare. Private pension provision is clearly unsympathetic to time away from the labour market and no entitlement builds while she is engaged in full-time childcare. Turning to look at the outcomes from solely relying on state provision, we see that second state pension entitlements are highest under the 2008 system, repeating early findings for the Lowes and showing the impact of S2P compared with the earlier versions of SERPS. Additionally, in 2008, Ms Meade would have such S2P entitlement recognised by the savings credit element of Pension Credit. Moving on to consider occupational pension outcomes, the underlying increases in real earnings clearly increase the value of defined benefits based on final earnings over the three systems but in 2008 there is additional state pension entitlement from S2P that recognises Ms Meade's time out of the labour market looking after children[11]. We estimate that means-tested help with rates in 1979 and 2008 would also be available in fairly small amounts (and thus subject to lower likelihood of take-up). Finally, turning to outcomes with personal pension, and again these are only modelled for 1997 and 2008, we see that Ms Meade receives less from her private pension in 2008 due to the factors of extended life expectancy and smaller National Insurance rebates that we saw applying to Mr Meade. However, in 2008, there are compensating state provisions that make up and exceed these shortfalls. S2P is received alongside some savings credit and council tax rebates. The 2008 system clearly has advantages for median earning women with interrupted working lifetimes when it comes to pension outcomes in retirement on these assumptions.

These four sets of pension results give a fairly clear picture of how the underlying assumptions of the 1979, 1997 and 2008 systems work alongside tax and social assistance benefits, but they are a partial picture for many reasons. First, we have not shown the higher-income Moores here, as they look very much like higher earning versions of the Meades and illustrate little underlying policy differences at this juncture. Second, we have shown our model earners as single people in order to clearly show the links between earnings levels and individual entitlements. In reality, our male and female lives overlap and join in long relationships and their

Figure 9.9: Ms Meade – retirement outcomes

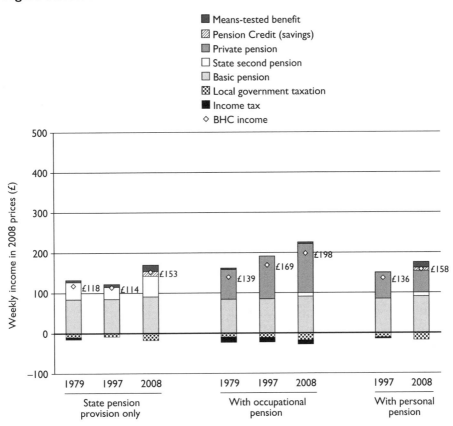

Source: Authors' calculations using LOIS.

pension outcomes will be joint ones. The other side of the coin is that we have not shown the outcomes of saving for retirement on income during working years and how this relates to earnings histories and family composition – clearly part of the pension story despite it being seen as a working age profile. Once again, we are trying to reconcile bits of the life story to fit the policy compartments that keep forming inadequate pigeonholes. It is time to turn to the lifetime perspective in this book's third and final part.

Summary

This chapter has considered the changing policies on pensions and retirement and benefits for death and survivorship.

• Basic flat-rate state pension has fallen in relative terms from 20% to 13% of average earnings, but has seen a small real rise in value since 2003.

- Social assistance for pensioners has, however, been at levels above that of basic pension since 1988 and has recently moved from 110% of state pension levels in 1997 to 137% in 2008.
- Secondary state pensions to supplement the basic pension have formed the main area of policy reform since the 1970s. The SERPS system was twice reformed by the Conservatives to make it less generous and then replaced by New Labour with S2P in 1999, which is more generous to those with the lowest earnings.
- Third-tier pensions from private sources were dominated by occupational pensions run on defined benefits as a percentage of final salary. Private personal pensions were reinvigorated in the 1980s through subsidies and mis-sold for a period to those who would have been better off remaining in SERPS or occupational schemes.
- New proposals for a state-subsidised, third-tier private personal pension aimed at low to modest incomes – 'personal accounts' – will come into force after pension reform in 2007.
- Outcomes from defined contribution private pensions rely on the performance of the fund, particularly at the point of retirement, annuity rates and estimated life expectancy. Annuities are not typically linked to rise with prices, although a large range of products have emerged in recent years. Outcomes from defined benefit occupational pensions tend to be price protected and based on earnings and give higher levels of outcomes because of employer subsidies in many instances.

Notes

[1] In addition, as noted in Chapter Seven, any SERPS entitlement built up (or any notional entitlement) became payable in the event of a claimant receiving Invalidity Benefit.

[2] The Fowler review proposed the phased abolition of SERPS and rejected proposals merely to restrict the scheme (DHSS, 1985a).

[3] In terms of housing costs for mortgages, 'pensioners' claiming social assistance can receive support towards mortgage interest payments without the waiting period that applies to claimants under 60.

[4] Free dental treatment is available for over-60s in Scotland and Wales but not in England.

[5] These are distinct from cold weather payments, receipt of which is dependent on receipt of a qualifying benefit along with other conditions.

[6] If inflation were taken into account over time rather than solely between the comparison years, then the 1979 and 2008M schemes would show the outcome of higher basic pension that had been uprated with earnings.

[7] The old age tax allowance was tapered more steeply in 1979 than in 1997 and 2008 and Mr Moore pays more income tax partly as a result of this.

[8] In the simple inflation-free world with no earnings progression that we are modelling at this stage, Mr Meade's final salary is the same as the salary he receives throughout his life. More complexity is introduced to the model in Part Three.

[9] We do not make any allowances for marriage, as estimates here reflect a single person.

[10] A real interest rate of 2%, an annual administration charge of 1% of fund value, 5% commission for annuity purchase and an annuity rate of 2.5%.

[11] This is calculated on the underlying assumption that she maximises her entitlement and contracts in and out as appropriate.

Part Three

A lifetime of difference?

TEN

Taxes, benefits and national profiles of inequality and poverty

In this chapter, the discussion shifts from one of descriptive policy formation and design towards one of analysis of outcomes and a comparison of policy between the systems in 1979, 1997 and 2008. This chapter acts as a bridge between the earlier discussion and our model lifetime analysis in Chapters Eleven to Fourteen. We consider the aggregate empirical profiles of policy outcomes over time for the whole of Britain and then illustrate how these will inform our later model lifetime analysis.

Policy change and the generation of change

The previous two sections of this book have described how far British social, economic and political life have changed since the 1970s and how social policy has changed alongside these other aspects. This third part of the book analyses changing policy systems by comparing the income and tax packages available in three key years 1979, 1997 and 2008 using a lifetime perspective. We now have the description of policy change as it affects the different parts of the lifetime from Part Two and it is time to align the lifetime view of policy and take our analysis forward. In Part Three, there are three main areas that most concern us:

- *The incidence of taxes and benefits.* How much is paid in tax and how much is received in benefits and how has this changed between 1979, 1997 and 2008?
- *The outcomes that arise from the different policy systems.* How does the changing incidence of taxes and benefits alter incomes? Comparing outcomes means both considering how net and gross income change for each individual (and how this cumulated over their hypothetical lifetime) and comparing such incomes in a relative way – placing them in the contemporary income distribution. This approach to outcomes means that we can look at the changing levels and incidence of relative poverty and other points in the income distribution since the 1970s and place our hypothetical lifetimes in such contexts.
- *Inequality.* Finally, we can then look at our low, median and higher earning families over the lifetime and see whether they are drifting further apart or not. Are the low-earning Lowes, the median-earning Meades and the high-earnings Moores more or less unequal over time and what are the roles of taxes and benefits?

The incidence of taxes and benefits

Earlier chapters have discussed how the design of taxation, social security and benefits and other elements of social policy has changed since the 1970s. What has been the impact of these changes on incomes and how has such impact changed?

Measures of incidence and of the extent of redistribution require the population to be ranked by income using equivalised household income that takes account of household size and composition[1]. The use of household-based incomes and the process of making incomes comparable across different households requires some basic explanation. The income distribution of the whole British population is profiled. It is statistically produced from a sample that for many years was the Family Expenditure Survey, which was replaced by the Expenditure and Food Survey from 2001. From 1992, the Family Resources Survey (FRS) has taken over as the main source of analysis of the income distribution and in particular the Households Below Average Income (HBAI) statistical time series that captures poverty incidence.

The use of equivalence scales allows us to compare and rank incomes of households of different size and composition. These scales adjust per capita income assumptions to allow for income to reflect underlying differences in needs by adjusting for economies of scale and recognising that adults and children have differing levels of need. The scaling of adult needs to allow for economies of scale recognises that co-resident people share some elements of costs experienced jointly so that, for instance, two people's needs are not twice but one and a fraction times those of a single householder. The scaling of children's needs currently adopts an assumption that children have equal needs as adults when they reach the age of 14. This is so in the 'modified OECD' (Organisation for Economic Co-operation and Development) equivalence scale that is adopted by the government in HBAI and poverty measurement and is adopted by us in the lifetime profiling of poverty in Chapters Twelve to Fourteen. Government statistics are not, however, consistent in their use of equivalence scales. The Office for National Statistics (ONS) analysis of tax and benefit incidence to which we now turn uses a different approach.

Like its predecessors, the ONS produces an annual independent assessment of the effects of taxes and benefits on British income distribution. At the time of writing, the most recent of these considers the programmes in place in 2006/07 (Jones, 2008) but the series goes back to 1961/62. Capturing the redistributive impact of taxes and benefits requires some careful and particular definitions of income and a clear logical sequence in estimating impact. The ONS approach is as follows:

- first, *original income* is that sourced from non-state activity – the gross earnings from employment and self-employment, investment income, occupational and other private pensions such as annuities;

- second, *gross income* is calculated by adding together all components of *original income* plus *transfers* from the state[2] for all members of the household;
- third, *disposable income* is gross income minus income tax, employee's National Insurance contributions and council tax (rates in Northern Ireland);
- fourth, *post-tax income* is disposable income minus indirect taxes paid by household members (duties on alcoholic drinks, tobacco, petrol, oil, betting, customs (import) duties, motor vehicle duties, air passenger duty and stamp duty, consumption taxes such as VAT, insurance premium tax, driving and television licenses and national lottery purchases equivalent to the distribution fund);
- fifth and finally, ONS analysis adds benefits in kind from non-cash social policy provision to come to a definition of '*final income*'; we will not use such analysis other than to point to its influence on underlying disposable income.

Figure 10.1 shows annual income in 2006 for each income quintile group ranked by disposable income. The incidence of transfers alongside original income clearly shows that transfers are disproportionately paid to those with lowest incomes and are thus progressive. The lowest decile receives £5,400 or 60% of gross income from transfers compared with £1,500 or just 2% of gross income for the highest decile group. Direct taxes show a clear pro-poor profile in the amounts but the lowest decile group, paying over £1,000 in direct tax (income tax, National Insurance and council tax), is paying 12% of its gross income in tax compared with a tax take of £24,000 or 25% of gross income for the highest decile group. The position of indirect taxation is less clear and the net amount of indirect taxes paid by the lowest decile group is more than £3,000 or 34% of gross income, compared with the £8,300 or only 9% of gross income paid by the

Figure 10.1: Incidence of taxes and cash transfers, 2006

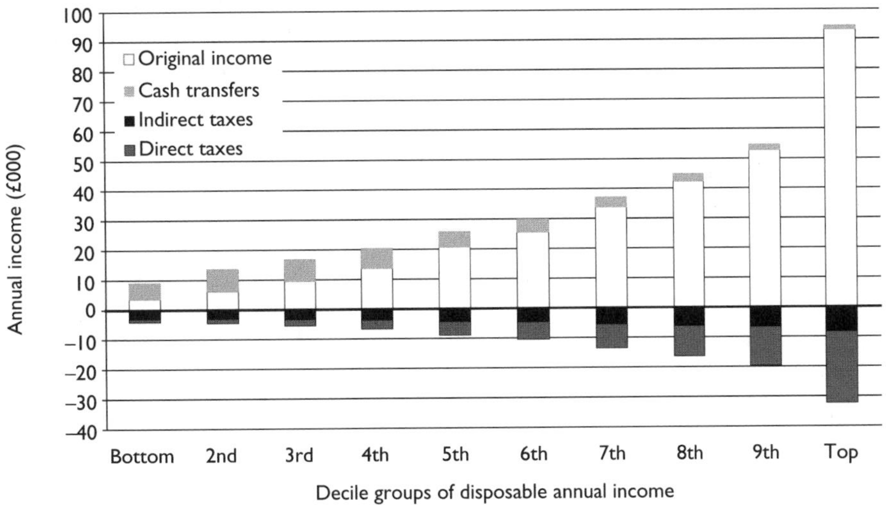

Source: Jones (2008, Table 14)

highest decile group. Transfers are thus the most progressive in impact, followed by direct taxation, while indirect taxation is, arguably, regressive – taking a higher percentage of income from the poor.

Overall, if we put these three elements of transfers and taxes together, we get a picture of overall progressivity of the tax and benefit system in 2006. We now move to compare 1979, 1997 and 2006 incidence. The following three figures show the results in consistent measures for incidence of taxes and benefits for these three years. Figure 10.2a shows transfers, Figure 10.2b shows taxation and Figure 10.2c shows the overall net impact when transfers and taxation are taken together. Transfer incidence has a roughly common shared profile for the top three quintiles across all three years, with 1979 having a slightly higher proportional impact on the higher deciles. The incidence of transfers in the middle of the distribution, from the third to the sixth decile groups inclusive, shows 1979 as the least generous, as the transfers reduce steeply from 44% of income for the third decile group down to 21%, 15% and then 10% for the sixth. This drop is not as steep for the 1997 and 2006 systems, which are very similar, with 1997 more generous overall. Transfer receipt at the bottom two decile groups shows a clear ranking, with the highest incidence occurring in 1979 – 87% of all gross income for the poorest and 72% of such income for the next lowest decile groups. By 1997, these proportions have fallen to 71% and 62% respectively and by 2008 they have fallen further, to 60% and 55% respectively.

Figure 10.2b shows how direct taxes differ markedly to indirect taxes over the three years. The overall pattern is that direct taxation is clearly progressive – the slope tilts upward as income rises and taxation takes a larger proportion of gross income. Indirect taxation is the opposite – the slope tilts downwards except for 1979, when indirect taxation is mostly 'flat', ranging from 17% of gross income for the poorest to 15% for the richest quintile groups with slightly higher incidence in the middle of the distribution. The move to increase indirect taxation in the early 1980s and subsequently, primarily from increased VAT, has disproportionately hit the lowest decile groups, of whom the poorest pay such taxes proportional to 33% to 34% of their gross income, and the second poorest around 23%, compared with only 10% to 8% for the highest decile group.

The incidence of direct taxation shown in Figure 10.2b clearly shows that the 1979 system taxed the middle of the distribution more than subsequent systems in 1997 and 2006. The higher direct tax take for 2006 compared with 1997 for middle and higher incomes comes largely from higher council tax rather than changes to income tax rates. At the bottom of the distribution, the lowest two decile groups have consistently paid 11% to 12% of gross income as direct tax over all three comparison years.

The overall effect of taxes and benefits taken together is shown in Figure 10.2c. The seventh to top decile groups are treated almost exactly the same over the three systems.

Figure 10.2a: Tax and benefit incidence by decile groups, 1979, 1997 and 2006 – transfers

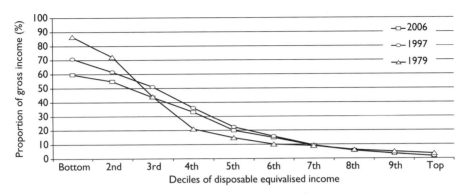

Figure 10.2b: Tax and benefit incidence by decile groups, 1979, 1997 and 2006 – taxes

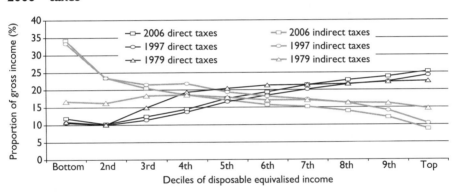

Figure 10.2c: Tax and benefit incidence by decile groups, 1979, 1997 and 2006 – net effect of transfers and all taxes

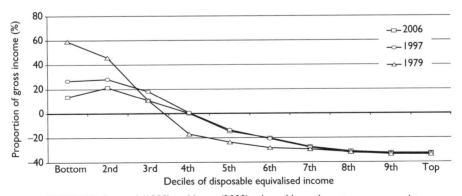

Source: ONS (1981), Stuttard (1998) and Jones (2008), adapted by authors to ensure consistency.

These results, with lower taxation for the better off and higher indirect taxes for the poorest combined with lower transfer income, have been confirmed by micro-simulation by Redmond and colleagues, who compared the systems of 1978/79 and 1996/97 using constant population assumptions to isolate the impact of changes in taxes and benefits (Redmond et al, 1998). The micro-simulation approach allows systems to be run on consistent population samples – the 1978/79 system on both contemporary and 1996/97 population samples. This isolates the changes that occur in incidence due to changes in underlying population composition of different parts of the income distribution. Such changes are crucial to understanding and interpreting the changing incidence of taxes and benefits shown in Figure 10.2.

There is a crucial point to note here for later chapters that look specifically and solely at income-based taxes and transfers using lifetime simulations. Such simulations will not capture indirect taxation or benefits in kind. The first of these is a significant omission that results from our methodology resting on relying on income levels and earnings histories to estimate the incidence of taxes and benefits. We will have to add in the context of indirect taxation to these results.

Figure 10.3 shows changing household composition across the income distribution in 1979 and 2006. Retired older people used to make up 80% of the bottom quintile of the distribution in 1979. Their relative position had increased greatly by 2006, when they comprised only 38% of the bottom quintile. This is largely a cohort effect, as those workers who had employer-based defined benefit occupational pensions have retired on much higher incomes than their counterparts, who built up smaller pensions prior to the Second World War. Households with children make up one third of the poorest quintile in 2006 but only 10% in 1979. Lone parents, 3% of all households, were mostly in the middle of the distribution in 1979. By 2006, they had doubled in overall incidence but were far more represented in the lower deciles of the population – 20% of the poorest quintile. The higher proportion of working age households without children in the poorest quintile in 2006 compared with 1979 reflects the higher incidence of non-employment (workless households) and of a higher level of low-quality (part-time, low-paid) employment.

The changes associated with the lifecycle have great importance but are also related to crucial changes in the origins of income across the income distribution. The move of pensioners upwards and away from the very bottom of the income distribution over time means that state pensions become less heavily concentrated in the bottom two deciles and that earnings from wages and self-employment now spread further down the income distribution, a quarter of the bottom two decile groups' incomes in 1996/97, rising to 30% and 34% in 2006/07 compared with 5% and 13% in 1979 (ONS, 1981; Jones, 2008). The other notable trend is for other forms of state transfers to grow in incidence in the later years, as families with children and workless households increasingly rely on transfers, often means-tested, at the bottom of the income distribution.

Figure 10.3: Household composition by income quintile, 1979 and 2006/07

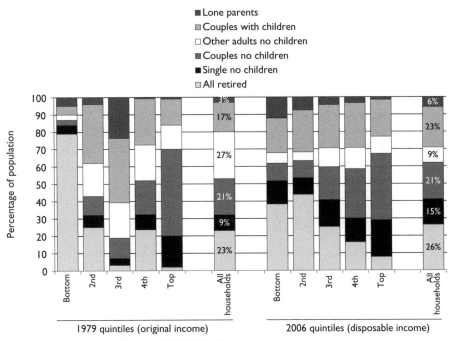

Source: ONS (1981, Table U); Jones (2008, Table 22).

Our approach using model lifetimes will look solely at incomes and direct transfers and thus does not include the changing impact of benefits in kind, services and subsidies provided as part of social policy alongside or in place of transfers. One clear change in policy since 1979 has been the revolution in provision and finance of social housing. Chapter Two showed how in the early 1980s the Thatcher government both encouraged social housing to be sold to sitting tenants of means and moved subsidies away from local authorities to other social landlords, primarily housing associations. At the same time, it replaced housing subsidies, to the 'bricks and mortar' of buildings in the form of lower rents, with income-related subsidy through Housing Benefit. Moreover, Chapter Six showed how eligibility levels and tapers for housing benefits have changed over time to reduce generosity. In 1979, 60% of the poorest and 40% of the next poorest deciles were in social housing (primarily local authority dwellings) and social tenure extended up the income distribution, with 18% to 19% of the richest deciles also living in social housing (ONS, 1981). We know that benefit support with rent (through both Supplementary Benefit paying rents and from rent rebates) added an aggregate total that was 55% of all general subsidies to housing in 1979 (Hills, 1998, Table 5A1). By 2006/07, social rented tenure had fallen to cover only a quarter of the lowest decile group and between 31% and 34% of the second and third decile groups respectively. General housing subsidies had fallen close to zero, representing only around 0.3% of the lowest decile groups' gross income (Jones, 2008). Housing Benefit spending had remained roughly constant or had fallen slightly across the poorest deciles – 8% of the poorest, 7% of the second poorest and 5% of the third poorest deciles' gross incomes on average. One way of partly addressing this issue is to use measures of income based on an after housing cost definition. We return to this point when discussing poverty and the methodological assumptions of the hypothetical model lifetimes later.

Other elements of social wage, from health and education, have a less direct effect on disposable income. Sefton's analyses of 1997 and 2002 allow a consistent comparison of the change in distribution of elements of the social wage between 1979, 1996/97 and 2001/02 and these show greater targeting of spending to lower-income groups in general (Sefton, 1997, 2002).

Income inequality and the incidence of taxes and benefits

So far, our discussion of the aggregate changes in the incidence of taxes and benefits has shown increasing regressivity resulting from lower rates of income taxation for higher incomes and the introduction of higher reliance on indirect consumption taxes that disproportionately tax low-income households. We have, however, seen some changes that have increased income-based housing subsidies to poorer households to replace benefits in kind and a marked increase in pro-poor spending on health and education over the period since 1979. What is the aggregate effect of these changes on the dispersion of income?

Figure 10.4 shows the gini coefficient over time from 1978 to 2006/07 based on four cumulative definitions of income to isolate the effect of taxes and benefits on income inequality. First, when we look at original income (before transfers), we see that underlying income inequality has risen significantly over time. In 1978, the gini coefficient for original income is 0.43; 18 years later, in 1996/97, it is 0.53, a rise of over 23%. Nine years further on, in 2006/07, the gini coefficient is 0.52, suggesting that inequality in original incomes has flattened out over the term of New Labour's tenure despite the evidence in Chapter Three that *earnings* inequality has risen. Inequality of 'gross income', including the overall progressive profile of transfers, is obviously lower, with the gini coefficient falling to 0.28 in 1978. The rate at which transfer payments reduce inequality over time will be subject to cyclical fluctuations and other changing reasons for demand for transfers as well as reforms to the benefit system. This means that transfers did most to reduce inequality on their own in the mid-1980s. Since then, the gross income inequality profile has remained roughly parallel with original income inequality and the gini coefficients in 1997/98 and 2006/07 were 0.37 and 0.38 respectively.

The greatest impact on inequality comes from the combination of direct taxes on income and transfers, producing 'disposable income'. In 1978, disposable income had a gini coefficient of 0.26, the lowest measurement of income inequality across

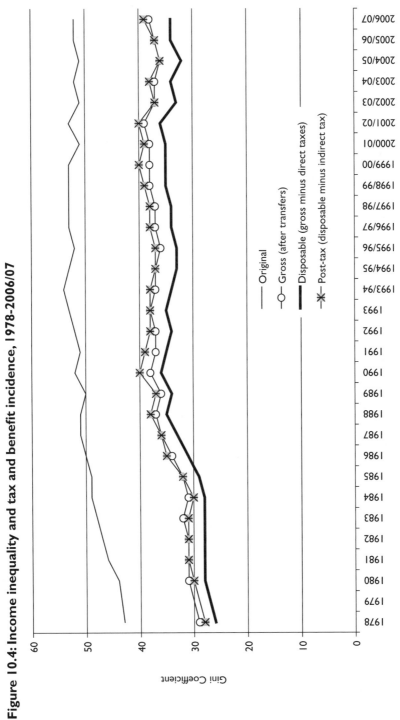

Figure 10.4: Income inequality and tax and benefit incidence, 1978-2006/07

Source: Harris (1999, Table 2); Jones (2008, Table 27).

the whole period. By 1996/97, inequality in disposable incomes had risen to 0.34, equivalent to a 31% increase. When we compare that to the increase in inequality in original incomes mentioned earlier, at 23% we see that the Conservatives are associated not only with an increase in original income inequality but also with an even higher rise in inequality in disposable incomes. Since 1996/97, the gini coefficient for disposable incomes has remained largely flat, at around 0.34, once more suggesting that growth in inequality has stabilised but not reduced since the mid-1990s.

Equality gained from the combination of transfers and direct taxation is eroded by the effect of indirect and consumption taxes. Inequality in post-tax incomes produced a gini coefficient of 0.28 in 1978 and this rose to 0.38 by 1996/97, a 38% increase, outstripping the rates of increase in inequality in both original and disposable income under the Conservatives. Since 1997/98, inequality in post-tax income has been flat in crude terms; 2006/07 saw a gini coefficient of 0.39.

The UK stands out as one of the industrial countries where inequality has risen most sharply since the 1970s – along with New Zealand and the US (Gottschalk and Smeeding, 2000). Many authors have shown how taxes and benefits played a role in increasing income inequality during the 1980s. Goodman and colleagues (1997), however, took a much longer time-frame for their overview – 1961 to 1991 – and showed that contributions to growth in inequality were primarily from increased inequality in earnings, but also from investment income (private pensions included) and self-employment. Indeed, greater dispersion in original income, between the growing poles of the very poor and the very rich self-employed, between pensioners with high and low private incomes from pensions, and growing earnings dispersion are the major factors driving original income inequality (see Hills, 2004, Chapter Four of this volume and the earlier discussion of earnings inequality in Chapter Three). Benefits had a slightly improved 'countering' effect, lowering overall inequality over the 1980s as they became more targeted on those with low income. However, this equalising effect was swamped by rises in original sources of income becoming more unequal and the removal of elements of progressivity in the tax system meant that there was no countervailing tax effect to reign back growing income inequality.

Inequality during the 1980s was also a result of growing unemployment and inactivity as the incomes of those in and out of work grew apart. However, the recession in the early 1990s hit a wider section of the income distribution (the so-called 'middle-class recession') and equalised incomes. Employment growth since the 1990s recession has been across the income distribution and has particularly benefited families with children, with widening female participation continuing (see Chapter Three). The effect of taxes and benefits on incomes has changed since New Labour's attempts to reintroduce more progressivity into fiscal policy in contrast to the 1980s. However, New Labour has failed to stop rising inequality altogether; although income inequality slowed in its first term (Brewer et al, 2004; Clarke and Leicester, 2004), it has risen again in recent years and 'has returned to its highest-ever level – last seen in 2000-01 – as measured by the gini coefficient' (Brewer et al, 2008, p 20)[3]. Phillips (2008) shows that overall, the effect of changes to taxes and benefits since 1997 have benefited the lowest decile of the population by raising net income after tax by around 13%, raising the second lowest decile income by 10%, and have been slightly negative to the middle of the distribution but have decreased net income by around 5% to 6% for the richest deciles.

Outcomes

How have the policy outcomes changed since 1979? The promises made by New Labour to end poverty for children and pensioners provide us with a set of outcomes that can be used retrospectively over the period since the 1970s: relative poverty and the associated position of non-poor people in the income distribution. Relative poverty is a standard and approach that is both cross-party in agreement in Britain and pan-European. The definition of poverty currently adopted by the European Union (EU) is set at 60% of median household income (equivalised for household size and composition)[4]. Of course, there are other measures of absolute poverty and of deprivation and a range of indicators that provide better context about the realities of poverty, social exclusion and deprivation (Atkinson et al, 2002). Annually produced HBAI statistics in the UK (DWP, 2007a) base poverty on this relative approach. Poverty measures for EU comparison and for domestic policy analysis need not coincide. The use of before housing costs (BHC) income definitions is best for the former, but arguably an after housing costs (AHC) measure better captures the workings of the British benefit system and its separate Housing Benefit for rent. However, the adoption of BHC or AHC measures is a question of capturing different profiles that provide different interpretations – neither is 'right' or 'wrong'. We will use both in different contexts, particularly to capture profiles of periods of the lifetime when housing costs have a potentially significant impact on living standards – during childhood when they are high and during retirement when for the majority of pensioners they are close to zero, as by this time homes have been bought outright.

Our use of median earnings as the core calibration for our lifetime profiles means that we put much attention on the 'typical' or median case and then develop richer and poorer profiles based on arithmetic fractions of median earnings. Of course, it is crucial to point out that median earnings is not equivalent to median income as earnings are a component of income when measuring the income distribution. Even so, we can see our hypothetical Meade family, who have median earnings, as being around the median in the income distribution (depending, of course, on the point in their lifetime). Relative poverty is also based on a fraction of median income to imply a comparison with the 'typical' case rather than an average that can be distorted by very high incomes.

How has median income grown since the 1970s compared with other measures of the income distribution? The most recent of these analyses at the time of writing takes us up to the 2006/07 financial year based on the Institute of Fiscal Studies' (IFS) consistent time series on the British income distribution dating back to 1961 (Brewer et al, 2008). Figure 10.5 shows BHC income since 1971 for the median and mean as well as the 5th, 10th, 90th and 95th percentile points, thus giving a clear indication of how the middle, top and bottom distribution levels have changed. Widening dispersion over time is evident from the growing distance between the mean and the median. Mean income is growing further away from the median as it is pulled upwards by faster growth in incomes at the highest points in the distribution. Figure 10.5 shows that the 90th percentile point in the income distribution is widening compared with the median and that the 95th percentile point is widening when compared with the 90th. At the other end of the distribution, the 5th and 10th percentile points have seen more modest growth over time, with the gap between these and the median growing, but more slowly than we saw between the 90th and 95th and the median. There is a slowly emerging gap between the 10th and 5th percentile points.

Table 10.1 breaks down the long-term trends into medium-term profiles linked to the periods prior to 1979 (essentially the Heath and Old Labour governments), the Conservative years and the New Labour post-1997 period. Table 10.1 shows the consistent average annual rate of income growth over these different periods and compares such growth across the income distribution to median income growth for each period[5].

Comparing average real income growth at the bottom of the distribution between the periods shows that the 5th and 10th percentiles grew fastest during the 1970s – around 2.5% per annum – and that such growth was faster than median income growth during that period – the poor were closing the gap with the median. Since 1979, the poorest have fared worst in terms of real income growth. Real incomes of the 5th percentile grew on average by 0.7% a year under 18 years of the Conservatives and have subsequently grown at around the same rate (by 0.8% a year) under New Labour. However, the 10th percentile, which also grew very slowly under the Conservatives – 0.9% annually – has had much bigger growth under New Labour – on average 1.9% annually. Even so, relative growth at the bottom, which had narrowed the gaps between the poorest in the 1970s, ended after 1979. Relative to median growth, the 5th percentile grew half as fast (a ratio of 0.5:1 or thereabouts) as the median under both the Conservatives and New Labour, widening the gap between the poorest and the middle of the distribution. The 10th percentile experienced similar relative widening of gaps under the Conservatives and have almost, but not quite, stayed relatively at the same distance from the median under New Labour – a ratio of 0.9:1.

The fortunes of real income growth for those in the upper parts of the income distribution have changed most dramatically since the 1970s. Prior to 1979, incomes of the 90th and 95th percentiles rose more slowly than the median

Figure 10.5: Real income growth at points in the income distribution, 1971-2006

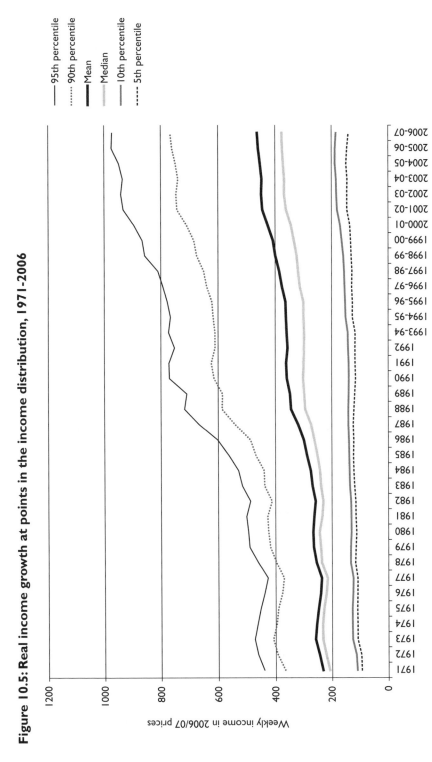

Source: IFS data for Brewer et al (2008).

Note: BHC income definition.

Table 10.1: Periodic real income growth rates at different points in the income distribution

	5th	10th	Median	Mean	90th	95th
1971-79						
Overall growth for whole period (%)	21	20	15	14	14	12
Average annual growth (%)	2.6	2.5	1.8	1.7	1.7	1.4
Ratio of average growth to median	1.4:1	1.3:1	–	0.9:1	0.9:1	0.8:1
1979-97						
Overall growth for whole period (%)	12	15	31	42	53	61
Average annual growth (%)	0.7	0.9	1.8	2.5	3.1	3.6
Ratio of average growth to median	0.4:1	0.5:1	–	1.4:1	1.7:1	2.0:1
1997-2006						
Overall growth for whole period (%)	8	19	20	23	20	23
Average annual growth (%)	0.8	1.9	2.0	2.3	2.0	2.3
Ratio of average growth to median	0.4:1	0.9:1	–	1.2:1	1.0:1	1.1:1

Source: Authors' calculations from Brewer et al (2008).

and, indeed, the 95th percentile rose most slowly. This meant a period of overall narrowing dispersion of the income distribution because higher income groups were trending down relatively towards the median at the same time as the low income groups were trending up – a situation reflected in the low overall inequality measures shown previously in Figure 10.4 for this period. The boom in inequality during the 1980s and early 1990s discussed earlier is clearly shown in the real income growth rates of the 90th and 95th income percentiles under the Conservatives – 3.1% and 3.6% a year respectively. Such growth was double the rate for the median and for the 95th percentile and slightly lower – 1.7% to 1% – for the 90th percentile. This level of divergent growth at the top of the income distribution has not been maintained since 1997, with incomes rising in line with the median for the 90th percentile and slightly ahead for the 95th percentile. But median income was growing at the fastest rate for the whole period since 1971.

Real annual median income growth is highest since 1997, mostly a direct consequence of sustained economic growth up to 2006 (but not reflecting later slowdown and recession). This fast rate of growth in median income has a direct effect on a relative poverty line, set at a fixed 60%, and coincides with the commitments to combat pensioner poverty and eliminate child poverty made by New Labour in 1999. These levels of median income growth also potentially confound the ability of tax and transfer programmes to consistently reduce poverty unless they maintain a value that rises at the rate of median income growth.

The Meades, median earnings and median income

The growth in median income affects our estimates for the model lifetimes. The gross earnings distribution and the household income distributions are totally different (but related) statistical distributions and this means that median income in the whole income distribution refers to the income of the typical *household* in the middle of the household income distribution. Median household income will rely on earnings (households around the median usually have earners in them) but will also rely on household composition (because income is equivalised) and on household-level employment behaviour. On the other hand, our calibration of model lifetimes is based on median earnings – and these are individual earnings of full-time male and female employees.

Figure 10.6 shows the changing relationship between male and female median full-time earnings and median household income from 1971 to 2006/07. Male median earnings have fallen relative to median household income over time by ten percentage points from 140% to 130%. Female median earnings have risen relative to median household income (and male median earnings) from 80% in the early 1970s to just over 100% by 2006/07.

We base our model lifetime profiles on contemporary median earnings in 1979, 1997 and 2008 and measure results against contemporary income distributions. This means that we have inputs of median earnings and outcomes that are measured against median income and are changing over time. Interpretation of

Figure 10.6: Median male and female earnings relative to poverty line at 60% of median household income

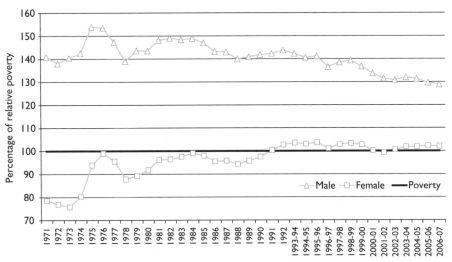

Source: Authors' calculations from Brewer et al (2008), Office for National Statistics long-term time series on New Earnings Survey and Annual Survey of Hours and Earnings provided to authors.

Note: Median household BHC income.

the tax and benefit systems' role in outcomes will also require care, as changing household composition, aggregate earning behaviour and household composition are all factors that alter the relationship between gross earnings and median income as well as changing incidence of taxes and benefits. For instance, the growth in two-earner households as women's labour market participation increased over the period means that a consistent relationship between household-level incomes and median earnings reflects such changes, a point we return to when reporting results from model lifetimes.

These changes mean that the relative poverty line, which is based on median income, is rising due to compositional and behavioural reasons as well as fiscal interventions.

Poverty

Figure 10.7 shows the poverty headcount, the proportion of individuals living below the relative poverty line, from 1971 to 2006 for both BHC and AHC incomes. This allows us to see the effect of rising housing costs over the period as well as the differences in fiscal treatment of benefits and rents and the lifetime incidence of housing costs. Taking Figure 10.7a first and looking solely at the BHC poverty profile, close to the 'disposable income' measure discussed earlier in the analysis of incidence of taxes and benefits, the overall trend for poverty from 1971 to 2006 is upward, from 15% of the population in 1971 to 18% in 2006. There are considerable fluctuations, however, some of which are clearly aligned (if slightly lagged) to the economic cycle, so that in 1980 poverty rose to a peak of 15% and peaks again at over 20% in the early 1990s. But there is no direct relationship over the period between the economic cycle and poverty, as unemployment itself is poorly related to relative poverty (Burgess et al, 2001) because unemployment is a minority experience even when rates are at their highest and the incomes of the employed affect relative measures of poverty far more than those of the unemployed. Moreover, around one quarter of the population are pensioners who rely mostly on fixed incomes and thus the relationship between such groups on fixed incomes linked to prices and median incomes growing with earnings has a bigger effect. This can clearly be seen in the steep rise in pensioner poverty during the 1980s as the economy came out of recession in a cyclical boom, increasing median income at a time when pensioners were the cohort of those retiring prior to the full maturation of occupational pension expansion in the 1950s onwards. Indeed, when we turn to more specific pensioner and child poverty, trends are in some ways easier to interpret.

Figure 10.7b shows similar trends in AHC poverty and there are three general points to note when comparing AHC and BHC poverty trends. First, aggregate AHC rates follow the same cyclical fluctuations as BHC rates. Second, aggregate AHC rates for the whole population are higher and this difference has grown over time as housing costs have risen. In 1971, AHC poverty rates were 6% higher than

Figure 10.7a: Relative poverty rates based on 60% of equivalised median income, 1971-2006/07 before housing costs

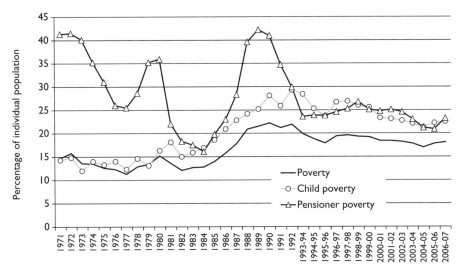

Figure 10.7b: Relative poverty rates based on 60% of equivalised median income, 1971-2006/07 after housing costs

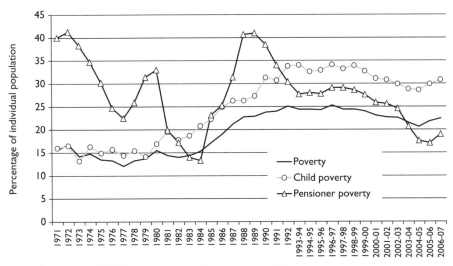

Source: Brewer et al (2008) and data supplied to authors by IFS.

Note: All data for Great Britain.

BHC rates. This difference rose by 30% in the mid-1990s but has subsequently fallen to around 25% higher. Third, AHC rates differ in ranking to BHC rates across the lifetime, with AHC rates higher than BHC for child poverty but lower than BHC rates for pensioners. This last point once again picks up the lifetime perspective difference in housing costs between the time when households with children are paying high housing costs (in rent or in mortgage interest early in the mortgage period) and retirement, when costs are lower (either lower rent for a smaller property or low housing costs for those who now occupy their home with the mortgage fully paid off). Overall, AHC poverty rates for the whole population fell from 16% in the early 1970s to 14% in 1979. During the 1980s, AHC poverty rose steeply, from 16% in 1980 to 24%, prior to the recession in the early 1990s. The peak of AHC poverty was 25% in 1992 and over the 1990s poverty gradually receded and fell to a low of 21% in 2004/05 before slowly climbing again to 22% in 2006/07. However, the trends in AHC poverty are best explored differently for pensioners and children.

Pensioner poverty

Pensioners rely on large elements of fixed income and thus are very sensitive to inflation and to comparison with an overall income distribution that is driven by earnings and thus by earnings growth over time. Pensioners in the early 1970s had a high risk of relative poverty – rates were 40% and over under both measures shown in Figure 10.7. Over the whole period, the pensioner poverty rate in both BHC and AHC terms trends downwards. However, there are large fluctuations in rates of pensioner poverty, with big falls in the poverty rates in the early 1980s followed by steep increases in the late 1980s that brought rates back up to the margins of the early 1970s levels. Since the 1990s, the pensioner poverty trend has been downwards, with a marked falling off since the early 2000s. However, interpreting these changes is difficult. It is obvious that falls since 2001/02 can be attributed to the introduction of the more generous social assistance system of Pension Credit, but over the longer term there are a large range of changes that make a simple story solely about pension or benefit levels inadequate. There are unobservable cohort effects as older, poorer pensioners become a smaller proportion of the population and increasing numbers of retiring workers with mature occupational pensions from the 1950s come into the pensioner population. However, it remains true that increasing ageing and longevity will dampen the effect of richer retirees over time, as the longer retirements on fixed incomes mean that relative income and risk of poverty increases for the older pensioners. Moreover, over most of the period, the increased value of occupational pensions is undermined only by real increases in underlying state pensions and this will reduce the extent to which better private pensions lift pensioners away from poverty. In the end, it is important to stress that the rollercoaster pensioner poverty profile is due in part to the sensitivity of pensioner incomes to the poverty measure. Many pensioners have incomes at the margins of the 60% of median income level and thus small nominal changes in benefits or incomes can shift significant numbers across the threshold. There are no data for 'poverty gaps', the distance of the poor pensioners from the poverty line, over time and thus it is difficult to interpret the whole period precisely. However, more recent data suggest a clearer story.

Consistent time series of data from 1994 show real incomes of pensioners rising by an average of 3% annually (DWP, 2008c, Table 2.2) and this growth, combined with underlying large increases in the means-tested safety net for pensioners, discussed earlier in Chapter Nine, can explain part of the overall reductions in pensioner poverty. Analysis in 2007 (Brewer et al, 2007) attributed one quarter of falls in pensioner poverty to younger, higher-income cohorts replacing older, poorer ones who die and three quarters to improved incomes alone. However, the most recent year, 2006/07, has seen a rise in pensioner poverty that confounds the overall rapid downward trend since the mid-1990s. This has arisen from the impact of inflation, which rose in 2006 and against which pensioner incomes are particularly sensitive, and in the non-payment of age-related winter payments in the winter of 2006. Because pensioner incomes are clustered so near to the poverty line, this alone accounted for an estimated 100,000 increase in the numbers of pensioners in poverty together with increased problems in identification of pensioners receiving means-tested safety net Pension Credit[6] (Brewer et al, 2008).

AHC measures of pensioner poverty shown in Figure 10.7 show overall lower rates of poverty for pensioners compared with BHC figures. They also clearly show that the relative risk of poverty for pensioners compared with the whole population and children is significantly lower over time as more and more pensioners retire with their mortgage costs paid and thus have lower housing costs compared with others in the AHC income distribution. Because poverty measures compare rates across the whole population, BHC measures best capture modern pensioners where the majority are full owner-occupiers. However, as one goes back to the early 1970s, the proportion with these characteristics declines.

The underlying pensioner poverty profile over time is thus driven by a huge number of factors that relate to cohorts of pensioner populations and their income profiles combined with the aggregate income performance of the remainder of the population.

Child poverty

We concentrate on the trends in AHC definition of income for profiles of child poverty, as this captures the combined changes to parental risks of low income (working age adults in the main) and housing cost changes over time. The overall trend is upward. In terms of crude child poverty rates, the 1970s saw rates of 12% to 24%, the 1980s saw child poverty climb steeply to double and by 1992 one third of children were poor and this remained so until 1998 when poverty began to fall consistently year on year until it was 28% in 2004/05. Since then, it has risen again, to over 30% in 2006/07. The political bravery of the 1999 pledge to eliminate child poverty is clear once the structural long-term legacy of high child poverty rates is understood. Table 10.2 shows both average rates of poverty and the underlying changes in numbers of children in poverty split between the three major periods, 1971 to 1979, 1979 to 1997 and 1997 onwards. Over the nine years to 1979, child poverty averaged 15.3% and this rate was only 1% higher than overall poverty for this period. The growth of child poverty in the 1980s and early 1990s meant that that period, which started low and ended high, had an average child poverty rate of 26%, but this rate was on average 8% higher than overall poverty. Inheriting high child poverty rates of 33% in 1997 meant that the period from 1997, even with declining poverty, has an average of 31% for the nine years since 1997 and that child poverty is, on average, eight percentage points higher than overall poverty. The impact that New Labour has made is easier to see in the trends on incidence, where child poverty has fallen fastest since 1997 – an average of 0.8% annually. However, it will take a long period of sustained continuous reduction to undo the 8% annual growth in child poverty between 1979 and 1997. These headline figures on reductions in the incidence of child poverty allude to the impact of programmes on lowering child poverty since 1997; these have been clearly shown and estimated elsewhere (Piachaud et al, 2003).

However, the ability of current approaches to reach the child poverty targets, of halving 1997/98 rates by 2010 and eliminating child poverty by 2020, are seriously in question. Hirsch (2006) estimated that additional spending of £4-5 billion is needed to meet the 2010 target and a further 1.6% of gross domestic product would be required to meet the target by 2020. However, it is worth reminding readers at this point that the target uses BHC, not AHC, definitions. While this is sensible, to allow for international comparison, the relevance to real living standards in terms of domestic policy performance has to be more circumspect.

Table 10.2: Periodic trends in AHC child poverty

	Risk %		Incidence – number of children	
	Average child poverty rate (%)	Percentage point difference between child poverty and all poverty	Period growth (%)	Average annual poverty growth (%)
1971-79	15	1	–5	–0.7
1979-97	26	6	142	8.3
1997-2006	31	8	–7	–0.8

Source: Authors' calculations from Brewer et al (2008).

The reason for this is that the relative risk of child poverty compared with overall poverty – one can think of this as the additional risk of poverty that comes from having children – is different for BHC and AHC measures. Figure 10.8 shows the percentage point *differences* between child poverty and overall poverty for both BHC and AHC measures since 1971. This clearly suggests that the differences are growing – that what is particular to the combination of children and housing costs in underlying poverty risk continues to grow even as inroads are made to the numbers of children who are poor.

Both child poverty and pensioner poverty will be crucial measures of outcomes for our profiles of 1979, 1997 and 2008 policy packages over the lifetime and it is clear that our profiles will have to look closely at these periods of the lifetime in addition to overall whole lifetime outcomes. This means adapting and expanding our hypothetical lifetime simulation approach to produce outcome measures that are able to reconcile our approach to the cross-sectional contemporary income distribution and poverty measures in these years. We do this in Chapter Eleven.

Figure 10.8: Differences in child poverty from total poverty

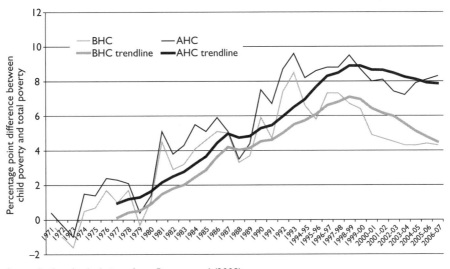

Source: Authors' calculations from Brewer et al (2008).

Note: Trendlines smoothed to moving averages over six years.

Summary

This chapter has looked at the time series data on changes to the whole population since the 1970s and focused on aggregate profiles of the incidence of taxes and benefits, income inequality and the changing income distribution and relative poverty measures. Our approach will use these time series and contemporary measures of inequality and poverty as indicators of outcomes for policy in our hypothetical lifetime simulations. We have shown how individual hypothetical cases relate to the cross-sectional population profiles and have discussed some of the difficulties in reconciling an approach based on hypothetical profiles with survey-based profiles of the whole population. The findings are as follows:

- The annual series of ONS profiles of the incidence of taxes and benefits across the income distribution gives a profile of how redistribution has changed from 1978 to 2006 and shows that overall there has been a less progressive outcome since 1979 in the net effects of both taxes and benefits. In 1979, this raised the incomes of the poorest 10th by 60% but in 1997 and 2006 these incomes had fallen to 26% and 18% respectively. Net incidence of taxes and benefits in the top deciles of the income distribution have hardly changed overall but the middle of the distribution had lower outcomes in 1979.
- The move to increase the role of indirect consumption taxes has been remarkably regressive, raising the proportion of the bottom decile's income paid in such taxes from less than 20% to around 50%.
- The composition of the bottom deciles of the income distribution has changed over the study period, and this helps explain some of the changing incidence as pensioners now make up much smaller shares of the poorest population and low earners and families with children much higher shares.
- Inequality in original incomes rose hugely, with gini coefficients rising from 0.43 to 0.52 between 1978 and 2006/07, an original rise of 21%; however, inequality after direct taxes and benefits rose faster overall, by 31% and by 39% when indirect taxation is additionally taken into account.
- Median income has risen significantly over the whole period but rose fastest from 1997 to 2006. However, the top of the distribution, which in the 1970s rose more slowly than the median, has, since 1979, raced ahead. It grew twice as fast as median income between 1979 and 1997 and since 1997 has grown by 110% of the median. By contrast, the bottom of the income distribution grew faster than the median in the 1970s but slowed down after 1979.
- Relative poverty rates have grown over the period. Child poverty in particular, which was on average 15% in the 1970s and falling in trend, rose on average by 8% per annum between 1979 and 1997 with an average of 26% for the period. Since 1997, there has been a decline of 7%.

Notes
[1] ONS employs the McClements equivalence scale to enable time series consistency and this means measures of income cannot be precisely compared with either HBAI or model lifetimes.

[2] These sums are estimated to represent an annual amount by ONS in its computation using a range of assumptions on annualisation (Jones, 2008).

[3] These measures of inequality are not directly comparable with the ONS estimates in Figure 10.7 because of differences in measurement, and in particular, the use of different equivalence scales.

[4] For some countries, such as the UK, such a measure is ambitious but for others, particularly some of the poorer, newly accepted EC countries from Eastern Europe such as Romania and Bulgaria, this 60% of median figure is actually below what they put forward as a minimum standard of living using a basket of goods. This is because the median household in such countries is poor or near poor in consumption terms and thus taking 60% of that income line merely draws a relative poverty line that is below an absolute one.

[5] It should be pointed out that the real income growth at the bottom of the income distribution during the 1970s was partly due to inflation and prices outstripping earnings for those with price-indexed incomes for this period. However, the expansion of entitlement to a wider range of transfers and their relative generosity during their early history of implementation also explains such real income growth.

[6] Increased levels of measurement error in FRS in regard to accurate reporting of means-tested benefits are also identified as a potential cause of increases in poverty.

ELEVEN

LOIS and model lifetimes

This chapter outlines the methodology and assumptions that will be used in Chapters Twelve, Thirteen and Fourteen to look at our analysis of the policy systems in 1979, 1997 and 2008 using a model lifetime approach.

A model lifetime profile captures a very large portion of a policy system, in this case on personal taxation and benefits and other income-related policy areas. The fundamental idea is to be comprehensive in order to profile the synthesised performance of as large a set of policy rules as possible and to show interactions and cumulative effects. This approach is similar to putting policy rules into a controlled test situation using simulated cases. If each policy system were a car, the approach would be analogous to testing each car on a testbed using different parameters and combinations of passengers and driving speeds. Each car tested in this manner could be compared consistently according to a pre-set agreed number of iterations comparing numbers of passengers, driving speed, fuel consumption, fuel efficiency and wear and tear. Rather than being realistic 'lifetimes', our model lifetime profiles are thus primarily heuristic devices used to compare policy systems. However, the idea of a lifetime is a resonant one; life histories evoke interest and empathy and allow readers to place themselves in the policy comparison in a way that a more abstract approach cannot. This is obviously not the real world and in the rest of this chapter we set out the assumptions that are used to consistently compare the tax and benefit systems of our sample years using a lifetime perspective. We then outline the measurements we use to compare the systems consistently.

Why turn to a hypothetical modelled world? The previous chapters have shown how difficult it is to separate the 'policy story' from the huge changes that have occurred in the economy and population since the 1970s. One huge advantage of simulation is thus to control for changes and to isolate the effects of policy change from other effects. It allows us to use *one* element of the empirical story of change, the policy rules, and apply them consistently to profiles of changing circumstances. This approach allows us to examine how the 1979, 1997 and 2008 policy design creates different outcomes if everything else is held constant.

LOIS and model lifetime methodology

Model lifetimes

At heart, using a hypothetical lifetime profile of policy rests on a simple question: 'What would it be like to live a whole life under the same policy rules? We ask readers to keep the fundamental simplicity of the question uppermost in mind for the remainder of this chapter because, as usual, deceptively simple questions belie considerable complication and uncertainty.

The reason we ask the question based on the lifetime is to capture the whole range of policy interventions that policy makers had in their minds when they designed programmes for their contemporary populations in 1979, 1997 and 2008. This in a way sets up measurements of policy using a grid of provision 'from the cradle to the grave' across our comparison years of 1979, 1997 and 2008. This approach allows us to synthesise analysis across the boundaries of different forms of provision and to look cumulatively at their outcomes. We cut across the current three-way government compartmentalisation of the lifetime into children, working age and elderly groups and join together the income-related, contributory and universal systems of social transfers with taxation, housing, private pensions and other elements of policy over the lifetime.

Lifetime hypothetical models have been a small but growing part of social policy analysis since the early 1990s. Their beginnings lie in profiling pension provision (Evans and Falkingham, 1997; Evans et al, 1999; Johnson, 1999; Rake et al, 2000) before they were expanded to incorporate wider elements of lifetime incomes in profiling women's experience of earnings and pension penalties (Joshi et al, 1996; Rake, 2000). Evans and Eyre (2004) widened the approach to look at all aspects of the 2003/04 tax benefit system in the form of 'model lifetimes' and Evans and Scarborough (2006) then moved on to analyse specific periods of the lifetime to assess the prospects for child poverty under 'model childhoods'.

Model lifetimes use hypothetical cases to analyse policy rather than real data. They are tax benefit models that produce profiles of the incidence of taxes and benefits and produce various measures of outcomes and of household budget constraints. Government and policy makers use similar tax benefit models to demonstrate and illustrate how the total income package changes as earnings rise for families of various types. In Britain, there is a continuous series of 'tax benefit model tables' produced currently by the Department for Work and Pensions that go back to 1971 (DWP, 2008d). One way of understanding the model lifetime approach is to think of such tax benefit model tables done repeatedly for every year of a lifetime.

It is crucial to differentiate our approach from micro-simulation, which is based on representative surveys of the population that can produce whole population-based estimates of government spending and revenue collection and of resulting changes in income distribution. British readers will recall that every Budget announcement is accompanied by an analysis of how many people gain and lose from changes in taxation and benefits and how much the changes will cost. These estimates are produced through micro-simulation but are also often accompanied by profiles of how 'typical' families will experience the changes, which are the individual profiles that more resemble our approach using hypothetical individuals. Micro-simulation can also be used to compare policy systems and Redmond et al (1998) compare Old Labour and the Conservatives (1978 and 1996/97 systems) to show the changes to benefits and taxation over that period. Such micro-simulation is purely cross-sectional. Thus, while excellent at capturing policies that rely on income levels and demographic status, such an approach cannot identify programmes that rely on underlying personal history, a particular problem for contributory benefits and pensions and investments. There are also dynamic micro-simulation models that have addressed this problem by allowing a sample population to age and change behaviour according to a set of behavioural assumptions prescribed by predictive regression (see Falkingham and Hills, 1995) for a British model that looks across a range of provisions such as social security, health and education. Most dynamic micro-simulations models have been used to simulate policy outcomes from demographic changes, in particular future pension provision and other aspects of long-term provision for a growing older population, such as care provision (see, for example, Curry, 1996; Wittenberg et al, 1998; Evandrou et al, 2001).

The strengths of the hypothetical lifetime profiles are that they can capture illustrative profiles of large sections of policy and are thus suited to looking at overviews of policy or large-scale structural changes such as those that have occurred since 1979. The key to interpretation is that they are illustrative rather than representative, as they are not based on samples of survey data. Indeed, there is no survey dataset available that covers lifetimes in Britain, only several birth cohorts that start in the late 1950s and panel data that start in the early 1990s. Such data provide us with empirical evidence to inform our hypothetical profiles and build a set of assumptions that reflect the contemporary evidence, but in the end these are not representative reflections of cross-sectional incidence in the actual contemporary population, nor a set of stochastic predictions. The lifetime profiles are a set of lifetime event parameters that are used to make illustrative and consistent comparisons of the underlying policy systems. We now outline our assumptions and methodology in some detail in the remainder of this chapter.

The Lifetime Opportunities and Incentives Simulation

We use a custom-built lifetime simulation model that can calculate entitlement to all aspects of social security, taxation and a range of other policies under a wide range of hypothetical lifetime events: LOIS, the Lifetime Opportunities and Incentives Simulation. Previous versions of LOIS have looked solely at single years of policy and moving to a comparative approach means that much more has had to be done on framing lifetime profiles to capture change over time.

LOIS is a computer simulation programme that uses Microsoft Excel spreadsheet workbooks. There are two main elements to the programme. First are the central core 'lifetime' parameters that are set by the user. These can be changed to input a whole range of circumstances for each three-month period of the subsequent lifetime. We work on an underlying unit of a quarter year as a rounding convention that best captures benefit entitlement rules and avoids the unnecessary complexity and computing task of a weekly approach to a lifetime or the loss of detail that would result from using annual inputs.

One of our core assumptions is to use a *single generation*, a single set of adult lifetime circumstances, and all model lifetimes start at the age of 16. If we were to start a profile at birth, apart from the most aristocratic of babies, there would be no income attributable to the child and we would have to make assumptions about parental incomes. This would require capturing two sets of adult lifetimes or portions thereof to profile a single lifetime. We avoid this and also capture the point at which the benefit system historically starts entitlement, school-leaving age, which is 16. One consequence of this is that 'childhood' periods of the lifetime refer to later periods when this hypothetical person has children of her own.

A lifetime is an incredibly complicated set of events and trends, and focusing on a set of key elements allows us both to focus on a small set of significant lifetime events for easier interpretation as well as consistent comparison.

The hypothetical person who starts from the age of 16 is assumed to be a woman in all simulations used in Part Three. We call this primary person 'Ms' rather than referring to her by differing marital status or names. But this also points out another crucial element of the hypothetical lifetime, which is that it is built around the concept of a 'benefit assessment unit', which is the core person plus their partner plus any children that reside with them. This means that the partner only appears in the model lifetime at the point of first cohabitation and then subsequently for the period that this cohabitation continues. The result of this is that we end up with 'one and a bit' lifetimes as the prior life of partners is not directly recorded in our original profile. However, the previous taxes, benefits and pension rights of the partner are included in the model lifetime outcomes, but profiles only look at the core unit throughout the lifetime. This could be very misleading if, for example, we based our lifetime on huge differences in age, say, of ageing rock stars and young consorts. We avoid the problem by matching incomes in partnership to a point where they are more stereotypical than any novel, a partnership of averages where Mr Meade and Ms Meade both have median earnings, the low earners marry other low earners and the rich marry the rich.

In this book, we concentrate on a core set of lifetime events that are consistent across our comparison of family types and policy systems. The core set of lifetime events is designed to be 'typical' but in many ways is stereotypical. Our desire to consistently compare rather than to look at the widest potential range of outcomes for each system means that we construct simple 'average' behaviours. But an average lifetime is a slippery concept, as the sequencing and mix of events and trajectories are not understandable as averages. Cross-sectional data can give us much information about contemporary populations; however, cumulatively building a set of 'average' behaviour can result in a nonsensical lifetime profile. We ensure that the profiles are a coherent set of parameters that produce interpretable results.

Simplification of profiles includes the following:

- partners of the same age and with equal life expectancy;
- a single house purchase rather than the multiple purchases and moves that are in reality a feature of the lives of higher-income families;
- a single average social rent assumption for low-income families that does not change with family composition;
- a single heterosexual life partnership rather than a series of cohabitations, separations, divorces and step-relationships;
- continuous membership of single pension schemes – either occupational or personal;
- savings behaviour that is only modelled to reflect payments for a deposit for mortgage and contributions into pension schemes.

Children continue to be counted as part of the core profile until they are 16 or, if they continue in secondary education, to their 19th birthday. Put simply, our hypothetical lifetime profiles capture tax and benefit incidence for the period in which young adults live with their parents but we do not start to profile outcomes that relate to overall income distribution and poverty until they form their own household.

For the main adult and her partner, there are a range of economic activity parameters in the model that trigger status for benefits and taxation. Hours and rates of earnings are computed at all points in time and status assigned to those periods where no employment takes place. This means that, from the age of 16, a whole range of behaviour can be simulated in education and work, in partnering and having children, in savings and pension uptake and in retirement. The earnings histories for the analysis in this part of the book weight earnings to reflect experience and productivity over the working life. Figure 11.1 shows the cross-sectional lifetime earnings profile for 2006 that is used to produce lifetime earnings profiles. This weighting of earnings by age is used consistently across all the versions of the lifetime models so that for the main comparisons of lifetimes in 1979, 1997 and 2008 the same earnings weightings are employed. One important point to note, however, is that the national minimum wage in 2008 will place a lower limit on potential lifetime curves for earnings of the lowest paid. This has particular relevance to the Lowes and is discussed further in Chapter Fourteen.

The second part of the LOIS programme uses the earnings and status profiles of the individuals present at each point in the lifetime to calculate all taxes, tax credits, benefits, and private and occupational pensions. These computations are made using the rules as they existed in 1979, 1997 and 2008 so that we are able to exactly replicate the workings of each tax and benefit system in its reflection of income and other characteristics that lead to entitlement to transfers and to liability for income taxation. The computation algorithms and formulae are very complex and details of the policy rules are not given here. Reference works include

Figure 11.1: Age weighting of earnings

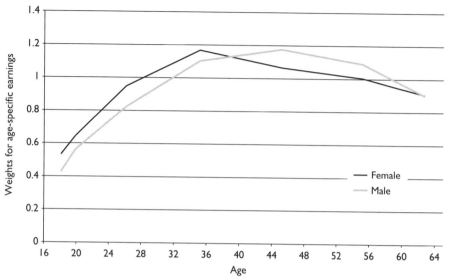

Source: Authors' calculations from ONS (2007e).

the Child Poverty Action Group annual guides to the benefit system and the long-standing HM Treasury's *Tax benefit reference manual* (HM Treasury, 2008b). We have had to make some assumptions about benefit and tax behaviour and we assume that individuals maximise their income by taking up all entitlement and by minimising their liability for tax at all times. This means that all means–tested benefits are taken up and all tax allowances are used optimally. In particular, for the 1979 system, we assume that married couples will optimally use the potential for joint or independent taxation. Such take-up assumptions reflect our approach of looking at overall policy performance as a set of ideal optimised outcomes over the lifetime.

We also have to make some assumptions about time and change and these are crucial to interpreting our results.

Lifetimes in a single year

The key assumption in our model lifetimes is to capture the theoretical position where the whole lifetime is lived in each of the single years 1979, 1997 and 2008. This means that lifetime events and ageing still occur but experience a frozen policy system. The lifetime resembles the plot of the film 'Groundhog Day', in which the main character relives the same day time and time again, but in our case, the model lifetime profile relives the same policy system year by year. This means that any lifetime profile does not represent a population cohort and this is a crucial distinction to make. In any given year, the population consists of a large number of cohorts who all have their own experience of social policy over their differing lifetimes. In, say 1979, we can look back and see that the rules in place in that year affected different age cohorts, some born listening to news of the Boer War and others to the English punk rock band, The Clash. In policy terms, some had paid into the graduated pension scheme, while others were just beginning to pay into the State Earnings Related Pension Scheme (SERPS), for instance. This means that in a frozen 1979, only The Clash and their contemporaries are on the radio and SERPS is the only state pension option.

But while a model lifetime profile does not represent a cohort, the key reason for having a lifetime history is to provide a range of illustrative circumstances that relate directly to policy intervention and capture the major events that occur in the majority of people's lifetimes and thus to compare the underlying policy systems and their treatment of both lifetime events and cumulative lifetime experience. We therefore adopt an approach that enables us to focus on these underlying analytical questions of comparison and formulate our lifetime profiles to allow the main questions concerning incidence, outcomes and inequality to dominate.

A lifetime under the same policy system

The central premise of a hypothetical lifetime profile is that it is based on an unchanging policy regime to allow comparisons of the systems in the comparison years. Yet freezing each year's policy system in 1979, 1997 and 2008 is somewhat at odds with the policy change and evolution we have shown in our discussions in previous chapters. What do we gain and lose when we freeze policy at a given point of time? We have seen in the earlier chapters that policy change has been driven both by a mix of ideological difference and by changing demographic and economic circumstances. Sometimes politicians like to confuse these two by using supposedly neutral terms like 'modernisation' or by asserting that 'there is no alternative', but essentially the policy rules in place at a point in time capture the way that policy makers see the world and have designed programmes to match. However, it is also the case that each system will inherit policy legacies that it will take time to reform and that policy makers will introduce programmes that take time to mature and are designed for the future, particularly on pensions. We approach the first two problems in the following ways.

First, there is no serious problem of policy legacies affecting the labelling of 1979 as 'Old Labour', as all of its major policies – especially Child Benefit and SERPS – had been legislated for. 1997 was the end of five years of Major government and 18 years of Conservative rule in which a large number of policies had been changed and implemented. 2008 also sees 11 years of New Labour and thus the implementation of many structural reforms. Second, transitional rules put in place to protect losers or other people affected by policy change are avoided because we model fully implemented versions of policy programmes. Put simply, we assume that all hypothetical individuals have no history prior to each policy year and can have new policies introduced without being in the position of a 'loser'.

Mature policy

Policies nevertheless in place in 1979, 1997 and 2008 may not exactly match contemporary policy makers' policy aims because they are a work in progress. Policy makers may set long-term policy change in motion and this may be expected to fully come into force a considerable period after the year in question. This problem, which we refer to as 'policy maturity', means looking at mature versions of 1979, 1997 and 2008 as well as purely contemporary models of policy. Our approach to allow for this and capture maturity in policy design is to distinguish two versions of each policy year – first, the purely cross-sectional policy rules that were in place in 1979, 1997 and 2008, and second, the 'mature' version of these policy years where all the policy that had been legislated for and agreed but not brought into effect is additionally modelled. The best way to explain this is through example. In 2008, there is in place a commitment to introduce 12 months' Statutory Maternity Pay and leave before 2010. In our cross-sectional version of 2008, we model the effects of what was in place in 2008 (nine months) and in our mature version we model the 12 months. A more significant example is in the area of pensions where in 1997 and 2008 policy makers had decided to raise the pension age for future pensioners but these raised pension ages had not come into practice. In our cross-sectional versions of 1997 and 2008, we have the contemporary pension age and in our mature versions of these years we have the raised pension ages. Clearly, the new pension policy that has been agreed following the adoption of most elements of the Turner Report (Pensions Commission, 2005) will also come into place in a mature version of 2008 policy.

Recalling our discussion in Chapter Two, the 1974-79 Labour government adopted a busy programme of social security reform, meeting, in fact, all of the major commitments of the October 1974 Labour manifesto in this area: introducing an inflation-proofed State Earnings Related Pension Scheme (SERPS) in place of the Conservatives' scheme; increasing family allowances to include the first child (achieved through the introduction of Child Benefit); and introducing new non-contributory benefits for the incapacitated and disabled people and carers (achieved through the introduction of Non-Contributory Invalidity Pension, Mobility Allowance and Invalid Care Allowance). However, the one area in which it makes definite sense to think of the 1979 system as not mature is the issue of funding for SERPS. In the real world of 1979, the SERPS scheme was in legislative place but no one had yet had time to build up any significant entitlement to benefit under it. As discussed in Chapter Nine, it would take in excess of 20 years for anyone to build up any full entitlement to SERPS and it would take much longer than that, a further 10 to 30 years (DHSS, 1974), for the scheme to reach its ultimate level of real expenditure. We can refer to government estimates made in 1985 for the cost of a fully mature SERPS scheme in terms of the rates of National Insurance contributions (NICs) required to pay for it. On the assumptions of the basic pension being linked to earnings (as would have been

1979 policy) and 1.25% per annum real earnings growth, such estimates suggest that a combined employee and employer National Insurance rate of 27.4% would be required to fund a fully mature SERPS (DHSS, 1985b). Maintaining the 1979 ratio between employee and employer contributions but assuming the 1985 level of contracted-out rebate that informed the estimate, this translates into a 4.3% increase in employee NICs for contracted-in employees and a 4.9% increase for contracted-out employees on actual 1979 rates. We apply these increases to arrive at our model for a mature policy 1979 system.

By 1997, it might be argued that after 18 years of Conservative rule the policy of the day might well already be considered mature. However, although this point can be well taken, again in the area of pensions, policies had reached the statute books for implementation in the future rather than at the present time. In particular, the 1995 Pensions Act provided for the equalisation of male and female pension ages at 65 to be achieved by the phasing in of higher pension ages for women between 2010 and 2020. Thus, for our mature policy 1997 system, we set the pension age at 65 for both men and women. We also complete the project of the phasing out of Mortgage Interest Relief at Source and the additional married couple's tax allowance and additional personal allowance begun by the Conservatives in 1994 and 1995, to leave our mature policy 1997 system without these tax concessions.

In respect of the 2008 system, the key area of policy maturity again concerns pensions. To model the mature 2008 system, we suppose the full enactment of the provisions of the 2007 Pensions Act, which is scheduled to take place over the next 30 to 40 years, notably including the introduction of the personal accounts scheme and the conversion of the State Second Pension to a flat-rate benefit (although these two measures will not affect the Meades) as well as the raising of the state pension age to 68, which in the real world will be fully phased in by 2046. We also model other forthcoming changes to which firm or statutory commitments have been made, for example, the above-mentioned extension of Statutory Maternity Pay and maternity leave to 52 weeks, due by the end of the current parliament. Our assumptions for the personal accounts pensions are discussed later in this section alongside the other assumptions used for non-state pensions.

To include these changes in our simulations in a meaningful way clearly requires us to make some assumptions about accompanying behaviour changes as well.

Changing lifetime behaviour

It is clear from Chapter Three that behaviour has changed considerably over time and that life expectancy has increased. A comparison between now and 1979, for instance, will have to take into account differing typical behaviour in the comparison years. In 1979, for example, it is more likely that a woman would take a longer period out of work after having a child and that the overall lifetime would be shorter, as life expectancy has grown considerably in the past

30 years. The different behaviours also reflects policy difference over time and this means that policy systems are best compared in two different ways: first, by comparing the systems with the same underlying set of lifetime events and second, adjusting the lifetime event histories to take account of behavioural differences. This approach allows us to analyse the differences in policy response to changing lifetime behaviour through comparison of consistent and altered versions of the modelled lifetimes.

Changing behaviour is partly the outcome of changing economic constraints and we do not change behaviour for the high-income Moores. We keep behaviour of the higher-income comparisons constant, to reflect, for instance, the fact that with more income the Moores can smooth out some of the risks of maternal earnings interruption by hiring a full-time nanny.

Modelling inflation

Inflation has a potentially huge effect on long-term lifetime outcomes and differences between the 1979 and later systems in their treatment of inflation and uprating have been established as fundamental in Parts One and Two of the book. Inflation has the biggest potential impact on living standards in retirement both because of the funding of pensions and because in retirement income from pensions is fixed. Money invested in pensions should plan to produce annuities that at least keep up with prices, although many provide only fixed nominal incomes.

Inflation has varied greatly over the past 30 years or more. The 1970s were infamous for high inflation and economic stagnation while the late 1990s and early 2000s have become synonymous with consistent economic growth and low inflation. 2008 has seen the macroeconomic climate take a turn distinctly for the worse, with a combination of higher inflation from international commodity prices and an economic downturn. Certain elements of prices, particularly house prices, have outstripped both price and earnings inflation in the short to medium term since the mid-1990s. Writing in 2008, what inflation profiles suit a comparison of long-term lifetime profiles of policy systems? There is no single correct answer and our approach is to adopt the following assumptions.

Each policy system in 1979, 1997 and 2008 will have that year's prices and earnings levels applied to it in any purely cross-sectional profile. This means the following. All prices can be set at 1979, 1997 and 2008 levels and applied to the tax and benefit rules also held at that year's amounts. This means, for instance, that contemporary house prices, social rent levels and other particular elements of consumption that directly affect benefits and taxes can be captured. This approach clearly captures the inflation that occurs between the comparison years and, where actual prices or monetary amounts are compared over time, the comparisons are made in constant 2008 terms. In this way, we are able to compare incidence of taxes and benefits and their outcomes in a purely cross-sectional, inflation-free view of a lifetime where there is no inflation over the lifetime but the changing contextual inflation for prices and earnings is captured in each year. These versions of lifetime profiles we term 'inflation-free' and are used in the basic 'Groundhog Day' baseline results for each of our three hypothetical lifetimes in Chapters Twelve, Thirteen and Fourteen.

To comprehensively assess and compare the policy systems, it is important also to compare tax and benefit incidence, outcomes and inequality that take account of longitudinal incidence of inflation over the lifetime and to compare each policy system's treatment of inflation. We additionally do this by applying consistent inflation parameters to each policy model, so that each policy year's prices, earnings and tax and benefit parameters are inflated and uprated from the starting point of actual prices, earnings and rates for that year. However, for consistent comparison, the same profiles of the exogenous elements of inflation – those relating to general prices and earnings and other macroeconomically reliant elements of inflation – must be given to each system[1]. Prices that are politically set as part of the policy system, such as social rents and private rents after Rent Act regulation in 1979, we term as endogenous and these can be set as part of the system's parameters, alongside uprating rules and rates for benefits and tax allowances and so on. Box 11.1 shows the rules we apply for inflation.

Box 11.1: Inflation assumptions

Inflation parameters for all three model systems

Prices	2% per annum (rounded average for period)
Earnings	4% per annum (rounded average for period)
House prices	6.5% per annum (rounded average for period)

Policy-related inflation parameters

1979 rents and rates	Prices
1997 and 2008 rents and council tax	Earnings
Childcare costs – all years	Earnings

Outcome inflation parameters

Median income and relative poverty line	Earnings

Applying these inflation parameters over the lifetime produces very large cumulative effects that have to be interpreted carefully. Given our assumption that a whole lifetime occurs within a repeated single year but that that year could have repeated inflation, it is additionally important to consider when to 'start' inflation for such a hypothetical lifetime profile. If we start inflation running from the earliest point of the hypothetical lifetime, the 16th birthday, a 2% inflation rate can lead to a 400% nominal increase by late retirement. We adopt an approach that more coherently balances the inherent compromise between the longitudinal and cross-sectional in hypothetical lifetimes in a single year. Inflation is balanced over the lifetime so that prices are neutral at the mid-point of the lifetime and inflation decreases ahead and increases beyond this point. We set the age of 40 as neutral with inflation either side.

Modelling uprating

We adopt two approaches to uprating alongside inflation. The first is to use whole lifetime profiles to assess the effect of inflation and uprating on long-term outcomes. The second is to use parts of the lifetime and look at inflation and uprating as they affect childhood and retirement. In the latter case, we start inflation from the point of birth (of the first child) and from the point of retirement respectively. These two approaches allow us comprehensively to assess the medium- and long-term effects of uprating and inflation together for each of the three policy regimes. However, these two approaches require different assumptions about uprating. Any policy maker is likely to have the electoral and governmental cycle as their main temporal mind-set for the majority of short- to medium-term programmes. Programmes that have fallen out of favour but are too risky to cut can be allowed to slowly erode in value. Tax thresholds can be allowed to rise with prices in the short term because fiscal drag will mean that as earnings rise more money is collected for future structural or other reforms (Sutherland et al, 2008). However, it would be misleading to extrapolate such behaviour over a lifetime unless there were explicit long-term commitments behind uprating policy.

For whole lifetime profiles, we thus employ the assumptions on uprating shown in Box 11.2. We assume no fiscal drag and thus that income tax thresholds and allowances rise with earnings over the long term. This reflects what we saw in Chapter Five and in particular Figure 5.1, which showed that personal tax allowances have been at a fairly constant 20% of male full-time earnings across 1979, 1997 and 2008. For transfers, we adopt different approaches according to the policy year in order to capture systemic difference across the comparison years. In 1979, all long-term contributory benefits and Child Benefit were uprated by earnings and all short-term benefits were uprated by prices (subject to there being some elements that were never uprated). For 1997 and 2008, most elements of benefits are either uprated by prices (either by the retail price index or using the Rossi price index to exclude housing costs for means-tested safety net benefits) or are not uprated at all. In the benefit system, in all years there are elements that are allowed to fall in real value through no or very intermittent uprating. These elements mostly relate to capital limits and to earnings disregards in means-tested benefits, although, as we have seen in Chapters Four to Nine, elements of the system are also allowed to wither in real value as part of a pattern of periodic long-term structural reforms. Our approach, based on the long-term lifetime, is thus to uprate all elements by prices unless there is a specific, justifiable reason not to across all three systems. The one element of the benefit system where a no-uprating policy is appropriate is the additional 25 pence pension for the over-80s, which was set at this amount in 1971 – when it was the price of a bag of coal – and has never subsequently been uprated.

Box 11.2: Uprating assumptions[2] for whole lifetime profiles

Income tax allowances and thresholds	Earnings
National Insurance limits	Earnings
1979 state retirement pension, Invalidity Benefit, long-term rate of Supplementary Benefit, Child Benefit, Family Income Supplement (FIS)	Earnings
1979 Unemployment Benefit, Sickness Benefit, Maternity Allowance, other Supplementary Benefit	Prices
1997 all contributory and non-contributory non-means-tested benefits	Prices
1997 Income Support, Jobseeker's Allowance (JSA) and Housing Benefit	Rossi prices
2008 all contributory and non-contributory non-means-tested benefits, all tax credit thresholds and elements	Prices
2008 Income Support, JSA and Housing Benefit	Rossi prices

For short- to medium-term profiles, childhoods and retirements, we use actual behaviour on uprating of the government of the time for the period up to 1979, up to 1997 and up to 2008 alongside explicit commitments that the government has made. These are shown in Box 11.3.

Box 11.3: Uprating assumptions for medium-term childhood and retirement profiles

As lifetime profiles (see Box 11.2) except:

Income tax allowances and thresholds all years	Prices
National Insurance limits all years	Prices
2008 Child Tax Credit family element and second income threshold	Current
2008 Child Tax Credit child element and Pension Credit guarantee	Earnings

---

Modelling occupational and personal pensions

Chapter Nine has discussed the changing history of private pension provision and our approach is to consider both defined benefit and defined contribution pensions for the median and higher earnings lifetime profiles of the Meades and the Moores. However, we will only consider defined contribution personal pensions for 1997 and 2008. To provide consistent measures of investment across both forms of pension, we assume constant levels of contribution for both. This provides consistent measures of outcomes against consistent inputs but is a strange method of comparison for several reasons. First, employers have historically subsidised their defined contribution schemes; this has led to low levels of contributions compared with the total costs of such pensions. However, the amount that employers contribute to their pension schemes differs according to the size and maturity of the scheme, and the number of contributors and beneficiaries and is not constant over time. The assumption of a constant, fixed employee contribution does not take into account such fluctuations. The same contribution paid into an individualised defined contribution personal pension creates a smaller fund and misses the historical and political points of such individuals having to pay more as employers pull out and pass the risk on to their employees. Second, we are unable to look at differences in investment risk and their effects on personal pensions. Thus, the 2008 stock market falls and differences in annuity rates are not considered, despite their crucial effect on the outcomes of such pensions. We use the simplest form of annuity – cash, not index linked – to illustrate the differences between inflation-protected and other forms of retirement income compared with occupational pensions. The consistent characteristics used to model private pensions are shown in Box 11.4.

Box 11.4: Private pension parameters used in LOIS comparisons of 1979, 1997 and 2008

Occupational pensions defined benefit (all years)	**Personal pensions defined contribution (1997 and 2008 only)**

Contribution rate

6% of gross earnings

Unknown employer contribution

6% of gross earnings

Zero employer contribution

Pension computation

Based on final year's salary

Accrual rate = 1/80th

Real interest rate 2%

Annual administration charge 1%

Commission annuity purchase 5%

Pension uprated with prices when in payment

Annuity rate 2.5%

Female life expectancy at retirement 24.1 years

Male life expectancy at retirement 17.4 years

Flat annuity

Personal accounts in 2008

Earning band lower limit £5,000

Earning band upper limit £33,000

Percentage of band earnings paid by employee 4%

Percentage of employee's band earnings paid by employer 3%

Personal accounts interest rate 2%

Annual administration charge 0.3%

Commission annuity purchase 5%

Annuity rate 2.5%

Flat annuity

Policy outcomes

We have looked at the details of the model lifetimes and their role as a comparative tool to compare changes in policy between 1979, 1997 and 2008. This section outlines the measures that will be used from the model lifetimes to analyse policy change. Throughout the book so far we have discussed how much people receive in benefits and pay in taxes and the overall coverage of these policy instruments and the outcomes. Capturing these policy outcomes is thus the key element of comparison.

Incidence

How do the 1979, 1997 and 2008 systems differ in the amounts that they tax and provide in transfers over the lifetime? Our model family approach has already allowed us to look at the incidence of tax and benefits at points of time or periods of the lifetime. Moving to the lifetime allows us to do this for longer periods and to provide cumulative totals. We do both to measure the inputs and outputs of fiscal policy, namely how much our hypothetical lifetime families pay in tax and how much they receive in transfers. Our approach allows us to match the majority of income definitions with the cumulative incidence of taxes and transfers that was demonstrated in Chapter Ten. We start by measuring gross earnings at the family level, so this includes both the male and female earnings profile over the lifetime. We can add transfers (assuming full take-up) and deduct income-based taxation and direct taxation from local government taxes. This gives us the same measure of 'disposable income' as used in official measurements of the incidence of taxes and benefits outlined in Chapter Ten. This measure of disposable income, when also adjusted for pension contributions, is equivalent to the official 'before housing cost' (BHC) income and we use this definition in our results.

The big difference between our approach and that of the Office for National Statistics, seen in Chapter Ten, is that we cannot estimate indirect taxation from consumption-based taxes such as VAT and excise duties. This is a significant limitation that arises from our approach of basing profiles purely on income-related policy responses. We considered modelling estimates of consumption taxes based on demographic and income characteristics at each point in the lifetime, but decided that this approach would add additional complexity and would mean using poor-quality estimated data. Our results are therefore given purely in terms of 'disposable income' after taxes and not in 'post-tax income', which would include consumption taxes. However, for each set of lifetime results, we clearly outline what the aggregate evidence is for the sorts of households on income levels appropriate to our three model lifetime profiles, the Meades, the Lowes and the Moores. This allows us to relate our results to the very considerable changes that increasing indirect taxation has made since 1979.

Outcomes

How do the outcomes of tax and benefit policies differ between 1979, 1997 and 2008 when measured over the lifetime? We measure two forms of outcome. First, we look at incentives to work and put together all of the tax, benefit and other rules to look at the marginal rewards from additional earnings. This approach cumulates all of the marginal tax rates and tapers for means-tested benefits and tax allowances to produce 'effective marginal deduction rates' and it is worth outlining these in more detail.

Effective marginal deduction rates

Having covered the issue of tax, social assistance, in-work benefits and housing benefits, it is worth joining up the potential effect of several overlapping areas of policy for low-paid employees at this point. In reverse order, we have seen how the tapers for rent support from housing benefits have risen and Chapter Five showed how this process works in the same way for local government taxation rebates. Together, these tapers for Housing Benefit and Council Tax Benefit form a combined taper of 85 pence in the pound – that means that for every additional pound of additional income, the rebates are reduced by 85 pence and thus net income (after housing costs) only rises by 15 pence. The expansion of in-work benefits from FIS through Family Credit and to the current system of tax credits operates alongside these tapers. These tapers interact with those of housing benefits where low-paid people are eligible for both housing and other in-work benefits. Income tax and National Insurance contributions, however, also interact with these in-work benefits. Benefit calculations differ on whether they use gross or net income after tax and Housing and Council Tax Benefit take tax credit income into account, so the overall combination of additional tax and reduced benefits for additional earnings is not immediately transparent, but together the interaction of taxation and means-tested benefit tapers produce an 'effective marginal deduction rate'. These marginal rates are important in their impact on households pursuing additional earnings; earners faced with only a net return of four pence for an additional pound of earnings – the highest possible marginal deduction rate, as outlined in the 2008 *Tax benefit model tables* (DWP, 2008d) – may quite reasonably decide not to work harder.

The term 'effective marginal deduction rate' is used from this point to distinguish between the combined effect of taxes and means-tested benefit on marginal gains from earnings and the underlying marginal rate of tax, which, as discussed in Box 5.1 in Chapter Five, refers solely to taxation. Others use the term 'effective marginal tax rate' but whichever term is used, this is a concept we will return to on many occasions during the remainder of the book. It was Field and Piachaud who first brought to light the problem of overlapping means tests and taxation producing a situation where increasing income had little or no effect on net income – the so-called 'poverty trap'. If caught in this trap, families on the margins of a poverty income could do little to earn more and escape the clutches of the proposed Family Income Supplement (Field and Piachaud, 1971). The rise of means testing over the subsequent years has both helped to create and been reformed to respond to the issue of high marginal deduction rates. For instance, the Fowler reforms in the 1980s sought to eliminate rates of over 100% (where someone is actually being worse off for earning an additional pound). Similarly, tax credits in the late 1990s were partly designed to be generous enough to lift many off entitlement to Housing Benefit or Council Tax Benefit and thus rely solely on tax credits and a lower effective marginal deduction rate.

However, it is crucial to point out that while poor effective marginal deduction rates affect those on low incomes most, those on higher incomes are not necessarily free of high rates. This is particularly true in 2008 with Child Tax Credits reaching up into the middle of the income distribution and beyond. However, it is also true of 1997 and 2008 when we take into account the issue of student loan repayments, which we treat as analogous to a tax to be consistent with 1979 when no repayment was necessary. Student loan repayments, especially if they interact with higher rates of tax or with Child Tax Credit entitlement, can raise the effective marginal deduction rates of our middle and higher earnings lifetimes, a point we illustrate in Chapters Twelve and Thirteen.

Replacement rates

Work incentives and the improvement of job entry incentives (not being 'better off on benefit') has been a constant theme of policy since 1979. The value of disposable income on benefits as a proportion of disposable income in work is thus a clear measurement of a replacement rate over time and we calculate these for all model families within LOIS. However, we only report results for the Lowe family, where their low earnings make such replacement rates a clear comparison that is relevant to policy makers' intentions over the period. To capture the effect of rent and housing benefits, we show these figures using 'after housing cost' (AHC) income definitions that are equivalent to disposable income.

Poverty outcomes

We match income definitions to those used in the Household Below Average Income (HBAI) series and thus we can show how incomes of our model families compare with the contemporary poverty lines in 1979, 1997 and 2008. However, when we do so, it is crucial to emphasise that the outcomes we capture are those based both on the changes in policies of taxation and transfers and on other factors that influence the contemporary median income. We discussed this point in some detail at the end of Chapter Ten and will not repeat those details here.

Which poverty line should be used over the lifetime? AHC measures clearly show the impact of housing expenditure and capture the rise in rent levels and house prices over time in three contemporary profiles. The AHC approach also illustrates clearly how the costs of mortgages decline over time compared with rents, which are set to keep pace with standards of living or market return, as discussed in Chapter Six. Crucially, an AHC definition is clearly a more accurate indication of disposable income and household budget constraints when children are present because children occur at that point in the lifetime when housing costs are mostly likely to be at their highest relative to parental income. However, on the other hand, BHC definitions best match the circumstances of retired pensioners who have no mortgage to pay. There is no 'best' measure. Both AHC and BHC measures are appropriate and we use them both to consistently show outcomes between the policy systems in ways that allow the clearest interpretation. We also look at poverty in three profiles for each model lifetime: whole lifetime poverty, childhood poverty and pensioner poverty. Each of these profiles is used alongside an appropriate policy model that takes into account inflation and policy maturity.

All of the poverty measures used in the analysis come from reported data, either the historic series of HBAI for 1997 or the Institute of Fiscal Studies time series data for 1979 (Brewer et al, 2008), that we use on a consistent basis. We extrapolate the poverty line for 2008 from 2006 data using earnings growth.

Inequality

Our lifetime models only use three illustrative families: the Meades, on median earnings; the Moores, on twice median earnings; and the Lowes, on half median earnings. Our use of arithmetic fractions and multipliers of mean gross earnings allows us to show the evolving differences in original and disposable income between the three families in 1979, 1997 and 2008. How far are the Lowes and Moores diverging from the Meades and how has this divergence changed between the policy years? Such findings on inequality cannot replicate those shown and discussed in Chapter Ten, but allow us to illustrate the changing income inequality since 1979 and demonstrate how far changes in policy have contributed to it.

Notes
[1] There is a macroeconomic argument that welfare spending in general is inflationary under some assumptions. Where any general effect is concerned, we still term this as 'exogenous' to distinguish it from politically determined prices.

[2] We will not model disability benefits in Chapters 12, 13 and 14 and do not outline them here.

TWELVE

The Meades

In this and the following two chapters, we finally turn to the results of our hypothetical lifetime simulations. This chapter considers the median-earning Meades. What would a median-earning family experience in taxes and benefits if they lived their whole lives under the 1979, 1997 and 2008 rules? The results for the Meades will be carried forward as a benchmark against which we will consider outcomes for the high-earning Moores and the low-earning Lowes respectively in the following two chapters.

Our main questions address the following issues:

- How and to what extent do benefits and taxation differ between the three policy systems when viewed from the lifetime perspective? How does their incidence differ between the 1979, 1997 and 2008 systems?
- What difference does allowing for different behaviour that has evolved since 1979 make?
- If the policy systems of 1979, 1997 and 2008 were fully matured, what difference would it make?
- What difference would inflation and uprating make to tax and benefit incidence?
- Do the Meades face different incentives under the three historical systems?
- How do the three historical systems leave the Meades in terms of their position in the income distribution? Are the Meades at risk of child poverty or pensioner poverty under any of the three systems?

The Meades' model lifetime

We begin by outlining the 'lifetime history' parameters that are used to create our hypothetical profile. It is worth re-emphasising the point made in Chapter Eleven that these simplistic life histories are designed for consistent comparison of the policy systems and not to reflect empirical lifetime profiles of actual people. The life history that we employ for the Meades runs as follows:

- The profile starts at age 16. Ms Meade continues her secondary education and then takes a degree. She thus remains in full-time education until 21.
- At age 21 she begins work. She works in the public sector and joins her employer's occupational pension scheme, contracting out from the State Earnings Related Pension Scheme (SERPS).

- She lives at home with her parents until age 22, when she moves into rented accommodation.
- At 26 she cohabits with Mr Meade (who is exactly the same age and has a very similar life history – he, too, works in the public sector, beginning work and joining his employer's occupational pension scheme at age 21).
- At age 28, they marry.
- At 30, they have sufficient savings for a 10% deposit on a house valued at the average contemporary purchase price for first-time buyers, which they buy, taking out a 25-year mortgage.
- At age 32, they have their first child. Ms Meade takes a total of nine months' maternity leave, returning to part-time work thereafter.
- At age 34, they have their second child, and again Ms Meade takes nine months' maternity leave.
- At age 39, when her youngest child is five, Ms Meade returns to full-time work. While Ms Meade is in work and her children are under 14, the Meades pay for childcare. Throughout their working lifetimes, the Meades work for the prevailing female and male median wages.
- Ms Meade retires at age 60. Mr Meade retires at age 65. They both die at age 85.

This profile is used throughout the first set of comparisons of the 1979, 1997 and 2008 systems. However, a variation to reflect behavioural differences is used later to illustrate '1979 behaviour' and to measure the potentially different outcomes that arise from changing behaviour over time.

The incidence of taxes and benefits

The Meades' lifetime in 2008

We begin by profiling the 2008 system in the simplest of ways. The Meades live out their entire lives in a 'Groundhog Day' world with no inflation. Every day of their lives the Meades will face the tax and benefit system as it stood in December of 2008 with exactly the same levels and rates of benefits and taxes alongside contemporary earnings levels and prices.

Figure 12.1 shows the resulting lifetime income profile and the underlying income components from earnings, taxes, benefits and pensions for the Meades. Gross earnings, state transfers and private pension income appear above the x-axis, and negative income components (taxes, private pension contributions and childcare costs) appear below. The black plotted line depicts the Meades' disposable income in terms of after housing costs (AHC) income with the tinted line section showing AHC income after childcare costs.

This simple profile allows us to bring out some general, although perhaps not unexpected, features of the Meades' lifetime income profile and to ensure that

Figure 12.1: The Meades' lifetime income profile, 2008 system

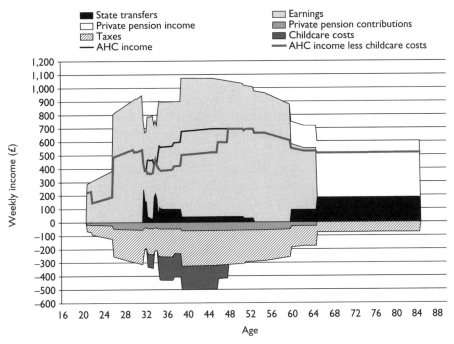

Source: Authors' calculations from LOIS.

the assumptions we have used in the profile are understood and their implications clear. First, the life history event assumptions have a clear effect on the level and composition of income. For example, we can see a fall in AHC income at age 22, as Ms Meade leaves home and faces significant housing costs for the first time; we can see the household's income in earnings more than double at age 26 as Ms Meade partners and Mr Meade becomes a part of the economic unit; we can see how the time that Ms Meade takes away from work through maternity leave and working part-time hours while the family has young children affects household earnings; and so on. Second, we can see the effect of the lifetime earnings weights that were outlined in Chapter Eleven, which, all else being equal, would serve to increase the Meades' earnings from starting work to a high point around their forties before a slight downturn in their earning power thereafter.

Taxes, private pension contributions and childcare costs are shown below the x-axis. The Meades pay taxes throughout their entire working lives and retirement. Looking above the x-axis, there are only two periods during which state transfers (benefits and tax credits) play any role: first, when the Meades have dependent children and, second, when one or both of the Meades have retired. Our standard assumption of final salary occupational pension means that their private pension income will prevent them facing an uncomfortable drop in income in retirement.

Incidence of tax and benefits across the 1979, 1997 and 2008 systems

Keeping this lifetime profile and fundamental structures in place, we can now compare the 1979, 1997 and 2008 systems. Table 12.1 shows the results of a comparison of the Meades' lifetime profile for these years with contemporary median earnings and price assumptions.

Taking direct taxation first, under all three systems the Meades pay tax from the moment they leave full-time education and begin work until their deaths. Direct taxes comprise income tax, National Insurance contributions (NICs), rates and council tax, but we also include repayment of student loans as analogous to tax to enable consistent comparison of 1979 (when there were no loans) and subsequent years. The repayment of student loans represents around 1.3% of the Meades' lifetime earnings under the 2008 system and 0.6% under the 1997 system. Total resulting lifetime taxation for the Meades is 28% of gross lifetime earnings under the 1997 system, 30% under the 2008 system and 32% under the 1979

Table 12.1: The Meades' lifetime under the 1979, 1997 and 2008 systems

	Percentage of lifetime earnings		
	1979	1997	2008
Direct taxation			
All direct taxes (including student loan repayments)	31.9	28.0	29.8
All direct taxes (excluding student loan repayments)	31.9	27.4	28.5
State transfers			
All	17.5	13.8	15.5
Maternity/dependent children	2.2	1.9	3.8
Retirement	15.3	12.0	11.8
Net effects of direct taxes and transfers	**−14.4**	**−14.2**	**−14.3**
Other transfers and payments			
Private pension contributions	6.0	6.0	6.0
Private pension income	25.9	26.1	26.2
Childcare costs	5.7	6.3	6.6
Housing costs	4.1	4.7	6.8
Lifetime income totals (£million, 2008 prices)			
Lifetime gross earnings	1.29	1.67	1.83
Lifetime disposable income after housing and childcare costs	1.26	1.59	1.70

Source: Authors' calculations from LOIS.

Note: Meades modelled with constant '2008 behaviour' across all three systems.

system. However, we only use income calculations to capture direct taxation. The significant changes to indirect taxation since 1979 will have an additional effect that we discuss after looking at other elements of the changes in direct taxation and at transfers.

The different lifetime incidence of direct taxes is affected not just by changing rates of income tax, the headline political story, but also by the changing nature of tax reliefs – primarily in the forms of allowances and set-offs against income tax and in rebated NICs. We know from Chapter Five that the underlying position of personal allowances and lower earnings limits (LELs) have not changed much in relation to median earnings but that tax allowances for marriage have disappeared, age allowances have been made more generous and mortgage interest tax relief has disappeared. On the other hand, tax relief on pension contributions, both from income tax and National Insurance, has been allowed to continue. We estimate the costs of all these additional elements of tax relief, above and beyond the basic personal allowances and LEL as 6.9% of lifetime earnings in 1979, 5.4% in 1997 and 3.8% in 2008. Tax reliefs clearly play the greatest role under the 1979 system, where in particular tax reliefs in respect of marriage and pension contributions serve to keep taxation for the Meades dramatically lower than it would otherwise be. For example, were the Meades to be modelled as an unmarried and never-marrying couple, their lifetime tax total would be over two percentage points higher.

State transfers only occur for childhood and retirement under all three systems. Transfer income is lowest in total under the 1997 system, at 13.8% of lifetime earnings compared with 15.5% under the 2008 system and 17.5% under the 1979 system. Different prioritisation of pensions and children's benefits are clear. Transfers for childhood (from pregnancy with the Meades' first child to their youngest child's 19th birthday) are far higher under the 2008 system – 3.8%, compared with 2.2% for 1979 and a mere 1.9% for 1997. The higher spending on child transfers reflects both the tax credits available to help with childcare and the increased generosity of maternity provision under the 2008 system. State spending on state pensions has declined from 15.3% under the 1979 system to 12% under the 1997 system and again to 11.8% under the 2008 system, principally due to the erosion of the relative value of the basic state pension over the intervening periods between the comparison years.

Table 12.1 also shows the combined impact of direct taxes and transfers, the overall net effect, as a percentage of gross lifetime earnings and the differences between the 1979, 1997 and 2008 systems are minimal. 1979 provides a net effect of −14.4%, 1997 −14.2% and 2008 −14.3%. Given that our methodology of estimation is a hypothetical model, it is safer to conclude that there are no significant differences between the three systems in their overall net effect of direct income-related taxation and transfers over the lifetime.

But at this point, it is necessary to consider the effects of indirect taxation. Outside our lifetime methodology, we can estimate figures for indirect taxation from available summary data discussed in Chapter Ten. Using these figures for disposable income, we can approximate indirect taxation at around 12.5% for the 1979 system, 16.5% for the 1997 system and 15.5% for the 2008 system. Given that the differences in net effects of direct taxation and transfers combined are minimal, additional consideration of the potential of indirect taxation would allow us to rank the systems according to the incidence of indirect taxation alone. We do not conclude that it is correct to do so but that this means that the 'low tax' outcomes of 1997, and less so of 2008, are pretty meaningless when compared with 1979 for the Meades. It is safer to conclude that the differences overall are marginal.

Employer-subsidised final salary occupational pension schemes clearly benefit the Meades greatly. For a fixed contribution of 6% of their earnings, they receive pensions that represent around 26% of their lifetime earnings. Their employers' contributions, along with fiscal subsidies and market investment, are making a huge impact on lifetime incomes, with a gain equivalent to a net 20% of lifetime gross earnings. The other costs that the Meades face – housing and childcare – rise as a proportion of gross lifetime earnings because underlying costs have risen faster than gross earnings over time. Inflation between 1979 and 2008 also clearly affects the lifetime totals for housing costs even when we keep interest rates constant across the comparison years. The rising childcare costs reflect rising female relative to male wages as childcare is assumed to be a fixed percentage of maternal earnings.

The final rows of Table 12.1 give an illustrative picture of how lifetime gross earnings and net disposable income after housing and childcare costs compare in constant 2008 prices. Gross earnings have risen over time as a result of the growth in real median earnings discussed earlier in Chapter Ten. When the effects of higher housing costs and childcare are taken into account alongside direct taxation, net disposable income in 2008 prices suggests that the Meades have 'never had it so good' as in 2008, in terms of disposable income and living standards. But this does not take into account the issue of indirect taxation, which may equalise outcomes between 1979 and the two later years and does not take into account the withdrawal of many employers from final salary occupational schemes. If the Meades relied on financing their own personal pensions in 1997 and 2008, their lifetime outcomes would be very different – a point we return to later.

This core set of results forms the basis for further discussion and analysis. What differences would occur if we used the behaviour of 30 years ago to profile 1979 and how would each scheme finally mature to provide different outcomes than those arising from the rules that were in place in 1979, 1997 and 2008?

Allowing for behavioural difference and policy maturation

So far we have used a constant set of lifetime events based on contemporary 2008 behaviour to consistently profile the three systems. As discussed in Chapter Eleven, we now adopt a different pattern of behaviour to capture the long-term changes in behaviour from 1979 and keep 1997 results to reflect 2008 behaviour.

The 1979 lifetime behaviour significantly includes three sorts of changes: timing of partnership; maternal employment; and life expectancy. As with our 2008 model behaviour, we allow our story to be informed by statistical evidence, in particular focusing on the differences between 1979 and 2008 statistics in respect of middle earners, but at the same time ensuring that our story remains a coherent one. In particular explanation of this 1979 behaviour, the Meades' early marriage is informed by the statistic that the median ages at marriage for both single men and single women were in 1979 six years lower than they are according to the latest available figures (ONS, 2008a). The decision not to have the Meades cohabit before marriage is informed by lower rates of cohabitation in the 1970s (see Chapter Three). The decision to have the Meades purchase their house at a relatively young age reflects a world of cheaper house prices before the repayment of student loans, and is informed by statistics produced by mortgage lenders showing the average age of first-time buyers rising between the 1970s and today[1]. The decision to have the Meades have their first child earlier is informed by the mean age of mother for first live births in marriage among those whose husband's social class is skilled non-manual, with this figure being four years younger in 1979 than it is according to the latest available figures (ONS, 2008c). Finally, of note, our decision to 'kill off' the Meades five years earlier for the 1979 behaviour model is informed by life expectancy at 65 being much higher today than it was in 1979. Figures from the Government Actuary's Department, for example, put the period life expectancy of men at 65 at 13 years for 1981 (the nearest year to 1979 with available data) and 17.8 years for 2008, a difference of 4.8 years (GAD, 2008a).

Earlier marriage, house purchase and childbirth, as well as there being no cohabitation prior to marriage, mean that the lifetime behaviour diverges from the 2008 pattern at age 24:

- At age 24, Ms Meade marries Mr Meade without any period of prior cohabitation.
- At 26, the Meades buy a house, having accumulated sufficient savings for a 10% deposit on it.
- At age 28, they have their first child.
- At age 30, they have their second child.

The changes to maternal employment mean part-time employment and zero childcare costs:

- Ms Meade does not return to work until the youngest child is aged five and starts primary school, at which point she returns to work *part time*.

- Once the youngest child starts primary school at age 11, Ms Meade returns to full-time work.
- The Meades do not at any point use any paid childcare.

The changes to life expectancy are based on constant pension age and retirement at 60 for Ms Meade and at 65 for Mr Meade:

- They both die at age 80 – reducing life expectancy by five years from previous 2008 assumptions.

The mature systems of 1979, 1997 and 2008 change in following ways:

- 1979: higher rates of National Insurance contributions (NICs) and reduced National Insurance rebates to pay for a fully mature SERPS system.
- 1997: full erosion of tax reliefs in respect of marriage and mortgage interest; equal pension ages for men and women at 65.
- 2008: extended pension age to 68 for both Mr and Ms Meade linked to a further five years of life expectancy; full enactment of the provisions of the 2007 Pensions Act; 12 months of maternity leave and Statutory Maternity Pay.

The set of further simulations produces another five sets of model lifetime results and the total eight model results are given in Table 12.2, including those from Table 12.1 shown in grey shading. The changing length of lifetime used across the different simulations is also shown.

How far do the 1979 results change if behaviour appropriate to that year is used rather than current assumptions? Lifetime housing costs are lower because the Meades purchase their home earlier and therefore spend less money on rent prior to purchase and enjoy more years as full owner-occupiers with no mortgage. Childcare costs are non-existent as an explicit cost because Ms Meade works part time and avoids them – but the effect of substituting her own lost wages for childcare charges can be seen in the lower levels of lifetime gross earnings and the knock-on effect that has on taxation and pension outcomes. However, pension income, both private and state, is lower under the 1979 behaviour because of the assumption of reduced longevity. Changing Ms Meade's earning behaviour lowers the tax take under the 1979 system, as that tax system favours the situation where a wife is either not working or working for part-time or otherwise low pay. This brings the 1979 direct tax take to exactly the same level as 2008 if each reflects contemporary behaviour of their time.

What would be the results if the 1979 system matured? Higher NICs, from both members and non-members of SERPS, would have been required to fund the mature SERPS scheme. The 1974 White Paper that introduced SERPS spelt out that contracted-out employees would be expected to share the burden of the mature scheme through a much lower contracted-out rebate once the scheme had reached maturity (DHSS, 1974). As discussed in Chapter Eleven, we use 1985 government estimates (DHSS, 1985b) to calculate these increases to the main and contracted-out rate of NICs (increases of 4.3% and 4.9% respectively). Thus, under the mature 1979 policy system, we do see the Meades being faced with higher levels of overall taxation – indeed, this is the only change introduced by modelling a mature system.

What differences would a maturation of the 1997 system make to the comparison? Ms Meade works an extra five years to reach the new equivalised pension age of 65 and more tax is taken through the removal of tax allowances for marriage and Mortgage Interest Relief at Source (MIRAS). The five years of additional work (compared with non-mature 1997 assumptions) means that the Meades have a higher lifetime earnings total, which provides a larger numerator for gross lifetime earnings and thus lower percentage tax takes and transfer levels over the lifetime. State pension income totals are lower because Ms Meade misses out on five years of pension income that she would have received had she retired at 60. Housing costs remain constant, as any fall that would have occurred has been entirely offset by additional costs due to the abolition of MIRAS. Direct taxation rises due to the removal of additional tax allowances for marriage. However, the taxation result for the mature 1997 is still the lowest in comparison with 1979 and 2008 system results.

How does the mature system assumption change our outcomes for 2008? The main effect is through extending the working life and consequent higher lifetime earnings that drive down all the percentage of lifetime earnings results (except the rate of private pension contributions), with, for example, childcare costs falling from 6.6% to 5.8% (which is actually below the 1997 mature system result) as the Meades spend additional years in work without dependent children.

Comparing the eight sets of results is best done using consistent measures of outcome and there are two that stand out. First is the net effect of taxes and benefits as a proportion of lifetime gross income. Our first set of results showed little difference between the three systems, with all net outcomes over the lifetime between −14.2% and −14.4% of gross earnings on both a constant behaviour and constant lifetime years assumption. Maturing the 1979 system has the biggest effect by raising net effects to −19% of gross earnings. However, maturing of both the 1997 and 2008 systems also raises the tax take and the overall net effects rise to −17% and −16% for 1997 and 2008 respectively. Once again, it is necessary to bring in the unseen factor of indirect taxation that is so much higher in the 1997 and 2008 systems compared with 1979. Even with the highest tax assumption of 1979 it is probable that the differences after indirect taxes would be considerable between the systems.

A second, more nuanced, measure of outcome is to take disposable lifetime income, which takes into account housing and childcare costs, and to express that in equivalent lifetime years to allow for the differences in longevity and working

Table 12.2: The Meades' lifetime under the 1979, 1997 and 2008 systems with behavioural change and policy maturation

	1979				1997		2008	
	1979 behaviour		Current behaviour		Current behaviour		Current behaviour	
	'79 rules	Mature	'79 rules	Mature	'97 rules	Mature	'08 rules	Mature
Total number of lifetime years modelled	120	120	128	128	128	128	128	138
Female	(64)	(64)	(69)	(69)	(69)	(69)	(69)	(74)
Male	(56)	(56)	(59)	(85)	(59)	(59)	(59)	(64)
Percentage of lifetime earnings								
All direct taxes								
(including student loan repayments)	29.8	34.5	31.9	36.6	28.0	28.9	29.8	29.5
(excluding student loan repayments)	(29.8)	(34.5)	(31.9)	(36.6)	(27.4)	(28.4)	(28.5)	(28.2)
All state transfers	14.6	14.6	17.5	17.5	13.8	11.9	15.5	13.6
Maternity/children	2.2	2.2	2.2	2.2	1.9	1.8	3.8	3.5
Retirement	12.3	12.3	15.3	15.3	12.0	10.1	11.8	10.1
Net effects of direct taxes and transfers	**-15.2**	**-19.9**	**-14.4**	**-19.1**	**-14.2**	**-17.0**	**-14.3**	**-15.9**
Other transfers and payments								
Private pension contributions	6.0	6.0	6.0	6.0	6.0	6.0	6.0	6.0
Private pension income	19.3	19.3	25.9	25.9	26.1	23.5	26.2	26.0
Childcare costs	–	–	5.7	5.7	6.3	6.0	6.6	5.8
Housing costs	3.8	3.8	4.1	4.1	4.7	4.7	6.8	6.2
Lifetime income totals (£million, 2008 prices)								
Lifetime earnings	1.25	1.25	1.29	1.29	1.67	1.75	1.83	2.05
Lifetime disposable AHC income after childcare costs	1.18	1.12	1.24	1.18	1.59	1.58	1.70	1.89
Disposable income per year of life (2008 £ rounded to nearest £100)	9,800	9,300	9,700	9,200	12,400	12,300	13,300	13,700

Source: Authors' calculations from LOIS.

histories across the models. This shows that 1979 outcomes differ mostly from maturity assumptions of paying for SERPS, rather than differences in behaviour. In 1997, disposable incomes have risen significantly, both from underlying earnings growth and lower direct taxation, but maturity assumptions make little difference to adjusted years of life outcomes. In 2008, once again earnings growth has raised disposable incomes despite higher housing costs and increasing the number of years of earnings, and even allowing for associated longer life expectancy, gives a substantial increase in disposable incomes.

Allowing for inflation and uprating

Chapter Eleven put forward the methodology for capturing the effects of inflation over each hypothetical lifetime based in 1979, 1997 and 2008. Our analysis so far already reflects differences in inflation over the 30 years since 1979 by highlighting the changing levels of benefits, house prices and so on. However, each system, in 1979, 1997 and 2008, will treat inflation differently and uprate benefits and taxes accordingly. Capturing this crucial aspect of policy differences between the systems is clearly important, as our policy discussions in Parts One and Two of the book makes clear. One of the best examples of such policy difference can be seen in government's treatment of the basic state pension over the 30 years. The 1979 system/Old Labour policy was to uprate the basic pension in line with the better of earnings or prices, while the approach of the Conservatives and early New Labour in the late 1990s was to abandon earnings uprating altogether and solely, up-rate with prices. New Labour's most recent commitment, however, is to return to earnings uprating of the state pension from a target date of 2012.

Table 12.3 shows the effect of inflation and uprating policies on our original benchmark profiles shown in Table 12.1 and based on a constant 2008 set of lifetime behaviour. The nominal effect of inflation is balanced over the hypothetical lifetime by setting true contemporary prices and earnings at age 40 with equal years of inflation either side over the lifetime. Table 12.3 clearly shows that inflation affects lifetime outcomes greatly. The most notable changes concern retirement outcomes, private pension income and state transfers during retirement (and consequently the 'all state transfers' results). The greatest impact is on occupational pension. When this is calculated on the basis of final salary, its value increases greatly in the world with inflation, raising it from what is effectively an average lifetime salary in the inflation-free world. This means that the value of the pension expressed as a percentage of lifetime earnings jumps from around 26% under all systems in the inflation-free models to around 40% under all systems when inflation is modelled.

The other dramatic change once inflation is introduced is to the result for state transfers during retirement under the 1979 system. This jumps from 15.3% in the inflation-free world to 32.5% with inflation modelled, whereas no comparable rise, and indeed a slight fall, is seen under the 1997 and 2008 systems. This reflects the

Table 12.3: The Meades' lifetime under the 1979, 1997 and 2008 systems with inflation modelled

	1979		1997		2008	
	Flat	**Inflation**	**Flat**	**Inflation**	**Flat**	**Inflation**
	Percentage of lifetime earnings					
All direct taxes						
(including student loan repayments)	31.9	33.7	28.0	27.0	29.8	29.9
(excluding student loan repayments)	31.9	33.7	27.4	26.5	28.5	28.6
All state transfers	17.5	34.7	13.8	11.9	15.5	13.4
Maternity/dependent children	2.2	2.0	1.9	1.6	3.8	3.2
Retirement	15.3	32.5	12.0	10.4	11.8	10.2
Other periods	0.0	0.2	0.0	0.0	0.0	0.0
Net effects of direct taxes and transfers	−14.4	+1.0	−14.2	−15.1	−14.3	−16.5
Other transfers and payments						
Private pension contributions	6.0	6.0	6.0	6.0	6.0	6.0
Private pension income	25.9	40.5	26.1	40.8	26.2	40.9
Childcare costs	5.7	4.9	6.3	5.5	6.6	5.8
Housing costs	4.1	2.8	4.7	3.2	6.8	4.8

Source: Authors' calculations from LOIS.

Note: Constant 2008 assumptions for behaviour.

huge lifetime impact of differences in uprating policy of the basic state pension and the move to uprate only in line with prices under the 1997 and (current) 2008 systems.

Higher income in retirement, through a combination of higher private pension income and a state pension that is uprated in line with earnings, leads to an increase in taxation in retirement under the 1979 system and amounts to a 1.8% increase in total lifetime taxation. Elsewhere the introduction of inflation has less dramatic consequences and the new results give us no cause to revise the conclusions we have already drawn. However, one final, notable anomaly is Ms Meade's rent and rate rebates when she is young and single. Reductions in the generosity of housing benefits over the 1980s mean that the post-1979 systems provide no equivalent entitlement.

Figure 12.2 illustrates our benchmark models with inflation in terms of the net effects of the tax and benefit systems on the Meades' original income. Original income means gross earnings prior to retirement and gross occupational pension thereafter. This means that net effects will be mostly negative (taxation mostly outweighing transfers) during working years and will be positive during retirement as state transfers will outweigh taxation and will be a larger proportion of private occupational pension income. For instance, at age 52 while earning, the results from all three systems give around a 71% net effect, meaning that the Meades keep this proportion of gross earnings after tax and benefits. On the other hand, turning to retirement and the change of lifetime income from earnings to pensions (effectively income from savings), Figure 12.2 demonstrates the effect of inflation in both its manifestations. First, the different relative values of state retirement pension income at the point of retirement are clear from the starting points for pension income at 60 (Ms Meade) and at 65 (Mr Meade). Second, over the period of retirement, the profiles differ between the price-indexed state retirement pensions in 1997 and 2008, which are effectively a flat proportion of price-protected occupational pensions, and the 1979 earnings uprated state pension, which rises as a proportion of the price-protected occupational pension over retirement.

Figure 12.2: The Meades' net effects of taxes and benefits over the lifetime

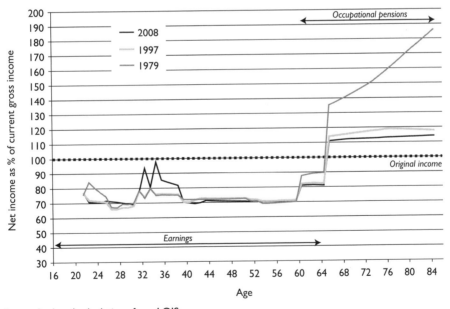

Source: Authors' calculations from LOIS.

Note: Simulation from the Meades' lifetime using benchmark models with inflation.

Figure 12.2 shows that results under the three systems differ dramatically during three periods of the Meades' lifetime. First, as mentioned above, rent and rate rebates occur in the early years before marriage in the 1979 system, which is unique to that year Second, greatest support for childhood occurs under the 2008 system, with its generosity of maternity and tax credit provision. Third, and most dramatically, retirement in the 1979 system provides an earnings uprated pension alongside an occupational pension that rises with prices. This means that the net effects of the state pension rise over time, even after taxation, because of the differential between earnings and prices that we model as 2% per annum.

The most striking thing about the remaining results is the similarity between the 1979, 1997 and 2008 systems. For the working age period, ignoring the five-year overlapping period when Ms Meade retires at 60 and Mr Meade still works, the Meades 'keep' around 70% of their gross earnings under all three systems.

Outcomes

We now move on to consider our second area of comparative lifetime profiles of 1979, 1997 and 2008 policy – the outcomes in terms of work incentives, and in terms of the final income position of the Meades in the income distribution and in relation to relative poverty.

Work incentives

Our policy history in Part Two of the book clearly showed several overlapping and potentially confounding trends. First, the move from contributory to means-tested approaches to social security and other transfers raised the risk of deteriorating work incentives. Similarly, higher National Insurance rates and the introduction of the repayment of student loans would take higher proportions of earnings for many and for longer periods of the lifetime. Second, the high-profile lowering of headline rates of income taxes was often heralded as reducing the burden on earnings, rewarding work further and allowing people to spend more. How do these trends affect the Meades?

Adding the tax rates and tapers from means-tested transfers allows the calculation of an effective marginal deduction rate as described in Chapter Eleven. This measure captures the portion of an additional £1 of earnings that would be left after tax and benefit deductions are applied. Figure 12.3 shows these effective marginal deduction rates for Mr Meade from the age of 26 when he joins the lifetime profile until he retires at age 65, using our consistent '2008' behaviour model previously shown in Table 12.1 and Figure 12.1[2]. Marginal rates include those for his occupational pension contributions, which are a fixed 6% of gross income across all three years. In 1979, an unchanging marginal deduction rate of 41% comes from the combination of income tax and National Insurance and in 1997 there is a similar flat profile at a lower but unchanging rate of 36%[3].

Figure 12.3: Mr Meade's effective marginal deduction rates

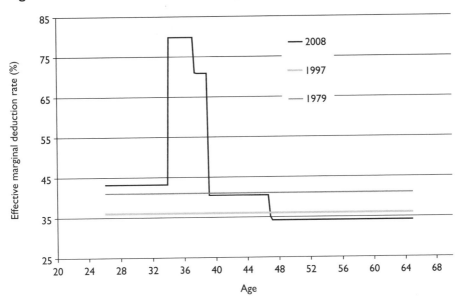

Source: Authors' calculations from LOIS.

Mr Meade is never a high-rate taxpayer under the 2008 system, but his overall marginal deduction rate is still higher than under the 1997 or 1979 systems at age 26 because of student loan repayments (9p of Mr Meade's extra £1 will go towards repaying his student loan). With the arrival of children and entitlement to tax credits, his overall marginal deduction rates (which combine the taper of tax credits with tax rates and student loan deductions) rise to 80%, fall to 71% when his student loan is paid off and then fall again to 40% when tax credits solely comprise the family element of Child Tax Credit. Only when children leave the household does he reap the full advantage of the 2008 system's lower underlying tax rates, from the age of 50.

The lifetime impact of such marginal deduction rates under the 2008 system means that they are highest and have the biggest potential for deterring additional earnings at the period in the lifetime when costs are highest from having children and purchasing a house. Lower rates in later life when the children have left home (ignoring for the sake of argument that those children will still represent significant costs while at university) will assist in saving for retirement but reflect a period in the lifetime when costs are lower. The additional problem for 2008 is that the rates that arise from tax credits are based on the earnings of both Mr and Ms Meade – and this means that Ms Meade will face high marginal deduction rates on additional earnings during her return to work after having children. The impact of incentives on children and child poverty is thus a theme we return to in our conclusions.

Another way in which we could consider incentives is in terms of replacement rates, asking what percentage of the Meades' income would be replaced by state transfers in the event of the household becoming workless. Such analysis would address the issue of whether it pays to work and thereby the validity or otherwise of any 'why work?' argument. However, these questions are clearly of greater relevance when we are talking about low-income families. We therefore postpone our analysis of replacement rates until we get to the Lowes and content ourselves for now with the knowledge that the Meades (and more so the Moores) will, to a greater or lesser extent under all three tax and benefit systems under consideration, always be better off in work.

How do the Meades fare in the overall income distribution?

We carry forward our three models with inflation shown in Table 12.3 to address how the Meades fare in the overall income distribution over their lifetime. Figure 12.4 thus illustrates the Meades' lifetimes using constant 2008 behaviour. We use AHC income to control for the changing levels of housing costs over time (see Figure 6.4 in Chapter Six) and express the Meades' income as a percentage of contemporary median equivalised AHC income for the whole population. This means that the comparison is with the changing level of survey-based data on median incomes over time and includes the underlying change in the relationship between median earnings and median income in 1979, 1997 and 2008 discussed in Chapter Ten (see Figure 10.6).

Figure 12.4 shows the Meades' position in the income distribution and their relative position to the contemporary poverty line in 1979, 1997 and 2008. The Meades never fall close to or below the poverty line in any of the years. The closest the household gets to poverty is under the 2008 system when Ms Meade is single and leaves home to move into rented accommodation; the second closest point is at the end of the Meades' retirement when their pension incomes fall against a rising relative poverty line in the 1997 and 2008 systems. Pension income in 1979 falls less quickly against the poverty line as state pensions are uprated in line with earnings and help cushion the relative fall of the price inflation-protected occupational pension. Elsewhere and in all three years the Meade household remains comfortably above poverty, and at or above median income level. The Meades enjoy the best outcomes in terms of relative income position as so-called 'DINKYs'[4], between the ages of 26 and 31 when they are both working full-time and have no children, and even more so at ages 53-59 when they are 'empty nesters', that is when the children have grown up and left home. For the Meades, this coincides with reduced mortgage costs as their loan matures.

Interpreting the ranking of the 1979, 1997 and 2008 systems during retirement is fairly straightforward. State pension value falls against poverty between all years and over time in 1997 and 2008 but not 1979. This means that 1979 has the most

Figure 12.4: The Meades' relative position in the income distribution

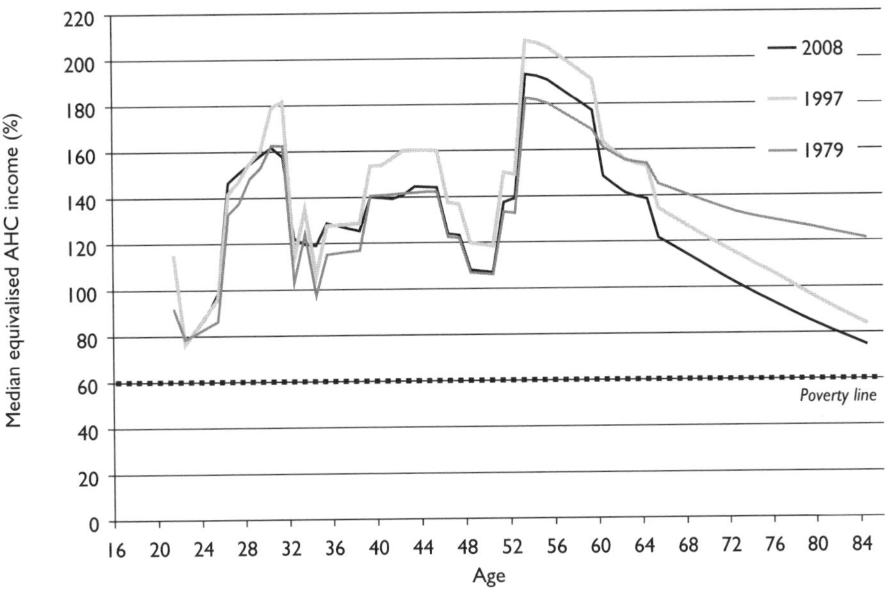

Source: Authors' calculations from LOIS.

Note: Simulation of the Meades' lifetime using 2008 behaviour models with inflation.

favourable characteristics for maintaining relative living standards in retirement when combined with final salary occupational pensions.

The ranking of the systems during working age is more difficult, as there are several underlying factors that combine with the effects of taxes and benefits. First, housing costs have risen faster than earnings over time and thus AHC incomes will not fully reflect underlying earnings growth. The AHC income distribution is cross-sectional for each year and thus represents a stock of owner-occupiers with a range of purchase and loan histories; in this scenario, the Meade family is placed as having purchased a home in contemporary prices. Second, we know that median household income growth and earnings growth are not aligned and thus the higher position in the 1997 income distribution compared with 2008 is partly due to the fall in the relative value of median income against median earnings (see Chapter Ten). Third, the increased generosity of the 2008 system in real and net effects for children's transfers, demonstrated in Chapter Four and earlier in Figure 12.2, does not do enough to keep relative income position, given the combined effects of housing costs and median income growth. One aspect of this latter problem is that the value of tax credits erodes over time and is thus very sensitive to assumptions about inflation and uprating. Here we have neutral inflation at age 40 and then deflate and inflate either side of this point to leave lifetime inflation profiles balanced. An alternative way to consider the effects of inflation would be to change the starting point to reflect the events that trigger changes in transfers and taxation and we adopt this approach in looking at childhood and retirement respectively.

Childhood and risk of poverty

Here we solely look at the childhood period of the Meades' lifetime in order to assess the position in 1979, 1997 and 2008 more distinctly against inflation and uprating beginning at the point of birth of the first child. We also use medium-term rather than long-term assumptions about benefit erosion and fiscal drag (see Chapter Eleven, Box 11.3). The childhood period begins with Ms Meade giving birth to her first child and ends at the point at which the Meades' second (and eldest) child becomes 19.

Figure 12.5 illustrates a child poverty profile for the Meades using this approach. Notwithstanding the government's preference for a BHC measure of child poverty, in large part in order to facilitate international comparisons, we show both AHC and BHC measures here, as housing costs are clearly a significant factor in dictating the Meades' disposable income during this period of their lifetime.

The income lines in Figures 12.5a and b reflect the assumptions of equivalisation used to account for change in household size as well as the common pattern of employment based on '2008' behaviour, with Ms Meade returning to full-time employment at age 39 (when her second and youngest child is five). Prior to this, the household relies on the full-time earnings of Mr Meade and on the part-time (50%) earnings of Ms Meade as well as her maternity pay. The equivalence scale used reduces income against the poverty line at age 34 when the Meades have their second child, and again at age 46 as their first child turns 14, and once more at 48 when their second child turns 14.

This leads to the underlying income profile against poverty being n-shaped over the period of childhood – lower and constrained earnings in early childhood but lower needs associated with younger children, followed by lower constraints on income allowing full-time work by both parents as children reach school age and mature, and finally by the higher needs of teenage children combined with full-time earnings that cause income to dip again. Obviously, the presence of more than one child causes 'steps' in the profile as they age over time.

Figure 12.5a shows the BHC income profile and this allows us to focus on the issues that give rise to childhood poverty clearance other than housing costs. The first point to note is that the 'generous' provision through tax credits in the 2008 system does not compare well with 1997 and 1979. Earlier profiles in this Chapter and Chapter Four showed performance of tax credits in periods where mothers were either not working or were working part time. There is no reason to expect the 2008 system to grant the Meades the strongest results in terms of poverty clearance once Ms Meade returns to full-time work at age 39, as two full-time median-earner incomes result in low levels of Child Tax Credit entitlement. Indeed, it is worth referring back to Figure 12.4 to remember that the 1997 and

1979 systems granted better outcomes for the Meades in terms of the net effects of the tax and benefit systems during the period when the Meades have dependent children and two full-time earners (from age 39 to age 52).

Figure 12.5a: The Meades' childhood poverty profile before housing costs

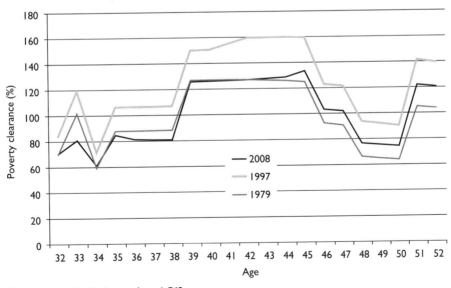

Figure 12.5b: The Meades' childhood poverty profile after housing costs

Source: Authors' calculations from LOIS.

Second, there is the crucial impact of inflation and benefit erosion. Allowing for benefit erosion and fiscal drag to occur from the point of birth of the first child means that any increased generosity in the 2008 tax credit system is eroded surprisingly quickly, to the point where the Meades no longer qualify for tax credits over the childhood period. Parts of the tax credit system are not uprated at all, despite the child credit element rising in line with earnings, and the overall effect for the Meades is that tax credits fall away. The anti-poverty impact of tax credits may thus erode in short order given earnings growth and a consequently rising poverty line. This is a crucial point and one to which we return in more detail in respect of the low-paid Lowe family.

Third, and in line with earlier findings, the 1997 results have the inherent advantage of a contemporary poverty line that is easier to beat than the 2008 poverty line. The 2008 system has to work that much harder just to obtain the same, let alone better, results in terms of poverty clearance.

Finally, as shown in Figure 12.5b, higher housing costs play an additional part in reducing the impact of taxes and transfers. High house prices and mortgage costs in 2008 mean that pressures on disposable income are highest over the childhood period. One of the combined effects of gradually declining mortgage payments over time is to counteract the impact of fiscal drag on incomes.

Outcomes in retirement and pensioner poverty

Moving forward to the other end of the lifetime, are the Meades ever at risk of pensioner poverty? The answer is less clear than for the childhood period. The Meades' income in retirement depends on their earlier pension planning decisions. In line with the discussion in Chapter Eleven, there are two basic pension-planning options for the Meades:

- lifetime membership of occupational schemes, as we have modelled them so far; and
- lifetime membership of personal pension schemes, which we only apply to the 1997 and 2008 systems.

A third option would be for the Meades to make no pension-planning decision and thus remain reliant on only state provision. However, only under the 1979 system would this be a conceivably sensible decision for the Meades to make. A policy since 1979 of failing to uprate the basic pension in line with earnings and deliberately cutting SERPS in order to encourage middle earners to save means that if the Meades relied solely on state pension provision they would fall into poverty within 10 years of retiring under the 1997 and 2008 systems. We can illustrate the effects of a consistent set of savings 'inputs' for the Meades as a couple for both occupational final salary pensions and defined contribution personal pensions and then look at the differences in 'outcomes' in terms of their position in the income distribution during retirement and their ability to avoid pensioner poverty.

However, it is crucial to realise that by consistently applying the same inputs or savings levels we will necessarily achieve different outputs and outcomes. Indeed, there is some doubt about how far NICs are 'inputs' in terms of pension savings. This is because state pensions are in reality funded cross-sectionally on a 'pay as you go' basis and NICs are increasingly treated as an alternative to income tax in raising revenue. The fact is that the National Insurance fund does not exclusively fund state pensions and nor are state pensions funded exclusively from it. Alongside NICs at the prevailing contracted-out rate, our assumption is that the Meades pay a constant 6% of their earnings into a private pension scheme. If this is a defined benefit occupational scheme, it is clear that employers make considerable contributions to defined benefit final salary occupational schemes to top them up. The alternative form of pension provision, defined contribution, is, by definition, not linked to a defined outcome as a percentage of salary but to the investment outcomes of the pension fund and the resulting annuity at the point of retirement. The rise of personal pensions of this type to replace occupational defined benefit systems thus transfers the investment risk to the individual and away from the employer. It is also bound to give a lower level of outputs and outcomes for the same level of contribution because there is no employer subsidy and because it is hard to ensure that investment outcomes will match rising earnings over time. For instance, if the Meades contribute a constant 6% of earnings into a final salary scheme, the lower pay penalty for female earnings will lead to higher outputs for such joint pensions over time relative to their final salaries with no discounting for longer life expectancy.

The outputs for a same 6% of earnings contribution into a defined contribution scheme will depend crucially on investment decisions, the state of financial markets at the point of retirement, the contemporary annuity rates in place and their underlying assumptions about life expectancy. Our assumptions for these factors are held constant over the lifetime and are shown in Chapter Eleven, apart from life expectancy that is allowed to rise between 1997 and 2008. The outputs in 2008 compared with 1997 from the same level of contributions will thus fall even when investment and return parameters are constant.

But there is another crucial difference in outputs and that is the underlying difference in the treatment of resulting pensions and inflation. Occupational pensions are generally inflation proofed up to a certain level of price inflation, but annuities depend on the product purchased. A price-protected annuity will give a much lower nominal level of pension at the point of retirement than one that is a regular cash sum of income, but inflation over retirement will soon erode the value of the cash annuity that is not protected. We illustrate this by using cash non-inflated annuities, the norm in 1997, although by 2008 these had been superseded by a range of ever more sophisticated annuity products.

The outcomes over retirement thus rely on the income package that results from the combination of state pension and private pension and the performance of this package against inflation in terms of real living standards and the performance of this package against rising median incomes when considering outcomes in terms of relative pensioner poverty. We show the latter in Figure 12.6. How do these investments in and returns from pensions affect the Meades' ability to avoid poverty in retirement?

Figure 12.6 shows potential pensioner poverty profiles for the Meades corresponding to the occupational and private pension choices we have modelled. Here we use a BHC income measure because in retirement housing costs are no longer a significant issue for the Meades, their mortgage having already been paid off in full. We start the inflation clock ticking at age 65 and adopt the medium-term assumptions for uprating (as discussed in Chapter Eleven) that allow fiscal drag and benefit erosion.

The first point to note is that Figure 12.6 demonstrates the main underlying problem of maintaining relative income standards during retirement. Pensioners have incomes that are, at best, uprated in line with prices. They do not benefit from general earnings growth that drives the relative poverty line. This means that their income over retirement will fall compared with a relative poverty line. The Meades' retirement poverty profiles are therefore determined by three overlapping factors: the original value of their retirement income package at the point of retirement; the ability of this income package to keep pace with inflation; and the underlying growth of a relative poverty line over time.

For reasons already discussed, occupational pensions give consistently higher outcomes at the point of retirement than personal pensions. The highest poverty clearance at this stage is under the 1997 system, followed by the 1979 and 2008 systems in that order. This reflects a combination of the higher value relative to earnings of the basic state pension under the earlier years' systems, especially 1979, and the above-mentioned inherent advantage of the 1997 system in having a poverty line that is easier to beat. Over time, however, the 1997 and 2008 results fall, so that from age 69 onwards the best results in terms of poverty clearance are under the 1979 system. Under the 1979 system when the basic pension was uprated by earnings, poverty clearance falls more slowly over retirement because at least part of the Meades' income package, the state pension element, is keeping pace with the poverty line, which rises with earnings. The pension packages in 1997 and 2008 fall parallel to each other because they are both based on keeping up with prices, both through the uprating of the state pension and the indexing of occupational pensions. The resulting profiles for the Meades with occupational pensions means that they never get to the margins of poverty, but that the 1979 system in the long run gives them best protection against relative poverty.

Turning to personal pensions, Figure 12.6 clearly shows that under our assumptions the Meades would have to contribute more to avoid poverty in retirement. However, one of our assumptions, introduced for the benefit of

Figure 12.6: The Meades' pensioner poverty profile before housing costs

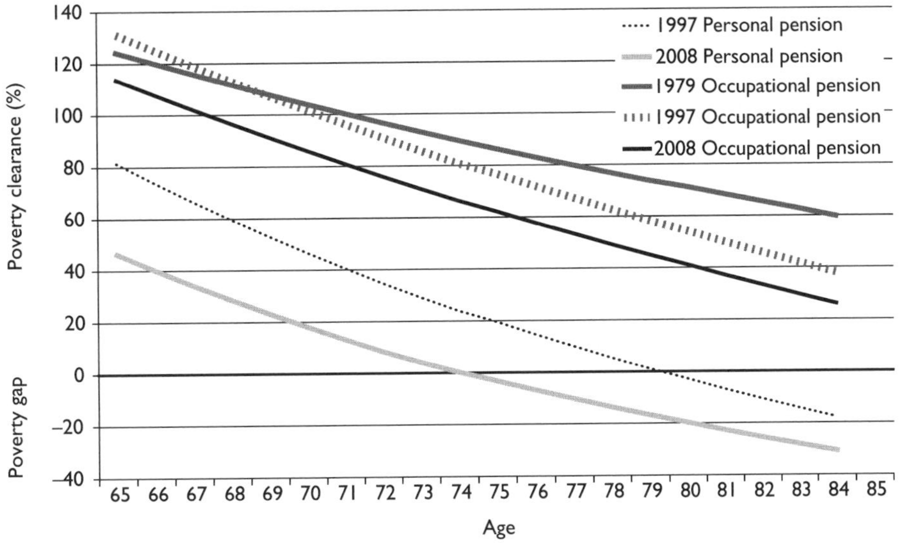

Source: Authors' calculations from LOIS.

simplicity, is that of flat annuity purchase, which means that the Meades' personal pension income retains the same nominal value year on year falling relative to prices, let alone earnings.

Generalisation from these results is difficult because they reflect our chosen assumptions and cannot take in the much wider range of options, particularly on personal pensions and annuities in the real world. However, two crucial conclusions do come out of these illustrations based on consistent levels of pension saving inputs. First, there is a growing need to ensure that state pension alongside such personal pension provision is uprated to ensure that pension incomes are protected over retirement against inflation, especially as the underlying composition of pensions moves from final salary calculations to annuities. The decision to move to earnings uprating of the basic state pension from 2012 or thereabouts is thus crucial to support a growth in reliance on riskier personal pensions. Second, the value of pension at the point of retirement is the crucial starting point for retirement provision, as income is a fixed matter from this point and will fall relative to a poverty line in almost all cases. Moving to a price-indexed annuity will give more relative protection over time at the cost of lowering the initial value of income, but the amount of pension one can purchase at the point of retirement is determined by the state of stock markets and pension funds at that point of time. A retiree in early 2009 will thus be faced with economic downturn, poor financial markets and significant reductions in the value of their retirement pot on which to fund their retirement and the attraction of a fixed-price rather than indexed annuity will be great in the short term – a higher immediate income.

The most crucial lessons to be taken from this discussion would, however, require moving to a different underlying assumption: of matching outputs and outcomes from pensions rather than inputs into pensions. How much would the Meades have to contribute to match outcomes from occupational pensions if they were personal pension investors? This would change the whole lifetime profile and would potentially drag the Meades further down the income distribution. But if households with median earnings were all paying much higher pension contributions, this alters median incomes and relative poverty lines in a manner that is beyond modelling using hypothetical individuals. At this point, the most we can conclude is that significant increases in the level of pension contributions necessary to match outcomes from occupational pensions would have very significant implications for the income distribution. It would also mean rethinking the balance between taxation and private contributions in measuring disposable incomes. Such a large structural change in pension finance has potentially significant lifetime impacts and significant cross-sectional impacts on incomes.

This discussion of pensioner poverty outcomes concludes our chapter on the Meades. In the next two chapters, we turn respectively to our family of high earners, the Moores, and our family of low earners, the Lowes.

Summary

This chapter has used lifetime simulation to synthesise all elements of tax and benefit provision in 1979, 1997 and 2008 for a profile based on median earners, the Meades. Our main findings are:

- Direct taxation levels are lowest in 1997 and highest in 1979, with 2008 positioned in between. However, the more generous transfers available in 1979 and 2008 mean that the net effects of taxes and benefits are no different between years for a consistent set of lifetime profiles, around a negative 14% of lifetime earnings under all three systems.
- The move to increase indirect taxation from 1979 is not captured in these net effects and means that the gains from 'low taxation' for the Meades in 1997 and 2008 compared with 1979 can be seriously questioned.
- Allowing for a set of behaviours that better represents 1979 lowers transfer income and maternal earnings but makes little overall difference to results in terms of lifetime disposable incomes.
- Maturing the 1979, 1997 and 2008 systems raises the tax burden in 1979 considerably to pay for SERPS but also significantly increases the overall negative effects of the 1997 and 2008 systems and the overall net effects move to −19% of lifetime earnings in 1979 compared with −17% and −16% in 1997 and 2008 respectively.
- Inflation raises the costs of transfers most in the 1979 system and this effect from uprating pensions by earnings takes the Meades into a neutral to positive

position on net effects over the lifetime in that year. Outcomes from 1997 and 2008 systems vary less with inflation.

- Effective marginal deduction rates are lowest, and thus the return on additional earnings is highest, in 1997. Effective marginal deduction rates in 1979 are higher but stable over the lifetime. However, in 2008 the low underlying marginal tax rate is overtaken by high withdrawal rates for tax credits while children are present.

- Over the lifetime, the 1979 system protects against pensioner poverty in retirement best, but in general early periods tend to benefit from the combination of low tax and the lower contemporary poverty lines of 1997. The 2008 system provides best coverage for young infants but increased generosity has not kept pace with underlying rises in relative poverty and underlying increases in median income.

Notes

[1] Two widely reported sets of results were first, 2002 research from the Halifax, putting the average age of the first-time buyer at 29 in 1974 and 34 in 2002, and second, 2007 research by GE Money Home Lending, putting the average age of the first-time buyer at 27 in 1977 and 34 in 2007.

[2] Plotting other results allowing for behaviour change and policy maturation yield no significant differences in these results, with the exception of the mature 1979 system and its higher rate of NICs.

[3] Under the 1979 system, 4p of Mr Meade's extra £1 of earnings goes in NICs, 6p goes in pension contributions and 31p goes in income tax (with his marginal tax rate of 33% being applied to the 94p of income on which Mr Meade does not get tax relief in respect of pension contributions). Under the 1997 system, 8.4p of Mr Meade's extra £1 goes in NICs, 6p goes in pension contributions and 21.6p goes in income tax (with his marginal tax rate of 23% being applied to the 94p of income on which Mr Meade does not get tax relief in respect of pension contributions).

[4] This popular acronym stands for Dual Income, No Kids Yet.

THIRTEEN

The Moores

How would the lifetime profiles of the richer Moores compare with those of the Meades in their lifetime experience of the 1979, 1997 and 2008 systems? The Moores have twice the earnings of the Meades and can afford to pay more for childcare alongside their bigger more expensive house and lifestyle. To reflect the lower economic constraints of the Moores, we take a simpler set of assumptions about lifetimes for them and do not vary their lifetime profile between 1979 and later years as we did for the Meades. However, to capture changes in taxation at the top of the earnings distribution, we do consider another version of the Moores' lifetime profile – that of their richer identical cousins, called the Evan-Moores, who earn twice as much again as the Moores and thus four times as much as the Meades.

The Moores' model lifetime

The simple life history we use for the Moores is as follows.

- At age 16 the profile starts. Ms Moore continues her secondary education and then takes a degree, thus remaining in full-time education until 21.
- At age 21 Ms Moore begins work. She works for an employer with an occupational pension scheme.
- At age 22 she moves into rented accommodation.
- At age 26 she cohabits with Mr Moore, who is her male doppelganger, with exactly the same age and background.
- At age 28 they marry.
- At age 30 they buy a house (which is twice as expensive as the Meades') and pay appropriate rates and council tax.
- At age 32 they have their first child. Ms Meade takes a total of nine months' maternity leave. After this she returns to work full time, employing a nanny.
- At age 34 the Moores have their second child and again Ms Meade takes nine months' maternity leave. After this' she returns to work full time, employing a nanny.
- Ms Moore retires at age 60.
- Mr Moore retires at age 65.
- They both die at age 87.

We begin our analysis of the Moores in the same way as we did the Meades, by considering results in the inflation-free 2008 'Groundhog Day' world.

The incidence of taxes and benefits

The Moores' lifetime in 2008

Figure 13.1 shows the income components and profile for the Moores living out their entire lives under the 2008 system. It is thus the equivalent of Figure 12.1 from the preceding chapter, which showed the income components and profile for the Meades. It should be noted, however, that Figures 12.1 and 13.1 use different y-axis scales. How does the Moores' lifetime income profile differ from that of the Meades? First and most fundamentally, the Moores clearly enjoy a higher income than the Meades, even after their higher housing costs. There are then differences that arise from the different behaviour pattern we have modelled in respect of the Moores. The different pattern of maternal work behaviour is reflected in Ms Moore's immediate return to full-time rather than part-time work, as well as the Moores' longer lives. In addition, state transfers are clearly a relatively much less significant income component for the Moores than the Meades. As with the Meades, there are only two periods where state transfers form any part of the Moore's income package, first, when there are dependent children in the household and second, when someone in the household retires. Under our 'default' assumption of occupational pension scheme membership, it can be

Figure 13.1: The Moores' lifetime income profile, 2008 system

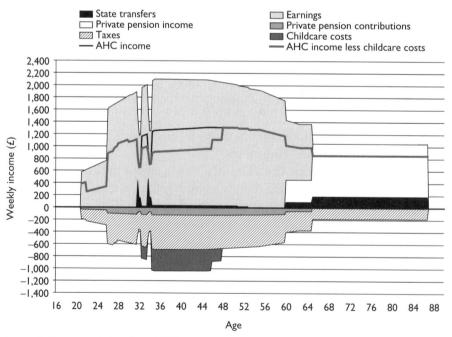

Source: Authors' calculations from LOIS.

seen that the Moores, like the Meades, do not face a particularly uncomfortable income drop in retirement.

Incidence of tax and benefits across the 1979, 1997 and 2008 systems

Table 13.1 presents the cumulative results of the Moores' lifetime lived out under the 1979, 1997 and 2008 tax and benefit systems. Many of these results simply show that some of the conclusions that we have drawn in respect of the Meades apply more or less equally to the Moores. The Moores receive proportionately the least in state transfers under the 1997 system, the equivalent of 7.3% of their lifetime earnings, compared with 7.5% under the 2008 system and 9.2% under the 1979 system. Transfers in respect of childhood and maternity are highest under the 2008 system as a result of longer maternity pay, followed by the 1979 and the 1997 system in that order. Transfers in respect of retirement are highest

Table 13.1: The Moores' lifetime under the 1979, 1997 and 2008 systems

	1979	1997	2008
	Percentage of lifetime earnings		
Direct taxation			
All taxes (including student loan repayments)	38.9	32.3	33.4
All taxes (excluding student loan repayments)	38.9	32.1	33.0
State transfers			
All	9.2	7.3	7.5
Maternity/dependent children	1.1	1.0	1.3
Retirement	8.1	6.3	6.2
Net effects of direct taxes and transfers	**−29.7**	**−25.0**	**−25.9**
Other transfers and payments			
Private pension contributions	6.0	6.0	6.0
Private pension income	28.3	28.5	28.6
Childcare costs	5.5	6.1	6.4
Housing costs	3.3	3.6	5.6
Lifetime earnings totals (£million, 2008 prices)			
Lifetime gross earnings	2.67	3.46	3.81
Lifetime disposable income after housing and childcare costs	2.24 (84%)	3.04 (88%)	3.22 (85%)

Source: Authors' calculations from LOIS.

Note: Moores modelled with occupational pension provision and constant '2008 behaviour' across all three systems.

under the 1979 system, and then fall over time as the basic retirement pension falls relative to earnings, thus being lowest under the 2008 system.

In terms of direct taxation, the story for the Moores differs from that of the Meades, for whom the differences across the three systems were small. The Moores have clearly higher direct taxation under the 1979 system, a lifetime total of 38.9% as opposed to 32.3% or 33.4% respectively under the 1997 and 2008 systems, and this difference would not be offset by a consideration of behavioural change or indirect taxes. Consumption-based taxation would be proportionally low for the Moores, as all evidence suggests that among higher earners less of their income goes towards indirect taxation. Figures from 1979 giving indirect taxes as a percentage of gross income report differences in the amount of indirect taxation faced by top and bottom quintiles as varying from 4.2% to 8.3%, depending on household type (ONS, 1981).

This change to lower direct taxation in 1997 and 2008 is obviously what would be expected, given the explicit political aims to reduce the rates of income tax and the history of policy shown in Chapters Two and Five. At higher incomes there is less substitution of other taxation for income tax, as National Insurance, local government taxation and consumption taxes are all essentially regressive in nature. The Moores are just unequivocally better off courtesy of lower income tax rates if they live their lives in 1997 or 2008 compared with 1979. The only way that fiscal policy could reduce this effect would be to target transfers away from them. However, apart from receiving very small amounts of Child Tax Credit under the 2008 system during the periods where they have a child under the age of one, the Moores have too high an income to receive any income dependent benefit. The erosion of Child Benefit and basic retirement pension is the only aspect of withdrawal of transfers that will result in these benefits making less proportional contribution to the Moores' lifetime income over time. Taking transfers and taxes into consideration with overall net effects, the negative impact of the 1979 package at −29.7% of lifetime earnings falls to −25% in 1997 and rises only marginally to −25.9% in 2008.

Disposable income differences are affected most by the assumptions of housing and childcare costs rather than underlying changes in the net effects of taxes and transfers. In 1979, they are 84% of lifetime earnings and in 1997 and 2008, 88% and 85% respectively.

Given that the main factor driving differences between 1979, 1997 and 2008 is direct taxation, it is worth introducing and comparing an even richer version of the Moores to see just how reductions in progressivity in direct taxation have affected the well off.

The Evan-Moores

The Evan-Moores earn twice as much as the Moores, which is to say that their underlying earnings levels are four times median wages. For simplicity, we use the same lifetime story for the Evan-Moores as the Moores, simply doubling income and the value of their property and its cost of purchase, and ignore any additional ways of reducing risks and liabilities the Evan-Moores might enjoy. Table 13.2 presents a further set of headline results for the Evan-Moores' lifetime.

The Evan-Moores pay higher proportions of their lifetime earnings in direct taxes than the Moores under all three systems, but the 1979 result shows the most dramatic increase. Under the 1979 system, the Evan-Moores pay direct taxes at a rate roughly 10 percentage points higher than the Moores, with almost half of their lifetime earnings paid as tax. This higher level of direct taxation drives down the lifetime disposable income result for the Evan-Moores under the 1979 system, entirely offsetting the 1979 system's advantage of lower childcare and housing costs.

The distinctly higher tax take for the Evan-Moores under the 1979 system arising from that system's distinct progressivity is vividly reflected in Figure 13.2.

Figure 13.2 shows the net effects of taxation and transfers as a percentage of concurrent original income (gross earnings and/or private pension income). Apart from a brief period during early adult life where the 2008 system results are negatively affected by repayment of Ms Evan-Moore's student loan, it can be seen that the 1997 and 2008 system results are generally close to one other,

Table 13.2: The Evan-Moores' lifetime under the 1979, 1997 and 2008 systems

	1979	1997	2008
	Percentage of lifetime earnings		
Direct taxation			
All taxes (including student loan repayments)	48.6	38.9	40.3
All taxes (excluding student loan repayments)	48.6	38.8	40.1
State transfers			
All	4.6	3.7	3.9
Maternity/dependent children	0.6	0.6	0.8
Retirement	4.0	3.1	3.1
Net effects of direct taxes and transfers	**–44**	**–35.2**	**–36.4**
Lifetime earnings totals (£million, 2008 prices)			
Lifetime gross earnings	5.35	6.92	7.61
Lifetime disposable income after housing and childcare costs	3.92 (73%)	5.66 (82%)	6.02 (79%)

Source: Authors' calculations from LOIS.

Note: Evan-Moores modelled with occupational pension provision and constant '2008 behaviour' across all three systems.

Figure 13.2: The Evan-Moores' net effects of taxes and benefits

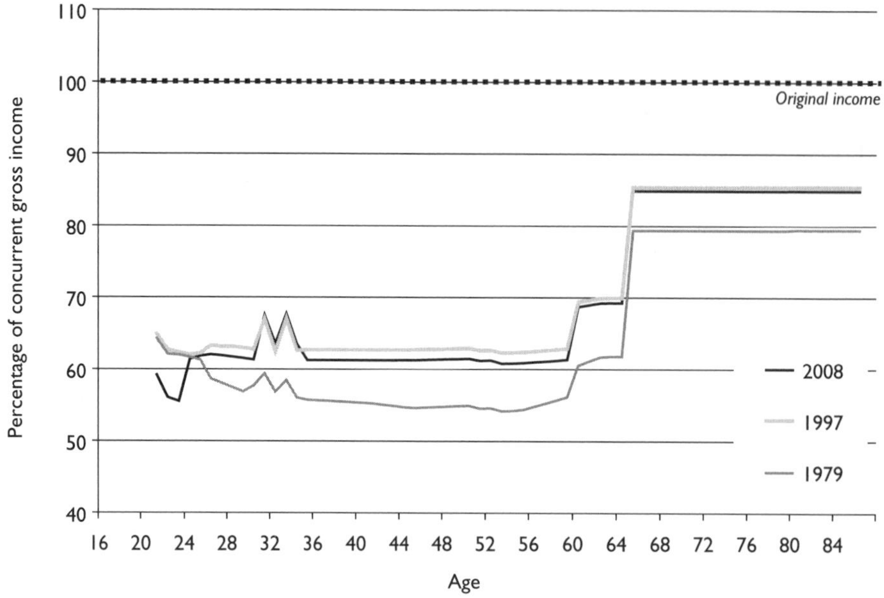

Source: Authors' calculations from LOIS.

Note: Simulation of the Evan-Moores' lifetime using benchmark models without inflation.

with the 1979 system results standing out as being very different and much lower. Clearly, the larger negative net effects under the 1979 system shown earlier in Table 13.2 operate across the whole lifetime and are driven by higher taxation at all points in the lifetime, including retirement.

Because the Moores and Evan-Moores potentially gain more from occupational and fiscal welfare, it is also interesting to see how far the changes in direct taxation are affected by tax relief for these higher income lifetimes. Tax reliefs decline in overall significance as we move from the 1979 system to 1997, and again from 1997 to 2008. The Evan-Moores receive no additional age allowance under any of the three systems, as their income in retirement is too high. Taking all the lifetime tax reliefs in total, it is again noticeable that they blunt the higher rates of taxation most in 1979. This effect is higher for the Evan-Moores than the Moores in that year, with a total of 5.5% of lifetime income offset against direct income-related taxes for the former compared with 5% for the latter.

Allowing for inflation and uprating

What impact does inflation have on our higher-income lifetime for the Moores? Here, as we did with the Meades' lifetime profiles, we model inflation as balanced over the lifetime with contemporary prices at the half-way point in the lifetime.

Table 13.3 shows the results alongside our original results from an inflation-free world from Table 13.1 highlighted in grey. As we saw with the Meades, inflation affects lifetime outcomes greatly. Occupational pensions based on final salaries are very significantly increased once inflation is modelled, as we saw earlier in the case of the Meades, rising from 28.5% of lifetime earnings to around 44.5%. Similarly, the 1979 system with automatic earnings uprating for basic retirement pension raises its value for the Moores from 8.1% of lifetime earnings to 17.7% once inflation and uprating are taken into account. As discussed in earlier chapters, this effect is not seen in 1997 and 2008 where uprating is based on prices. Taxation rises with inflation modelled, but not because of fiscal drag, which is neutral over the lifetime in our assumptions; rather, this result reflects the higher taxation of the higher pension incomes the Moores enjoy in retirement with inflation modelled. This applies particularly to their income in retirement under the 1979 system, but in that year such higher taxation in retirement is more than offset by the higher state pension income under that system. This is better illustrated

Table 13.3: The Moores' lifetime under the 1979, 1997 and 2008 systems with inflation modelled

	1979		1997		2008	
	Flat	**Inflation**	**Flat**	**Inflation**	**Flat**	**Inflation**
	Percentage of lifetime earnings					
All direct taxes						
(including student loan repayments)	38.9	43.8	32.3	32.8	33.4	34.6
(excluding student loan repayments)	38.9	43.8	32.1	32.7	33.0	34.0
All state transfers	9.2	18.8	7.3	6.3	7.5	6.5
Maternity/dependent children	1.1	1.0	1.0	0.8	1.3	1.1
Retirement	8.1	17.7	6.3	5.5	6.2	5.4
Net effects of direct taxes and transfers	**−29.7**	**−25.0**	**−25.0**	**−26.5**	**−25.9**	**−28.1**
Other transfers and payments						
Private pension contributions	6.0	6.0	6.0	6.0	6.0	6.0
Private pension income	28.3	44.5	28.5	44.7	28.6	44.8
Childcare costs	5.5	4.9	6.1	5.4	6.4	5.7
Housing costs	3.3	2.2	3.6	2.3	5.6	3.6

Source: Authors' calculations from LOIS.

by a graphic depiction of the net effects of taxes and benefits over the Moores' lifetime in Figure 13.3.

Figure 13.3 shows the net effects of taxes and benefits on the Moores' original income over the lifetime with inflation modelled. For the majority of the Moores' lifetime, the 1997 and 2008 systems yield comparable outcomes in terms of net effects, with the 1979 system distinctly different. Differences in the first part of their lifetime concern first, the repayment of student loans and second, benefits during maternity. No student debt exists in 1979. Under the 1997 system, the Moores have a lower student debt to repay than under the 2008 system, but repayments that are less sensitive to income. This leads to longer repayment at lower rates under the 2008 system, with repayment going on into the Moores' late twenties. By the time the Moores have children, their student debts are only just fully repaid under the 2008 system. The greater generosity of the 2008 system in terms of maternity benefits puts it clearly ahead of the 1979 and 1997 systems in terms of net effects at the points where the Moores have a child under the age of one in the household. But from this point on in the lifetime, the 1997 and 2008 systems are very similar and the 1979 system stands out in contrast. During working age, the 1979 system's higher taxation spells more negative net effects for the Moores; during retirement, its higher relative value state pension spells more positive net effects. Results for net effects during retirement 'improve with age' for the Moores. This is clearly true under the 1979 system by virtue of the earnings uprating of the state retirement pension, but it is also true under the

Figure 13.3: The Moores' net effects of taxes and benefits (with inflation modelled)

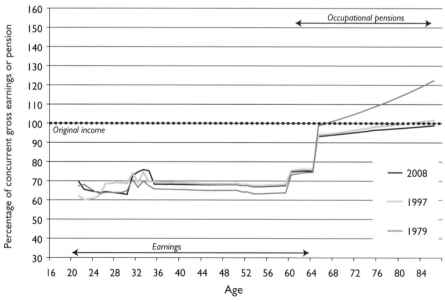

Source: Authors' calculations from LOIS.

other years' systems because the income threshold that determines the tapering of age allowances in income tax is following earnings while pensions in 1997 and 2008 are only rising with prices, thus leading to rising net effects.

Outcomes

What are the outcomes for the high-earning lifetimes? Once again, we consider overall marginal effective deduction rates and the position in the contemporary income distributions. We focus the majority of our results on the Moores but use the Evan-Moores where appropriate to show results for the highest of our lifetime earning profiles.

Incentives

Figures 13.4a and b show the effective marginal deduction rates for Mr Moore and Mr Evan-Moore respectively. To aid interpretation, let us consider Figure 13.4b for Mr Evan-Moore first because this best demonstrates the differences in underlying marginal tax rates between 1979, 1997 and 2008. Because his student debt is already paid off by the time he joins the household at age 26 and because transfer income is not an issue, Mr Evan-Moore's marginal deduction rates are simply his marginal tax rates. The stepped pattern of the 1979 line reflects the greater number of income tax bands present in that system interacting with the lifetime earnings curve. The steps in marginal rates thus move upwards while Mr Evan-Moore's earnings levels rise and then downwards in the latter half of the working life. Total marginal rates for Mr Evan-Moore in 1979 are between 62% and 77% and thus mostly reflect the higher rates in upper income bands of income tax. Our simulation assumes that the Evan-Moores optimise their tax position by electing to be taxed independently and thus these rates are lower than would be seen if they were jointly assessed for income tax, a possible marginal rate of 83%. The 1997 and 2008 systems for Mr Evan-Moore are both low by comparison and more simple, with flat profiles over the lifetime at 44% in 1997 and 45% in 2008, the difference being the 1% additional rate of National Insurance.

Keeping the tax structures in mind from the description of Mr Evan-Moore's marginal deduction rates, we can now turn to Mr Moore's profile, as shown in Figure 13.4. In 2008, he is subject to the interaction of taxation first with student loan repayment and second with brief periods of entitlement to Child Tax Credit when his children are under one year old. This adds three steep peaks to the profile of effective marginal deduction rates as they rise to 54% with student loan repayments before falling to the underlying 45% rate in 2008 and then rise twice to 51% before falling again to the same underlying rate. In 1997, Mr Moore's earnings in the early years attract the lower rate of income tax, but from the age of 28 onwards he reverts to the underlying top marginal rate of tax at 44%. In 1979, the stepped changes of marginal tax rates and the lifetime

Figure 13.4a: Marginal deduction rates for Mr Moore

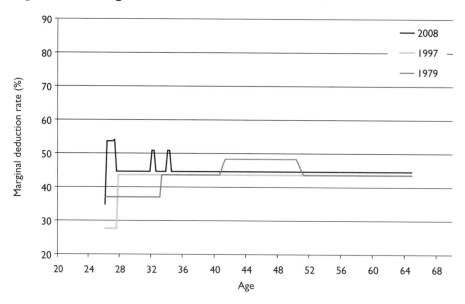

Figure 13.4b: Marginal deduction rates for Mr Evan-Moore

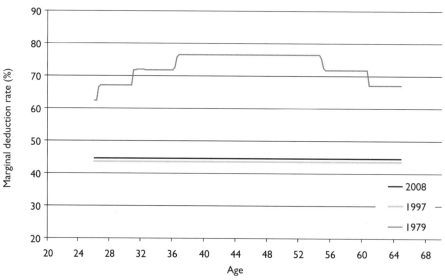

Source: Authors' calculations from LOIS.

earnings profile interact in a similar manner to that seen for Mr Evan-Moore but he crosses into fewer bands of income tax and has marginal rates of 38%, 44% and, at the highest, 48%.

The Moores in the overall income distribution

Figure 13.5 shows the lifetime profile of the Moores' income as a percentage of contemporary median income after housing costs (AHC). To give an indication of the relative gap between the Moores and the Meades, the figure also shows the comparative 2008 outcome for the Meades. As it did for the Meades, our analysis for the Moores goes beyond the net effects of tax and benefit systems to take in the additional factors of housing costs and different levels of median household income in the real-world populations of 1979, 1997 and 2008. The underlying events and changes in the lifetime give rise to the peaks and troughs of relative position against the unchanging medians, but under all three systems the Moores never get close to the 60% of median poverty line and spend all of their lifetime above median income.

Overall, the pattern emerging from Figure 13.5 is one of the Moores enjoying the strongest outcomes under the 1997 system, followed by the 2008 system and then the 1979 system in that order. There are exceptional periods where this ranking differs, notably in retirement where the 1979 system result with its earnings uprated basic state pension overtakes the 1997 results from age 76 onwards. Overall, however, the 1997 system comes out on top for the Moores. This result is predictable given three considerations: first, in terms of net effects,

Figure 13.5: The Moores' relative position in the income distribution

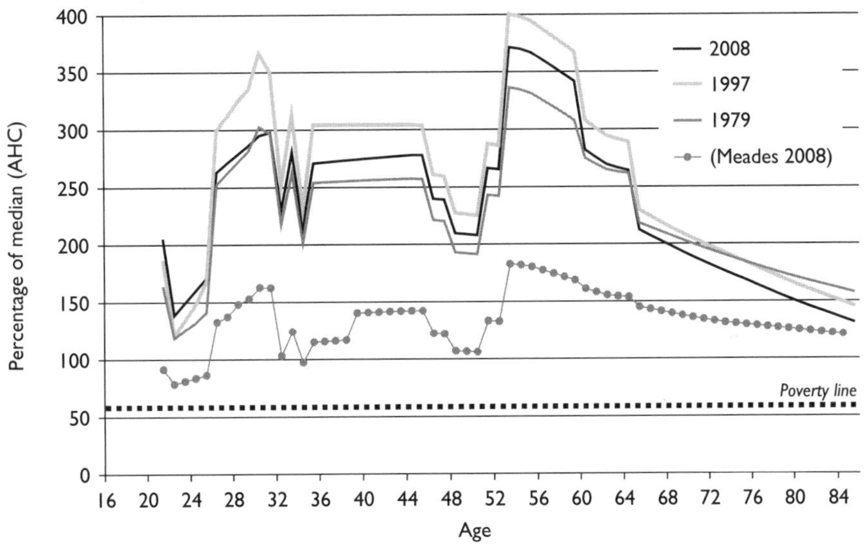

Source: Authors' calculations from LOIS.

the 1997 and 2008 systems have treated the Moores similarly at least from their mid-30s onwards; second, as discussed in Chapter Twelve, the relatively lower median income in the real world of 1997 will yield a 1997 poverty line that is easier to beat than the 1979 and 2008 poverty lines; and third, higher housing costs under the 2008 system will drive down 2008 system results in early to mid-adult life.

Childhood income profile

Remembering that the Meades never experience child poverty, we can be assured that the Moores, on double their income, will have even higher levels of income above the poverty line during the period that they have dependent children. Figure 13.6 confirms this, showing that the Moores at their lowest equivalent income position have incomes that are more than 200% above the poverty line. This clearance rises to 400% when both the Moores work full time and their children are not teenagers. The biggest dip in income is around the birth of the second child. This suggests that, in reality, high-income families like the Moores may be more inclined to employ the services of a nanny to smooth their incomes during this period – paying a low-earning nanny or au pair when they are able to earn twice the median wage makes clear economic sense even if it potentially erodes parenting and quality time with their infant children. Figure 13.6 also gives the Meades' childhood outcomes under the 2008 system as an indication of the

Figure 13.6: The Moores' childhood income profile (AHC) and poverty clearance

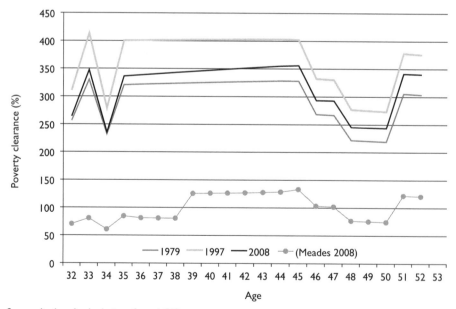

Source: Authors' calculations from LOIS.

gaps between the two families. Here it is clear that having two full-time earners in early childhood makes a big difference when compared with the Meades' move to part-time work – the combination of higher earnings levels and the lower relative costs of childcare make the Meades and the Moores draw apart across the income distribution and reinforces inequality, a point we return to discuss later.

The Moores consistently enjoy the best outcomes for childhood under the 1997 system, followed by the 2008 and then the 1979 system. This partly reflects the changing underlying relationship between median earnings and median equivalised income previously highlighted in earlier profiles. The move to include the effect of inflation over the childhood period, with true contemporary prices at the point of childbirth and modelling fiscal drag, does not introduce significant changes to outcomes for the Moores. The effect of fiscal drag would, all else being equal, be to drive down outcomes gradually over time, but such an effect is being offset by the combined positive effects of earnings rising and housing costs falling.

Outcomes in retirement and pensioner poverty

How would the Moores fare in retirement? As discussed in Chapters Nine and Eleven, the Moores are a difficult case to profile consistently over time, as their enrolment in private personal pensions in 1979 makes no sense in terms of tax subsidies – they would end up with high state pensions from the State Earnings Related Pension Scheme alongside private pensions that received nothing in terms of National Insurance rebates during their working lives. We therefore look at comparable defined benefit final salary and defined contribution private pensions alongside each other, but do not model the latter for 1979.

Following the example for the Meades in the previous chapter, and for consistent comparison between systems and between hypothetical lifetimes, we take a constant private rate of contribution of 6% of earnings into both forms of private pension over time. In 1979, the Moores pay 4.9% of lifetime earnings as National Insurance contributions (NICs); in 1997, they pay 6.5% and in 2008, 7.8%. These contributions are for more than just their pension but as they are only claiming basic pension alongside their private pensions, they reflect different underlying assumptions about the cost of a contributory record for such a basic pension. Of course, compared with the Meades, they pay less in percentage terms – emphasising again the underlying regressivity of NICs, although the higher level in 2008 captures the 1% of income above the upper earnings limit that now operates.

Occupational pensions would provide around a constant 60% replacement rate at age 65 (based on earnings at 59) and this reflects the consistent set of assumptions used for final salary calculations across all three years. Private personal pensions under consistent assumptions of contributions of 6% of earnings would decline under 2008 rules compared with 1997 and fall from 41% to 37% of earnings (using the same assumptions as for the Meades and as given in Chapter Eleven) due to both reduced NIC rebates and longer life expectancy assumptions.

The outcomes for the Moores of occupational and personal pension packages are shown in terms of retirement incomes relative to the poverty line in Figure 13.7. Discussion of the fundamental nature of these profiles echoes our earlier findings for the Meades in the previous chapter. Occupational pension membership secures a higher level of pension at the point of retirement and greater protection against price inflation than defined benefit annuity pensions that are lower in comparative value for the same contributions at the onset of retirement and are not price indexed over retirement. Occupational pensions of this level are taxed more heavily in income tax in 1979, but the combination of a price-indexed occupational pension and earnings-uprated state pension gives greater protection against relative poverty over retirement. This results in the highest income in the later years of retirement compared with the 1997 and 2008 systems where state pension is only uprated by prices.

Once again, the lower levels of income from personal pensions at the point of retirement reflect the assumption of a matched consistent contribution of 6% of earnings to the occupational pensions. In reality, the Moores could afford, and would probably contribute more, into pension saving as their tax incentives to do so are high. The problem of relying on non-inflation-proofed annuity and incomes falling fairly rapidly against relative poverty lines during retirement is brought home in the Moores' case: in 2008, with a higher poverty line relative to

Figure 13.7: The Moores' pensioner poverty profile

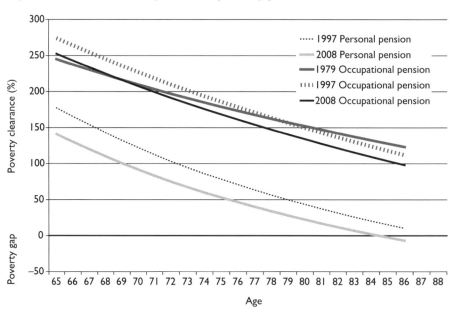

Source: Authors' calculations from LOIS.

original retirement income due to rising median incomes over time, the Moores' pension income will fall below the poverty line at the age of 85. Of course, they could afford a better annuity product – one with both higher original retirement income and price indexation – but the underlying principle is well illustrated here: even those on relatively high incomes can potentially slide into pensioner poverty over the length of their retirement. Given longer life expectancy, much of what the Moores pay in additional pension provision may well end up giving them additional years of pension but there is still a risk that they will slide into the margins poverty in their final years of retirement. The move to earnings-uprated state pension from 2012 will help militate against this problem by providing better poverty clearance for private pensions across the board.

Inequality

How do these high-income lifetime profiles compare in outcomes to the Meades? Our assumptions start with the Moores having twice the median earnings of the Meades and the Evan-Moores four times. Does this difference in original income widen or narrow between the systems in 1979, 1997 and 2008? Table 13.4 shows the simplest comparison of outcomes using consistent assumptions of lifetime behaviour (that is, 2008 for the Meades).

The underlying sets of lifetime behaviours of the Moores and the Meades are not exactly the same and this leads to underlying difference in gross lifetime earnings that are larger than the assumed 200% and 400%. This reflects the underlying reality that growth in income inequality reflects different constraints on income generation. The Moores and Evan-Moores can hire nannies after the birth of children and thus maximise their income generation in this example. This assumption leads to an illustrative difference that raises overall differences in lifetime earnings between the Meades and the higher-earning Moores and Evan-Moores, whose respective lifetime earnings are 207% and 415% of the Meades'. Our profiles put in consistent assumptions that offset such earnings with housing and childcare costs across the three systems and thus the difference in lifetime disposable incomes provides us with clear inferences about the impact of the different policy systems on inequality between the Meades and their higher-income counterparts. Table 13.4 clearly shows that these differences were smallest in 1979, when the Moores' and Evan-Moores' lifetime disposable income was 178% and 311% of the Meades' respectively. These differences are much larger in 1997, 191% and 356% respectively. In 2008, there is some small reduction in difference, to 189% and 354% respectively, but these are at levels that do not unequivocally support a more general conclusion of reducing inequality from 1997 levels, as they are very small in comparison with the huge differences between 1979 and 1997.

Table 13.4: Lifetime differences in outcomes of the Moores and Evan-Moores compared with the Meades'

	Income as percentage of Meades		
	1979	1997	2008
Moores			
Gross lifetime earnings	207	207	208
Disposable income after housing and childcare costs	178	191	189
Evan-Moores			
Gross lifetime earnings	415	414	416
Disposable income after housing and childcare costs	311	356	354

Source: Tables 12.1, 13.1 and 13.2.

Summary

This chapter has used lifetime simulation to synthesise all elements of tax and benefit provision in 1979, 1997 and 2008 for a profile based on the Moores, who earn twice median income, and for comparison, the Evan-Moores, who earn twice as much again. Our main findings are:

- Direct taxation levels for high-income lifetimes are highest in 1979 by a considerable amount: 39% and 49% of lifetime earnings for the Moores and Evan-Moores respectively. In 1997, these fall to 32% and 29% respectively and are not very different in 2008.
- The higher income lifetimes are less affected by the increase from indirect taxation after 1979.
- Effective marginal tax rates are highest in 1979, with rates of 62% and 77% during peak earnings for the Evan-Moores.
- The gains from low taxation and the relatively minor role played by transfers in the Moores' lifetime mean that 1997 provided the best relative income standards. However, earnings uprating of state pensions still helped the Moores' relative income position to be maintained best in 1979 in the latter part of their retirement.
- Using the simplest of the lifetime profiles we found that lifetime inequality had grown when we compared the differences between original and disposable incomes of the Moores and Evan-Moores with those of the Meades – the gap was smallest in 1979 and highest in 1997, with just a small narrowing from 1997 levels in 2008.

FOURTEEN

The Lowes

This chapter considers model lifetime simulations for our low-paid family, the Lowes, whose wage is 50% of median earnings. How far do these profiles differ from those of the median and higher earners, the Meades and the Moores, and what differences arise between the outcomes of the policy systems of 1979, 1997 and 2008? We answer these questions for the Lowes by using the same set of analyses seen in Chapters Twelve and Thirteen.

The Lowes' model lifetime

The simplified life history that we use to construct a lifetime profile for the Lowes in 2008 is as follows:

- At age 18 Ms Lowe begins work.
- At 22 she leaves the parental home and moves into rented accommodation.
- At 26 she sets up home with Mr Lowe (who, as her male doppelganger, is the same age as her and has a similar background).
- At age 28 they marry and have their first child. Ms Lowe leaves work to undertake full-time childcare.
- At age 30 they have a second child.
- At 33 she returns to part-time work.
- At 37 she returns to work full time and until their youngest child reaches the age of 13 the Lowes pay for some childcare.
- Both children remain in full-time secondary education until they are 18.
- Throughout, Ms Lowe works for 50% of the female full-time median weekly wage weighted according to her age[1]. Part-time is pro rata half of her full-time wage.
- Mr Lowe works for 50% of the male full-time median weekly wage weighted according to his age.
- Mr Lowe has an uninterrupted history of full-time employment up until his retirement.
- Neither of the Lowes makes any private pension provision, so they will rely entirely on state pensions in retirement.
- The Lowes live in social housing rented accommodation throughout their lives and pay contemporary average local authority rent.
- Ms Lowe retires at age 60.
- Mr Lowe retires at age 65.
- They both die at age 83.

This profile, which is based on an assumption of continuous uninterrupted lifetime employment for Mr Lowe and an assumption that Ms Lowe's employment is solely interrupted for household childcare, is optimistic because low-paid workers face a relatively high risk of periods of being out of work. Figures for 2008 suggest that low-skilled workers in elementary occupations are more than four times as likely to be unemployed than the highest-skilled managers and senior officials, and that overall their risk of being unemployed is one-and-a-half times the average (ONS, 2008d, Table 6.11). Moreover, Evans and Harkness (2009) report that inactivity from long-term ill health is heavily skewed to the lowest-skilled workers. Later in this chapter we take account of such risks and show the effects of interruptions in the working life due to unemployment and incapacity for work.

We start our profile of the Lowes in the same way as we did for the Meades and the Moores, with the simplest case, considering the profile of income, taxes and benefits for an inflation-free 2008 'Groundhog Day' lifetime before moving on to impose these same assumptions on the 1997 and 1979 systems and comparing the incidence of taxes and benefits between these years.

The incidence of taxes and benefits

The Lowes' lifetime in 2008

Figure 14.1 shows the lifetime profile of earnings, taxes and benefits for the Lowes' lifetime under the 2008 system. This shows how various life events and overall lifetime earnings profiles combine with the tax and benefit system to give a clear impression of the overall incidence of taxes and transfers. Unlike the Meades and the Moores, the Lowes receive considerable levels of transfers when children are present. These are at their highest at the two births, when they comprise maternity provision and high levels of Child Tax Credit, and are high again later in childhood on Ms Lowe's return to work, when Working Tax Credit rises to meet the considerable childcare costs (shown below the x-axis after taxes). The Lowes also receive state pensions, Ms Lowe from age 60 and Mr Lowe from age 65. The disposable income lines show how income is raised with Ms Lowe's decisions to return to work and then to move to full-time work, although the 'after childcare costs' line clearly demonstrates that the net gain from working while paying for childcare is small for the Lowes. Also shown in Figure 14.1 is the considerable amount of tax paid by the Lowes over their lifetime, although liability for tax during retirement arises solely from council tax.

Figure 14.1: The Lowes' lifetime income profile, 2008 system

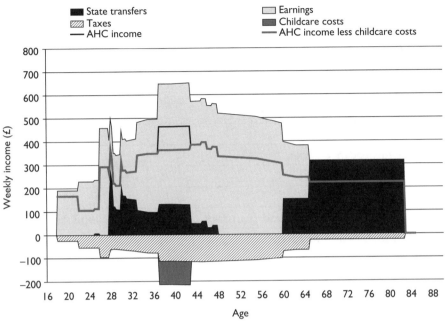

Source: Authors' calculations from LOIS.

Incidence of tax and benefits across the 1979, 1997 and 2008 systems

Table 14.1 shows the summary lifetime cumulative results for tax and benefit incidence if the 2008 lifetime profile is repeated in the 1979, 1997 and 2008 systems in contemporary fixed prices. Direct taxation represents around 21% of lifetime earnings under both 1979 and 1997 systems, but is higher in 2008, mostly as a result of higher local government taxation. It is predictable, but worth reporting, that under all three systems the Lowes face lower levels of *direct* taxation in lifetime terms than the Meades. However, this result is an obvious one only if one ignores that the Lowes' tax burden will be significantly changed by the growth of indirect taxation, especially VAT, post-1979. Earlier discussion in Chapter Ten showed that indirect taxation of the lowest income quintile represented around 25% to 30% of disposable income in 1997 and 2008 compared with only 17% in 1979. Such huge increases in tax regressivity from indirect taxation make any clear conclusions about change over time being based purely on direct taxation rather tentative.

Tax reliefs for the Lowes relate only to income tax allowances for marriage and old age, but provide significant levels of underlying support, especially in 1979. Tax relief in respect of marriage, whatever its virtues or otherwise, provided a key element of support for families under the 1979 system that is present to a much lesser extent under the 1997 system and not available at all under the 2008 system. However, the role of tax reliefs for marriage has to be set against

Table 14.1: The Lowes' lifetime under the 1979, 1997 and 2008 systems

	Percentage of lifetime earnings		
	1979	1997	2008
Direct taxation			
All direct taxes	20.9	20.9	24.6
State transfers			
All	43.4	34.4	47.4
Maternity/dependent children	5.7	4.9	12.1
Retirement	36.9	29.2	35.3
Other periods	0.8	0.3	0.0
Net effects of direct taxes and transfers	**+22.5**	**+13.4**	**+22.9**
Other transfers and payments			
Childcare costs	3.0	3.3	3.3
Housing costs	13.7	23.9	27.6
Lifetime income totals (£million, 2008 prices)			
Lifetime gross earnings	0.64	0.83	0.95
Lifetime disposable income after housing and childcare costs	0.67	0.71	0.92

Source: Authors' calculations from LOIS.

Notes: Constant '2008 behaviour' across all three systems.

the countervailing impact of transfers, and in particular the increased incidence of transfers that are associated with children. Marriage allowances provide an equivalent of 5% of lifetime earnings in 1979 and 1.7% in 1997. Age allowances are very small in 1979 – 0.2% of lifetime earnings – and provide no value in 1997, as the Lowes pay no income tax in retirement, but are equivalent to 1.5% of lifetime earnings in 2008.

Table 14.1 clearly reflects the evolving policy story discussed to date in this book – that of a move towards selectively prioritising childhood and old age, which is strongest in the 2008 system. State transfer income during periods of the lifetime associated with childhood is much higher under the 2008 system, at 12.1% of lifetime earnings, twice the level in 1979 (5.9%) and even further ahead of the least generous 1997 system (just under 5%). However, it is important to stress that much of this increased spending comes in the form of tax credits and as such can be seen as counteracting the higher direct taxation of 2008. In addition, a fair proportion of this spend goes towards meeting childcare costs.

Turning to old age and pensions, Table 14.1 shows that the value of state pensions is highest in 1979, at almost 37% of lifetime earnings. However, unlike the situation for the higher-earning Meades and Moores, the intervening decline in the value of the basic state pension relative to earnings does *not* mean that 2008 pension results fall as a percentage of lifetime earnings for the Lowes. The 2008 system provides substantially higher pensions – 35% of lifetime earnings compared with 29% under the 1997 system. The reason for this is the explicitly redistributive nature of State Second Pension (S2P). As noted in Chapter Nine, S2P, which was New Labour's 2002 replacement for the State Earnings Related Pension Scheme (SERPS), grants a more generous accrual rate on low earnings, which, in the long term, has the potential to significantly improve outcomes in retirement for low earners like the Lowes. Here, the effect is seen to be sufficient to more than offset the effect of the declining relative value of the basic pension, at least over the period since 1997.

However, transfer coverage for pure 'working age' periods of the lifetime have fallen over time and were 0.8% of lifetime income in 1979 from rent rebates and 0.3% from housing benefits in 1997. No transfers of any significant value in lifetime terms are given to the working age Lowes in 2008.

The net effects of combined taxes and transfers given in Table 14.1 show that the 2008 system has a lifetime cumulative net effect of a positive 22.9% of lifetime earnings that is almost at the same level as 1979 (22.5%) and is way ahead of 1997 (13.4% of total lifetime earnings). Figure 14.2 shows how this net effect operates over the working age part of the lifetime both with and without children. Net effects for pension age cannot graphically be shown, as we assume zero savings. Thus there is no 'original income' for that period; state pension income is the sole income, leaving net effects as an incalculable infinite.

Figure 14.2 clearly shows the effects of tax credits in 2008 operating as true tax credits by providing transfers that take the family out of taxation and into positive net effects when it has children. The two peaks clearly show the increased level of tax credits for each child in its first year and the continuing positive transfer balance continues while childcare is being paid for. It then falls into a negative overall effect and only rises against the other years' profiles when the Lowes' children receive Education Maintenance Allowance payments at ages 16 to 18 (when Ms Lowe is aged 44 to 48). Over other periods of working age, the 2008 system has the largest negative effect, net direct tax, but it is important to remember that this is partly due to underlying support from the national minimum wage, which is keeping earnings higher relative to tax thresholds than in other years. Both 1979 and 1997 systems are quite similar in profile. There is a small jump in positive 1979 subsidies when rent rebates are paid at age 22, but apart from that, the systems largely run very close together, with some gains from Family Credit during the period of part-time work for Ms Lowe aged 33 to 37. At age 60, when Ms Lowe draws her pension and Mr Lowe continues to work, there is a clear illustration of the changing value of state pensions for Ms Lowe compared with overall earnings and taxation. Her pension is clearly highest in 2008 for reasons previously outlined, lowest in 1997 and somewhere in between in 1979 with SERPS.

Figure 14.2: The Lowes' net effects of taxes and benefits over the working age lifetime (no inflation)

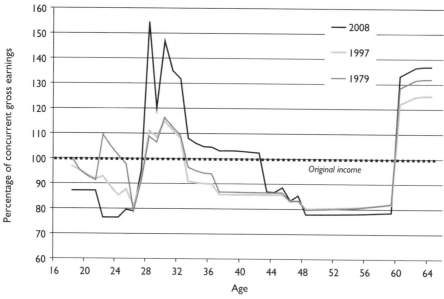

Source: Authors' calculations from LOIS.

Note: Constant 2008 behaviour without inflation.

Disposable incomes

However, taxes and benefits are not the whole story and it is easier to interpret the differences between the systems when we consider the issue of rent over the lifetime. Chapters Two and Six outlined how housing subsidies had moved from subsidising rents across the board to subsidising low incomes and that rents were allowed to rise substantially in real terms in social housing. Table 14.1 shows the value of housing costs as a percentage of lifetime earnings and clearly shows that they double between 1979 and 2008, from 13.7% to 27.6% (based on our assumption of average local authority rent levels in England). This is a direct result of changing social policy and, together with the issue of childcare costs, means that disposable incomes after housing costs (AHC) are probably the best overall illustrative measure of the changing policy profile. Lifetime gross earnings have risen for the Lowes over the years, as they have benefited from overall earnings growth. There is the need to pause at this point because 2008 gross earnings will also be affected by the national minimum wage and our estimates for 1997 use a consistent underlying profile of earnings mobility from the underlying age weighting of earnings that may not accurately reflect the extremely poor state of low-paid earnings progression in 1997. With these caveats in mind, we can see that the relationship between gross earnings growth and disposable income after housing costs is pegged back hugely between 1979 and 1997 – a rise from

0.67 to 0.71 million pounds in total or an effective rise of 6% compared with an underlying rise in gross earnings of 30%. Given that indirect taxation is not taken into account in these increases in disposable incomes, the change between the 1979 and 1997 systems appears to be a very precarious one in terms of overall disposable incomes for the low-earning Lowes' lifetime profile. The 2008 figures for gross earnings and disposable incomes, even after allowing for housing and childcare costs, show the Lowes' lifetime profile as having largely improved since 1997 in no small part due to the introduction of the national minimum wage and the 2008 child-focused tax credit system. Overall gross income growth between 1997 and 2008 is assumed to be 113%, but disposable incomes after housing and childcare costs have risen by 129%.

Of course, these results reflect our assumption of constant contemporary 2008 behaviour and the issue of childcare costs is particularly important in discounting the value of transfers in 1979 for the Lowes because there were no transfer-related subsidies at that time and low-income parents were unlikely to pay for childcare. We will now control for such differences in lifetime behaviour in a further set of comparisons.

Allowing for behavioural difference and policy maturation

As we did for the Moores in Chapter Thirteen, we now consider differences in behaviour over time for the Lowes, whose income is far more constrained and who, like the Meades, will more clearly demonstrate and illustrate some of the changes in economic and social life since the 1970s. Once again, as we did for the Meades, we adjust the Lowes' lifetime profile in 1979 to represent a different behaviour set to compare to the 2008 behaviour set that is used for both 1997 and 2008. The Lowes' 1979 life story includes different patterns of earlier marriage, earlier childbirth, reduced maternal employment, lower school leaving for their children and shorter lives. It differs from our original 2008 life story in the following respects.

Earlier marriage and childbirth mean that the lifetime behaviour profile diverges from the 2008 pattern at age 22:

- At age 22 Ms Lowe marries and sets up home with Mr Lowe (again her male doppelganger).
- From this point they live in rented accommodation, paying average social rent (local authority) and average rates and council tax for such a property.
- Their first child is born at age 24 and their second at age 26.

The changes to maternal employment mean a longer period away from employment and no return to part-time work in the first instance:

- Ms Lowe does not return to work after the birth of her first child until the youngest child reaches age 11 and instead undertakes household childcare full-time.
- At age 37 Ms Lowe returns to work full-time.

There are further changes to reflect the Lowes' children leaving full-time education at the minimum school-leaving age:

- The Lowes' children will remain in full-time secondary education only until they each respectively reach age 16.

And finally there are changes to reflect lower life expectancy:

- The Lowes both die at age 78 (five years earlier than 2008).

The mature systems of 1979, 1997 and 2008 change in the same way as earlier assumptions for the Meades.

Table 14.2 shows the changed lifetime incidence of taxes and benefits using all sets of modified assumptions, with the original results shown in grey shaded cells. The first thing to consider is the effect of moving from 1979 to 2008 behaviour on the 1979 results. Direct taxation falls slightly as a result of lower maternal earnings but benefits also rise during childhood as the family receives more help from Family Income Supplement (FIS) and rent and rate rebates to make up for Ms Lowe's lost earnings. Transfers for this childhood period rise from 5.7% to 8% of lifetime earnings, a rise of 2.3%. However, transfers for pensions fall to reflect Ms Lowe's reduced lifetime earnings, from 36.9% to 28.4% of lifetime earnings. There is a reduction in the small level of transfers during working age without children because there are no longer periods where Ms Lowe is both single and renting, thereby qualifying for greater assistance with housing costs. The overall net effects of direct tax and benefits are thus to reduce the overall net positive effect from 22.5% to 16.2%, and this almost entirely results from pension reduction.

Lifetime earnings totals do not differ greatly because the change in Ms Lowe's earnings history is based on a fairly short period of low part-time earnings in 1979. Differences in disposable lifetime incomes after housing and childcare costs are also small because the 1979 profile of behaviour avoids childcare costs and gains from transfers during childhood redress some of the overall losses to lifetime income from differences in pension income.

What difference does policy maturity make across all three years? In 1979, the difference purely lies in the additional direct taxation that arises from higher National Insurance contributions (NICs) to pay for SERPS. In constant 2008 behaviour terms, the total of direct taxes over the lifetime rises to 25.1% of lifetime earnings and this reduces the overall net effect from 22.5% to 18.4% of lifetime earnings in positive transfers over the lifetime. A mature 1997 system,

Table 14.2: The Lowes' lifetime under the 1979, 1997 and 2008 systems with behavioural change and policy maturation

| | 1979 | | | | 1997 | | 2008 | |
| | 1979 behaviour | | Current behaviour | | Current behaviour | | Current behaviour | |
	'79 rules	Mature	'79 rules	Mature	'97 rules	Mature	'08 rules	Mature
Total number of lifetime years modelled	116	116	124	124	124	124	124	130
Female	(62)	(62)	(67)	(67)	(67)	(67)	(67)	(70)
Male	(54)	(54)	(57)	(57)	(57)	(57)	(57)	(60)
Percentage of lifetime earnings								
All direct taxes	20.4	24.6	20.9	25.1	20.9	22.1	24.6	23.5
All state transfers	36.5	36.5	43.4	43.4	34.4	29.9	47.4	38.6
Maternity/children	8.0	8.0	5.7	5.7	4.9	4.9	12.1	10.8
Retirement	28.4	28.4	36.9	36.9	29.2	24.8	35.3	27.8
Other	0.2	0.2	0.8	0.8	0.3	0.3	0.0	0.0
Net effects of direct taxes and transfers	**+16.2**	**+11.9**	**+22.5**	**+18.4**	**+13.4**	**+7.8**	**+22.9**	**+15.1**
Other transfers and payments								
Personal accounts contributions	–	–	–	–	–	–	–	2.3
Personal accounts income	–	–	–	–	–	–	–	8.1
Childcare costs	–	–	3.0	3.0	3.3	3.1	3.3	2.9
Housing costs	12.7	12.7	13.7	13.7	23.9	22.7	27.6	24.3
Lifetime income totals (£million, 2008 prices)								
Lifetime earnings	0.63	0.63	0.64	0.64	0.83	0.87	0.95	1.08
Lifetime disposable income after housing and childcare costs	0.66	0.63	0.67	0.65	0.71	0.71	0.92	1.05
Disposable income per year of life (2008 prices rounded to nearest £100)	5,700	5,400	5,500	5,200	5,700	5,700	7,400	8,100

Source: Authors' calculations from LOIS.

with equalised pension ages, means higher taxation and lower pensions (with life expectancy held constant) and reduces the overall net effect of taxes and benefits to 7.8% of lifetime earnings. Maturity under the 2008 system importantly means longer working lives for the Lowes and the consequently higher level of earnings reduces the significance of transfer income in lifetime terms. However, the large fall in transfer income in retirement is due both to this effect and to fewer years in retirement (notwithstanding an increase in life expectancy) as well as S2P becoming a flat-rate benefit under mature pensions policy. Of course, compensating for this will be the new personal accounts pensions. Their outcome will in reality depend on how such funded pensions perform at the time. However, given the assumptions we have used (as outlined in Chapter Eleven), such a pension will, at an additional cost of 2.3% of lifetime earnings, yield an estimated pension equal to 8.1% of lifetime earnings. Adding personal accounts into the net effects of the mature 2008 system would give a positive total of 20.9%, just two percentage points lower than the original 2008 result. In terms of lifetime disposable income, the impact of additional working years is significant – £8,100 compared with £7,400 per annum – even when the additional years of life expectancy are allowed for.

Allowing for inflation and uprating

Table 14.3 shows the baseline lifetime profiles from Table 14.1 with outcomes adjusted for inflation and uprating assumptions over the lifetime. Tax totals rise with inflation modelled under the 1997 and 2008 systems but not in 1979. This is not because of fiscal drag, which we do not model in our lifetime as opposed to medium-term profiles, but because under the 1997 and 2008 systems council tax is rising in line with earnings, whereas local government taxation under the 1979 system rises with prices. Transfers for children in 1979 and 1997 maintain their relative value and, indeed, slightly improve with the impact of inflation and uprating. This similar effect comes from opposing reasons, with earnings uprating of Child Benefit primarily responsible in 1979 and price uprated Family Credit compensating for low earnings under the 1997 system. In the 2008 system, where the national minimum wage provides a floor below which wages cannot fall, the far larger and more generous package of childhood benefits does not keep its relative value after inflation is modelled. State pensions in 1979 rise dramatically to 62.5% of lifetime earnings once basic state pension is uprated with earnings, while the 1997 system sees the opposite, with a fall in value of state pensions to 26% of lifetime earnings. The 2008 system has a higher result for transfer income in retirement once inflation is modelled, but, in terms of benefit to the Lowes, this is deceptive, as the rise is accounted for by their Housing Benefit and Council Tax Benefit rising but only to keep pace with rising rent and council tax. Overall, in terms of net effects, this means that inflation has the largest positive effect on net outcomes for 1979, small positive effects in 1997 and significant negative effects

Table 14.3: The Lowes' lifetime under the 1979, 1997, 2008 systems with inflation modelled

	1979		1997		2008	
	Flat	**Inflation**	**Flat**	**Inflation**	**Flat**	**Inflation**
	Percentage of lifetime earnings					
All direct taxes	20.9	20.3	20.9	23.0	24.6	27.3
All state transfers	43.4	69.9	34.4	32.7	47.4	50.6
Maternity/dependent children	5.7	6.1	4.9	5.4	12.1	11.4
Retirement	36.9	62.5	29.2	26.4	35.3	39.0
Other periods	0.8	1.3	0.3	1.0	0.0	0.3
Net effects of direct taxes and transfers	**+22.5**	**+49.6**	**+13.4**	**+9.7**	**+22.9**	**+23.3**
Other transfers and payments						
Childcare costs	3.0	2.5	3.3	2.8	3.3	2.9
Housing costs	13.7	11.8	23.9	30.7	27.6	31.4

Source: Authors' calculations from LOIS.

Note: Constant 2008 assumptions for behaviour.

in 1997. Another issue for the Lowes, at least during periods when they are not in receipt of full housing benefits, is the cost of housing. Under the 1979 system, where rents are rising with prices, housing costs fall slightly in lifetime terms once inflation is modelled. Under the 1997 and 2008 systems, the reverse is true, with housing costs under both systems rising to above 30% of lifetime earnings.

Outcomes

How would outcomes for the Lowes change between the systems? We look at two forms of work incentives for this low-paid lifetime as well as their final position in the income distribution and against child and pensioner poverty.

Work incentives

The Lowes spend considerable periods of their working life receiving means-tested benefits alongside their low wages, especially when they have children. This means that they are likely to face combinations of marginal tax rates and benefit tapers that produce high effective marginal deduction rates as outlined in Chapter Eleven. Figure 14.3 shows this to be the case for Mr Lowe, but to differing extents according to the year of comparison. In 1979, the arrival of children

Figure 14.3: Mr Lowe's effective marginal deduction rates

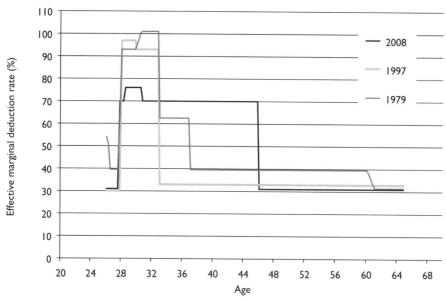

Source: Authors' calculations from LOIS.

Note: Simulation of the Lowes' lifetime using benchmark 2008 lifetime profiles without inflation.

leads to a combination of rent and rate rebates and FIS, and this pushes marginal rates up to over 100% for Mr Lowe. When Ms Lowe returns to part-time work, entitlement changes and the rates fall to 63% and then again to 40% when she moves to full-time work. When Ms Lowe retires at 60, Mr Lowe's marginal rates fall to 30%. In 1997, the arrival of children means that Family Credit, Housing Benefit and Council Tax Benefit are paid and these in combination raise marginal rates to 93% until Ms Lowe returns to work part time. At this point entitlement to all these benefits ends and rates fall to the underlying marginal rate of income tax and NICs. In 2008, the highest marginal rates Mr Lowe faces are once again during the early years after the birth of his children, when they peak at 76% reflecting Child Tax Credit, Working Tax Credit and Council Tax Benefit receipt. From the point of his second child reaching the age of one, Council Tax Benefit entitlement falls away and marginal deduction rates fall to 70%, reflecting the combined rate of tax credit tapers, income tax and NICs. However, they stay at this rate until age 46 through the majority of the Lowes' whole period with dependent children. This potentially has significant effects on Ms Lowe's return to work, as she will face the same 70% marginal deduction rate on her earnings at all times when there are two children present.

At this point, it is important to remember the higher risks that the Lowes face of interruption of earnings and to look at the replacement rates of out-of-work benefits to earnings over the Lowe's working age lifetimes. We calculate these in terms of disposable income after housing costs and compare incomes in work and out of work if Mr Lowe does not work and Ms Lowe continues working.

Figure 14.4 shows family income out of work as a percentage of income in work assuming that Mr Lowe is unemployed (Figure 14.4a) or inactive due to incapacity for work (Figure 14.4b) but that Ms Lowe's earning behaviour is not affected in either case. The profiles in Figure 14.4 are difficult to interpret in the first instance because the age-weighted earnings profile puts an underlying n-shaped profile to earnings that are used to calculate the replacement rates. This confirms one underlying assumption that we make about replacement rates – that they are the value of the benefit package relative to earnings immediately prior to unemployment or inactivity – and thus do not reflect any wage reduction that may happen on re-entry into the workforce. Figure 14.4a can be simplified into four main periods, the first of which is the period before children are born. At this point, the value of Mr Lowe's unemployment benefits alongside Mr Lowe's full-time earnings is compared with the outcomes from two full-time earners. Clearly, 1979 has the highest replacement rate as expected because benefit levels are historically highest in relative terms and there is an earnings-related supplement. The second comparison period relates to the presence of children and under all three systems shows the effect of replacing one full-time earner with one unemployed and the effect of means-tested assistance alongside Ms Lowe's earnings. Here, 2008 and 1979 are broadly similar in terms of replacement rates (despite much 'noise' in peaks and troughs), which hover between 70% and 80%. In 1997, the replacement rate is much lower, plummeting at the point where Ms Lowe enters work at age 36. Rates rise over time as the earnings curve changes underlying comparison earnings. The third comparison period relates to the time when the children have left home. Here we see the ranked values of unemployment benefits over time against earnings, with 1979 highest, but with 2008 higher than 1997 because of the Working Tax Credit that would supplement Ms Lowe's earnings. Finally, once Ms Lowe is of pension age, the comparison is once again with means-tested benefits and higher rates of social assistance for 60-year-olds – Pension Credit in 2008 and Income Support in 1997 raises replacement rates relative to 1979.

Figure 14.4b shows the similar calculations for the situation where Mr Lowe is claiming incapacity benefits. The 1979 system stands out clearly as having extremely high replacement rates – the Lowes are better off if Mr Lowe is on Invalidity Benefit (not taxable in 1979) and especially so if the system provides him with SERPS additional pension. Replacement rates are lower in 1997 and 2008, but are still at 80% to 90% when children are present in the 2008 system and tax credits supplement Ms Lowe's low wages and slightly lower in 1997, with greater fluctuation as Ms Lowe changes her employment hours.

These replacement rates reflect a better comparison of employment incentives than a pure comparison of earnings and underlying benefit levels – it is the overall income package that is crucial and this changes over the working lifetime, with

**Figure 14.4a: Replacement rates for the Lowes if Mr Lowe is not working
– unemployment**

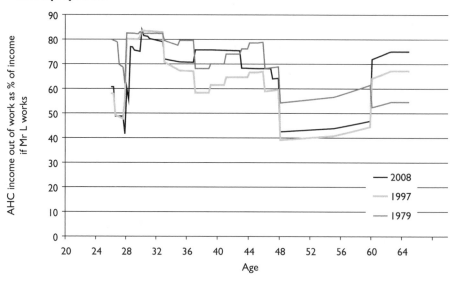

**Figure 14.4b: Replacement rates for the Lowes if Mr Lowe is not working
– incapacity**

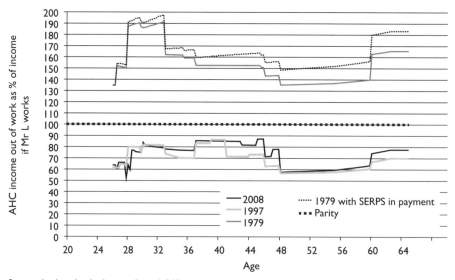

Source: Authors' calculations from LOIS.

Note: Simulation of the Lowes' lifetime using benchmark models without inflation.

childhood transfers and means testing undermining incentives to work even under the least generous and more means-tested systems of 1997 and 2008. If we combine this consideration of replacement rates with the earlier discussion of effective marginal gains from work, we can see that part-time employment may indeed be increasingly producing a poverty trap and supporting worklessness.

How do the Lowes fare in the overall income distribution?

As with earlier profiles, we now turn to show the Lowes' position in the income distribution and ask how far they are at risk of poverty using our underlying assumptions about inflation.

Despite illustrating a situation where the Lowes do not suffer any unemployment or incapacity, Figure 14.5 nevertheless shows a family lifetime lived near the poverty line, with various peaks and troughs under all three systems and actual falls into poverty under the 1997 and 2008 systems. The figure can be considered in terms of four periods. First, there is the period up until age 26 when the household simply comprises a single Ms Lowe. Here high housing costs clearly put the 2008 system in last place, at least until Ms Lowe turns 25 and benefits from receiving Working Tax Credit. Second, there is the period with dependent children, which generally shows the 2008 system providing the strongest outcomes and which period we will shortly address separately under slightly different terms. Third,

Figure 14.5: The Lowes' relative position in the income distribution

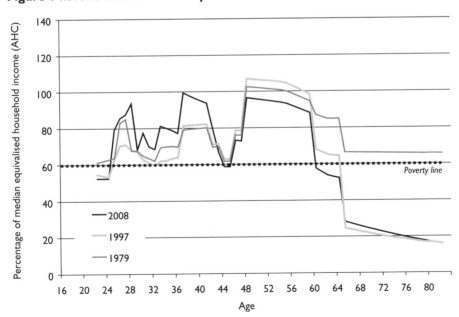

Source: Authors' calculations from LOIS.

Note: Simulation of the Lowes' lifetime using benchmark models with inflation.

there is a period where the Lowes both work full time but have no dependent children to support. Here the 1997 system, with its lower than 2008 direct taxation and 'inherent advantage', leads the pack. However, as we move into the Lowes' retirement years, it is the 1979 system with its earnings uprated state pension that provides the best outcomes; indeed, these are the only results that do not have the Lowes sliding into poverty. Under the 1997 system, this is clearly the result of the state retirement pension having been uprated with prices and having fallen dramatically in value in relative terms, with the reformed SERPS in no way able to provide a top-up pension income to bridge the poverty gap. Our simulation of the 2008 system is arguably unfair here. Although the improvement of S2P over reformed SERPS results is a visible improvement in outcomes, despite the ever-continuing decline of the state pension in relative terms, what is not reflected in Figure 14.5 is either any future commitment to uprate the state pension in line with earnings or any benefit from the generosity of Pension Credit. In the latter case, this is because our lifetime inflation assumptions are to uprate Pensions Credit with prices only, meaning that by the time the Lowes retire the level of income it guarantees is one far below the poverty line. We consider the alternative to this assumption and earnings uprating of the Pension Credit guarantee at the end of this chapter.

How would the risks of unemployment and incapacity for work affect poverty during working life? The answer largely depends on when such risks occur and how they interact with other circumstances such as age, the presence of children, whether one of the parents continued to work and so on. Figure 14.6 gives an overview of five unemployment and incapacity events spaced at different times in the Lowes' working lifetime and the poverty gaps or clearance that would occur if such an event were to affect only Mr Lowe's ability to work.

Unemployment while the children are very young and where there are no maternal earnings to protect family income leads to poverty under all three systems, but to differing degrees. In 1979, the poverty gap would be 9%. In 1997, this will have grown to 12%, but in 2008 would be only 5%, as a result of more generous provision for children through Child Tax Credit. Eight years on at age 40, when maternal earnings are assumed to be full time, poverty gaps are 3% in 1979 and 12% in 1997. The 2008 system, however, protects the family against poverty, yielding a narrow poverty clearance of 3% as a result of the family receiving tax credits alongside Jobseeker's Allowance. However, as the children age, their needs increase and the poverty measurement through equivalence scales treats them as adult from 14 onwards. At this point, with Mr Lowe aged 44 and unemployed, the family would sink deeply into poverty under all three systems. The worse outcome would occur under the 1997 system, but even the higher relative female earnings and tax credits in 2008 do not greatly improve the Lowes' relative fortunes in the face of a poverty line that rises with earnings. In older working age when there are no children, poverty is still certain under all three systems. Here the 2008 system's generosity in respect of children is clearly no longer relevant. What

Figure 14.6: Unemployment and incapacity events and poverty outcomes

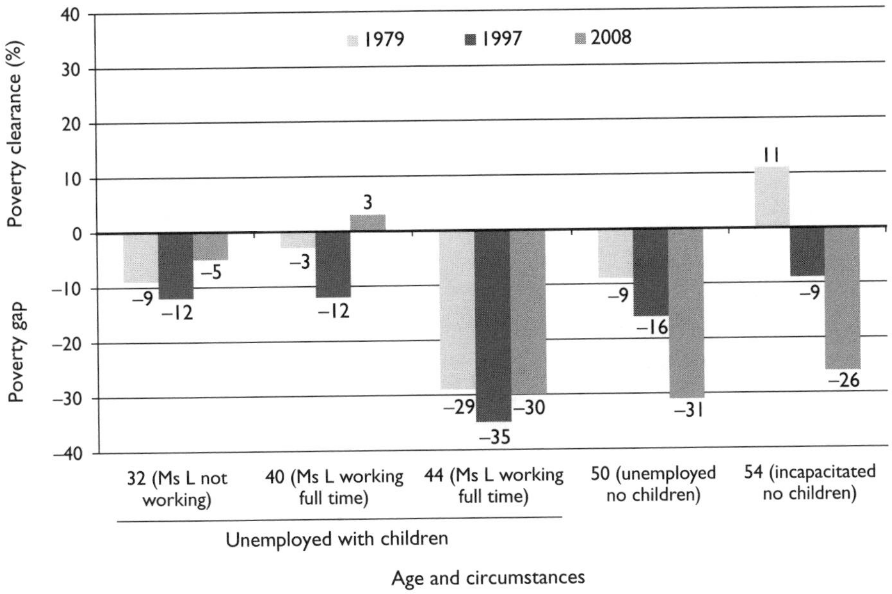

Source: Authors' calculations from LOIS.

does remain relevant is the declining relative value of adult out-of-work benefits, which leaves a clear ranking of the worst outcome by far under the 2008 system and the best, albeit still in poverty, under the 1979 system. At age 54, we suppose Mr Lowe to be incapacitated for over a year and the poverty gaps for this age and circumstances are very different in terms of magnitude but retain the same ranking between systems. The 1979 system provides an outcome of 11% poverty clearance (even without including any SERPS payment for which Mr Lowe might qualify), whereas the 1997 and 2008 systems present the Lowes with poverty gaps of 9% and 26% respectively. Again, the driving factor is the relative decline in underlying out-of-work benefits, with the added factor of the new, less generous Employment and Support Allowance under the 2008 system.

Childhood and risk of poverty

We now turn specifically to address child poverty. Figure 14.7 illustrates a child poverty profile for the Lowes using our short- to medium-term inflation assumptions that include the effects of fiscal drag and benefit erosion.

Figure 14.7, of course, does not simply repeat the analysis of earlier results, but has the Lowes facing contemporary prices at the time their first child is born with the inflation clock beginning to tick from that point on. It indicates that child poverty is a high risk for the family at two crucial points in childhood under all three systems. The first period relates to infancy and periods where there are

Figure 14.7: The Lowes' childhood poverty profile (AHC)

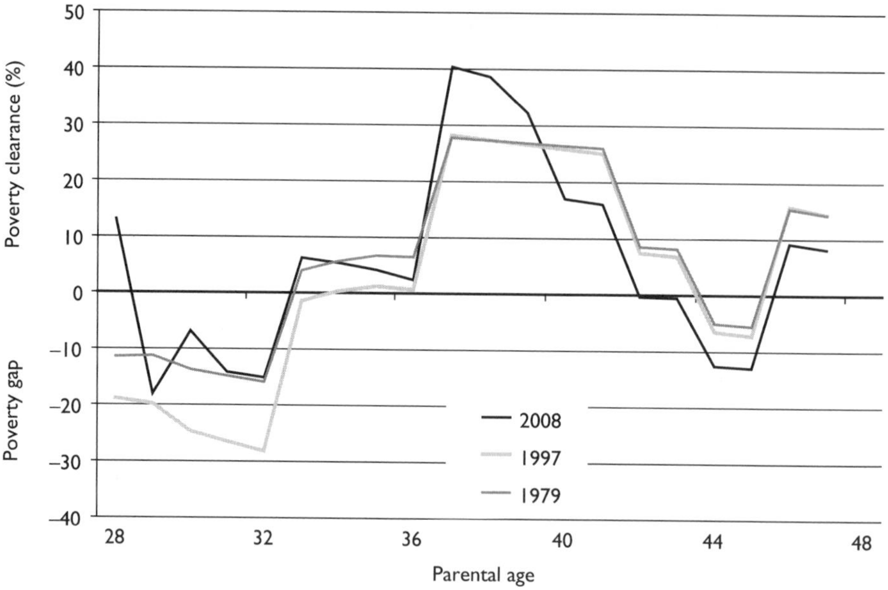

Source: Authors' calculations from LOIS.

no maternal earnings. The 2008 system prevents poverty at birth due to high maternity benefits and Child Tax Credit in the first year and gives 13% poverty clearance. This is clearly an improvement on both 1997 and 1979 positions, where poverty gaps of 19% and 13% arise at birth. The other main period of risk is when children reach teenage years and are treated as equivalent to adults from the age of 14 in the measurement of poverty. This clearly erodes the poverty clearance under all three systems even when there are two full-time, low-paid earners. The 2008 system fares worst during this period, partly because of the changing underlying relationship between median earnings (and fractions thereof) and the relative poverty line, discussed earlier in previous profiles, and partly because the system just does not keep up with a rising poverty line as children age.

The 2008 system makes the biggest impact at the points of change – rewarding maternal returns to work and the subsequent increase in earnings when full-time work starts. However, it is clear that these rewards erode more quickly in their anti-poverty effect than in comparison years – a reflection of the underlying elements of tax credits either rising with prices only or not being uprated at all. These underlying assumptions serve to erode the effect of uprating the child element of Child Tax Credit with earnings (see Sutherland et al, 2008, for a full discussion).

Outcomes in retirement and pensioner poverty

Moving to the other end of the lifetime, will retirement promise a poverty-free outcome for the Lowes? For the low-paid lifetime profile of the Lowes, we use both the current and the mature version of the 2008 system to illustrate the effect of the proposed personal accounts.

Figure 14.8 shows retirement outcomes from 65 under the 1979, 1997 and 'immature' 2008 systems and retirement outcomes from the later retirement age of 68 onwards under the mature 2008 system. Under all systems, we model the inflation clock as starting to tick at age 65. At 65, the highest state pension income relative to the poverty line is provided by the 1979 system, with its state retirement pension higher in relative terms and the contribution of SERPS under its original set of rules. All else being equal, the decline in the relative value of the basic pension serves to drive this outcome down towards the poverty line over time. In fact, come the 1997 system, when the situation is exacerbated only by cuts to SERPS, the Lowes begin their retirement on the poverty line. Under the 2008 system, the deliberately redistributive replacement for SERPS, S2P, serves to improve fortunes for the Lowes. However, whereas under the 1979 system clearance against poverty declined only slowly due to the combined package of earnings uprated basic pension and price uprated SERPS additional pension, under the 1997 and immature 2008 systems the sole price uprating of both basic and state secondary pensions means that outcomes quickly decline against a poverty

Figure 14.8: The Lowes' pensioner poverty profile (BHC)

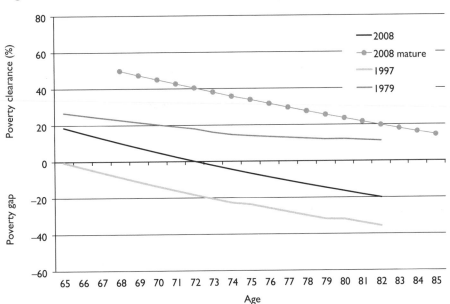

Source: Authors' calculations from LOIS.

line that rises with earnings. Under the 2008 system, this means that the Lowes fall into poverty at age 72 and sink further thereafter – a situation that the receipt of means-tested benefits at this stage, including some Pension Credit, actually does little to arrest. Under the 1997 system, the Lowes, who are already in poverty on retirement, simply sink further into it as their retirement progresses.

Despite such gloomy outcomes, Figure 14.8 promises a brighter retirement for the Lowes under the mature 2008 system. Our results here show the Lowes beginning retirement at 68 with a poverty clearance of 50% and a more gradual decline of income relative to poverty. Such outcomes, however, are a very long-term prospect – we are supposing working lifetimes lived out under a set of rules that will not even be in place until 2012, and depend on a number of assumptions. One such assumption is that the figures used to model personal accounts (as outlined in Chapter Eleven) are at best based on promised future policy and at worst on estimates of how such pensions may perform in practice in the distant future. A further key assumption is the promised future uprating of the basic state pension with earnings that will potentially provide a more stable relative income base in retirement on which additional pensions can provide longer-lasting poverty clearance.

Inequality

How do these low-income lifetime profiles compare in outcomes to the Meades? Our assumptions start with the Lowes having half the median earnings of the Meades. Does this difference in original income widen or narrow between the systems in 1979, 1997 and 2008? Table 14.4 shows the simplest comparison of outcomes using consistent assumptions of lifetime behaviour (that is, 2008 for both the Lowes and Meades).

The underlying earnings histories used in the lifetime profiles of the Lowes and the Meades do not differ greatly and this leads to a consistent difference in gross lifetime earnings of 50% for the Lowes when compared with the Meades. (The exception to this is under the 2008 system where the existence of the floor provided by the national minimum wage actually means that the Lowes' lifetime earnings work out at 52% rather than 50% of the Meades'.)

Our profiles put in consistent assumptions that offset such earnings with housing and childcare costs across the three systems and thus, once again, the difference in lifetime disposable incomes provides us with clear inferences about the impact of the different policy systems on inequality between the Lowes and the Meades. Table 14.4 clearly shows that these differences were highest in 1997 when the Lowes' lifetime disposable income was 45% of the Meades'. These differences are much smaller in both 1979 and 2008, at 53% and 54% respectively. This clearly suggests that the policy impact of 2008 programmes is similar in outcome to those of 1979 on incomes of the low paid compared with the median paid over the lifetime. Of course, this assumes a constant set of behaviours, and we have already

Table 14.4: Lifetime differences in outcomes of the Lowes compared with the Meades'

	Income as percentage of Meades		
	1979	**1997**	**2008**
Gross lifetime earnings	50	50	52
Disposable income after housing and childcare costs	53	45	54

Source: Tables 12.1, 14.1.

seen that maternal earnings and childcare costs are offset against each other if we alter the 1979 assumptions and that improvements in lifetime outcomes for 1979 also arise if shorter life expectancies are included. The turnaround of the relative fortunes of the low paid since 1997 under the 2008 system is also understated in this comparison because our assumptions include earnings progression in 1997 that is above that suggested by underlying contemporary data. In other words, adjustments that we could make to allow for differences between 1997 and 2008 would make 1997's performance potentially worse.

Summary

This chapter has used lifetime simulation to synthesise all elements of tax and benefit provision in 1979, 1997 and 2008 for a profile based on the Lowes, who earn half median income. Our main findings are as follows.

- Direct taxation levels in 2008 are highest and represent 25% of lifetime earnings compared with 21% in 1979 and 1997.
- Much of the additional tax burden in 2008 is offset by higher transfers, and a good proportion of these are acting as real tax credits. Transfers for childhood are 12% of lifetime income in 2008 compared with 5.7% and 4.9% in 1979 and 1997 respectively. Transfers for retirement are highest in 1979, at 37% of lifetime earnings, followed by 2008 (35%) and 1997 (29%).
- The combination of direct taxes and transfers means that 2008 provides the highest net effect, at 22.9% of lifetime income, followed closely by 1979 (22.5%) and a long way ahead of 1997 (13.4%).
- Low-income lifetimes will face the highest additional tax liability from indirect taxes, which are far higher in 1997 and 2008 and would easily wipe out the small net additional fiscal gain from the 2008 system compared with that of 1979.
- Work incentives in terms of effective marginal deduction rates yield longer-lasting periods of high marginal rates of 70% to 80% in 2008, but the peak

rates under all systems occur in early childhood and are highest in the 1979 system at 100%, with the 1997 system having peak rates of 95%.

- Changing replacement rates and their work incentives are primarily driven by falling values of out-of-work benefits relative to earnings over time and thus improve as job entry incentives between 1979 to 2008 due to periodic structural changes and underlying benefit erosion. Incapacity benefits in 1979 could result in higher than 100% replacement rates and these were removed by 1997 and 2008. However, these declining relative rates of benefit interact with family circumstances so that the presence of children and maternal part-time earnings and tax credits make 2008 rates rise above those of 1997.

- The risk of unemployment and inactivity is almost certainly linked to poverty in all three systems and poverty gaps will result unless one full-time earner remains and then only so in 2008. Poverty gaps grow over time and as children age, and for periods of working age without children.

- The risk of child poverty is greatest when children are very young, and mothers work less, and when children are over 14 and cost more in poverty measurement terms. The 2008 system provides best anti-poverty impacts in early childhood up to the point where there two full-time earners. However, these impacts erode quickly against rising relative poverty. The 1979 system performs better than 1997 in early childhood and then has equal effects, ahead of 2008 in the latter part of childhood.

- The 1979 system provides best coverage against poverty during retirement, while the 2008 system starts with good poverty clearance but then slides into poverty, and the 1997 system begins at or near the poverty line, with the whole of retirement spent in poverty. The proposed personal accounts will potentially lead to higher levels of sustained poverty clearance from a later age of retirement.

- The Lowes in 1979 had lifetime disposable incomes that were 53% of the Meades' despite their earnings being 50%. The gap grew hugely to 43% in 1997 and had returned to 1979 levels by 2008 (54%). Part of the 2008 difference is due to the national minimum wage.

Note

[1] For Mr and Ms Lowe, the age weighting calculation under the 2008 system cannot lead to an hourly wage that is less than the applicable national minimum wage, which is used as a wage floor.

FIFTEEN

Conclusion: a generation of change, a lifetime of difference?

The big picture

It is undeniable that there has been huge change in policy and underlying social and economic life since the 1970s and that our lives today are different in many ways. Clearly, 1979 stands out as a point when a momentous shift in British politics and in its social policy and welfare state occurred. Thirty years on and facing the fourth economic recession since the Second World War, we have tried in this book to look across the period, to put it in context and to measure some of the changes that have occurred in social policy. So much has been said about the 'isms' of Thatcher and Blair and so much emphasised about the differences between Old and New Labour that this focus on the rhetoric and ideology of change has resulted in little detailed analysis of what has actually changed and for whom. Of course, there have been historical descriptions of social policy change – the broad changes that we outlined in Chapter Two give but a whistle-stop tour of ground that has been covered in well-written accounts by Timmins (2001), Glennerster (2000) and others. We have aimed to bring history up to date – to the end of 2008 at the time of writing. However, our main aim has not been solely an historical one, but one that joins the historical overview of policy change with the detail of what has happened to the rules of social policy, and of taxes and benefits in particular – of what has been said *and* what has been done. This approach has meant turning to the rules of policy rather than just the aims. Rather unfashionably, we have focused on a reconstruction of the rules of welfare rather than a deconstruction of its discourse. More importantly, we have then used those rules to compare analytically the outcomes of policy at the turning points of 1979, 1997 and 2008. This approach has enabled us to get beneath the ideology and rhetoric and to document what has changed and with what effect. But a focus on rules potentially misses the bigger picture and much of the changes to this bigger picture have been dominated by changing economics.

The economic assumptions since the 1970s have most obviously changed and like most books on social policy this one has inevitably focused on the second-order responses to the impacts of such huge macroeconomic economic changes – with social policy continually having to readjust to respond to the changing risks to individual livelihoods that result from such macroeconomic changes. The most obvious economic story since the 1970s is of economic growth and a consequent growth in employment and living standards. Real earnings and incomes on average have grown very significantly for the majority of the population. The other obvious stories concern the pattern of such growth. There have been four major economic recessions since 1970 if we count the one that began in mid-2008 and the majority of the population have lived through at least two downturns. The recent period of sustained economic growth fooled many into thinking that such growth was inevitable, but bust we have, and in a spectacular downturn. But the conspicuous economic success of the majority in rising incomes, house prices and consumption has not been equally shared and income inequality has grown spectacularly. Those with marketable skills and qualifications have seen their incomes roar ahead of those of their unskilled and low-skilled counterparts and the economic divide discussed in Part One of the book has clearly grown beyond recognition since the 1970s. The Home Counties and the inner cities have never been further apart socially and economically.

One way to interpret social policy since the 1970s is to see it as a reflection of such division in economic fortunes. Indeed, one way to interpret many of the changes in fiscal and benefits policy that we document and model in this book since the 1970s is of microeconomic responses to macro changes. The labour market is the most central and obvious case in point, where huge structural shifts away from manufacturing to the service sector, from secure to flexible work, from full-time to part-time jobs, from the public to the private sector, from low-skilled to high-skilled jobs, from high-cost to low-cost employment and from men to women have ensured both adaptability to world and national markets and gains in efficiency. The gains to efficiency, however, have had some externalities in social costs. Those with high skills levels have gained and their earnings have grown hugely. But it is the most 'inefficient' workers who have benefited least and it must be acknowledged that the resulting fall in demand for low-skilled jobs has led to increased selectivity in employment. The privatisation of the low-skilled public sector workforce has led to gains in efficiency but at the expense of the least efficient workers, those with poor skills and poor health who used to empty your dustbins, or did other menial tasks in the official mediocracy. Benefits have replaced state employment as a last resort for many. Jobs have not disappeared in aggregate, but there are fewer opportunities for a significant group: those with low skills who are in poor health, are older, are living in the wrong location or have other constraints on being employed from family or caring responsibilities. They have been at the rear of a queue for work as the economy has expanded.

Faced with economic restructuring, the 1980s saw policy relatively happy to have the victims of the economic step-change raise the benefits bill. The low-skilled unemployed bore the brunt of the new economic reality of low and stagnating pay levels, worse terms of employment and the high probability of lay-off and repeated unemployment. The outcome, quite predictably, was a rise in economic inactivity caused by greater selection out of those with ill health or caring responsibilities as well as the differentials in benefit levels. The microeconomic policy changes described in Chapter Seven, aimed at increasing conditionality and financial incentives to work, were thus a necessary but not sufficient response to the problem; a response that additionally created externalities, including a rise in those who could not meet the new conditions of an efficient, more selective labour market and stricter regime. In the 1990s, policies slowly evolved to take on the problem of wider 'worklessness' so caused and the New Labour government in the 2000s has been even more determined to enforce labour market rationality on those who are not employed. This approach was boosted by the long economic boom from the mid-1990s that demonstrated how far growth could reach down and draw in those at the margins of employability. This remarkable return to 1975 levels of unemployment in the mid-2000s has since slowed down. The continued reliance on a technocratic ability to continually improve the labour supply side in order to reduce 'exclusion' has begun to suffer and New Labour is unlikely to achieve its idealistic vision of eradicating all the lumps from the lumpenproletariat.

The unnerving truth is that the market recruits labour but does so selectively according to its own determinants of 'efficiency'. At the same time, the rhetoric of fecklessness of the non-employed is now firmly established as the main causal factor in worklessness. 'Tebbit's bicycle' – the myth based on anecdotal precedent that anyone can find work if they look long and hard enough, irrespective of the number of other fitter people on better mountain bikes doing the same – has never really been put back in the shed since the 1980s. Enforcing labour market attachment to the ultimate point, even in times of economic growth, creates only partial employment gains at the bottom of the labour market, a fact we know from the experience of some states in the US where benefit safety nets were withdrawn to increase labour market participation, but where, even so, many were only ever partially employed in the short to medium term and substantial numbers never worked (Danziger and Kossoudji, 1995).

Perhaps it will only be in 2009 – now that it is clear that the causes of the recession are structural and worldwide – that such assumptions will begin to be questioned more fundamentally. Pension funds have crashed and annuity values have plummeted at a time when life expectancy is growing, thus stretching the funds built up over a working life that started out with different expectations. Imagine someone who opted out of SERPS in the 1980s, mis-sold or otherwise, who is now facing retirement on a personal pension whose value is far lower than they expected. The state stepped back and encouraged such people to be risky when they would actually have been better off in a national risk pool underpinned by today's taxpayers, who in any case will be picking up a larger bill from means-tested pensions to make up the shortfall. The state as the bank of last resort for capital may also have to become the employer of last resort – either directly or indirectly.

Trends in the lifetime design of policy

Our detailed history of provision from childhood to retirement, from the cradle to the grave, in Part Two clearly showed how much of policy had changed away from a comprehensive approach to risks over the lifetime for the whole population to one based on selective additional support for childhood and old age alongside a more market-based set of provisions for those of working age. But much of what was 'comprehensive' and 'universal' in 1979 was blatantly sexist and women's social rights to tax and benefit programmes have hugely improved over the so-called generation of change.

Maternity provision has similarly improved, both in generosity and in coverage, over the first year following birth. But this improvement has been for those who are in work and employment rights have improved alongside it. Tax credits now weight additional assistance towards babies aged under one year in a clear acceptance of the constraints on maternal employment in the earliest stages of childhood. Maternity benefits have also improved for those not in work, but to a lesser extent, and each step-change in improvement in maternity grants has been allowed to wither in real value over time as if no government is ever committed to meeting an absolute standard of needs for the arrival of children – a rather shocking indictment of all governments since the 1970s, given the consensus on the relative nature of child poverty.

The combination of Child Benefit, social assistance and in-work, means-tested supplements as the basis for income maintenance to families with children has been consistent since 1979 but the balance has changed. Child Benefit was allowed to wither and social assistance and in-work support were readjusted in the 1980s to promote work incentives. Child poverty grew hugely and since 1997 the introduction of higher benefits across all three areas has improved the gross incomes of families with children and targeted most help to the poorest children and families on low wages. But the new, more generous provision under New Labour has two inherent weaknesses: first, gross gains to income from transfers are taxed back at higher levels and second, such provision does not hold its value over time when compared to a relative poverty line. Both of these are severe impediments to ending relative child poverty.

The trends in taxation are perhaps the most radical of all changes in policy since 1979. A deliberate aim of policy has been to make taxation more regressive. Of course, it is not termed in this way. Lower taxes have been achieved by reducing rates of income tax and this has reduced progressivity, as those on the highest incomes have gained most. But this headline lowering of rates to benefit high incomes has been accompanied by a shift of the tax burden to more regressive forms: National Insurance contributions and local government tax have risen and consumption taxes have faced a revolution – in 1979, the bottom fifth of the income distribution paid 17% of their consumption in VAT and other forms of indirect tax, while in 1997 and 2006 this figure was in the region of 30%. This means that the trend to target transfers on the poorest has been accompanied by the ability to gain more back from them in indirect taxes. These changes in taxation have reduced the effect of the state on income inequality, which has been driven by the huge rise in earnings dispersion over the period.

The role of social insurance and the contributory principle in responding to the main risks to adult earnings has been reduced to a minor role (Williams, 2009). Means testing came to dominate provision for unemployment and incapacity. This trend began in the early 1980s with the ending of earnings-related benefits for sickness and unemployment. The rise of long-term mass unemployment meant that social insurance had a lesser role and this was reinforced by policy that cut back on coverage from 12 to six months. Means-tested and contributory unemployment benefits were then joined under a single Jobseeker's Allowance from 1996. Conditionality for the unemployed was continually ratcheted up over the 1980s and 1990s. Sickness benefit was privatised for all those in work from 1984. Benefits for incapacity grew in coverage as more non-employed people qualified under long-term, ill-health provisions rather than unemployment. From 2007, a new unified system for those with incapacity for work, Employment and Support Allowance, has been introduced for both means-tested and contributory support and is focused on employability and employment.

Across all benefits, both means-tested and contributory, there was the move to abandon earnings uprating for long-term needs. Short-term benefits, such as unemployment and sickness benefits, were not changed and have been continually uprated by prices. However, safety net social assistance was also reformed in the 1980s to make unemployed people relatively worse off and to cut back on expenditure. Benefits to help pay rent and rates/council tax were also made less generous despite underlying liabilities for these rising ahead of prices. Help with mortgage costs when out of work was slashed. All these changes reduced the value of benefits in relation to earnings and improved incentives to work.

Disability benefits are the one notable area where entitlement to, and generosity in, non-means-tested provision has improved over the 30 years. The expansion of schemes for extra needs for care and mobility under Heath and Callaghan in the 1970s was followed by real rises in benefit rates until the early 1980s, since when they have remained price uprated, despite higher rises in costs for care services and transport. In the mid-1990s, entitlement was extended to a wider spectrum of disability needs, with the creation of benefits for lower levels of needs. In-work benefits for disabled people were introduced to supplement low pay, along with new anti-discrimination laws.

The 30-year period covered by the book has also seen a rise in the number of lone parents, many of whom have relied on means-tested social assistance. Since the early 1990s, the number of lone-parent families has levelled off and the proportion working has increased dramatically as a result of improved incentives to work and better employment services.

Pension policy over the period began with the introduction of the State Earnings Related Pension Scheme (SERPS), which was cut back in the mid-1980s to both reduce future liabilities and to encourage the growth of private personal pensions. Occupational pension provision has fallen over the period and private personal pensions have risen to partly take their place, although they fell from grace in the mis-selling scandal of the late 1980s. There have since been repeated attempts to reform second- and third-tier pensions to encourage those on modest incomes to save for retirement. SERPS continued to be cut back and New Labour then introduced a revised second state pension (S2P) that is more generous to those on the lowest earnings. However, its original plan to expand third-tier 'stakeholder pensions' failed and in 2007 a broad consensus was achieved with new subsidised 'personal accounts' operating for those with no other private pension provision in the future, unless they actively opt out of such provision. Alongside these and other third-tier pensions will be a renewed commitment to uprate state pension by earnings in the near future.

We have shown how each set of policies for periods of the lifetime has interacted and how taxes and housing costs have affected outcomes for model families alongside changes to benefits. These profiles for 1979, 1997 and 2008 have clearly shown how inflation has reduced the impact of most state benefits over time, as in each comparison year intervening earnings growth has meant that their relative value has shrunk. For those who encounter lifetime risks of reduced or interrupted earnings, this means that the risk of relative deprivation has grown over time. This is most acute where the risk leads to an interruption of earnings, prolonged unemployment or inactivity where relative poverty risk and poverty gaps have grown. In order to understand the distributional effects it is crucial to recognise that those with low skills are disproportionately more likely to be unemployed or inactive and such structural differences in relative risk have at least remained constant over time if not worsened. During the 1980s and early 1990s, this was accompanied by stagnating levels of pay for low-skilled workers, although the introduction of the national minimum wage and the recent period of earnings growth have led to some improvement in the earnings progression of low-paid workers.

A lifetime of difference?

Part Two of this book has provided a comprehensive and updated overview of the whole tax and benefit position for individuals and families since the 1970s. The comparisons made between 1979, 1997 and 2008 of the various components of the system have then been cumulatively assessed using whole lifetime profiles in Part Three. This approach has allowed us to stand back and look at the whole remit of policy from the cradle to the grave and assess its impact on theoretical profiles of median, high and low earning families. It has also enabled us to join up the big pictures of policy change and to test what the outcomes would be for each political 'system' in place: the system that incorporated Old Labour's reforms in the mid- to late 1970s and was present in 1979, the system after 18 years of radical Conservative government in 1997 and the system in 2008 after 10 years of New Labour.

This represents a very large and ambitious canvas, despite being built on the 'small story' of the rules of policy rather than the words and actions of policy makers. But, given the huge investment in hyperbole and generalisation of politicians and a corresponding approach in some commentators on social policy and political change since the 1970s, it is useful to do so. But the heady rhetoric should not unduly sway readers to up the ante with the findings from our analysis. Given the predisposition to ideological investment and preconception about 'good' and 'bad' policies, it is essential that the limitations as well as the strengths of our approach and analysis be fully understood. Yes, we approach and answer big questions about policy change, but no, this is not a definitive study that provides *the* answer – far from it. We look forward to others replicating and amending our findings using alternative approaches to analysing policy change.

Our approach is based on hypothetical tax benefit models so that whole lifetimes are lived out under single sets of rules in 1979, 1997 and 2008. This means that we can test the design of programmes and how they interact, and chart their potential outcomes in illustrative comparisons. They are not empirical findings other than being based on 'actual rules'. The assumptions we use to simplify a set of consistent lifetime profiles drive results, but do so in a common way across 1979, 1997 and 2008 rules to allow direct comparison. In this way, the loss of empirical inputs is countervailed by the ability to compare the cumulative sets of rules of these three systems in a rigorous and consistent way. The lifetime 'stories' of our three comparative families are thus not intended to be real but to provide a consistent set of parameters for the calculation of tax and benefit outcomes over the lifetime to capture the greatest set of policy components for comparison.

One crucial factor for interpretation is that we place each hypothetical lifetime in a frozen contemporary setting – with house prices, income distribution and other crucial determinants static around them as the hypothetical people age and cumulatively receive their entitlements to benefits and liabilities for taxes based on profiles of contemporary earnings. This approach means that changes in underlying earnings and prices between the comparison years are important to the results – the fact that median earners who buy an average house pay a higher proportion of their earnings for the mortgage in 2008 than in 1997 because of escalating house prices being ahead of earnings, for example. It also means that the changing relationship between median earnings and median incomes over time – partly due to the changing behaviour of dual earnings in households – makes policy outcomes based on fractions of median income change over time when compared with earnings. For instance, relative poverty, based on 60% of median income, rises ahead of median earnings over time and becomes a more difficult target to hit.

The illustrative nature of our profiles has actually performed rather well in bringing out and illustrating the changes in policy and its outcomes. Our findings are neither surprising nor entirely original in their impact, but retelling the policy story of the past 30 years using a lifetime approach has brought home once again what has been lost and gained, and, more importantly, who the losers and gainers have been.

For our median earners, the Meade family, circumstances have remained remarkably consistent over the years, although they have gained greatly from underlying economic and earnings growth. There are small differences in terms of direct taxation, but, allowing for student loan repayments, the maximum difference is around 2% of total lifetime earnings between the systems, with 1979 the highest. We are unable to model indirect taxation but it is obvious that rises in VAT and other consumption taxes will make a 2% reduction from 1979 null and void. Basically, the median earners pay around 30% of lifetime earnings in direct tax under all three systems – it is just the composition that has changed. The headlines about reducing income tax rates are just that – headlines with no underlying story – and the overall tax burden will have risen with the move to higher levels of indirect tax. Once transfers are taken into account, there is even less difference in income for the Meades over the three comparison years – they experience a net effect of –14% of their lifetime earnings after taxes and transfers. In retirement, the Meades are best off in 1979, as their state pension is earnings linked and gives them by far the best outcome.

Overall, the median earner can be seen as having fairly constant outcomes overall throughout one of the periods of most radical change yet seen in British social policy. Much has been shuffled and rearranged, but the end results look very similar. All of the high-profile attacks by the Right on the issues of tax and spend that have been aimed at the median voter to suggest that they are better off in *any* subsequent system than the one in 1979 are mostly political conceit and fiscal deceit.

How do the higher-earning Moores, on twice median earnings, fare over the lifetime? Very nicely, thank you; they are big gainers. Their tax situation has improved hugely since 1979 due to the overall changes in moving to a less progressive system. The Evan-Moores, with twice the earnings again of the Moores but with identical lifetimes, show this change in even clearer terms: their lifetime direct tax bill fell from 49% in 1979 to 39%–40% in 1997 and 2008. The low tax regime of 1997 together with historical lower median income means that both these model lifetimes have their best outcomes in childhood and retirement in 1997, but interestingly, the latest part of their retirement would be better under 1979 rules, as underlying state pension would protect their incomes in the latter stages of their lives. However, when we measure the Moores and Evan-Moores against the Meades and look at the gaps between them, the narrowest gap was in 1979 and the highest in 1997, with some small reductions in 2008.

The low-paid Lowes compare quite differently and can be seen as clear losers, especially when comparing 1997 with 1979, but appear to have gained ground in 2008. We have shown them as continuously employed over their lifetimes in the main, a clear understatement of their risk of non-employment, but we have also shown how the risks of poverty from such interruptions to work make them clear losers whose losses get progressively worse over time.

In terms of direct taxation, 2008 stands out as worst for the Lowes, but, after transfers are taken into account, 2008 matches and just outstrips 1979's overall generosity, while 1997 is by far the worst. This matching of 1979 levels by the 2008 system, however, comes about by targeted transfers at childhood and retirement. However, if the Lowes face unemployment or incapacity during their working lives, 1979 offers them the best coverage against income loss, to the point where incentives to return to work following incapacity in 1979 are negative. The erosion of benefit values over time mean that 2008 is the worst year to be unemployed or incapacitated and it is worse the older the Lowes are. Child poverty risk for the Lowes differs between years due to a range of different assumptions about Ms Lowe working and the in-built erosion of the 1997 and 2008 systems against the poverty line during childhood. Maternity is clearly better in 2008, but the 1979 system supports the family on Mr Lowe's sole earnings best – thanks to low rents, earnings-uprated Child Benefit and lower income tax from marriage allowance. The 2008 system provides the best anti-poverty coverage when Ms Lowe returns to work but this does not keep up over time and erodes as the children age, leaving the 1979 system ahead in poverty protection against contemporary poverty lines for the majority of the childhood overall. Pensioner poverty was best avoided in 1979 and was most certain in 1997, with 2008 improving things and pointing the way forward to better-off retirements in the future with personal accounts.

However, any gains to the Lowes in incomes since 1979 will be very largely offset by increases in indirect consumption taxes that we do not capture in our lifetime models. These could be between 20% and 30% of lifetime disposable income and would completely wipe out any gains from the increased generosity of 2008 and further undermine the worst results for the Lowes in 1997.

Inequality between the Lowes and the Meades when considered by the disposable income gap between them is highest under the 1997 system and lowest under the 2008 and 1979 systems, with 2008 benefiting from higher house prices reducing comparative disposable incomes of the Meades and the national minimum wage underpinning the earnings of the Lowes in addition to the gains from the tax and benefit system.

Disincentives to work if based purely on marginal rates of tax are highest for the Evan-Moores and Moores in 1979. But for the Meades and the Lowes, other factors are brought into play alongside tax rate, means-tested benefits and student loan repayments. Tax credits in 2008 generally raise effective marginal deduction rates for long periods when children are present but the highest rates and worst incentives to work exist under the 1979 system when they are around 100% for a shorter period of childhood.

A strength of these results is that they clearly match the expected outcomes that would be predicted from the changing policy profile. Lower taxes for the better off make them even better off and increased taxation of the poor, despite higher transfers that are increasingly means-tested to target them, will undermine any gains they have in income terms from such transfers. It is clear that the change from 1979 to 1997 is best for the higher-income and worst for the lower-income lifetime profiles and that 2008 redresses some of the worst of these changes for the poor but leaves the better off largely untouched. But the lifetimes of difference are clear. The change in economic policy away from full employment and redistributive social policy since 1979 is lucidly played out and those with the highest risk of low income are now more firmly locked into low-income lifetimes than they were in 1979 due to a combination of risk and policy response. There is a clear bettering of position for poor families since 1997, but it is also clear that the increased generosity is not keeping up with the targets set for it. Relative poverty in times of economic growth means that more investment is needed to make and maintain an anti-poverty impact than is currently being made.

The next generation

We have shown some of the expected outcomes from mature policy assumptions that are currently in place and although there seems to be the potential for better pension outcomes for those on low and modest incomes, these will take a full lifetime to come into play. We have also shown that, in the short to medium term, there are real problems with meeting relative poverty targets such as the one of ending child poverty by 2020. Increasing employment rates of parents will help, of course, but the current system, just as much as the 1979 and 1997 systems, has real problems in helping with the dynamics of employment for low-paid people. Underlying rates of benefit when out of work are now very low and will continue to worsen, given that the risk of interruptions from low-paid employment, and subsequent reliance on such benefits, is high. In addition, there is no underlying system to lift lifetime trajectories, as too much is concentrated on the step-change from non-employment into low-paid work. Of course, underlying profiles of education and skills may change in the medium to long term, but current evidence suggests that progress is slow, given the number of poorly qualified young people who leave school with no vocational qualifications let alone academic ones. The workers of the future must have higher skills levels and the tax and benefit system must support the poorest more to improve skills and progress the labour market.

It is too early to say whether 2009 is a turning point – either electorally or in the wider sense of economic and social policy. There are signs that some elements of the macroeconomic rulebook of the past 30 years have been put to one side.

Higher income tax rates for the highest earners and a reduction in consumption taxes clearly indicate a small step towards greater progressivity, even if taxes will have to rise in the long term with rises in National Insurance contributions to accompany them, as outlined in the November 2008 pre-Budget report (HM Treasury, 2008a). What is clear is that the economic downturn is severe and will affect many.

One lesson from the history of British social policy is worth remembering here. When confronted by the reality of poorer people's lives, the middle classes have traditionally been supportive of progressive change rather than swayed by lazy rhetoric and biased reporting. Conscription for the Boer War caused people to realise that poor health was a real problem in finding fit soldiers and the condition of wartime evacuee children from the inner cities was a revelation. When Mr Meade is made redundant and turns up at the Jobcentre Plus, his shock at the assumptions of adequacy of benefits for his family's needs, the selective sample and short-termism of the job offers presented to him and the inflexibility of the system may just be enough to build more of a bridge with Mr Lowe sitting alongside him.

As the generation of change ends and the 30-year anniversary of Mrs Thatcher entering 10 Downing Street is upon us, it is an apt time to recognise how far people's lives and lifetimes have diverged. The unfettered, or lightly touched and regulated, free market is a risky thing to rely on to the extent that ideology and belief outplay common sense and sound empirical evidence. We have lost and gained in aggregate since then and we are mostly all hugely better off, but the losers and the gainers are further apart than ever. A new architecture for financial risk suggests new structures for sharing risk and social policy must respond accordingly.

References

Addison, P. (1975) *The road to 1945: British politics and the Second World War*, London: Jonathan Cape.

Agulnik, P. and Le Grand, J. (1998) *Tax relief and partnership pensions*, CASE Paper 5, London: Suntory and Toyota International Centres for Economics and Related Disciplines, London School of Economics.

Arulampalam, W., Gregg, P. and Gregory, M. (2001) 'Unemployment scarring', *The Economic Journal*, vol 111, no 475, pp 577-84.

Atkinson, A. and Micklewright, J. (1989) 'Turning the screw: benefits for the unemployed 1979-88', in A. Dimnot. and I. Walker (eds) *The economics of social security*, Oxford: Oxford University Press.

Atkinson, A., Cantillon, B., Marlier, E. and Nolan, B. (2002) *Social indicators, the EU and social inclusion*, Oxford: Oxford University Press.

Audit Commission (1986) *Making a reality of community care*, London: HMSO.

Barnes, C. (1992) *Disability and employment*, Leeds: Centre for Disability Studies, University of Leeds.

Barnett, C. (1995) *The lost victory: British dreams, British realities 1945-50*, London: Macmillan.

Bennett, F. (2006) *Child Benefit: Fit for the future*, CPAG Policy Briefing, London: CPAG.

Berthoud, R. (2007) *Work-rich and work-poor: Three decades of change*, Bristol: The Policy Press.

Blanden, J. and Gibbons, S. (2006) *The persistence of poverty across generations: A view from two British cohorts*, Bristol: The Policy Press.

Blanden, J., Gregg, P. and Machin, S. (2005) 'Educational inequality and intergenerational mobility', in Vignoles, A. and Machin, S. (eds) *What's the good of education? The economics of education in the UK*, Princeton, NJ: Princeton University Press.

Blundell, R. and Reed, H. (2000) *The employment effects of the Working Families Tax Credit*, London: Institute of Fiscal Studies.

Bradshaw, J., Middleton, S., Davis, A., Oldfield, N., Smith, N., Cusworth, L. and Williams, J. (2008) *A minimum income standard for Britain: What people think*, York: Joseph Rowntree Foundation.

Brewer, M., Goodman, A., Muriel, A. and Sibieta, L. (2007) *Poverty and inequality in the UK: 2007*, IFS Briefing Note 73, London: Institute of Fiscal Studies.

Brewer, M., Muriel, A., Phillips, D. and Sibieta, L. (2008) *Poverty and inequality in the UK: 2008*, IFS Commentary C105, London: Institute of Fiscal Studies.

Brewer, M., Goodman, A., Myck, M., Shaw, J. and Shephard, A. (2004) *Poverty and inequality in Britain 2004*, Commentary 96, London: Institute of Fiscal Studies.

Brown, J. (1983) *Family Income Supplement*, London: Policy Studies Institute.

Burgess, S., Gardiner, K. and Propper, C. (2001) *Why rising tides don't lift all boats: An explanation of the relationship between poverty and unemployment in Britain*, CASE Paper 46, London: Centre for Analysis of Social Exclusion, London School of Economics.

Campbell, N. (1996) *The decline of employment among older people in Britain*, CASE Paper 19, London: Suntory and Toyota International Centres for Economics and Related Disciplines, London School of Economics.

Chung, W., Disney, R., Emmerson, C. and Wakefield, M. (2005) *Public policy and saving for retirement: Evidence from the introduction of stakeholder pensions in the UK*, Centre for Policy Evaluation Working Paper 5/05, Nottingham: University of Nottingham.

CIPFA (Chartered Institute of Public Finance and Accountancy) (1977) *Return of rates 1976-77*, London: CIPFA.

CIPFA (1982) *Financial, general and rating statistics 1977/78-1981/82*, London: CIPFA.

CIPFA (1990) *Finance and general statistics 1982/83-1989/90*, London: CIPFA.

Clarke, T. and Leicester, A. (2004) 'Inequality and two decades of British tax and benefit reforms, *Fiscal Studies*, vol 25, no 2, pp 129-58.

Clasen, J. (2007) *Distribution of responsibility for social security and labour market policy – country report: United Kingdom*, AIAS Working Paper 2007-50, Amsterdam: University of Amsterdam.

CLG (Communities and Local Government) (2007) *Housing in England 2005/06: A report principally from the 2005/06 Survey of English Housing*, London: CLG.

CLG (2008a) *Live tables on rents, lettings and tenancies housing statistics*, London: CLG.

CLG (2008b) *Levels of council tax set by local authorities in England statistical release*, London: CLG.

Conservative Party (1970) *A better tomorrow*, Conservative manifesto 1970, London: Conservative Central Office.

Conservative Party (1974) *Putting Britain first*, Conservative manifesto October 1974, London: Conservative Central Office.

Conservative Party (1979) *The Conservative manifesto 1979*, London: Conservative Central Office.

CPAG (Child Poverty Action Group) (1978a) *Guide to contributory benefits and Child Benefit* (2nd edn), London: CPAG.

CPAG (1978b) *National welfare benefits handbook* (8th edn), London: CPAG.

CPAG (1980) *National welfare benefits handbook* (10th edn), London: CPAG.

CPAG (1997a) *Rights guide to non-means-tested benefits* (20th edn), London: CPAG.

CPAG (1997b) *National welfare benefits handbook* (27th edn), London: CPAG.

CPAG (2007) *Welfare benefits and tax credits handbook* (9th edn), London: CPAG.

CPAG (2008) *Welfare benefits and tax credits handbook* (10th edn), London: CPAG.

CSO (Central Statistical Office) (1990) *Family expenditure survey: 1988*, London: HMSO.

Curry, C. (1996) *PENSIM: A dynamic simulation model of pensioners' incomes*, Government Economic Service Working Paper, Newcastle: Department of Social Security, Analytical Services Division.

Danziger, S.K. and Kossoudji, S. (1995) *When welfare ends: Subsistence strategies of former GA recipients*, Ann Arbor, MI: University of Michigan.

Deacon, A. and Bradshaw, J. (1983) *Reserved for the poor: The means test in British social policy*, London: J. Basil Blackwell and Martin Robertson.

Department of Employment (1989) *Family expenditure survey 1987*, London: HMSO.

DoE (Department of the Environment) (1984) *Housing and construction statistics 1973-1983 Great Britain*, London: HMSO.

DoE (1989) *Local government financial statistics England No 1*, London: HMSO.

DEWO (Department of the Environment and the Welsh Office) (1976) *Rates and rateable values in England and Wales 1973/74-1975/76*, London: HMSO.

DfES (Department for Education and Skills) (2007) *Raising expectations: Staying in education and training post-16*, Cm 7065, London: The Stationery Office.

DH (Department of Health) (1992) *Health of the nation: A strategy for health in England*, Cm 198b, London: HMSO.

DH (2003) *Fairer charging policies for home care and other non-residential social services: Guidance for councils with social services responsibilities*, London: DH.

DH (2005) *Independence, well-being and choice: Our vision for the future of social care for adults in England*, Cm 6499, London: The Stationery Office.

DH (2008a) *Departmental report 2008*, Cm 7393, London: DH.

DH (2008b) Department of Health website (www.dh.gov.uk).

DHSS (Department of Health and Social Security) (1972) *Proposals for a tax-credit system*, Cmnd 5116, London: HMSO.

DHSS (1974) *Better pensions, fully protected against inflation, proposals for a new pensions scheme*, Cmnd 5713, London: HMSO.

DHSS (1978) *Social assistance: A review of the Supplementary benefits scheme in Great Britain*, London: DHSS.

DHSS (1980) *Social security statistics 1980 (incorporating 1979)*, London: HMSO.

DHSS (1985a) *Reform of social security*, Green Paper following Fowler review in three volumes, Cmnd 9517, 9518, 9519, London: HMSO.

DHSS (1985b) *Reform of social security, programme for action*, Cmnd 9691, London: HMSO.

DHSS (1987) *Social security statistics 1972-1987*, London: HMSO.

Dickens, R. and McKnight, A. (2008) *Changes in earnings inequality and mobility in Great Britain 1978/9-2005/6*, CASE Paper 132, London: Centre for Analysis of Social Exclusion, London School of Economics.

Disney, R., Emmerson, C. and Wakefield, M. (2007) *Pension provision and retirement saving: lessons from the United Kingdom*, SEDAP Research Paper 176, Ontario: McMaster University.

Donkin, A., Goldblatt, P. and Lynch, K. (2002) 'Inequalities in life expectancy by social class 1972–1999', *Health Statistics Quarterly*, vol 15, pp 5-15.

DSS (Department of Social Security) (1997) *Social security statistics 1997*, London: The Stationery Office.

DSS (2000) *Social security statistics 1988-2000*, London: The Stationery Office/ Corporate Document Services.

Dunnell, K. (2007) 'The changing demographic picture of the UK: National Statistician's annual article on the population', *Population Trends*, no 130, pp 9-21.

Dutton, D. (1997) *British politics since 1945* (2nd edn), Oxford: Blackwell.

DWP (Department for Work and Pensions) (2006a) *A new deal for welfare: Empowering people to work*, Cm 6730, London: DWP.

DWP (2006b) *A new system of child maintenance*, Cm 6979, London: DWP.

DWP (2006c) *Security in retirement: Towards a new pensions system*, Cm 6841, London: DWP.

DWP (2006d) *Income related benefits estimates of take-up in 2004/05*, London: DWP.

DWP (2007a) *Households below average income 1994/95-2006/07*, London: DWP.

DWP (2007b) *The abstract of statistics for benefits, National Insurance contributions, and indices of prices and earnings*, Newcastle: DWP.

DWP (2007c) *Disability equality impact assessment*, London: DWP.

DWP (2007d) *Report of the Statutory Sick Pay Review Working Group*, London: DWP.

DWP (2007e) *Pension Credit estimates of take-up in 2005/06*, London: DWP.

DWP (2008a) *No one written off: Reforming welfare to reward responsibility*, Cm 7363, London: The Stationery Office.

DWP (2008b) *Work and pension statistics 2001-2008*, London: DWP.

DWP (2008c) *Pensioners incomes series 2006/07*, London: DWP.

DWP (2008d) *Tax benefit model tables April 2008*, Newcastle: DWP Information Directorate.

Etzioni, A. (1993) *The spirit of community: The reinvention of American society*, New York, NY: Touchstone, Simon & Schuster.

Etzioni, A. (1996) *New communitarian thinking: Persons, virtues, institutions, and communities*, Charlottesville: University of Virginia Press.

Evandrou, M. and Falkingham, J. (1998) 'The personal social services', in Glennerster, H. and Hills, J. (eds) *The state of welfare* (2nd edn), Oxford: Oxford University Press.

Evandrou, M., Falkingham, J., Rake, K. and Scott, A. (2001) 'The dynamics of living arrangements in later life: evidence from the British Household Panel Survey', *Population Trends*, no 105, pp 37-44.

Evans, M. (1994) *Not granted? An assessment of the change from single payments to the Social Fund*, Welfare State Discussion Paper 101, London: Suntory and Toyota International Centres for Economics and Related Disciplines, London School of Economics.

Evans, M. (1996) 'Fairer or Fowler? The effects of the 1986 Social Security Act on family incomes', in Hills, J. (ed) (1996) *New inequalities: The changing distribution of income and wealth in the United Kingdom*, Cambridge: Cambridge University Press.

Evans, M. and Eyre, J. (2004) *The opportunities of a lifetime*, Bristol: The Policy Press.

Evans, M. and Falkingham, J. (1997) *Minimum pensions and safety nets in old age: A comparative analysis*, Welfare State Discussion Paper 133, London: Suntory and Toyota International Centres for Economics and Related Disciplines D, London School of Economics.

Evans, M. and Glennerster, H. (1994) 'Beveridge and his assumptive world: The incompatibilities of a flawed design', in Ditch, J., Glennerster, H. and Hills, J. (eds) *Beveridge and social security: An international retrospective*, Oxford: Clarendon Press.

Evans, M. and Harkness, S. (2009) 'Employment, worklessness and unemployment', in McLean, I., Halpern, D., Uberoi, V. and Coutts, A. (eds) *Options for a new Britain*, London: Palgrave Macmillan.

Evans, M. and Scarborough, J. (2006) *Can current policy end child poverty by 2020?*, York: Joseph Rowntree Foundation.

Evans, M., Falkingham, J. and Rake, K. (1999) *Tightropes and tripwires: New Labour's proposals and means-testing in old age*, CASE Paper 23, London: Centre for Analysis of Social Exclusion, London School of Economics.

Evans, M., Eyre, J., Millar, J. and Sarre, S. (2003) *New Deal for Lone Parents: Second synthesis report of the National Evaluation*, Sheffield: Department for Work and Pensions.

Falkingham, J. and Hills, J. (1995) *The dynamic of welfare: The welfare state and the life cycle*, Brighton: Harvester Press.

Field, F. and Piachaud, D. (1971) 'The poverty trap', *New Statesman*, 3 December, pp 772-3.

Fraser, D. (2000) 'The postwar consensus: A debate not long enough?', *Parliamentary Affairs*, 53, pp 347-62.

Fry, V., Hammond, E. and Kay, J. (1985) *The taxation of occupational pension schemes in the UK*, IFS Report Series 14, London: Institute for Fiscal Studies.

GAD (Government Actuary's Department) (1986) *Occupational pension schemes 1979: Seventh survey by the Government Actuary*, London: HMSO.

GAD (1999) *Occupational pension schemes 1995: Tenth survey by the Government Actuary*, London: The Stationery Office.

GAD (2008a) *Cohort expectation of life, 1981-2056*, London: GAD.

GAD (2008b) *Occupational pension schemes annual report 2007 edition*, London: Office for National Statistics.

Ginn, J. and Arber, S. (2000) 'Personal pension take-up in the 1990s in relation to position in the labour market', *Journal of Social Policy*, vol 29, no 2, pp 205-28.

Glennerster, H. (1998) 'Education: reaping the harvest', in Glennerster, H. and Hills, J. (eds) *The state of welfare* (2nd edn), Oxford: Oxford University Press.

Glennerster, H. (2000) *British social policy since 1945* (2nd edn), Oxford: Blackwell.

Glennerster, H. (2005) 'The health and welfare legacy', in Seldon, A. and Kavanagh, D. (eds) *The Blair effect 2001-5*, Cambridge: Cambridge University Press.

Glennerster, H. and Hills, J. (eds) (1998) *The state of welfare* (2nd edn), Oxford: Oxford University Press.

Goodman, A., Johnson, P. and Webb, S. (1997) *Inequality in the UK*, Oxford: Oxford University Press.

Gottschalk, P. and Smeeding, T. (2000) 'Empirical evidence on income inequality in industrial countries', in Atkinson, A. and Bourguignon, F. (eds) *Handbook on income distribution, volume 1*, Amsterdam: North Holland-Elsevier.

Griggs, J. and Walker, R. (2008) *Estimating the costs of child poverty for individuals and society: A literature review*, York: Joseph Rowntree Foundation.

Hannah, L. (1986) *Inventing retirement: The development of occupational pensions in Britain*, Cambridge: Cambridge University Press.

Harris, T. (1999) 'The effects of taxes and benefits on household income 1997/98', *Economic Trends*, no 545, pp 27-63.

Haskey, J. (2002) 'One-parent families and their dependent children in Great Britain', *Population Trends*, no 109, pp 46-57.

Hills, J. (ed) (1996) *New inequalities: The changing distribution of income and wealth in the United Kingdom*, Cambridge: Cambridge University Press.

Hills, J. (1998) 'Housing: a decent home within the reach of every family?', in Glennerster, H. and Hills, J. (eds) *The state of welfare* (2nd edn), Oxford: Oxford University Press.

Hills, J. (2004) *Inequality and the state*, Oxford: Oxford University Press.

Hirsch, D. (2006) *What will it take to end child poverty? Firing on all cylinders*, York: Joseph Rowntree Foundation.

HMRC (Her Majesty's Revenue and Customs) (2007) *Child and Working Tax Credits statistics December 2007*, London: HMRC.

HMSO (1942) *Social insurance and allied services: Report*, Cmd 6404, London: HMSO.

HMSO (1968) *Report of the Committee on Local Authority and Allied Personal Social Services*, Cmnd 3703, London: HMSO.

HM Treasury (1998) *Budget report 1998*, London: HM Treasury.

HM Treasury (2002) *The Child and Working Tax Credits: The modernisation of Britain's tax and benefit system*, London: HM Treasury.

HM Treasury (2008a) *Facing global challenges: Supporting people through difficult times, pre-Budget report November 2008*, Cm 7484, London: The Stationery Office.

HM Treasury (2008b) *Tax benefit reference manual 2008-09*, London: HM Treasury.

Holmes, M. (1997) *The failure of the Heath government* (2nd edn), London: Macmillan.

Holz, V. and Scholz, J.K. (2003) 'The earned income tax credit', in Moffitt, R. (ed) *Means-tested transfer programmes in the United States*, Chicago, IL: University of Chicago Press.

Hotopp, U. (2005) 'The employment rate of older workers', *Labour Market Trends*, vol 113, no 2, pp 73-88.

House of Commons (1974) *Report of the Committee on One Parent Families*, Cmnd 5369 (The Finer Report), London: HMSO.

House of Commons Library (1998) *Working Families Tax Credit and Family Credit*, Research Paper 98/46, London: House of Commons.

House of Commons Treasury Committee (2006) *The design of the National Pension Savings Scheme and the role of financial services regulation*, Fifth Report of the Session 2005-06, London: The Stationery Office.

IFS (Institute of Fiscal Studies) (2006) *A survey of the UK tax system*, London: IFS.

IFS (2007) *Winners and losers from personal and indirect tax changes*, London: IFS.

IFS (2008a) 'Fiscal facts: tax tables and benefit tables' (www.ifs.org.uk/fiscalfacts. php).

IFS (2008b) *Poverty and inequality in the UK*, London: IFS.

Johnson, P. (1999) 'The measurement of social policy convergence, the case of European public pension systems since 1950', *Journal of Social Policy*, vol 28, no 4.

Jones, F. (2008) 'The effects of taxes and benefits on household income, 2006/07', *Economic and Labour Market Review*, vol 2, no 7.

Jones, H. and Kandiah, M. (eds) (1996) *The myth of consensus: New views on British history 1945-64*, London: Macmillan.

Joshi, H., Davies, H. and Land, H. (1996) *The tale of Mrs Typical*, London: Family Policy Studies Centre.

Kavanagh, D. and Morris, P. (1989) *Consensus politics from Attlee to Thatcher*, Oxford: Blackwell.

Kay, J.A. and King, M.A. (1980) *The British tax system* (2nd edn), Oxford: Oxford University Press.

Labour Party (1974) *Britain will win with Labour*, Labour manifesto October 1974, London: Labour Party.

Labour Party (1976) *Labour Party annual conference report*, London: Labour Party.

Le Grand, J. and Vizard, P. (1998) 'The National Health Service: crisis, change or continuity?', in Glennerster, H. and Hills, J. (eds) *The state of welfare* (2nd edn), Oxford: Oxford University Press.

Le Grand, J., Mays, N. and Mulligan, J. (1998) *Learning from the NHS internal market: A review of the evidence*, London: King's Fund.

Le Grand, J., Winter, D. and Woolley, F. (1990) 'The National Health Service: safe in whose hands?', in Hills, J. (ed) *The state of welfare*, Oxford: Clarendon Press.

Lissenburgh, S. and Smeaton, D. (2003) *Employment transitions of older workers: The role of flexible employment in maintaining labour market participation and promoting job quality*, Bristol: The Policy Press.

Lonsdale, S. (1986) *Work and inequality*, London: Longman.

Lowe, R. (1996) 'The social policy of the Heath government', in Ball, S. and Seldon, A. (eds) *The Heath government 1970-1974: A reappraisal*, London: Longman.

Marsh, A. (2001) *Earnings top-up evaluation: The synthesis report*, Department of Social Security Research Report 135, Leeds: Corporate Document Services.

McConnell, H. and Wilson, B. (2007) 'Families', in Smallwood, S. and Wilson, B. (eds) *Focus on families 2007*, London: Office for National Statistics/Palgrave Macmillan.

Mead, L. (1993) *The new politics of poverty: The non-working poor in America*, New York, NY: Basic Books.

Mead, L. (1997) *The new paternalism: Supervisory approaches to poverty*, Washington, DC: Brookings Institute.

Mesher, J. (1981) 'The 1980 social security legislation: the great welfare state chainsaw massacre?', *British Journal of Law and Society*, vol 8, no 1, pp 119-27.

Nationwide (2008) 'UK housing prices since 1952' (www.nationwide.co.uk/hpi/historical.htm).

Nickell, S. (2001) 'Introduction', *Oxford Bulletin of Economics and Statistics* 63 (special issue), pp 617-27.

ODPM (Office of the Deputy Prime Minister) (2005) *Levels of council tax set by local authorities in England 2004-05 statistical release*, London: ODPM.

ONS (Office of National Statistics) (1981) 'The effects of taxes and benefits on household income, 1979', *Economic Trends*, January, pp 104-31.

ONS (2001) *Family expenditure survey 1971-2000*, London: ONS.

ONS (2003) *New earnings survey 1971-2003*, London: ONS.

ONS (2004) *Labour force survey 1979-2004*, London: ONS.

ONS (2005) *Births: 1970-2001, mean ages of women at live births within marriage (according to social class of husband) and birth order*, Series PBH114, London: ONS.

ONS (2006) *General Household Survey 2005*, London: ONS.

ONS (2007a) *Mid-2006 UK population estimates*, Titchfield: ONS.

ONS (2007b) *Birth statistics: Review of the Registrar General on births and patterns of family building in England and Wales*, Series FM1 35, Newport: ONS.

ONS (2007c) *Social trends 1970-2007*, London: ONS.

ONS (2007d) *Expenditure and food survey 2001-2007*, London: ONS.

ONS (2007e) *Annual survey of hours and earnings 2004-2007*, London: ONS.

ONS (2008a) *Marriage, divorce and adoption statistics FM2 (historical series)*, London: ONS.

ONS (2008b) *Labour market statistics 1971-2008*, London: ONS.

ONS (2008c) *Population trends 1975-2008*, London: ONS.

ONS (2008d) *Economic & Labour Market Review*, November, London: ONS.

OPSI (Office of Public Sector Information) (2007a) *Welfare Reform Act 2007*, London: OPSI.

OPSI (2007b) *Welfare Reform Act 2007 explanatory notes*, London: OPSI.

Parckar, G. (2008) *Disability poverty in the UK*, London: Leonard Cheshire Disability.

Pensions Commission (2004) *Pensions: Challenges and choices, the first report of the Pensions Commission*, London: The Stationery Office.

Pensions Commission (2005) *A new pension settlement for the twenty-first century, the second report of the Pensions Commission*, London: The Stationery Office.

Phillips, D. (2008) 'The impact of tax and benefit reforms to be implemented in April 2008', in Chote, R., Emmerson, C., Miles, D. and Shaw, J. (eds) *The IFS green budget: January 2008*, Commentary 104, London: Institute for Fiscal Studies.

Piachaud, D., Sutherland, H. and Sefton, T. (2003) *Poverty in Britain: The impact of government policy since 1997*, York: Joseph Rowntree Foundation.

Pimlot, B. (1988) 'The myth of consensus', in Smith, L. (ed) *The making of Britain: Echoes of greatness*, London: Macmillan.

Powell, M. (ed) (2008) *Modernising the welfare state: The Blair legacy*, Bristol: The Policy Press.

PPI (Pensions Policy Institute) (2004) *Tax reliefs and incentives for pension saving*, London: Pensions Policy Institute.

Rake, K. (ed) (2000) *Women's income over the lifetime*, London: The Stationery Office.

Rake, K., Falkingham, J. and Evans, M. (2000) '21st century pensions – a partnership or a marriage to the means-test?', *Social Policy and Administration*, vol 34, no 3, pp 296-317.

Redmond, G., Sutherland, H. and Wilson, M. (1998) *The arithmetic of tax and social security reform: A user's guide to microsimulation methods and analysis*, Cambridge: Cambridge University Press.

Rendall, M. and Smallwood, S. (2003) 'Higher qualifications, first-birth timing and further childbearing in England and Wales', *Population Trends*, no 111, pp 18-26.

Ritchie, J. and Snape, D. (1993) *Invalidity Benefit: A preliminary qualitative study of the factors affecting its growth*, National Centre for Social Research Paper P5200, London: National Centre for Social Research.

SBC (Supplementary Benefits Commission) (1976) *Supplementary Benefits Commission annual report 1975*, Cmnd 6615, London: HMSO.

Sefton, T. (1997) *The changing distribution of the social wage*, STICERD Occasional Paper 21, London: Suntory and Toyota International Centres for Economics and Related Disciplines, London School of Economics.

Sefton, T. (2002) *Recent changes in the distribution of the social wage*, CASE Paper 62, London: Centre for Analysis of Social Exclusion, London School of Economics.

Sinfield, A. (2007) 'Tax welfare', in Powell, M. (ed) *Understanding the mixed economy of welfare*, Bristol: The Policy Press.

Smithers, A. (2005) 'Education', in Seldon, A. and Kavanagh, D. (eds) *The Blair effect 2001-5*, Cambridge: Cambridge University Press.

Stuttard, N. (1998) 'The effects of taxes and benefits on household income, 1996-97', *Economic Trends*, no 533, pp 33-67.

Sutherland, H., Evans, M., Hancock, R., Hills, J. and Zantomio, F. (2008) *The impact of benefit and tax up-rating on incomes and poverty: Keeping up or falling behind?*, York: Joseph Rowntree Foundation.

Timmins, N. (2001) *The five giants: A biography of the welfare state* (2nd edn), London: Harper Collins.

Titmuss, R. (1958) *Essays on the welfare state*, London: George Allen & Unwin.

Vaux, G. (2001) *Community Care*, 16 May, p 3.

Walker, R. and Howard, M. (2000) *The making of a welfare class? Benefit receipt in Britain*, Bristol: The Policy Press.

Williams, L. (2009) 'Fair rewards or just deserts? The present and future of the contributory principle in the UK', *Benefits: The Journal of Poverty and Social Justice*.

Wittenberg, R., Pickard, L., Comas-Herrera, A., Davies, B. and Darton, R. (1998) *Demand for long-term care: Projections of long-term care finance for elderly people*, Canterbury: Personal Social Services Research Unit, University of Kent.

Young, K. and Rao, N. (1997) *Local government since 1945*, Oxford: Blackwell.

Index

Page references for figures and tables are in *italics*; those for notes are followed by n

A

adulthood 99
after housing costs (AHC) poverty 207, 212, *213*, 214, 238-9
  children 215-17, *216*, *217*
  pensioners *213*, 215
ageing *see* older people
alcohol excise duty 96, *96*
Arulampalam, W. 10
Attendance Allowance 15, 145, 146, *147*, 148, 152, *152*
Audit Commission 22

B

basic state pension 23, 167-8, 169, *169*, 171, 191
before housing costs (BHC) poverty 207, 212, *213*, 214, 239
  children 216-17, *217*
  pensioners *213*, 215
behavioural difference 229-30
  Lowes 289-90, *291*, 292
  Meades 246-9, *250*, 251
benefits
  carers 151-3, *152*, 165
  caring
  children 58-62, 64-7, *64*, *65*, *66*, *67*
  death and funeral expenses 176
  disability 143-6, *147*, 148-51, 164-5
  lone parents 153-7, *155*, *157*, 165
  maternity 55-8, 62, *63*, 64
  owner-occupation 111, 112-13
  pensioners 172-5, *174*, *175*
  renting 107-11, *111*
  safety net 99-105, *104*, *105*, 119
  sickness and long-term incapacity 128-32, *133*
  unemployment 123-8, *125*, *126*, *127*
  see also tax and benefit system; uprating
Bereavement Allowance 176
Bereavement Payment 176
Bevan, Nye 1, 13
Beveridge, William 2, 14
  death and funeral expenses 176
  family allowance 58
  lone parents 143, 153
  maternity provision 77n

  pensions 167, 171
  rent 107-8
  social assistance 99, 144
  unemployment 123
births 37-9, *38*, 51-2
Black papers 19, 33n
Blair, Tony 4, 26-32, 62, 64, 305
Brewer, M. 207
Brown, Gordon 4, 5, 26-32, 64, 83

C

Callaghan, James 4, 17
care in the community 22, 25, 144
Carer's Allowance 151, *152*
  relative value 127-8, *127*
caring 18, 143, 151-2, 165
  coverage of benefits 151-3, *152*
  Meades and Lowes 163-4, *164*
Child Benefit 18, 26, 59, 76, 308
  lone parents 154, 156
  Lowes 72
  Moores 71
  New Labour 31, 60
  value 64-5, *66*, 77n
child poverty 2, 10, 58, 308, 314
  Lowes 299-300, *300*, 304
  Meades 258-60, *259*
  Moores 278-9, *278*
  New Labour 27, 31
  outcomes *213*, 215-17, *216*, *217*, 218
  and parental employment 60
  tax credits 61
Child Poverty Action Group 108, 226
Child Support Act 1991 155
Child Support Agency 155-6
Child Tax Credit 31, 60-1, 76, 102, 107
  disability 150, 151
  effective marginal deduction rates 238
  generosity and coverage 65-6, *67*, 77n
  Lowes 72
  Meades 69
  Moores 71
  Nunns 74
Child Trust Fund 61
childcare 31, 61, 77n
children 2, 55, 76-7, 308
  dependency ratio 35, 37, *37*
  disability 149-50

family types 40, *41*, 52
generosity and coverage of benefits 64-6,
    64, 65, 66, 67, 77n
Lowes 72, *72, 73*, 74
maternity provision 55-8, 62, *63*, 64
Meades 68-9, *69, 70*, 71
model families 67-8
Moores 71-2, *71*
Nunns 74, *75*
policy 58-62
in population 35, *36*
Children Act 1989 55
Chung, W. 182
Citizen's Charter 24, 25
claimant count 125, *125*, 126, *126*
Clark, Kenneth 82
cohabitation 40-2, *41*, 52
  and social assistance 102-3
  see also partnership
Colwell, Maria 19-20, 33n
Commission for Health Improvement 30
community care 22, 25, 144
community charge 24, 26
comprehensive schools 15, 17
Conservative Party 4-5, 227, 311
  children 58-60, 64, *65, 66*, 77n
  disability 148
  Evan-Moores 270-2, *271, 272*
  Heath 14-16, 32
  housing 13, 108-10, *110*, 203
  income growth 208, 210, *210*
  income tax 81-3, 84, 97
  local government taxation 90, 92
  lone parents 154-6, *157*
  Lowes 285-7, *286, 288*
  Major 24-6, 33
  maternity provision 56-7, *63*
  Meades 244-6, *244*
  minimum earned income guarantees 106
  Moores 269-70, *269*
  mortgage interest tax relief 113-14
  National Insurance contributions 86, 87,
    88, 89
  pensioner benefits 174, *174*
  pensions 168, *169*, 170, 181-2, 192, 229
  post-war welfare state 14
  savings 178
  sickness and long-term incapacity 128,
    129-30
  social assistance 100-2
  Thatcher 19-24, 33
  unemployment 124
  VAT 95
consumption 50-1, *50*, 52

indirect taxation 79, 95-7, *96*, 206, 315
council housing 42, *43*, 203
  Major 25
  New Labour 34n
  Old Labour 18
  post-war welfare state 13
  rent 108
  rents and affordability 109-11, *110, 111*
  Thatcher 19, 20-1
council tax 79, 90-1, 94
Council Tax Benefit 77n, 150, 156, 175, 237
Crossman, Richard 15
CTC *see* Child Tax Credit

D

death 176
Death Grant 176
defined benefit pension schemes 172, 179-
    80, 181, 192
defined contribution pension schemes 172,
    181, 182, 192
Department for Education and
    Employment 60, 102
Department for Work and Pensions (DWP)
    31, 60, 102
  state pensions 167
  Tax benefit model tables 222, 237
Department of Health and Social Security
    (DHSS) 100
Department of Social Security (DSS) 30,
    31, 60, 102
dependency ratio 35, 37, *37*
devolution 28
Dickens, R. 48
direct taxation
  Evan-Moores 271, 282
  incidence 200, *201*
  Lowes 285-6, *286*, 303
  and marriage 92-4, *93*
  Meades 94-5, *94*, 244-5, *244*, 264
  Moores 270, 282
  see also income tax; local government
    taxation; National Insurance
    contributions
disability 26, 143-4, 164-5, 309
  changing value of extra-cost benefits 146,
    147, 148
  coverage of benefits 152-3, *152*
  extra-cost benefits 15, 144-6
  in-work benefits 150-1
  Meades and Lowes 162-3, *162, 163*
  out-of-work benefits 18, 148-50
  Severe Disablement Allowance 129-30
Disability Discrimination Act 1995 150

Disability Living Allowance (DLA) 26, 77n, 145-6, *147*, 148, 152-3, *152*
Disability Working Allowance (DWA) 150
Disabled Persons (Employment) Act 1944 150
Disabled Person's Tax Credit 150
Disney, R. 182
disposable income 199
  Lowes 288-9
divorce 40-2, *41*, 52, 153
  see also lone parents

E

early retirement 10, 184
Earned Income Tax Credit (EITC) 27, 77n
earnings
  age weighting 225, *226*
  growth and dispersion 48-9, *49*, 52
  inflation 49, *49*, 52, 78n
economic inactivity 46-8, *46*, *47*, 52
economy 43-4, *44*, *45*, 46-8, *46*, *47*, 51, 52
  earnings growth and dispersion 48-9, *49*
  Heath 16
  New Labour 27
  Old Labour 16-17
  prices and consumption 49-51, *50*
  recession 1-2
  and social policy 305-7
  Thatcher 19
education 5-6, 314
  Major 24
  New Labour 26, 28-9
  Old Labour 17
  post-war welfare state 13
  subsidies 62
  Thatcher 19, 21, 33n
  see also higher education
Education Act 1944 13
Education Act 1976 21
Education Act 1988 24
Education Maintenance Allowance (EMA) 28-9, 62, 66, 77n
  Lowes 72
  Nunns 74
Education Reform Act 1988 21
effective marginal deduction rates 81, 237-8, 313-14
  Lowes 293-4, *294*, 303-4
  Meades 254-5, *255*, 265
  Moores and Evan-Moores 275, *276*, 277, 282
effective tax rates 81
elderly people *see* older people
employer-sponsored pensions 181

employment 43-4, *45*, 52, 306-7, 314
  disabled people 143-4, 150
  lone parents 156-7
  Major 26
  New Labour 26, 31-2
  older people 184
  see also unemployment
Employment and Support Allowance (ESA) 32, 102, 131, 140
  disability 148, 165n
  lone parents 157
Etzioni, A. 26
European Union
  equal treatment 103
  VAT 95
Evan-Moores 6, 312
  1979, 1997 and 2008 systems 270-2, *271*, *272*
  inequality 281, *282*
  work incentives 275, *276*, 277, 313
Evans, M. 3
excise duties 95-6, *96*
Expenditure and Food Survey 198
Eyre, J. 3

F

Family Allowance 14, 58
Family Allowance Act 1945 14, 58
Family Credit 23, 26, 59-60, *67*, 77n, 170
value 65, *65*
Family Expenditure Survey 198
family formation 40-2, *41*
Family Income Supplement (FIS) 15, 18, 23, 58-9, 106, 237
  lone parents 154
  Lowes 72
  value 65, *65*
Family Resources Survey (FRS) 198
family wage 58
fertility 37-9, *38*, 51-2
final income 199
Finance Act 1921 178
Finer Report 153-4
fiscal drag 84, 98n, 232
Fowler reforms
  death and funeral expenses 176
  effective marginal deduction rates 237-8
  housing 92, 108-9, 111, 112
  lone parents 155
  maternity provision 56
  means-tested benefits 23, 59, 100, 106
  pensions 23, 170, 181, 192n
Fraser, D. 14
fuel excise duty 96, *96*

funeral expenses 176

G

Glennerster, H. 14, 305
Goodman, A. 206
Griggs, J. 10
gross domestic product (GDP) 43, *44*
gross income 199

H

Harman, Harriet 156
health *see* National Health Service
Health and Social Care Act 2008 57
Health Commission 30
Health in Pregnancy Grant 57
health of the nation, The (DH) 25
Healthy Start 57
Heath, Edward 14–16, 32, 60
  children 58-9
  housing 108, 109, *110*
  income growth 208, *210*
  sickness and long-term incapacity 128
Her Majesty's Revenue and Customs 34n,
  87
higher education 6, 21, 24, 29, 37
Hirsch, D. 216
HM Treasury 30-1, 60, 167, 226
homelessness 18, 25-6
Hospital Foundation Trusts 29
House of Commons Treasury Committee
  183
household composition 40-2, *41, 42, 43,* 52
  by income quintile 202, *203*
household expenditure 50-1, *50,* 52
Households Below Average Income (HBAI)
  198, 207, 238, 239
Housewives' Non-Contributory Invalidity
  Pension 129
housing
  Heath 16
  Major 25-6
  New Labour 30
  Old Labour 18
  post-war welfare state 13
Housing Act 1980 20
Housing Act 1996 25-6
housing associations 21, 25, 30, 42, *43*
Housing Benefit 59-60, 91, 108-9, 119, 203,
  204, 207
  childcare costs 77n
  disability 150
  lone parents 156
  lower capital limit 178
  pensioners 175

tapers 237
housing costs 5, 26, *50,* 51, 107, 119-20,
  203-4, 207
  model families 115
  owner-occupation 111-14
  pensioners 192n
  renting 107-9
  rents and affordability 109-11, *110, 111*
Housing Finance Act 1972 16, 108
Housing (Homeless Persons) Act 1977 18
Howe, Geoffrey 20, 82, 83, 95
hypothetical model lifetimes *see* model
  lifetimes

I

ill health 47, *47,* 48
in-work benefits 23, 26-7, 31, 32, 105-6,
  107
  children 59, 60-1, 65-6, *65,* 76
  disability 144, 150-1, 165
  lone parents 156, 165
In-Work Credit 156
incapacity 128-31, 140, 141, 143, 309
  coverage and generosity of benefits 127,
  127, 131-2, *133*
  Lowes 299, *299*
  Meades and Lowes 137-9, *138, 140*
Incapacity Benefit 32, 130-1
  coverage 132, *133*
  disability 148, 149
  pensioners 184
  relative value *127,* 132
income
  incidence of taxes and benefits 198-200,
  199, 201, 202-4, *203,* 218
  outcomes 207-8, *209,* 210-12, *210, 211,*
  213, 214-17, *216, 217*
income distribution
  Lowes 297-9, *297, 299*
  Meades 256-8, *257*
  Moores 277-8, *277,* 282
Income Support 1, 23, 32, 59-60, 100-2,
  120n
  caring 151
  children 60, 61, *67*
  disability 149-50, 165n
  lone parents *155,* 156, 157
  Nunns 74
  and owner-occupation 112
  pensioners 173, 174
  rates 104, *104*
  rent 109
  unemployment 124
income tax 79, 80-5, *84,* 97, 308

child allowances 58-9
and marriage 92-4
and National Insurance contributions 86-7
New Labour 27-8
and owner-occupation 111, 113-14, 120
pensioners 176-7, *177*
progressivity 315
Thatcher 20
Independent Living Funds 146
indirect taxation 79, 95-7, *96*, 97, 308-9
Lowes 303
Meades 245-6, 264
regressivity 206, 218
inequality 27, 51, 218
earnings 48-9, *49*, 52
and incidence of taxes and benefits 204, *205*, 206-7
life expectancy 39, 42
lifetime models 239
Lowes and Meades 302-3, *303*, 304
Lowes and Moores 313
Moores, Evan-Moores and Meades 281, 282, *282*
inflation 16-17, 49, *49*, 52, 78n, 310
Lowes 292-3, *293*
Meades 251-4, *252*, *253*, 264-5
modelling 230-2
Moores 272-5, *273*, *274*
Inland Revenue 31, 34n, 60
Institute of Economic Affairs 15
Institute of Fiscal Studies (IFS) 27, 77n, 208, 239
International Labour Organisation (ILO) unemployment 46, 125, *125*
International Monetary Fund (IMF) 17
Invalid Care Allowance (ICA) 18, 151, *152*
Invalidity Benefit 15-16, 26, 128-9, 130, 140, 141n
coverage 132, *133*
disability 148
relative value *127*, 132
and SERPS 192n
ISAs (Individual Savings Accounts) 178

J

Jobcentre Plus 2, 102, 124
Jobseeker's Allowance (JSA) 26, 32, 101, 102, 124
children *67*
lone parents 157
Nunns 74
relative value *127*, *127*
Jones, H. 14

Joseph, Keith 15

K

Kandiah, M. 14
Keynesianism 1, 14, 16, 17

L

Labour Party *see* New Labour; Old Labour
Lawson, Nigel 82
Learning Skills Council 29
Liberal Party 16
life expectancy 39, *40*, 51, 229-30
lifetime 2-3
and policy change 3-4
see also model lifetimes
Lilley, Peter 155
Lissenburgh, S. 10
local authorities
housing 18, 25-6, 30
personal social services 22, 30
post-war welfare state 13
privatisation 20
rent revenue 108
reorganisation 15
local government taxation 79, 89-91, *90*, 97, 308
disability 146
and marriage 94
rate rebates 91-2
and social assistance 101
LOIS (Lifetime Opportunities and Incentives Simulation) 7, 223-6, *226*
lone parents 26, 40, *41*, 52, 143, 153-7, *155*, *157*, 165, 309
Meades and Lowes 158-62, *159*, *161*
New Labour 30, 31-2, 60
social assistance 102, 103
tax allowances 82-3
long-term incapacity *see* incapacity
longevity 39, *40*, 51
Lowes 6, 283, 313
1979, 1997 and 2008 systems 285-7, *286*, *288*
behavioural difference and policy maturation 289-90, *291*, 292
caring 163-4, *164*
and childhood 67, 72, *72*, *73*, 74, 76
childhood and risk of poverty 299-300, *300*
disability 162-3, *162*
disposable incomes 288-9
inequality 302-3, *303*, 313
inflation and uprating 292-3, *293*
lifetime in 2008 284, *285*

lone parenthood 160-2, *161*
model lifetime 283-4
in overall income distribution 297-9, *297, 299*
pensions 185-8, *186, 187*
replacement rates 238
retirement and pensioner poverty 301-2, *301*
sickness and incapacity 133, 137, 139, *140*
taxes, benefits and housing costs 118-19, *118*
unemployment 133, 134-5, 136-7, *137*
work incentives 293-5, *294, 296*, 297, 313

M

McKnight, A. 48
Macmillan, Harold 51
Major, John 4, 5, 24-6, 33
  children 59, 64, 65
  disability 148
  income tax 82-3
  lone parents 156
  mortgage interest tax relief 114
  unemployment 124
  wage supplements 106
Making a reality of community care (Audit Commission) 22
marginal deduction rates 81
  see also effective marginal deduction rates
marginal tax rates 81
marriage 40-2, *41*, 52
  and income tax 82-3, 92-4, *93*, 97, 98n
  social assistance 102-3
Maternity Allowance 55-6, 57-8, 69
  Moores 71
  value 62, *63*
Maternity Expenses Payment 56, 57
  value 62, *63*
Maternity Grant 55, 56
  value 62, *63*
maternity provision 55-8, 76, 308
  generosity and coverage 62, *63*, 64
  Lowes 72, *72*
  Meades 68-9, *69*
  Moores 71
  policy maturity 228, *229*
Mead, L. 26
Meades 6, 241, 264-5, 312
  1979, 1997 and 2008 systems 244-6, *244*
  behavioural difference and policy maturation 246-9, *250*, 251
  caring 163-4, *164*
  and childhood 67, 68-9, *69*, 70, 71
  childhood and risk of poverty 258-60, *259*
  cumulative direct taxation 94-5, *94*
  disability 162, 163, *163*
  inequality 281, 282, *282*, 302-3, *303*, 313
  inflation and upgrading 251-4, *252, 253*
  lifetime in 2008 242-3, *243*
  lone parenthood 158-60, *159*
  marriage and income tax 93-4, *93*
  model lifetime 241-2
  modelling occupational and personal pensions 234, 235
  in overall income distribution 256-8, *257*
  pensions 188-91, *189, 191*
  retirement and pensioner poverty 260-4, *263*
  sickness and incapacity 133, 137-9, *138*
  social assistance 105
  taxes, benefits and housing costs 114-16, *116*
  unemployment 133, 134-6, *135*
  work incentives 254-6, *255*, 313
means testing 14, 18, 23-4, 59, 309
  families with children 66, *67*
  maternity provision 76
median earnings and median income 207, 211-12, *211*, 218
  see also Meades
men
  economic inactivity *47*, 52
  employment 44, *45*, 184
  life expectancy 39, *40*, 51
  pension age 167, 184
  pensions 185-6, *186*, 188-90, *189*
  in population *36*
  social security 103
  widowers 176
Mesher, J. 124
micro-simulation 222-3
minimum earned income guarantees 105-6
Minimum Income Guarantee (MIG) 32, 173
minimum wage 106-7, 119
MIRAS (Mortgage Interest Relief at Source) 21, 25, 30, 82, 83, 113-14
Mobility Allowance 18, 145, 146, *147*, 148, 152, *152*
model lifetimes 4, 6-7, 221-3, 310-14
  caring 163-4, *164*
  changing lifetime behaviour 229-30
  and childhoods 67-9, *69, 70*, 71-2, *71, 72, 73, 74, 75*, 76
  disability 162-3, *162, 163*
  a lifetime under the same policy system 227
  lifetimes in a single year 226-7

LOIS 223-6, *226*
lone parenthood 158-62, *159*, *161*
mature policy 228-9
modelling inflation 230-2
modelling occupational and personal
  pensions 234, 235
modelling uprating 232-3
policy outcomes 235-9
and retirement 185-91, *186*, *187*, *189*, *191*
taxes, benefits and housing costs 114-19,
  116, *117*, *118*, 120
unemployment, sickness and incapacity
  133-9, *135*, *137*, *138*, *140*
see also Lowes; Meades; Moores; Nunns
Moores 6, 267, 312
  1979, 1997 and 2008 systems 269-70, *269*
  changing behaviour 230
  and childhood 67, 71-2, *71*
  childhood income profile 278-9, *278*
  inequality 281, *282*
  inflation and uprating 272-5, *273*, *274*
  lifetime in 2008 268-9, *268*
  model lifetime 267
  modelling occupational and personal
    pensions 234, 235
  in overall income distribution 277-8, *277*
  retirement and pensioner poverty 279-81,
    280
  taxes, benefits and housing costs 117-18,
    117
  work incentives 275, *276*, 277, 313
  see also Evan-Moores
mortgage interest tax relief 21, 25, 30, 82,
  83, 113-14
Motability 146

N

National Assistance Act 1948 1, 14, 99-100
National Health Service 1, 13
  Heath 15
  Major 24-5
  New Labour 26, 29-30
  Old Labour 17-18
  Thatcher 19, 20, 21-2
National Health Service Act 1946 13
National Health Service and Community
  Care Act 1990 22, 25
National Institute for Clinical Excellence
  (NICE) 29-30
National Insurance Act 1911 55
National Insurance Act 1946 14, 85
National Insurance Act 1948 123
National Insurance contributions (NICs)
  79, 85-7, *88*, 89, *89*, 97, 308, 315

and marriage 94
New Labour 27, 28
Old Labour 18-19
pensioners 176
and SERPS 228-9
Thatcher 20
national minimum wage 106-7, 119
National Minimum Wage Act 1998 107
National Service Frameworks 30
National Union of Mineworkers 16
NEETs (not in education, employment or
  training) 29, 62
neighbourhood renewal 30
New Deal 124
New Deal 50 Plus 184
New Deal for Disabled People (NDDP)
  131, 165n
New Deal for Lone Parents 157
New Deal for Young People (NDYP) 31
New Labour 26-32, 33, 227, 305, 311
  children 60, 64, *65*, *66*, 216, 308
  disability 148, 150-1
  education 62
  employment 307
  Evan-Moores 270-2, *271*, *272*
  housing 109, 110, *110*, 114
  in-work benefits 107, 119
  income growth 208, 210, *210*
  income tax 82, 83, 84, 93, 97
  and inequality 206-7
  local government taxation 92
  lone parents 156-7, *157*
  Lowes 284, 285-7, *285*, *286*, *288*
  maternity provision 57-8, 62, *63*
  Meades 242-3, *243*, 244-6, *244*
  minimum wage 106-7, 119
  Moores 268-9, *268*, 269-70, *269*
  National Insurance contributions 86, 87,
    88, 89, *89*
  pensioner benefits 174, *174*, 175
  pensions *169*, 170-1, 179, 182-3, 192, 310
  savings 178
  sickness and incapacity 130-1, 141n
  social assistance 102
  unemployment 124
  VAT 95
New Zealand 206
NHS *see* National Health Service
Nickell, S. 33n
Non-Contributory Invalidity Pension
  (NCIP) 18, 127, *127*, 129
  disability 149, *152*
Nunns 6
  and childhood 67, 74, *75*, 76

social assistance 105, *105*

O

occupational pensions 168, 172, 179-81, *180*, 310
  modelling 234, 235
Office for National Statistics (ONS) 198-9
Ofsted (Office for Standards in Education) 24
old age *see* older people
Old Labour 5, 227, 305, 311
  1974-79 16-19, 32-3
  children 58, 59, *65*, *66*, 77n
  death and funeral expenses 176
  disability 145, 309
  education 15
  Evan-Moores 270-2, *271*, *272*
  housing 109, *110*, 113
  income growth 208, *210*
  lone parents 153-4, *157*
  Lowes 285-7, *286*, *288*
  maternity provision *63*
  Meades 244-6, *244*
  minimum earned income guarantees 106
  Moores 269-70, *269*
  National Insurance contributions 85, 87, *88*, *89*
  pensioner social benefits *174*
  pensions 167-9, *169*, 228-9
  post-war welfare state 13-14
  sickness and long-term incapacity 128-9
  social assistance 99-100, 103
  unemployment 123
  VAT 95
older people
  dependency ratio 35, 37, *37*
  life expectancy 39, *40*, 51
  longer lives and longer working lives 183-4
  in population 35, *36*
  tax allowances 83
  see also pensioner poverty; pensioners
One Parent Benefit 154
original income 198
owner-occupation 42, *43*, 52, 111-12
  and benefits 112-13
  Heath 16
  and income tax 113-14, 120
  Major 25
  Old Labour 18
  Thatcher 21

P

part-time employment 44, 46, 60

partnership
  and direct taxation 92-4, *93*
  and income tax 97
  social assistance 102-3
  see also cohabitation
paternity pay 57
Pathways to Work programme 131
Patient's Charter 25
pension age 167, 183-4
Pension Credit 32, 102, 173, 175, 184, 214, 215
  caring 151
pensioner poverty 2, 174, *213*, 214-15
  Lowes 301-2, *301*, 304
  Meades 260-4, *263*, 265
  Moores 279-81, *280*
  New Labour 27, 32
pensioners 2
  social assistance 172-5, *174*, *175*, 192, 192n
  state benefits 167-72, *169*
  taxation 176-7, *177*
pensions 2, 183, 191-2, 307, 310
  Heath 16, 33n
  lifetime approach 3-4
  model families 185-91, *186*, *187*, *189*, *191*
  modelling 234, 235
  New Labour 32
  Old Labour 18
  policy maturity 228-9
  private provision 177-83, *180*
  state pensions 167-71, *169*
  terminology 172
  Thatcher 23
Pensions Act 1995 170, 229
Pensions Act 2007 170, 171, 183
Pensions Agency 173
Pensions Commission 170-1, 183
Pensions Policy Institute 179
personal accounts 171, 183, 192, 229, 292, 302, 304, 310
Personal Equity Plans (PEPs) 178
personal pensions 171, 172, 181-3, 192, 310
  modelling 234, 235
personal social services
  Heath 15
  New Labour 30
  Old Labour 13, 17
  Thatcher 19-20, 22
Philips Curve 17
Phillips, D. 207
Pimlot, B. 14
policy maturation 228-9
  Lowes 289-90, *291*, 292

Meades 246-9, *250*, 251
poll tax 24, 26
population 51-2
  ageing and longevity 39, *40*
  births and fertility 37-9, *38*
  family and household formation 40-2, *41*, *42*, *43*
  size and composition 35, *36*, 37, *37*
post-tax income 199
poverty 207
  Lowes 298-9, *299*, 304
  New Labour 27
  outcomes 212, *213*, 214, 218, 238-9
  and rent 107
  see also child poverty; pensioner poverty
poverty trap 237
Powell, M. 10
prices 49, *49*, 52
Primary Care Trusts (PCTs) 29
Private Finance Initiative (PFI) 25, 28, 30
private pensions 23, 169-70, 192, 310
  modelling 234, 235
  occupational pensions 179-81, *180*
  personal pensions 181-3
  saving and contributing 177-9
private rented housing 13, 21, 25, 42, *43*
privatisation 20-1, 23, 180
progressivity 80, 81, 84, 200, 315

R

rates 79, 89-90, 91
  and marriage 94
  rebates 91-2
Rathbone, Eleanor 58
Redmond, G. 202, 222-3
registered social landlords 25
regressivity 81, 178-9, 218, 285
relative poverty 207, 212, *213*, 214, 218
rents 107-9, 119
  affordability 109-11, *110*, *111*
replacement rates 134, 141, 238, 294-5, *296*, 297
  Lowes 304
  Meades 256
  Meades and Lowes 134-7, *135*, *137*
Resource Allocation Working Party 18
retirement 183-4
  see also pensioners
Retirement Annuity Contracts 181
right to buy 20, 25
rough sleeping 30

S

S2P (State Second Pension) 170, 171, 192

safety nets 119
  benefit safety net and minimum income guarantees 99-105, *104*, *105*
  minimum earned income guarantees and minimum wage 105-7
savings 178
Savings Gateway 178
Scotland 29
Security in retirement (DWP) 183
Seebohm Report 15
Sefton, T. 204
selective universalism 31, 61, 76
SERPS (State Earnings Related Pension Scheme) 18, 23, 168, 170, 192, 192n, 228-9, 310
  contracting out 181-2
  Invalidity Benefit 141n
  National Insurance contributions 85
  sickness and long-term incapacity 129
Severe Disablement Allowance (SDA) 127, *127*, 129-30, 165n
  disability 149, *152*
Sheltered Placement Scheme 150
sickness 128-31, 140, 309
  coverage and generosity of benefits 127, *127*, 131-2
  Meades and Lowes 137-9, *138*, *140*
Sickness Benefit 16, 23, 128, 129, 140
  relative value 128, 131
  taxation 82
Smeaton, D. 10
smoking ban 30
social assistance 119, 309
  children 65-6, *66*
  disability 144, 148-50
  evolution of safety net 99-102
  living standards 103-4, *104*
  lone parents 154, 156, *157*, 165
  lower capital limit 178
  Major 26
  marriage and partnership 102-3
  Nunns 74, 105, *105*
  pensioners 172-5, *174*, *175*, 192, 192n
  post-war welfare state 13-14
  rent 107-8
  Thatcher 23-4
Social Care Institute for Excellence 30
social class
  and fertility 38-9
  and life expectancy 39, 42
social exclusion 27
Social Fund 23, 101, 109
  death and funeral expenses 176
  Maternity Expenses Payment 56

social housing *see* council housing
social inclusion 30
social insurance 309
  disability 143
  sickness and long-term incapacity 128-32,
    133
  unemployment 123-8, *125*, *126*, *127*
  see also National Insurance contributions
social policy 5-6, 32-3
  and economy 305-7
  first 25 years 13-14
  Heath 14-16
  Major 24-6
  New Labour 26-32
  next generation 314-15
  Old Labour 16-19
  Thatcher 19-24
  trends in lifetime design 308-10
social security 5
  Health 15-16
  Major 26
  New Labour 26, 30-1
  Old Labour 18-19
  Thatcher 20, 22-4
Social Security Act 1986 56, 100, 109, 170
Social Security (No 2) Act 1980 129
stagflation 17
stakeholder pensions 170, 182-3
state pensions 167-71, *169*
State Second Pension 170, 171, 192
Statutory Maternity Pay (SMP) 23, 56-7,
  69, 76
  generosity and coverage 62, *63*, 64
  Lowes 72
  Meades 69
  Moores 71
Statutory Paternity Pay 57
Statutory Sick Pay (SSP) 23, 56, 129, 141n
  relative value 127, *127*, 128, 131-2
student loans 238
Supplementary Benefit 19, 100, 105
  change to Income Support 100-1
  children *67*, 77-8n
  disability 149
  lone parents 154, *155*
  maternity provision 56
  Nunns 74
  pensioners 172-3
  rates 16, 91, 103, 104, *104*
  sickness and long-term incapacity 128
  taxable 124
Supplementary Benefits Commission 91,
  108, 149
Sure Start Maternity Grant 57, 62, *63*

Sutherland, H. 62

T

tax allowances 80, 232
tax band 80-1
Tax benefit model tables (DWP) 222, 237
Tax benefit reference manual (HM Treasury)
  226
tax and benefit system
  and housing costs 114-19, *116*, *117*, *118*
  incidence 198-200, *199*, *201*, 202-4, *203*,
    218, 236
  and income inequality 204, *205*, 206-7
  Lowes 284-90, *285*, *286*, *288*, *291*, 292-3,
    293
  Meades 242-9, *243*, *244*, *250*, 251-4, *252*,
    253
  model families 310-14
  Moores 268-75, *268*, *269*, *271*, *272*, *273*,
    274
  outcomes 236-9
  see also benefits; taxation
tax rates 80-1
tax relief 81
taxable income 80-1
taxation 5, 79, 97, 308-9
  cumulative direct taxation and the Meades
    94-5, *94*
  income tax 80-5, *84*
  indirect taxation 95-7, *96*
  local government taxation 89-92, *90*
  marriage, partnership and direct taxation
    92-4, *93*, 98n
  National Insurance contributions 85-7,
    88, 89, *89*
  pensioners 176-7, *177*
  policy maturity 229
  see also uprating
Tebbit's bicycle 307
TESSAs (Tax Exempt Special Savings
  Accounts) 178
Thatcher, Margaret 4-5, 19-24, 33, 305, 315
  children 59-60, 64
  education 15
  housing 108-9, 203
  income tax 81-2
  lone parents 154-5
  maternity provision 56-7
  mortgage interest tax relief 113-14
  National Insurance contributions 86
  pensions 170, 181-2
  savings 178
  social assistance 100-2
  unemployment 141n

VAT 95
Timmins, N. 305
Titmuss, Richard 5, 15
tobacco
  excise duty 96, *96*, 97
  smoking ban 30
Treasury 30-1, 60, 167, 226
Turner Commission 32

U

unemployment 46-8, *46*, *47*, 52, 123-4, 140,
    141, 309
  Heath 16
  levels and coverage by benefits 101-2,
    125-8, *125*, *126*, *127*
  Lowes 298-9, *299*, 304
  Major 26
  Meades and Lowes 134-7, *135*, *137*
  Old Labour 16-17
  Thatcher 23
  see also employment; Nunns
Unemployment Benefit 82, 123-4
    relative value 127, *127*
unions 23, 106
uprating 232-3, 309
  Lowes 292-3, *293*
  Meades 251-4, *252*, *253*, 264-5
  Moores 272-5, *273*, *274*
US
  benefit safety nets 307
  Earned Income Tax Credit 77n
  inequality 206
  minimum wage 106
  policy models 26-7
  welfare-to-work 26

V

VAT (value added tax) 95-7, *96*
Vaux, G. 149
vehicle excise duty 96, *96*

W

Walker, R. 10
Welfare Reform Act 2007 102, 131
Welfare Reform and Pensions Act 1999 182
welfare-to-work 26, 31-2
WFTC *see* Working Families Tax Credit
Widowed Mother's Allowance 176
Widowed Parent's Allowance 176
widowers 176
widows 153, 176
Widow's Allowance 176
Widow's Benefit 153
Widow's Payment 176

Widow's Pension 176
Wilson, Harold 58
women
  earnings 49, 52
  economic inactivity 47, *47*, 52
  employment 44, *45*, 46, 48, 184
  fertility 37-9, *38*
  Income Support 120n
  income tax 80, 98n
  Invalid Care Allowance 151
  life expectancy 39, *40*, 51
  maternity provision 55-8
  National Insurance contributions 98n
  Non-Contributory Invalidity Pension
    (NCIP) 129
  pension age 167, 184
  pensions 168-9, 187-8, *187*, 190-1, *191*
  in population *36*
  Severe Disablement Allowance 149
  social security 103
  widows 153, 176
work incentives 23, 33, 59, 106, 313-14
  Lowes 293-5, *294*, *296*, 297, 303-4
  Meades 254-6, *255*
  Moores and Evan-Moores 275, *276*, 277
work-rich households 48
Working Families Tax Credit 60, 61, 65, *65*,
    67, 77n, 107
Working Tax Credit (WTC) 31, 107, 119
  50-plus element 184
  disability 151
  families with children 61, *67*, 76
  lone parents 156
workless households 48

Y

young people 99
  Income Support 100-1
  NEETs 29, 62

Contemporary social evils
Joseph Rowntree Foundation

Which underlying problems pose the greatest threat to British society
in the 21st century? A hundred years after its philanthropist founder
identified poverty, alcohol, drugs and gambling among the social evils of
his time, the Joseph Rowntree Foundation initiated a major consultation
among leading thinkers, activists and commentators, as well as the wider
public. The findings have now been brought together in this fascinating
book.

Individual contributors, ranging across the political spectrum, include
Sean Bailey, Zygmunt Bauman, Anthony Browne, Chris Creegan,
A.C. Grayling, Neal Lawson, Anna Minton, Ferdinand Mount,
Julia Neuberger, Jeremy Seabrook, Matthew Taylor and Stephen Thake. But the book also reports the
results from a web survey of more than 3,500 people and a specially commissioned consultation
with groups whose voices are less often heard, including care leavers, carers, people with learning
difficulties, former offenders, and people with experience of homelessness or unemployment.

The results are eloquently and passionately expressed. They suggest that while some evils – like
poverty – endure as undisputed causes of social harm, more recent sources of social misery attract
controversy. Not least among them are an alleged rise in selfish consumerism driven by economic
liberalisation, and a perceived decline in personal responsibility and family commitment.

PB £17.99 US$29.95 **ISBN** 978 1 84742 408 2 · **HB** £60.00 US$80.00 **ISBN** 978 1 84742 409 9
234 x 156mm 256 pages June 2009

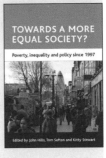